CANADIAN PUBLIC ADMINISTRATION
SERIES
COLLECTION ADMINISTRATION PUBLIQUE
CANADIENNE

J. E. Hodgetts, *General Editor / Directeur général*
André Gélinas, *Directeur associé / Associate Editor*

The Institute of Public Administration of Canada
L'Institut d'administration publique du Canada

This series is sponsored by the Institute of Public
Administration of Canada as part of its constitutional
commitment to encourage research on contemporary
issues in Canadian public administration and public
policy, and to foster wider knowledge and understanding amongst practitioners and the concerned citizen.
There is no fixed number of volumes planned for the
series, but under the supervision of the Research
Committee of the Institute, the General Editor, and
the Associate Editor, efforts will be made to ensure
that significant areas will receive appropriate attention.

L'Institut d'administration publique du Canada com-
mandite cette collection dans le cadre de ses engagements statutaires. Il se doit de promouvoir la
recherche sur des problèmes d'actualité portant sur
l'administration publique et la détermination des politiques publiques ainsi que d'encourager les praticiens
et les citoyens intéressés à les mieux connaître et à
les mieux comprendre. Il n'a pas été prévu de nombre
de volumes donné pour la collection mais, sous la
direction du Comité de recherche de l'Institut, du
Directeur général, et du Directeur associé, l'on s'ef-
force d'accorder l'attention voulue aux questions
importantes.

The Biography of an Institution:
The Civil Service Commission of Canada, 1908-1967
J. E. Hodgetts, William McCloskey, Reginald Whitaker, V. Seymour Wilson

An edition in French has been published under the title *Histoire d'une institution: La Commission de la Fonction publique du Canada, 1908-1967* by Les Presses de l'Université Laval

Old Age Pensions and Policy-Making in Canada
Kenneth Bryden

Provincial Governments as Employers:
A Survey of Public Personnel Administration in Canada's Provinces
J. E. Hodgetts and O. P. Dwivedi

Transport in Transition:
The Reorganization in the Federal Transport Portfolio
John W. Langford

Initiative and Response:
The Adaptation of Canadian Federalism to Regional Economic Development
Anthony G. S. Careless

Canada's Salesman to the World:
The Department of Trade and Commerce, 1892-1939
O. Mary Hill

Conflict over the Columbia:
The Canadian Background to an Historic Treaty
Neil A. Swainson

L'Economiste et la chose publique
Jean-Luc Migué
(Published by Les Presses de l'Université du Québec)

Federalism, Bureaucracy, and Public Policy:
The Politics of Highway Transport Regulation
Richard J. Schultz

Federal-Provincial Collaboration:
The Canada-New Brunswick General Development Agreement
Donald J. Savoie

Judicial Administration in Canada
Perry S. Millar and Carl Baar

The Language of the Skies:
The Bilingual Air Traffic Control Conflict in Canada
Sandford F. Borins

An edition in French is distributed under the title *Le français dans les airs: le conflit du bilinguisme dans le contrôle de la circulation aérienne au Canada* by Les Presses de l'Université du Québec

L'Analyse des politiques gouvernementales:
trois monographies
Michel Bellavance, Roland Parenteau et Maurice Patry
(Published by Les Presses de l'Université Laval)

Getting It Right

Regional Development in Canada

R. HARLEY McGEE

The Institute of Public Administration of Canada

McGill-Queen's University Press
Montreal & Kingston • London • Buffalo

© McGill-Queen's University Press 1992

ISBN 0-7735-0921-6

Legal deposit fourth quarter 1992
Bibliothèque nationale du Québec

∞

Printed in Canada on acid-free paper

This book has been published with the help of
grants from the Social Science Federation of
Canada, using funds provided by the Social
Sciences and Humanities Research Council of
Canada, and the Institute of Intergovernmental
Relations / Institut des relations
intergouvernementales, Queen's University.

Canadian Cataloguing in Publication Data

McGee, R. Harley (Robert Harley), 1927-
    Getting it right: regional development in Canada
    (Canadian public administration series,
    ISSN 0384-854X)
    Includes bibliographical references and index.
    ISBN 0-7735-0921-6
    1. Regional planning – Canada. 1. Economic
    assistance, Domestic – Canada. 3. Canada. Dept.
    of Regional Economic Expansion. I. Title.
    II. Series.
    H1395.C3M33 1992   338.971   C92-090385-1

This book is dedicated
to the late Gilles Chiasson,
who gave unselfishly of himself
so that the regions of Canada
may be better places to live.

Contents

Tables and Charts

Abbreviations

AC	Agriculture Canada
ACOA	Atlantic Canada Opportunities Agency
ADA	Area Development Agency
ADB	Atlantic Development Board
ADC	Atlantic Development Council
AEP	Atlantic Enterprise Program
APEC	Atlantic Provinces Economic Council
APMA	Agriculture Processing and Marketing Agreement
ARDA	Agriculture Rural Development Agreement
ARLEC	Atlantic Region Labour Education Centre
BCNI	Business Council on National Issues
BEDM	Board of Economic Development Ministers
CCED	Cabinet Committee on Economic Development
CCERD	Cabinet Committee on Economic and Regional Development
CDP	Comprehensive Development Plan
CEIC	Employment and Immigration (Canada)
CFIB	Canadian Federation of Independent Business
CFS	Canadian Forest Service (Forestry Canada)
CIRB	Canadian Industrial Renewal Board
CLC	Canadian Labour Congress
CMA	Canadian Manufacturers' Association
CMP	Council of Maritime Premiers
DEVCO	Cape Breton Development Corporation
DFO	Department of Fisheries and Oceans (Canada)
DIPP	Defence Industry Productivity Program
DREE	Department of Regional Economic Expansion
DRIE	Department of Regional Industrial Expansion
EA	External Affairs (and International Trade)

ABBREVIATIONS

EC	Environment Canada
ECB	Enterprise Cape Breton
ECC	Economic Council of Canada
EDI	electronic data interchange
EDP	Enterprise Development Program
EMR	Energy, Mines and Resources Canada
ERDA	Economic and Regional Development Agreement
FBDB	Federal Business Development Bank
FEDC	federal economic development coordinator
FEDNOR	Federal Northern Ontario Development Corporation
FMC	First Ministers' Conference
FPRO	Federal-Provincial Relations Office
FRED	Fund for Rural Economic Development
FTA	free trade agreement
GAAP	General Adjustment Assistance Program
GATT	General Agreement on Tariffs and Trade
GDA	General Development Agreement
HWC	Health and Welfare Canada
IDAP	Industrial Design Assistance Program
ILAP	Industry Labour Assistance Program
IRAP	Industrial Research Assistance Program
IRDP	Industrial and Regional Development Program
ISTC	Industry, Science and Technology Canada
ITC	Industry, Trade and Commerce
JAB	Joint Advisory Board
LDI	local development institution
LEDA	Local Economic Development Assistance
LRIS	Land Registration and Information Service
MMRA	Maritime Marshland Rehabilitation Act
MNE	multinational enterprise
MOU	memorandum of understanding
MPIP	Manufacturing Productivity Improvement Program
MSED	Ministry of State for Economic Development
MSERD	Ministry of State for Economic and Regional Development
NENB	Northeast New Brunswick
NORDCO	Newfoundland Ocean Research and Development Corporation
OGD	other government department
PCO	Privy Council Office
PDAS	Physical Distribution Advisory Service
PEMD	Program for Export Market Development
PFRA	Prairie Farm Rehabilitation Act
PMO	Prime Minister's Office

PPP	Promotional Projects Program
PWC	Public Works Canada
RDIA	Regional Development Incentives Act
RDIP	Regional Development Incentives Program
REXD	regional executive director
SME	Small and Medium Enterprise
TB	Treasury Board
TBS	Treasury Board Secretariat
TC	Transport Canada
UIC	Unemployment Insurance Commission
WD	Western Diversification
WEDC	Western Economic Diversification Canada
WEOC	Western Economic Opportunities Conference
WTIDP	Western Transportation Industrial Development Program

Preface

The federal government established the Department of Regional Economic Expansion (DREE) in 1969 and moved it out of the traditional Ottawa-based departmental mould in 1973, introducing a bold new decentralized approach in its mode of operation. In 1982 the department was disbanded. I realized at an early stage that the DREE regional development experiment was something special. As time went on, and as the end of the experience came ever nearer in 1982, I became concerned that the policy underlying the approach and the lessons learned in its implementation might be lost forever, as had happened with so many other governmental experiments, leaving history to be recorded only by observers external to the process. During the five-year interval that followed the demise of DREE, 1982–87, my concern heightened as I witnessed, from an Ottawa base, the government's half-hearted attempt to correct regional economic problems without the advantage of one agency dedicated to the task. That same five-year period, during which I no longer carried any direct responsibility for regional development, permitted me to refine my thinking on the issue and to observe it with a greater analytical detachment than I might have been capable of in 1982.

Sometime in 1987 I made the decision to write an insider's account of regional development in Canada as represented by the DREE concept. When I started to execute that intention early in the following year, I soon realized that the DREE story could not be told in isolation from the rest of the federal efforts directed to righting regional disparities in Canada. Further, my telling of any such story would be incomplete unless I revealed my own thoughts on how the policies and programs of the national government might be applied to improving regional economies. The book that was hazily aimed at recording the DREE experiment in regional development in Canada in the period 1973–82 now reaches into 1992, with only two of its eight chapters directly detailing the DREE interval. The remaining chapters set the stage for discussing regional development in Canada (particularly but not exclusively at the federal level), review policies, theories, and ideas that have prevailed in the literature on the subject, assess federal efforts at improving regional circumstances following the DREE episode, discuss a number of factors that influence regional economies and governmental efforts to improve them, and offer proposals for getting regional development right.

In reaching my decision to write a book on regional development, I had also to decide what kind of book I wanted it to be. It was above all to be a book that only someone with firsthand knowledge of the subject could write. The original idea was to capture what turned out to be a unique policy and administrative approach to regional development, one not likely to be repeated. The uniqueness of the approach was founded on a premise that the federal and provincial governments could work together as partners in the absence of political interference in the implementation of government policy. It worked—to a degree that will not be believed. Whether the understanding that existed between politicians and public servants was based on a degree of trust that has not prevailed since that time, on a realization that this was a winning formula, or on some other factor, officials operated with the confidence that they had backing at the political level. The regional development effort was the better for it. Politicians, however, felt that they did not receive proper credit for the DREE effort. Eventually, their discontent in this respect overwhelmed the validity of the DREE approach to regional development. Such paranoia persists to this day.

The views expressed in this review rely significantly on my own experience, one that included responsibility and accountability for the management of the largest single operating entity and regional development budget in the department; and daily contacts over an eight-year period with many individuals, provincial premiers, federal ministers, members of Parliament and provincial legislatures, federal and provincial officials at every level of the hierarchy, leading business-people, small entrepreneurs, and representatives of institutions and associations. Consequently, it will carry some of my biases on the practice of regional development. In no instance, however, is the accuracy of description of operational practices diminished by my closeness to the subject; rather I have been able to shed light on many practices that have been incorrectly reported by others. In setting the record straight on DREE, I have had to be critical of the opinions of some individuals who may not have had the same opportunity as myself to be exposed on such a continuous and wide-ranging basis to

DREE operations at both the bureaucratic and political levels. Such criticism is set forth as accurately as possible and is supported by substantiated information. Information sources include my own experience throughout almost all of the DREE period and many primary and secondary sources of information.

In writing this book, it would have been tempting to recall many personal accounts of my dealings with politicians at all levels in both the federal and the provincial governments. I early decided not to do that, notwithstanding the growing tendency of others with government experience to tell all, once outside the system. The story is perhaps less enriched on this account, but I have felt more comfortable for it.

Regional economic development in Canada is not well understood, even though the literature on the subject is considerable. Regional development is usually practised by governments or their agents, despite attempts to engage the participation of the private sector and other elements of the economy. Government thus becomes the butt of most of the criticism, but receives little credit even when it is due. Not enough has been written about the positive aspects of regional development effort and the people that made it happen. This book is not a defence of government policies and activities. Its aim is to describe the reality of the practice of regional development in Canada over almost twenty years, to scrutinize the origins of regional development policy and its translation into action over that period of time, and to prescribe an approach that could work in the future. Governments are assigned their share of the blame for past failures.

Organized regional development in Canada reached its zenith in the 1970s with the establishment and operation of the Department of Regional Economic Expansion. Notwithstanding DREE's accomplishments during its life, politicians and a good number of bureaucrats were not satisfied with it. DREE gave way in 1982 to a series of experiments that have yet to match its innovativeness or successes.

Acknowledgments

I am indebted to a number of people for their assistance in bringing this book to the publication stage. When I first undertook this project, Peter Leslie, past director of the Institute of Intergovernmental Relations, Queen's University, provided valuable suggestions on objectives, structure, and subject matter, which helped keep me on the straight and narrow throughout the book's subsequent writing and revision. Ronald Watts, who followed as institute director, gave me his steadfast support and encouragement from the outset. I am particularly grateful to J. E. Hodgetts, general editor of the Institute of Public Administration of Canada's Canadian Public Administration Series, Doug Brown of the Institute, and Jack Francis, respected former federal public servant, for their patient and meticulous reading of the first draft of this manuscript, which led to a substantial rewrite of the document. Ted Hodgetts's continuing patience in reading and providing detailed comments on subsequent iterations of the manuscript led to a much improved final document. Ted Hodgetts and Joan McGilvray merit special mention for their assistance in guiding me through the intricacies of document preparation, and Peter Goheen, of McGill-Queen's University Press, for expediting the movement of the manuscript through the review process.

My research was greatly facilitated by the permission of the now Department of Industry, Science and Technology to access DREE files and the assistance of the director and staff of the Halifax/Dartmouth Regional Records Centre of the National Archives in retrieving them. I am warmly appreciative of the contribution made by many past colleagues and other public servants who verified my recall, or suggested other versions, of a number of events and practices relating to regional development in Canada. I thank them too for sharing their own views on regional development with me. The final opinions expressed in this book are nevertheless my own.

From a technical point of view, I must also express my thanks to the staff of the Institute of Intergovernmental Relations for their advice and assistance on manuscript structure and production, especially to Valerie Jarus, who repaired diskettes for me and otherwise aided in manuscript production, to Darrel Reid, and to Anne Poels, who located so many library reference documents for me.

This book was brought to fruition with the assistance of a research grant from the Institute of Intergovernmental Relations and a publication grant from the Aid to Scholarly Publications Programme, both of which are gratefully acknowledged.

Introduction

Ever since Confederation, the notion of "balanced regional development" has been an implicit, if not explicit, objective of national policy.

—Economic Council of Canada, *Living Together: A Study of Regional Disparities*, 1977

Students of regional development will find a richness of resource material on the subject in libraries across the country. The Economic Council reference above, which is a quotation from its own first annual review of 1964, puts in perspective the influence that geography, geology, and climate have had on settlement patterns and economic activity in Canada. What is also apparent in reviewing the literature is the sometimes prominent, sometimes subtle, but always present federal-provincial relations aspect of the regional development effort and the political compromises that have prevailed over time. This book includes discussion of that relationship and of the role, and how it has been exercised, of the respective levels of government. Of significance is the degree to which the British North America Act attributed certain jurisdictions to the federal government and to the provincial governments. This separation of power has, since 1867, brought these two levels of government into continual contact in the management of the national and regional economies and in the consequent well-being of the country's citizens. The book also chronicles the frustration of the federal government in its efforts to be pre-eminent in planning and managing the economic destiny of Canada, if necessary (and very often deliberately) at the expense of the provinces.

This book is also about the economic well-being of Canada's peripheral regions. The thesis presented here is that government, through the development and application of national and regional development policies, can make a difference in regional economies. It is further argued that the federal Department of Regional Economic Expansion (DREE), created in 1969, represented the best approach to both regional development policy and its implementation. DREE came the closest to getting it right. The corollary of this contention is that all subsequent governmental organizations for regional economic development either failed or were unnecessary. This work, which focuses primarily on the period 1973–92, will dispel some of the myths and illuminate some of the policies and thinking that have prevailed on the subject.

A brief look at regional development programming after the Second World War, particularly after 1960, will bring us to the point of departure for this book, the decentralized DREE experiment that started in 1973. The decade following the war evidenced strong central government tendencies, expansionist policies, resource development, and large, federally funded infrastructure projects, including the Trans-Canada Highway system, telecommunications, and airport construction. All regions of the country were sharing, in relative terms, in the prosperity brought about in the postwar boom; regional development, as recognized by disparity measures, was not a preoccupation of governments.[1] This abruptly changed with the 1956 recession, which ushered in a period when government concentrated on stimulating development and studied the causes of regional disparities. Harvey Lithwick says that the approaches taken at the time did not recognize that the severity of the regional economic downturn was attributable in large part to the recession and that the proposed solutions therefore centred on development rather than anti-cyclical policies. He concluded that "this flawed diagnosis was to prove costly both to the regions and to the conservative party itself." He said that the government attempted to solve what were essentially short-run cyclical problems with long-run economic development policies.[2] The same could not be said of many of the unrelated program efforts later taken by consecutive governments up to 1973, when a broader, multi-dimensional approach to regional economic development was introduced. We will later see that criticism of the Department of Regional Economic Expansion in the late 1970s also took little account of the international recession then sweeping across Canada.

The short Diefenbaker period did place some emphasis on regional development and to some extent evidenced a return to federal-provincial cooperation, the same cooperative federalism that later characterized the Pearson era. Indicative of the inconsistent federal government approach to regional economies, however, was the fact that regional development policy resumed an overall lower profile with the 1966 economic recovery and the introduction of new social policy measures in health care and old age pension protection.

When the regional disparity issue emerged from time to time in readily identifiable form, a plethora of measures was brought forward to meet it, with a flurry of program activity in the 1960s. Thus came the Agricultural Rehabilitation and Development Act (ARDA) of 1961 (known later as Agriculture Rural Development Agreements), aimed at alleviating rural poverty and managed primarily by the provinces (refurbished with a wider mandate in 1964); the Atlantic Development Board (ADB) in 1962–63 for Atlantic Canada; and the Fund for Rural Economic Development (FRED) in 1966, which though carrying a rural bias had the mandate to support programs in areas of social infrastructure. For the manufacturing sector, the Area Development Agency (ADA) was born in 1963–64 to encourage regionally differentiated industrial development.[3]

Non-government organizations were also preoccupied with the apparently insoluble problems of economic inequality among Canada's parts. The Economic Council of Canada, in its 1966 third annual review, looked beyond the program-specific initiatives of government represented by ARDA, ADB, FRED, and the like to ask why such divergent activities as rural development, manpower training and mobility, area industrial grants, and transportation subsidies, each falling under a distinct federal departmental jurisdiction, could not be brought together to mutually reinforce levels of income and productivity in the Atlantic provinces. The council endorsed the need for better federal-provincial liaison in regional policies, improved administrative coordination, and an emphasis on a growth-oriented approach so that there could be greater spillover effects from the more prosperous areas to the more depressed ones. The council advocated the development, within the federal administration, of a deliberate and consistent focus on the regional problem. Further, the council emphasized "the need for collation and analysis of activities in a horizontal or area perspective, as well as from a vertical or functional point of view."[4]

The stage was set for a comprehensive attack on economic inequality in Canada. Federal regional development policy, based on creating economic opportunity, began to take shape. The first move of the government of the day was to bring several of the disparate regional development programs together under the newly formed Department of Regional Economic Expansion in 1969. Tom Kent, the department's first deputy minister, would later say that "the role of the new department would be to inject the purpose of lessening regional disparities into the whole structure of federal action and into arrangements with the provinces."[5] The department was to facilitate economic expansion and social adjustment in designated areas to improve opportunities for productive employment and access to those opportunities.[6] After a period of experience, Kent admitted that "the result could fairly be criticized as a hodgepodge of measures, too little coordinated. That did not worry me in the early stages." Kent did reveal his intention to move to more thorough planning as soon as was practicable.[7] In 1972, J. P. Francis reported that this more thorough planning would result in a more effective regional development policy based on a coordinated set of special programs operating as complements to national economic and social policies.[8] Even at this early stage the expectation was that DREE regional development initiatives would operate within, or complementary to, national policies. Francis said that within such a framework a new federal regional development policy had emerged, the goal being to assist in the dispersion and stimulation of economic growth across Canada to bring employment and earnings opportunities in the slow-growth regions as close as possible to those in the rest of the country.[9] A new era in regional development had been launched. It would lead to more or less continual policy change right into the last decade of the century.

The many theories, concepts, and proposals that have come forward over the years for improving regional economic circumstances have not necessarily, if at all, coincided with the directions that consecutive federal governments have taken in addressing the regional development dilemma in Canada. This has not discouraged political scientists and others interested in Canada's regions from continuing to come up with new ideas or from providing their opinion on the suitability of the government policies in place. Chapter 1 of this book examines some of the most commonly advanced ideas on regional development in Canada and provides the context within which the subject is explored in the remainder of the book. The various views are examined with respect to their theoretical legitimacy and the practicality of their implementation. Many are found to hold ideas of value to policy makers and some practical suggestions for application. Others are seen as repetitions of earlier hypotheses, unfounded in fact and unrealistic in the context of the make-up of the country. The chapter also probes the constitutional obligations and the jealousies of the two levels of government most involved with regional development, concluding that the Constitution presents no barriers to the two orders of government working together or individually to better regional circumstances. And the chapter challenges the often-suggested migration or mobility solution to regional disparity as being impractical in the Canadian context.

Chapters 2 and 3 deal with the outcome of the policy determination begun in 1972. The centralized DREE of 1969 gave way in 1973 to a decentralized, deconcentrated organization that for a period of nine years brought a new force to bear on regional disparity in Canada, a force that captured the attention of politicians, bureaucrats, and academics alike, attracting much praise and a lot of criticism. These two chapters detail how the organization really worked, cover the bureaucratic and political processes at play, and reveal the truths about federal interdepartmental and federal-provincial relations. The discussion demonstrates the uniqueness of the federal-provincial collaborative approach to solving the difficult problems of the less economically endowed parts of the country. This approach was based on a new concept embodied in the General Development Agreements (GDAS), under which subsidiary agreements to accomplish identified objectives were executed. The discussion proves the degree to which the integrity of federal regional development policy was protected and concludes that DREE came as close as it has yet been possible to getting it right.

Chapter 3 touches on the accomplishments of DREE and provides a new assessment of the changing policy orientations of the department over time, leading to the declaration that DREE was well poised to carry federal regional development programming through the 1980s and into the 1990s. The chapter explores the reasons prevailing at the time for the demise of the department and argues that there was much less validity in them than their authors would wish to admit. Chapter 3 also unequivocally demonstrates that DREE has been the most successful instrument to date for bringing credit to federal regional development efforts in the regions.

Chapter 4 covers the critical post-DREE period 1982–87, during which time regional development efforts languished in a partial no-man's-land, with responsibility shared by all and fully accepted by none. In 1982 DREE and Industry, Trade and Commerce were merged to form a new Department of Regional Industrial Expansion (DRIE), carrying a dual role of national and regional industrial development. The Ministry of State for Economic and Regional Development (MSERD) was formed in 1982 to oversee all economic development in Canada. It was dismantled in 1984, having failed to accomplish its mission. Individual departments carried the responsibility of taking initiatives that would improve regional economies, including entering into joint development agreements with the provinces. This chapter looks at the consequences of these actions and shows that better political management would have produced better results. The management and mismanagement of regional development programs, the ammunition of regional development policy, is also dissected in chapter 4, which reveals that politically approved programs can only be effective if placed in the hands of administrators who have adequate levels of knowledge and authority and are free of political interference.

In 1984 the Liberal government gave way to a Conservative regime that brought few new ideas to the conundrum of regional inequality in Canada. In 1987 Conservative Prime Minister Brian Mulroney, determined to put his stamp on regional development in Canada, created two new departments of government to lead federal initiatives in the Atlantic and the western provinces, and strengthened federal efforts in Quebec and Ontario. These moves are examined in detail in chapter 5, and a number of questions are raised on whether such structural change was necessary, or any more effective, than earlier approaches had been. The omission of any meaningful national coordination of effort is assessed, as is the distinctly more aggressive federal attitude to unilateral action in the field.

Chapter 6 pauses to assess federal efforts in regional development and admits that, in quantitative terms, an accurate evaluation is close to impossible to accomplish. It is nevertheless concluded that many of the past federal program activities showed recognizable results, with DREE having been the most efficient and effective approach taken. Because direct incentives to business have carried such a high profile in regional development programming, they are also evaluated in this chapter, along with the corporate motivation in accepting government incentives and the factors that companies consider in making their business decisions. It is shown that while incentives can have a beneficial impact on regional economies, governments would be better advised to concentrate their efforts on improving the environment for business through generic hard and soft infrastructure support, which would have wide application to business, industry, institutions, and even local government and community development commissions.

Chapter 7 brings to the fore, in implementation terms, a number of the most significant regional development policies that have either been tried or suggested over the years. Several are recommended for further use and consideration, and it becomes evident that there are few new ideas to be found. The conclusion is that existing ideas must be better implemented and that the ordering of priorities must change to recognize changing regional, national, and international economic realities. Valid theories of self-help, community and urban development, and concentration on medium and small business are each examined and endorsed, with qualification. It is demonstrated that the impact on regional economies of technology, information, service industries, and telecommunications is a major uncertainty for Canada's peripheral regions. Above all, a move towards self-reliance and away from dependency, through a blend of government and resident effort, is shown to be essential for the regions in a global economy.

Chapter 8 provides an optimistic conclusion to the book. With dedication, the unfailing support of government, and efforts to encourage the people of the regions to help themselves, continued progress can be made in improving regional circumstances. The efficiency and magnitude of that progress is in the hands of both the government and the public. It is argued that government must better manage its involvement in regional development through a long-term commitment to its policies for the regions and an improved ability to marshal all of its activities in a coordinated manner.

One question of definition needs attention before we launch into this story. The word "region" carries a number of different connotations, depending on its use. It can mean a grouping of more than one province or a territorial entity of such size that it may be considered in regional as opposed to provincial terms. Thus, DREE operated two multi-provincial regions, the Atlantic and the West, and two single-province regions, Ontario and Quebec. An area within a province will sometimes be designated subregional rather than subprovincial; thus we have "the northeast region" of a particular province. After 1982 "region" was employed in the new federal organization of economic departments to denote a province. In this book, every effort has been made to avoid confusion on this point, with the word "region" qualified in each instance of its use.

Getting It Right

Chapter One

Regional Development: The Canadian Context

ONE THING THAT STRIKES a researcher of regional development policies in Canada is the range of opinions held by those having any connection with the subject, be it politician, bureaucrat, academic, economist, business, or casual observer. Governments form a separate category because they represent the combined views of politicans and bureaucrats and they may be influenced to a greater or lesser extent by all the others who see fit to express a point of view. It is only governments, however, that make deliberate policies and take specific actions aimed at influencing regional economies. This does not prevent everyone else from second-guessing government policies, being largely critical and all too often making their own prescriptions for improvement in quite general terms, with little regard for implementation realities. There are exceptions, and this chapter will deal with them, as well as comment on other views that are either so widely held or echoed that they cannot be ignored.

A conceptual framework for studying regional development policy allows an assessment of what has gone before and what may be contemplated for the future. It takes into account the well-being of individuals and the reliability of regional economies in terms of productivity and competitiveness and meaningful consultation with participants, including the provinces, which hold their own jurisdictional responsibilities for regional economies. Also pertinent are the regional development policy fit within the total federal scheme of things, public perceptions of the policies (including the cost to taxpayers), and how well the policies facilitate the ultimate objective of all regional development schemes, economic self-reliance through gainful employment and the use of capital.

In a review of regional development policies for Canada, whether of those that have been tried or those that have only been proposed, it would be desirable to have an evaluation model against which all concepts could be assessed. Unfortunately, regional development policy, not unlike most governmental policies, is so influenced by externalties that it has been virtually impossible to isolate the impact of specific actions on regional circumstances with any degree of accuracy. Measurable indicators of economic well-being, while helpful in determining relative economic achievement over time and even the status of individuals, cannot be solely related to actions undertaken in the name of government policy. Government programs, however, and to an even greater extent government-assisted projects, can be evaluated in their own right, and the addition of their impact is sometimes used to assess a government policy in the absence of anything better. The coherence of a regional development policy in its application in more than one region and the policy's relationship to other government policies that may affect regional circumstances are both vital considerations in attempts to judge its success. Another measure of government policy in the field of regional development is what may be called the satisfaction level. This is an indicator frequently employed by politicians to gauge the success of their actions; imperfect as it may be, it is often the measure that guides governments in the course they chart to improve regional circumstances. We will see that individuals' and provinces' real or imaginary disenchantment with federal regional development policies has often dictated premature changes in policy direction.

This book does not employ quantifiable criteria for testing regional development approaches. It does attempt to assess degrees of success and failure by employing all of the foregoing ideas, recognizing that the outcome will be imperfect but satisfied that useful conclusions can be drawn from the effort. It assesses policies and programs against their stated objectives, the degree to which federal-provincial relations aided or hindered actions intended to improve regional economies, and, in particular, program and policy success in fostering self-reliance in the regions.

There is no unanimity on the definition of "regional disparity." Economists have for years used the measurable indices of income, earned income, employment and unemployment levels, participation rates, fiscal capacity of provincial governments, and subsidies to persons and governments (transfers) as proxies for economic well-being.[1] Some add the dollar value of government expenditures intended to correct these measured disparities. Productivity is always uppermost in the minds of most analysts.

Satisfaction levels are different for different people. What pleases in Toronto is not necessarily what pleases in Kirkland Lake, nor do the people of Burgeo, Newfoundland, aspire to life in the capital, St John's. Just about everyone wants to be economically independent, however, and that is what regional disparity is all about. Disparity has come to mean "unacceptable" levels of unemployment, low levels of income, and, directly related, low levels of productivity, and the inefficient use of capital and labour. Both the cause and result of these conditions are lower levels of education, insufficient use of new technologies, and a myriad of other factors that preoccupy those who wrestle with the disparity question. Disparity is the lack of economic opportunity. What is important is what to do about it.

In descriptive terms, there is some consensus on what the objectives of regional development policy should be. The Constitution Act of 1982, in those paragraphs of section 36(1) and 36(2) that relate to regional circumstances, enshrines the national objective as furthering economic development to reduce disparity in opportunities, providing essential public services of reasonable quality to all Canadians, and maintaining a commitment to the principle of equalization payments. This commitment was reaffirmed in the government's constitutional proposals of 1991. In 1972, federal regional development policy was described by DREE as the dispersion and stimulation of economic growth across Canada to reduce unemployment, underemployment, and low productivity and to increase labour force participation.[2]

By 1974, with the signing of General Development Agreements (GDAS) between DREE and nine of the ten provinces, the objectives were stated generally as increasing job opportunities and raising levels of earned income. Two GDAS mentioned the "stay option," which would permit residents to work in the geographic area of their choice. Only one specified closing the income disparity gap as an objective. A new generation of Economic and Regional Development Agreements (ERDAS) signed in 1984 did not significantly deviate from the GDA principles of raising the levels of earned income and increasing employment opportunity.

The Federal-Provincial Task Force on Regional Development Assessment phrased regional development policy objectives as the equitable provision of comparable public services across regions and the provision of the means to stimulate growth and achieve a more equitable distribution of income and employment among regions.[3] The Macdonald Commission (the Royal Commission on the Economic Union and Development Prospects for Canada) suggested that "regional policies are generally understood to include those policies aimed explicitly at changing the underlying relationships among regions." It added that economic development referred to the structural transformation of an economy in that it would become increasingly capable of sustaining its capacity for expansion through its own resources.[4] Any number of additional references may be quoted on the definition of regional disparity and how it should be overcome.[5] The general idea is more or less the same for all of them, with the possible exception of the free-market forces concept.

There is a remarkable degree of similarity, if not agreement, in the suggestions that have been advanced for policy and program solutions to the regional disparity question. It has also been acknowledged that there is no magic solution, no panacea, for this persistent conundrum in the Canadian economic make-up.[6] There are few dimensions of the regional development problem that practitioners have not already encountered elsewhere—thus, it becomes a matter of emphasis or degree. Two things do stand out: the importance of taking long-term positions and the degree to which just about everyone looks to government to be the agent for change in regional economies.

It is logical that governments should be in the forefront of policy change specifically directed to regional circumstances. Although the actions of the private sector may well have more impact on regional economies than those of governments, such actions are hardly deliberate in this regard, one way or the other. Private sector companies may be encouraged to do certain things that will aid regional economies if they stand to gain. On the other hand, certain detrimental actions sometimes taken by such companies in the name of efficiency exhibit little or no regard for the regional consequences. Abraham Rotstein, in his introduction to *Forced Growth*, said that governments must assume full responsibility for strategies of regional development, given that the private sector conscience was different than that of governments and that "normal commercial ventures imply a quite different economic setting and different rules of the game from development ventures sponsored by government."[7] Thus, most policy prescriptions stipulate that the government "must" or "should" do so-and-so. A legitimate criticism of government, and there are many, is the propensity to change direction before any one policy prescription has had a chance to work.[8]

Regional economies exist in a changing national and international environment. Along with the rest of Canada, they are highly influenced by forces external to their borders. In particular, their fortunes closely track those of the United States, in both good times and bad. Canada is more dependent than most countries on events that occur and decisions that are taken beyond its borders. Our high level of exports in certain product and commodity categories provides much of the life-blood of the economy. We are affected by currency rates, at home and in our target markets, growth rates and product preferences in target markets, and tariff and quota regimes. Long-standing purchase-preference tactics between nations, based on relationships that predate the Canadian Confederation, further complicate the Canadian trade picture. The industrialization of Third World countries, technological advances, and new sources of resources that compete with Canada are other areas that pose threats to regional economies.[9]

Targeted regional development policies must be constantly evaluated so that they keep up with changing times. This has been at the root of much of the criticism of earlier programs aimed at rural and agricultural development, infrastructure upgrading, and resource exploitation. Some of the criticisms have been valid. At the same time, it is not possible for a regional economy, already lagging behind the rest of the country in educational levels and the use of new technologies, to leap-frog into the forefront of new technology and sophisticated service industry sectors. This has become the theme of a number of writers on the future for regional development in Canada.[10]

Predictions are made about what future economies will look like or, more accurately, what factors will be at play in determining the make-up of national economies—not to mention those of the regions. It is already a serious concern whether Canada can hold its own in a global economy highly dictated by technology, with particular emphasis on communications, information technology, microelectronics, biotechnology, and advanced industrial materials. World leaders are emerging in all of these areas. Ownership patterns are changing along with these events. For many of these activities, companies need not have a physical presence in a country in order to be competitive in its market.

William J. Coffey, in a study of sectoral shifts in the Canadian economy, raises questions on the role of service industries, the changing geography of economic activity, and shifts in the demand for labour. He concludes:

> In sum, the scope of regional development policy needs to be expanded to include these new sectoral, spatial and occupational realities. In particular, the various elements of service activity need to be explicitly included in policy initiatives, which up to now have addressed only the goods-producing sector. The critical elements of a development policy for an economy in which high-order services play a major role are largely removed from older approaches involving incentives and infrastructure for industrial firms. Such a development policy may need to be aimed, at least in part, at improving the skills and the environment of the work-force.[11]

7

Coffey questions the degree to which government can influence the location of high-order services in terms of decentralization to peripheral regions.

THEORETICAL APPROACHES

It is fashionable for writers on regional development to proclaim the need for clear and precise regional development objectives, sometimes suggested as being separately defined for each region.[12] These writers, however, have failed to articulate such objectives in a form permitting their translation into action. Governments have steadfastly rejected the phrasing of objectives in terms of measurable indicators, such as relative levels of earned income or reduced unemployment, since these are generally seen to be either unobtainable or politically unpalatable. Factors over which governments and planners have no control make such concrete objectives too uncertain and the life of policians too uncomfortable. It is also too simplistic to state that someone (governments, it seems, bear the brunt of these statements) "should" set clearer objectives. If measurable targets are dismissed, other objectives should logically be adopted: to create an environment for growth, to remove constraints, to realize opportunities, and to build on comparative advantage. Strategies then put flesh on the objectives.

According to Richard Higgins, a regional development strategy contains a statement of the problems, a discussion of alternative ways to confront them, a discussion of these alternatives in terms of the responsibility of concerned parties, a statement of the role and responsibility accepted by the federal government, a set of objectives and targets, a statement of the overall strategy to be employed, the implementation strategy to be used, and a review provision. (Higgins digresses from this policy framework to presume block funding to the provinces, specific federal government development initiatives, federal-provincial initiatives, and provincial initiatives.)[13]

The strategy proposed by Higgins follows the classical textbook approach: problem identification, development and discussion of possible solutions, objectives setting, selection of preferred alternative, assignment of roles and responsibilities, and definition of the implementation strategy. It is a good approach, best suited to problems falling into relatively describable frameworks, less so for broad problem areas such as regional disparities. The approach nevertheless recommends itself as a good discipline by which to attack the study of any problem area. In regional development terms, it should certainly be employed in situations like transportation, the non-competitiveness of the Atlantic fisheries, low levels of technical competence in the peripheral regions, inadequate levels of service industries infrastructure, and so on. These individual problem areas can be aggregated up to, or disaggregated down from, larger concepts of regional development.

Most books on regional development either refer to the theoretical frameworks that have been applied to the subject or lament their absence. Too often the discussion of the theories of regional development clouds the realities under which regional development approaches must operate and becomes side-tracked from the actual issues of the problem, the causes, and the possible solutions.

The once popular and subsequently maligned growth-pole concept, hardly a revolutionary idea, has a basic logic to it. Certain activities have a tendency to cluster, feeding on themselves as the efficiency inherent in bringing like things together in one location becomes apparent and ever-higher-quality members are brought into the fold. There will normally be some catalyst to set the clustering off, usually population centres. Note that the activity itself does not guarantee clustering. Resource industries have traditionally been associated with single-industry communities, which have been built almost entirely on the exploitation of the resource and on activities related directly to it. Very little diversification accompanies such industries, and the communities dependent on them often disappear when the resource ends. Sometimes a high level of success or a particular achievement in science, academe, or business will trigger clustering.

In regional development, growth pole has too frequently been equated with induced industrial development, with insufficient attention paid to whether there is either a natural nucleus for such development or whether it can realistically be implanted. In the early growth-pole experiments in Atlantic Canada, who can say what influence DREE-related efforts had in making Halifax the now clearly dominant economic centre of the region? Certainly, the DREE support helped, perhaps significantly, this natural growth pole to succeed. The growth-pole theory also implied, and therefore accepted, intraregional mobility—implicitly from rural to urban areas. As the growth-pole concept matured, it broadened beyond its manufacturing and industrial connotation to include other activities that come together to make a particular place exciting enough to attract new entrants.[14]

Theoretical frameworks have been categorized by several authors.[15] In addition to the growth-pole theory, the development approach, trade theory, and the ever-present neoclassical theory, have all been discussed. The most enduring approach to regional development, from both a theoretical and practical point of view, is the multidimensional concept. It is timeless because it permits the implementation of everything that one might wish.[16]

The multidimensional approach can be employed to encompass comparative advantage, the trade theory, a variation on growth centres, community development—everything except, perhaps, the neoclassical theory. That idea promotes the free-market doctrine, which is what permitted regional economic differences to be accentuated in the first place, as naturally occurring comparative advantage based on resource endowment shifted to industrial development, region by region. Comparative advantage was the underlying premise of DREE in the 1973–82 era; DREE used the multidimensional approach to raise a region to a position where it could build on its strengths.

The multidimensional concept as applied to regional development does not exclude support of the free-market theory in all instances. Direct incentives to companies, for example, should not be used to prop up weak companies or even weak sectors unless there is a strong, analytically supported argument that a turn-around can be achieved. Even here a cold financial analysis might reveal that the best way of securing the future of an operation is to let it go bankrupt and allow the pieces be picked up debt-free by a stronger-managed and better-financed enterprise.

Speculation is the closest one can come to accuracy in predicting the right course for government intervention in project, company, and even sector-specific situations. But there is a role for government in supporting generic or horizontal activities aimed at upgrading communities, skills training, technology, industrial, social, transportation, education, and even municipal infrastructure so that a region has a reasonable chance to improve its own environment for economic opportunity.

The role for government includes actively assisting the adjustment process. It cannot, however, stand aside and simply let the free market dictate the outcome. The marketplace has no conscience. Industrial and business adjustment can be facilitated within the framework of the multidimensional approach and the theory of comparative advantage. By one definition, regional development is economic adjustment. Thus, being preoccupied with numerical gap-closing gives way to building on strength and upgrading regional infrastructures, leading to individuals helping themselves.

Donald Savoie, quoting several sources, has posited that there is no underlying theory of regional development and no panacea for it. He says that different situations in different regions require different approaches, that planners "had better keep [their] eyes on the patient as the treatment proceeds and be prepared to change it if it appears not to work."[17] Any practitioner would readily agree. There is no need for effective regional development to be postponed for lack of a theory—lack of a policy, lack of an approach, lack of a strategy (or strategies), yes, but not lack of a theory. Knowing that there is no panacea is poor reason to do nothing. Those who promote regional development strive for improvement over what exists at a given time. The broadest policy or approach is aimed at identifying the (economic) shortfalls of a region, finding out why, and initiating remedial action; it is also directed towards removing constraints to economic development and identifying and exploiting economic opportunity. Building on comparative strengths is axiomatic, as are flexibility and tailoring actions and solutions to identified situations.

POLICY INTEGRATION

Mario Polèse writes, "A full-blown regional development policy for Canada would take into account the regional consequences of all federal and provincial programs ... we must accept that direct regional policy is only one of the many policies, and not necessarily the most important one, influencing regional development in Canada."[18] Harvey Lithwick relates regional development policy to the well-being of the national economy and suggests that the focus be shifted from regional development to a program of national development in which all of the regions could participate. He follows up on this thesis with more precise recommendations on improved transportation and communication links to facilitate the mobility of capital and labour, ensuring access by producers to all markets in Canada and eliminating barriers that prevent interprovincial competition.[19] Charles McMillan, while agreeing that federal macroeconomic policies and particular policies to promote development within the Atlantic region must work in concert, expressed the following concern:

> It is now an open question whether macroeconomic policies aimed at maximizing total output and income at the national level, despite the concentration of impact on Central Canada, have the assumed consequence of bringing long-term prosperity to the Atlantic Region ... it was this central concern that the regional economies of Canada did not prosper proportionately with economic growth in Central Canada that inspired federal initiatives such as the Atlantic Canada Opportunities Agency and the Western Diversification Initiative.[20]

McMillan also quoted the C. D. Howe Institute to the effect that

11

evidence indicated that rather than providing a stabilizing influence, federal government policies have aggravated differences in regional performance. The institute referred to the impact of monetary and fiscal policies on regional interest rates and the value of the Canadian dollar as being detrimental to the resource-based provinces in the Atlantic and the West.[21]

Courchene,[22] Savoie,[23] the Macdonald Commission,[24] the Federal-Provincial Task Force on Regional Development Assessment,[25] and others have also commented on the critical importance of harmonizing regional economies with the national economy and of integrating regional economic development policies with national economic development policies.

Any publicly announced deliberate shift of emphasis from regional development to a national strategy, however well-founded, would not be well accepted by several provinces and would be politically untenable at the federal level. At the same time, the federal government came close to such an approach twice in the 1980s, first with its November 1981 budget paper, "Economic Development in the 1980s," and shortly thereafter in the reorganization of economic departments in 1982. In both instances, however, it hedged its bets with pronouncements on a priority position for regional economies within the national framework.

Unfortunately, one cannot stop the world while waiting for such ideal solutions to the regional dilemma. The next-best thing is to at least ensure that national and regional policies, while under development and in the implementation stages, recognize one another. Theoretically, a hierarchy of national economic objectives, regional economic objectives, derived strategies, and identified initiatives makes eminent sense.[26] Successive Canadian administrations have been unsuccessful in structuring an all-embracing national economic development policy, and little would be accomplished in regional development terms if one were to wait for it. Regional development policy inherently includes the selective use of national and provincial government policies in the attainment of regional development objectives.[27] Region-wide development strategies, which may encompass provincial aggregations to form a multi-provincial region, can recognize national sector strategies, and the converse is also true. There is no doubt that as efforts are made to bring more technology to the regions and to improve what is already there, national and international markets have to be taken into account.

If it is reasonable to expect regional development policy and national (particularly sectoral) policy to co-exist with a degree of mutual recognition and consideration, it is equally reasonable to expect region-specific programming to be tailored to the identified needs and opportunities of the peripheral parts of the country. It is generally considered that national and regional policies come into conflict in sector-specific policies and programs such as industrial development, resource exploitation, and transportation. The situation has as well been characterized as a political dilemma.[28] Later chapters of this book demonstrate that the political conflict between regional and national economic development policies has been misunderstood and greatly exaggerated. Regional development policy on its own, on the other hand, has caused much political discomfort for federal politicians. When too much attention is directed at the regions, the national efficiency syndrome (maximizing efficiency at the national level) has been sometimes effectively used to postulate a less efficient economy. Hugh Thorburn has said, "If a country is to develop some kind of industrial strategy, it must reconcile the need for developing the depressed areas and decentralizing industry against the need to maximize productivity on the national level."[29] This argument can be proven with national efficiency economic models if sufficient assumptions are made on the relative weights and quality of factors of production.

The two streams of national and regional economic development policy go hand in hand. An obvious adjunct is the need to coordinate the policies and actions of government as practised by individual departments. In an ideal world the government would maintain a broadly based economic development policy for Canada, its thrust to enhance regional economies would be an integral part of the overall plan, and all departments of government would conduct themselves in such a way as to support stated objectives. One might even envisage a centralized operation by which an appropriate agency of government would map and coordinate every single major action and policy of every department, testing them against the master plan. Alas, neither Treasury Board in its heyday, nor the Ministry of State for Economic and Regional Development, nor the Privy Council Office, nor the Department of Finance has ever undertaken such an endeavour, let alone succeed at it.

EXPLICIT REGIONAL DEVELOPMENT VERSUS NATIONAL POLICIES IMPACT

It is helpful to understand the relationship between national policies and regional development policies. A direct, or explicit, regional development policy is built on the selective application of specific programs, such as the Regional Development Incentives Program (RDIP), the Industrial and Regional Development Program (IRDP), the Area Development Agency (ADA), ARDA, and FRED, as well as the GDA and ERDA subsidiary agreements, with the objective of improving regional circumstances. The GDA multidimensional approach, which embraced a range of federal and provincial programs (written into the subsidiary agreements), the activities of a number of other federal departments, opportunity identification, and the removal of constraints to economic development constituted a cohesive application of such a policy of regional development. Until the advent of the DREE GDA era, no coherent regional development policy existed in Canada to envelop the activities being pursued.

The creation of DREE marked a move by the national government towards a more coherent regional economic development policy for Canada. Prior to DREE the best efforts of the federal government did not involve a broad or coordinated approach to either the geographic regions of the country or the various elements that comprise an economy. Industrial development was viewed as separate from spatial, rural, and urban development, and infrastructure development as separate from resource exploitation. Skills, educational levels, and social amenities stood apart from those efforts represented by a panoply of assistance programs. Federal planning and decision making took little account of provincial government views and capabilities and exhibited a less than desirable knowledge of real regional or local circumstances, other than a familiarity with the cold statistics that were used to quantify regional disparity.

National policies fall into the familiar categories of monetary and fiscal policy, trade and foreign affairs, defence, the environment, transportation, energy, human resources, and industrial and resource development. When a federal line department enters into regional development agreements, it is then implementing an explicit regional development policy and practising "explicit" regional development programming. The fact remains, however, that such activities do not comprise the bulk of that department's activities.

In 1980 the Liberal administration, after being back in power for four months, enunciated a rather unimaginative eight-point agenda for economic development in Canada: human resources, capital investment, energy, natural resources, technology, infrastructure, institutions, and market development. It stressed the horizontal issues of transportation, communications, and distribution.[30] The possible impact on regional development of the government's intended thrust could be assessed in several ways. For instance, the human resources item stressed skills upgrading for greater labour mobility, thereby

threatening regional development efforts to upgrade regional economies so as to keep people at home. Capital investment, depending
upon the area selected, could either aid regional economies (energy,
natural resources, decentralization of manufacturing, and infrastructure) or be detrimental to them (if region-neutral manufacturing and
infrastructure were emphasized). Similarly, technology, institutions,
and market development could either be region-neutral or lend themselves to regional tilting. These eight points cut across several departmental lines. As it turned out, they did not last long as guidelines to
economic development in the 1980s, and they were eclipsed by the
further policy changes of 1982 and 1984.

It is worth recalling Polèse's statement cited earlier that a full-blown
regional development policy for Canada would take into account the
regional consequences of all federal and provincial programs. There
is no argument that explicit regional development policies could not,
in themselves, right regional economic inequalities. That is why so
much effort has been expended in trying to muster the programs of
many departments for regional development purposes and to sensitize
departments to the impact their policies have on regional economies.
National policies present a fair target for everyone concerned about
Canada's peripheral regions. Some macro-level policies, in particular,
lend themselves to criticism. Monetary and fiscal policies are regularly
attacked by peripheral regions' provincial governments as being injurious to provincial economic growth.[31] Defence policy (but not the
awarding of defence contracts) and foreign affairs may be considered
region-neutral, but environmental policies are viewed as tilted against
regional economies (yet the regions are thought to be where the
environment remains slightly less scarred). Transportation, energy,
technology, and industrial and resource development are all fertile
areas for regional exploitation. Human resources development has
moved into the forefront as its potential for uplifting regional economies has become recognized.

Canada's continuing preoccupation with trade is a lively topic in the
peripheral regions. Is trade a help or a hindrance to regional development? Instances may be cited where the federal government has
been perceived as having taken actions detrimental to one region in
the name of the "national good." An equal number of cases can be
brought forward where actions have been taken to favour a region over
the national good. The 1987–88 Canada-France fisheries dispute was
seen as an example of the conduct of foreign affairs interfering with
the economic interests of the Atlantic region, to the latter's detriment,
Newfoundland's in particular. Tariffs and quotas are seen as working
against the national good, at least as measured by the well-being of

the general consumer. Textile and clothing import restrictions are usually cited to support this line of argument. The Canada-US Free Trade Agreement adds a whole new dimension to the trade debate, with no part of Canada exempt from its impact.

Federal government facilities bestow an economic advantage on the area in which they are located (National Defence is often mentioned in this regard). The withdrawal of such facilities has an equally significant impact.

All these federal policies, and the subsequent decisions taken outside the normal context of regional economic development, have immense consequences for regional circumstances. Although there is little room to influence macroeconomic policy in the name of regional development, modest success has been achieved in sensitizing sectoral departments to this objective.

THE TRANSFER SYSTEM AND LABOUR MOBILITY

The frustrations that accompany government actions to correct regional disparities in Canada have been well documented, backed up with an array of data illustrating the lack of success in closing measurable gaps in indicators of regional economic performance. Recent analyses have addressed the question of whether the gaps can ever be eliminated or substantially reduced. Mario Polèse has added to the evidence on the difficulties policy makers encounter in attempting to balance the Canadian economy. He writes, "Despite two world wars, a major depression, dramatic technological changes and varying government attempts to manage the Canadian economy, the relative economic weight of the two 'central' Canadian provinces has remained largely unaltered." As evidence, he shows that personal income by province as a percentage of the national total remained almost unchanged from 1910 to 1983, in Quebec moving from 23.2 to 24.2 percent and in Ontario from 41.3 to 38.7 percent. In terms of people, the combined population of Ontario and Quebec only moved from 62.9 to 61.6 percent of the Canadian total over the same period.[32]

On the other hand, Polèse reveals a consistent long-run relative decline of the three Maritime provinces, with their share of Canada's national income falling from 16.1 percent in 1890 to 10.1 percent in 1910 (measured as gross value added), 6.9 percent in 1926, and 5.3 percent in "recent years" (the early 1980s). He draws a similar profile for Manitoba and Saskatchewan. With regard to per capita income levels, Polèse's data show that in general these follow the trends in the share of national income for the Atlantic provinces, Manitoba, and Saskatchewan. Analyses focusing on the post-1945 period reveal

16

cyclical patterns of boom and bust, the Atlantic region, in particular, taking longer to recover from adverse economic conditions and the measurable gaps changing only with painful slowness.[33] Polèse concludes that the long-term stability of central Canada's share of the national whole is an indication of deep-seated locational advantages, going beyond resource endowments or other natural factors. Nevertheless, as 1992 began, Ontario residents had cause for serious concern as the province's concentration of manufacturing industry was buffeted by structural adjustment and job loss. The attributes that endow one region of the country over another and the ability of government policies to influence the endowment of the less-favoured areas of Canada are considered in subsequent chapters.

The social well-being of Canadians in all parts of the country has been relatively assured through the system of transfer payments to both governments and individuals.[34] A concern for the well-being of all Canadians has not been without cost to the nation and, coupled with the inherent preference of Canadians to be productive and self-supporting, has prompted the repeated efforts of governments to help individuals to help themselves. The enormity of the task was identified by a 1986–87 jointly commissioned task force formed to assess regional development in Canada. Its work showed just how out of balance transfers had become in relation both to direct funding and to certain indices of disparity, such as earned income and unemployment rates. The task force computed resources allocated directly to regional and industrial development at $30 per person per year (constant 1981), as compared with $1,700 per person per year in federal transfers to individuals and provincial governments and some $1,600 per person per year from provincial and local governments to individuals and from provincial to local governments. The task force assessed other federal expenditures that have an impact on regional economies and estimated that in 1984 these federal expenditures, including grants and subsidies, in such disparate sectors as agriculture, fisheries, transportation, housing, training, and research and development, were roughly six times the level of "regional development" expenditures on a per capita basis.[35]

These data paint a pessimistic picture, but there is room for optimism. Many of the expenditures in transportation, training, the resource sectors, research and development, and the like are expenditures accruing to a nation. It remains a national objective that each of Canada's regions contribute to national wealth and productivity and that individuals have the opportunity of gainful and productive employment. As the task force data indicate, proportionately little funding has gone into the explicitly regional economic development effort.

Greater effort, properly channelled, may yet lead to the attainment of regional development objectives.

Few aspects of the regional development question have received as much attention as the labour mobility/transfer payments conundrum, with the arguments being fuelled with the foregoing kinds of data. The proposition is frequently advanced that transfer payments make life too easy in the less economically advantaged regions, thus retarding outward mobility. Thomas Courchene is most associated with this concept through his expounded views (1981) that "the failure over time to submit the provinces and regions to the discipline of the market has exacerbated regional disparities and has tended to rigidify our industrial structure." Courchene postulates that transfers impede the process of regional adjustment and that decades of interrupting the process of regional economic adjustment have left some provinces increasingly dependent upon government transfers for their economic well-being.[36]

The strength of peripheral economies, the likelihood of raising them to national levels, the influence of equalization and transfer payments, externalities that go beyond the borders of Canada, and the personal preferences of individuals on where they live and how they gain their livelihood all lie at the root of the regional disparity problem. Analyses of the labour mobility/transfer payments phenomenon and the underlying premise of letting free-market forces work fail to take into consideration the even more fundamental question of what Canadians want for the federation. Do we really want to depopulate the peripheral regions of this country with a view to developing a primarily urban society and lifestyle? Would that automatically produce a stronger economy?

Mario Polèse states what most politicians, academics, and practitioners of regional development already know when he draws this conclusion to his analysis of long-term trends of regional economic development in Canada: "There are definite limits to the capacity of public policy to alter long-run patterns. ... The locational advantages and disadvantages which accrue to the various regions of Canada, including the externalities built up over many decades, are in large measure the reflection of now well established patterns and geographic realities."[37] He predicted that regional per capita income disparities would not disappear in Canada in the foreseeable future.

Accepting the inevitability of long-term per capita income disparities does not mean accepting per capita income as a sole proxy for an equality of standard of living. The standard of living is influenced by cost-of-living factors, including the degree of self-sufficiency in food and accommodation (well developed in many of the peripheral areas), the environment, social ambience, culture, and tradition. All should weigh importantly in an analysis of the out-migration solution proposed by some economists or of the concept that free-market forces would bring peripheral regions into comparative line in terms of relative wage rates. These are not workable solutions in the Canadian federation for very practical reasons.

With forced or encouraged out-migration, the mix of skills and other essential attributes carried by individuals would become even further out of balance in a region. With an exiting of these skills and entrepreneurial talent, the economy of the losing region would further deteriorate, calling for even higher levels of transfer payments to sustain an acceptable standard of living.

Lower, market-determined wages in the regions would not effect equilibrium; rather, as the inhabitants' ability to purchase consumer goods and pay the taxes to maintain essential services was further reduced, regional disparities would increase. There is also no logic in presuming that out-migration would raise the overall per capita income levels of those remaining in the regions. This presupposes that the unemployed, denied transfer payments or offered lower levels of assistance, would leave, reducing unemployment rates and increasing resident per capita income. Their leaving, however, is by no means a certainty. Other variables come into play: whether the unemployment was structural or cyclical, the composition of the economic base of the region, and the degree to which entrepreneurship is discouraged as the regional population base erodes. In a global economy, with its emphasis on skills, technology, and entrepreneurship, reduced regional or national population levels is not the answer to economic survival. Thus, to encourage out-migration from Canada's peripheral regions, so as to lower the tax level for the more prosperous regions of the country, would be to accept a reduction in the standard of living in the peripheral regions.

Mario Polèse takes cautious exception to the thesis put forward by Courchene. He acknowledges the neoclassical premise that labour will, on the whole, move from regions of low relative labour demand to areas of high relative demand and high relative wage rates. By using the important qualifier "unless otherwise motivated," he says that "labour will normally seek to adjust its supply to changing labour demand conditions, and migration is one of the possible avenues of adjustment."[38] In his analysis of the labour demand and cost-of-labour elements of the neoclassical theory, Polèse acknowledges that the theory's application would suggest that the adjustment of labour supply via migration would cause interregional disparities in unemployment and reductions in wages, and even that a policy that discouraged adjustment via migration, such as government programs, would only serve to maintain disparities.[39] In abandoning the neoclassical model, however, Polèse argues that theoretically it would not be difficult to devise a dynamic model—which would include the economic, social, cultural, and entrepreneurial costs of mobility—in which migration acted to increase regional economic disparity.[40] Polèse concludes that the state should not see migration as necessarily an efficient means to combat regional disparities and that transfer payments, which may keep people from moving, may not be as negative as is sometimes feared.[41]

In 1982 the Senate Standing Committee on National Finance had this to say on the rights of Canadians: "We believe that it is the fundamental right of Canadians to live where they choose, and that forced urbanization should not constitute an element of the government's efforts to reduce regional disparities."[42] The committee did not assess the cost of its conclusion, but did acknowledge the potential for greater productivity efficiency in urban areas. It concluded with the somewhat contradictory remark that governments should not be expected to support communities in perpetuity.

The Economic Council of Canada (ECC), in a special study of the Newfoundland economy, discussed migration in terms of out-migration and back- (or return-) migration, concluding that both work sometimes for and at other times against regional economies and that society should best remain neutral in such circumstances (it concluded that the Unemployment Insurance Commission, for example, was decidedly not neutral).[43] The ECC observed that migration can be a productive mechanism to raise opportunities for Newfoundlanders and to upgrade the skills of the province's labour force but that forced migration is not an efficient or desirable way to solve the problems of unemployment and low average incomes.[44] The ECC recommended "that migration be neither encouraged nor discouraged ... policies should be reconsidered with a view to removing incentives or disincentives to migration, either within provinces or between provinces."[45]

To give equal time to these various opinions, it is important to stress the validity of Courchene's underlying premises, namely: "Rationalization of the system to encourage initiative, efficiency and growth is a realistic goal, even if it is the case that from a political standpoint this rationalization will have to be implemented incrementally," and, "The critical issue on the regional front still remains one of encouraging provinces to move from dependency to self-reliance."[46] These very words are reflected in the Economic Council's report title, *Newfoundland: From Dependency to Self-reliance*. The council, in its most important conclusion, echoes Polèse and Courchene:

The main hope of Newfoundland lowering its unemployment and
raising its productivity does not lie in the resource industries.
Rather ... it lies with the people in the province and with the
ways in which they organize themselves and their activities. ...
It depends ... on the education, training, and experience of labour
and management alike. ... In the end, it will require some
reorientation of the economic system. ... With the benefit of
hindsight, we can see that subsidies, transfers, poor resource management, and bad business decisions have contributed to
inefficiencies in the system of economic organization and to
individual economic responses, which have intensified the unemployment problem.[47]

It can be assumed that the council believed its remarks on Newfoundland had substantial, if not complete, application to all of Canada's
peripheral regions.

The literature shows differences of opinion on the workforce
mobility/transfer payments issue. Yves Rabeau quotes the work of
Buchanan et al. to the effect that transfer payments to the provinces
constitute an efficient allocation of resources in the federation by
discouraging excessive interregional migration of labour.[48] Courchene
comments on the inefficiencies of excessive migration to resource-rich
regions.[49] Rabeau, in examining the theory that transfer payments to
the provinces and individuals reduce provincial government initiative
in the field of regional development, adds that provincial efforts to
close the measurable disparity gap could adversely affect the receipt
of federal transfer payments.[50] The theory of transfer-payment-induced
inertia is not new, but it seriously demeans the integrity of provincial
government leaders and their citizens. People want to work, and
working citizens and a flourishing economy make the lives of politicians, federal or provincial, a good deal easier. Regional development
policy should therefore strive to develop an economic environment
within which the people of the region are free to choose where to
work and what lifestyle to pursue. In a global economy, it is not
realistic to tailor strategies to keep the people of the regions "home,"
nor is it appropriate to pursue policies aimed at forced migration.

What of the political attitude on out-migration? In 1960, at what
became known as the Kingston Liberal Party Conference (erroneously
so labelled, according to Tom Kent), Kent proposed an eleven-point
agenda for development for the party under the title "Towards a
Philosophy of Social Security." An item on regional development held
that moving people was economically wasteful and socially disruptive.
Kent suggested that government should moderate adjustments by

making public investments and offering inducements to moving some jobs to where the workers were.[51] Kent also spoke of the ingrained beliefs in Ottawa in the Pearson years that central management was good management and that people would move to where the jobs undoubtedly existed. Believing these ideas incompatible with the new federalism, he set about trying to change them.[52]

In a briefing session some twenty-six years later, Sinclair Stevens, then minister of regional industrial expansion in the Mulroney Conservative government, suggested half-seriously (although with Stevens one could never quite be sure) that the department adopt a position of ensuring adequate levels of well-being and job opportunity in the less-developed regions, but not so high as to discourage out-migration. Officials reminded the minister of the deleterious effects of such an approach on the people remaining in the region and of the consequent difficulties in sustaining the services and the economy of such a depopulated region—the critical-mass argument, in other words. The idea never resurfaced with Stevens. His subsequent actions in Atlantic Canada, particularly in Cape Breton, would indicate that he did not dwell too long on the out-migration idea. Stevens had very good political antennae and would be the first to recognize the political dangers of any federal endorsement of a regional emigration stance. Thus, with all the academic discussion on the subject, it will not become a deliberate plank in any federal regional development policy.

The Constitution and Federal-Provincial Jurisdictions

The perennial controversy that surrounds federal-provincial relations in the Canadian federation requires that these relations be taken into account in any discussion of the theories of regional development. It has been said that intergovernmental relations in a cooperative federalism such as Canada are based on each of the two senior levels of government (federal and provincial) formulating its own policies and initiatives, then meeting together as equals to negotiate mutually agreed upon adjustments. Donald Savoie concludes that the General Development Agreements process "manifestly departs from this tradition" with consequences for both political and administrative institutions of Canada.[53] At both levels of government, ministers enter negotiations with all aspects of an idea having been thoroughly explored by officials, no matter where the idea originated. Before an understanding is reached or an agreement signed, officials from the two levels will have examined the policy alternatives and the consequences of the proposals on the table, and they will likely have met together both before and after ministerial meetings.

A review of federal-provincial conferences and negotiations, from first ministers down and covering such diverse topics as fiscal arrangements, health care, manpower training and employment, the environment, agriculture stabilization, energy, resource development and management, science policy, and economic and regional development, reveals an array of formats but with one thing in common — extensive contact at both the political and bureaucratic levels. Thorburn reports an increasing level of contact between 1957 and 1977, with formally registered ministerial contacts increasing from 5 to 31, and contacts between officials from 59 to 127.[54] Kernaghan and Siegel record 482 federal-provincial liaison bodies as early as 1972 and more than 1,000 federal-provincial committees of varying degrees of importance by 1987. During the twelve months following the September 1984 election, there were 438 federal-provincial meetings, 13 being meetings of first ministers, 353 of ministers, and 72 of deputy ministers.[55] Peter Leslie refers to a 1985 inventory of cost-shared federal-provincial programs that exceeded 300 pages and lists.[56] It would be hard to believe that the GDA stood out so dramatically among all the others, notwithstanding its flexibility and uniqueness.

The GDA approach to regional development has been viewed by some as seriously blurring constitutional responsibilities in Canada, resulting in the setting aside of constitutional niceties.[57] Whether or not that is the case, and there is no convincing argument to support the contention, this discussion on federal-provincial relations and regional development needs to address constitutional assignments to the respective levels of government. From the advent of the GDA to the present day, both levels of government have implemented programs in areas of the other's jurisdiction, the federal side perhaps taking the greatest liberties in this regard. During this time there has been little dispute of a jurisdictional nature, only scattered, politically motivated disagreements.

The Division of Power

The division of powers in a federal state may create areas of "policy vacuum" where neither order of government can deal effectively with certain problems or act efficaciously to achieve certain policy aims. Conversely, it may create areas of overlap in which both levels of government become active. In either case, there may be governmental interaction in policy formulation, so that policy is really a joint product of the activities of two governments. Peter Leslie observes that many commentators and even government actors have complained about duplication, confusion, and delay under such circumstances, where governments may be working at cross-purposes.[58] The converse, however, may be equally true. Any argument based on a clear separation of areas of policy responsibility presumes that one head is better than two and that one government working alone would always have the best response to any particular situation. Even where the priorities for action of two levels of government are at cross-purposes, it is in the public interest to have a reconciliation of views rather than a less than fully effective policy outcome, with the actions of either of the two levels of government detracting from those of the other. David Milne, in his observations on the tug of war that goes on between governments, concludes that "one of the most serious consequences of this political warring between the two orders of government is a decline in policy effectiveness in tackling problems. Not only can politically inspired unilateralism send the governments off in costly and inefficient duplication or contradiction of each other, it can materially injure the public interest groups caught in the government crossfire."[59] During the era of the GDA system, and to a lesser extent thereafter, it is probably safe to say that both levels of government exercised policy responsibilities, separately and together, the results generally being to the common good.

Leslie also emphasizes that the practical realities of policy making dictate that political support is frequently as important as the possession of constitutional powers in determining the distribution of policy responsibilities in a federal system.[60] The federal government has received political support for its intervention in the field of regional development policy, where it has assumed prime decision-making authority in areas of clear provincial jurisdiction. Provincial governments have acquiesced to this arrangement where the federal level held the required spending power, accepting a program delivery role for themselves.

Leslie brings federalism and the constitutional question into the present when he says in his discussion of entanglement, "Federalism has often been equated with the division of powers. Today, however, there is no federal state in which policy responsibilities are allocated in even moderately watertight compartments to the two (or more) orders of government. Both the division and the sharing of powers have become essential aspects of contemporary federalism."[61] The two senior levels of government may have difficulty in establishing their authority to operate in areas not clearly delineated by the constitution, legal interpretation, or precedent. There may be areas where neither order of government has clearly recognized jurisdiction, areas where both have interlocking, yet exclusive powers in a single policy field (for regional development, certain of the resource sectors, such as agriculture, forestry, mining, and fisheries), and areas of overlapping constitutional powers, which might include industrial development. Leslie says that entanglement is frequently criticized as complicating the lives of citizens and interest groups and as decreasing the likelihood of good actions (things get done more slowly or not at all) and the attainment of policy objectives. If governments do work together under these circumstances, they may be criticized for being undemocratic.[62] Some of these reactions were present in the response of politicians and academics to the close working relationships that existed between the federal and the provincial governments during the GDA era. Interest groups frequently felt left out of the picture, partially because of their inability to gain access to opportunities available to them.

With regard to economic development and the constitution, Milne says, "From the strict perspective of intergovernmental relations, there is wide latitude for philosophical disagreement about the role to be played by each level of government in relation to economic development. The constitution provides very little guidance on the appropriate balance of responsibilities and, in this respect, might be looked upon as a power reservoir for the different policy goals of provincial and federal politicians rather than an authoritative guide for distributing economic responsibilities."[63] Canadians have made it clear that they expect their federal government to take responsibility for improving regional economies, and they are not deterred by arguments of constitutional jurisdiction at the various levels of government that serve them.

Government Interaction and Policy Formulation

In elaborating his views on government interaction in policy formation, Leslie describes three ranges of performance that have particular relevance to regional development. The federal and provincial governments may share the same goals, they may have policy differences but share underlying objectives, or they may be at variance on both counts. All three situations have existed in the regional development arena. Leslie observes that governments may move closer to each other through dialogue and information exchange followed by independent action by one of the parties or by the joint funding of activities. In the instance where joint funding has been determined to be appropriate or necessary, Leslie suggests that nothing gets done unless the inducements work and a program is launched by mutual agreement, resulting in reciprocal action, notwithstanding the degree of goodwil that may or may not exist.[64] We know that the goodwill that generally existed during the era of the GDAs was not present in the more heavy-handed

initiatives consummated prior to 1973–74. Anthony Careless emphasizes this in his work *Initiative and Response*.[65] Federal unilateralism
emerged in regional development again in 1980, subsided in 1984,
and re-emerged as a concept in 1987. By 1989, strong political over-
tones clouded federal actions when the monotonous expressions of
federal disenchantment with provincial credit-taking once more surfaced.

Under DREE cost-shared arrangements, the provinces vacated certain
areas they had previously jealously guarded, reluctantly before 1973–
74, somewhat more willingly thereafter under the GDAs. Full consultation took place, followed by independent action by one party or the
other; full collaboration was effected in both policy and programming;
but antagonism was also observed. One constant remained over the
1973–82 period irrespective of the climate that prevailed: federal-
provincial agreements to improve regional economies continued to be
concluded.

At whatever stage of harmony or disharmony during a particular
period of federal-provincial collaboration, however, Leslie rightly
points out that "the history of shared-cost programs does reveal that
federal policy in these areas has been considerably influenced by
provincial demands. There is enough common ground in the areas
covered by joint funding arrangements to produce extensive bargaining."[66] What Leslie shows is that the GDA practice was not so very
different from other federal-provincial arrangements of cost-shared
programs (see the section on federal-provincial negotiation in
chapter 2 for a discussion of this point).

Levels of Influence

The degree of influence exercised by one level of government or the
other on economic development in Canada has been a subject of debate
under both centralized and decentralized models of the federation.
Leslie concludes that in regional development the potential for national
economic integration, and the integration of development strategies
based on it, is inhibited when provincial governments exercise policy
autonomy in economic development—the suggestion being that
provincial actions (in areas in which they exercise control) may be
incompatible with national economic integration. Leslie claims that even
centrally directed policies of regional development, other than those
aimed at economic adjustment, are similarly retrogressive.[67] He says
that, on the whole, regional development policies retard adjustment to
changing technologies and market conditions rather than promote it.[68]
This is a view that the author does not share. There is a strong argument

to be made that adaptation of technologies and adjustment to market conditions can be completely compatible with the objectives of improving regional economies; indeed, that they must be. Leslie implies that accepting adjustment for regional economies is tantamount to giving up on the potential of the regions to capitalize as well as on technology and the changing demands of the world marketplace. If the regions are not accorded equal opportunity (with central Canada) in this regard, however, the alternative again becomes out-migration.

The location of the control of the Canadian economy is seen in an ominous light by some observers. In commenting on the Trudeau agenda for economic renewal that was played out during and after the Liberals' successful election campaign of 1980, Milne says,

> The federal drive to strengthen the national economy had a decidedly centralist bent. As early as the summer of 1980, during the constitutional talks with the provinces, Ottawa unveiled a new constitutional agenda item intended to strengthen its powers to protect the domestic economy from provincial restrictions and infringements. In a lengthy attack on the damaging effects of provincial economic development policies on the economy, Ottawa sought constitutional instruments to curtail these practices and thus, indirectly, to tame the ambitions of the provinces. These initiatives were followed up by an array of policy decisions in the general area of economic development, the net effects of which were to circumvent, contain or undermine the provinces in their previous economic roles and/or to give Ottawa itself a more forceful and direct role in the economy.[69]

One action related to this federal intent was the introduction in 1980 of direct program delivery under the GDAS (and subsequently the ERDAS). This was designed to give the federal level a front-line involvement in regional development in the provinces. As is discussed in later chapters, direct program delivery did not succeed in bringing the government the kind of attention it had hoped for. In the admittedly narrower field of regional economic development, the national government was able to exercise greater control by employing cooperative instruments such as the General Development Agreements.

Regional development practice has not been as great a source of federal-provincial disagreement as such issues as the structure and content of the Constitution itself or energy policy, which more readily inflame passions at both levels of governments.[70] Leslie does not conclude that the Constitution carries any serious blame for problems that might occur in economic development policy. Rather, he sees it as underpinning a process that still provides a sufficient framework within which politicians can work to discharge assumed or assigned responsibilities in economic policy. In other words, the practical can prevail without contravening the constitution.

The GDAS recognized the constitutional assignment of jurisdictions pertinent to economic development, to the degree that they existed. The provinces delivered programs in assigned jurisdictions and in areas where no assignment had been specifically made, such as direct financial incentives to business, an area in which the federal government had long exercised an independent role. The federal government assisted in physical infrastructure (including schools, roads, and municipal systems), rural development, education, and training. The process of federal-provincial negotiations by which these positions were reached could not blur constitutional responsibilities or contradict the Constitution, since the Constitution never spelled out such practices. There were, and continue to be, areas where dispute goes beyond political bickering, but falls short of challenging respective constitutional or other acknowledged jurisdictions. The basis of much of the provincial concern, especially from the less wealthy provinces, has been the principle of undeniable right to federal support.

It is clear that the Constitution, recognized jurisdiction, and even historical precedent have not stood in the way of governments' attempts to remedy regional economic shortcomings. There is much to be encouraged about in this. The evidence shows that the two levels of government can set aside political, ideological, and economic policy differences in the interest of improving regional economic circumstances. Inevitably, there have been, and continue to be, problems when political imperatives intrude into the common-sense arena of regional development—concerns with visibility, taking credit, the provincial distribution of funding, short-term expediencies over long-term strategies—but these relate to human failings, not constitutional jurisdictions, and are both a test and a measure of the goodwill of our political leaders.

The management of the Canadian economy became an important component of a new federal constitutional proposal revealed in September 1991 titled *Shaping Canada's Future Together*. One offer made by the national government was to recognize the exclusive jurisdiction of the provinces in the areas of tourism, forestry, mining, recreation, housing, and municipal/urban affairs. The proposal that the federal government assume a lead role in managing the economic union received short shift from provincial governments.

The uneasiness that surrounded the more frantic constitutional discussions of 1991 was further revealed when a somewhat routine, jointly funded $300-million extension to a Canada-Quebec subsidiary agreement drew fire as being a ploy to further curry favour with Quebec in the constitutional contest.

THE REGIONAL DEVELOPMENT FUND

Of all of the ideas put forward for regional development, none has been more fanciful than the regional development fund. There is the presumption that funding in this way is somehow easier, that all of the problems of regional economic inequalities would be taken care of just by the fund's existence. It is a fitting subject with which to close this chapter on the Canadian context for regional development.

The level of federal funding dedicated directly to economic development in the less-endowed regions of Canada and the method by which funding is made available are subjects of almost universal interest. Recipients of such funding, in whatever form, usually suggest it is not enough. Provincial governments regularly cite data to prove that historic levels of funding have been eroded both in absolute terms and by inflation. The outcry that followed the April 1989 federal budget, which cut funding and cost-sharing levels for federal-provincial agreements, is such an example. Organizations with a particular attachment to a recipient region have made many analyses and recommendations for higher levels of expenditure on regional development.[71] Dedicated funding is important in regional economic development. Explicit regional economic development expenditures, however, are dwarfed by the total federal expenditures (excluding transfer payments) that have an influence on regional economies. But this is only part of the story. Much of what the federal government does within its national mandate is done, first and foremost, within a national context. Although a federal expenditure's impact on regional economies is usually recognized, this is generally not the primary reason for the expenditure, other than its being part of a national policy or program thrust. Thus, it may or may not accord with provincial, or even federal, regional economic development priorities.

The greatest benefit of dedicated funding is its discretionary nature. Notwithstanding charges that provinces have manipulated federal-provincial agreements to their advantage by using the funding to supplement their provincial departmental budgets and even to undertake projects envisaged in their own budgets, the dedicated federal funding generally makes things happen that otherwise would not happen or would be indefinitely delayed. Even if the federal funding does substitute for provincial funding, it nevertheless frees up monies for other things in support of regional economies. Explicit federal expenditures, properly managed, can have a disproportionately high level of impact on regional economic activities, opening up new and exciting development opportunities and removing blockages to economic development.

The idea of a regional fund, by which the federal government would dispense funds for regional development purposes in an orderly fashion, is largely a myth, but the concept manifests itself in many forms. The Royal Commission on the Economic Union and Development Prospects for Canada (the Macdonald Commission) recommended that provinces qualifying for equalization payments would be eligible for regional economic development grants determined by a formula on a per capita basis related to the equalization formula. The provinces would be free to use the grants for place-specific employment measures as part of their own approach to regional development, subject to their signing a code of conduct and to a federal-provincial plan for the province.[72] The suggestion is naive in concept and is in inherent contradiction with the principles of accountability.

A recurring suggestion in regional development circles over the years, particularly at the provincial level but even in some circles of the federal level, has been the idea of transferring a block of funds to a province on a non-accountable basis, other than it be used for regional development purposes, and letting the province decide its regional development priorities. There is, however, no compromise position between this approach and that of the federal government exercising its responsibilities in the field of regional development, not to mention the complete loss of visibility that the federal government would face by such a move. Nevertheless, Donald Savoie speculated on such an approach in 1981, suggesting that "conceivably, a federal unconditional grant to the have-not provinces would be satisfactory. The provinces would have the freedom to spend within limits of the federal grant and, as a result, they would be accountable for their expenditures."[73] If Savoie uses "accountable" in the sense that the provinces would have full responsibility for the use of the funding, then he advocates block funding. It would not be possible for the federal government to attach a condition—for example, that the province be accountable to the federal government on how it spent the money—to an unconditional grant. Savoie went on to say that perhaps a special economic development fund, by which federally managed funds could be provided to provinces, federal departments, and the private sector (as proposed by Richard Higgins to the Senate Standing Committee on National Finance in 1978), might be more palatable to the federal government.[74] He shifted his view somewhat later when he said, along with John Chénier: "In our view, a new mix of federal initiatives should be designed and implemented; a federal role beyond that of merely passing money on to the provinces according to some formula is an absolute necessity. Programmed commitment towards goals is preferable to a flat payment, which may quickly be interpreted as absolving the federal government of any responsibility for the outcome."[75]

James McNiven rejected the Macdonald Commission's recommendation that the regional development grant formula be linked to the equalization formula, believing that this would be self-defeating for provincial treasuries. He proposed, instead, a system based on a province's economic standing relative to the national average, with development bonuses paid to those provinces whose growth rates exceeded the standings in any given year—in other words, an incentives system. The bonuses, according to McNiven, would have to more than offset any reduction in equalization payments.[76]

Proposals for block-funding solutions are included under the aegis of a regional fund because block funding is a form of dedicated funding for the specific use of regional economic development. The concept has many weaknesses, however, and little to commend it. Block funding almost certainly has to be province-specific, thus removing the potential for any truly region-wide planning, and it negates the possibility of a national framework for regional development. Furthermore, block funding does not involve federal responsibility. Federal government attempts to do something on its own in the face of several, probably different, provincial approaches would end in chaos. Not only is block funding inconsistent in concept with block transfer of funds to a province with an accountability proviso, it is unworkable without a federal co-planning and approval role; the provinces would have no difficulty in doing what they wanted with the funding.[77] The federal government would no longer be in the game unless it chose to compete with the provinces—a wasteful and no-win position.

Most regional fund proposals envisage a separate allocation of funds set aside for regional development purposes, with decisions taken by ministers, to whom submissions may be made on behalf of provinces, federal government departments, and the private sector.[78] For example, all funding committed to subsidiary agreements under the Economic and Regional Development Agreements would be a charge against the regional fund. Although it was said at the outset that the regional fund idea is a myth, a regional fund did in fact first exist as the dedicated budget of DREE in the period 1974–82. During the DREE period, the decision function was taken by ministers—first by Treasury Board, a committee of cabinet, and after 1978 by committees of cabinet charged with regional development responsibilities (Cabinet Committee on

31

Economic Development and later the Cabinet Committee on Economic and Regional Development). The reason a regional fund works under a one-responsibility-centre arrangement is that raiding is held to a minimum.

The greatest weakness of a broad-based regional development fund to which all federal departments have access is that it is vulnerable to raiding. Almost any departmental project or program may be cloaked in the guise of a regional development initiative, and without an experienced focal point for assessment purposes, it may well be allocated funding from the regional reserve. It is virtually impossible, despite the checks and balances that Treasury Board or some other designated authority might suggest, to determine whether the initiative would have gone forward under the department's regular activities (formerly known as its "A" base) or would have been a new proposal (formerly a "B" budget item) within the departmental mandate. It would probably be accurate to say that virtually no departmental proposal, other than those from a department specifically charged with regional development responsibilities, is put forward first and foremost as a regional development project intended to enhance regional economies.

Raiding can be avoided by having all regional development proposals flow through one department charged with the regional development responsibility, with control of the budget, and with an implementation role in its own right. In this way projects of other departments judged supportive of the main thrust of regional development policy may be entirely funded, or "topped up," if clearly within the mandate of the sponsoring department.[79] The regional fund approach is also vulnerable to political raiding in situations where there is no one responsible minister fo fend it off.[80]

Finding examples of regional funds is difficult. With DREE and regional development agencies that were to follow, their assigned budget was and is a regional fund, clearly identifiable and visible. In every other form, regional funds have been much less so, being supplemented or eroded at the whim of ministers. The western development fund that emerged from the Western Economic Opportunities Conference (WEOC) of the 1970s never did exist. The regional fund associated with the 1982 reorganization of economic departments remained shadowy for the years that MSERD existed. This is hardly surprising. When ministers congregate to decide the ordering of priorities of government activities, whether within the envelope system while it existed or via the expenditure priorities committee structure, they are not overly constrained by bookkeeping parameters, which is all that a reserve fund is. They will do what they want, particularly if politically driven. They will reallocate funds between reserves, adding or subtracting as needed. Although dedicated departmental budgets are also subject to change, upwards or downwards, such change must be a deliberate action, reflected in the Estimates that go before Parliament for approval. This is therefore a public process, unlike the cabinet process.

Summary

The context within which regional development in Canada has been pursued has been politically complicated and vigorously scrutinized by academics and other observers of the federation. The analysis that follows attempts to remain cognizant of this context. Many of the regional development concepts recounted in this chapter have found there way into practice, in whole or in part. Many others have not. In the eye of the beholder, much may be imagined. The following four chapters describe and assess the policies implemented and the efforts made by federal governments to right regional economic disparities in Canada during the period 1973–92.

Chapter Two

DREE: Dispelling the Myths

INTRODUCTION

Under no other mantle has the federal government, aided and abetted by provincial governments, focused such deliberate, coordinated attention on regional economic development as it did under the Department of Regional Economic Expansion, created on April 1, 1969. Numerous other federal actions over time acknowledged the economic differences that existed and continue to exist across Canada. DREE was, however, to be the government's intended solution to regional economic inequality in this country. The solution was to be achieved by focusing and consolidating the full attack on the problem in this one central department. This was the intent, despite the fact that at no time in its short history was the department allocated even as much as 1 percent of the federal budget to discharge its awesome responsibility.

Then prime minister Pierre Trudeau, speaking in the House of Commons on the establishment of DREE said:

> We know ... that regional disparities have existed since the very first days of Confederation. We also know that the federal government has attempted, especially for a few years now, to reduce such disparities by having recourse to equalization payments, cost sharing programs and an increasing number of regional development projects. Most of those regional development programs were the responsibility of five Ministers, I should say of several departments and various agencies. Mr. Speaker, after all such programs have been consolidated under the sole Department of Regional Economic Expansion, we shall be clearly in a better position to achieve real coordination and centralization of our endeavors and

undertakings in such a worthy and vital sphere in respect of our country's future.[1]

Jean Marchand, the minister who was to run the new department, saw its objective as being to ensure that Canadians had good opportunities to earn their living at roughly comparable standards wherever they lived in Canada. He concluded that organizational and mandate change was a logical embodiment of the objective: "This legislation will, therefore, firmly charge the new department ... with the central responsibility for federal regional development programs. This is the only way to secure the co-ordination of federal effort which is essential to the achievement of the most effective results."[2]

There were other ideas about regional development in the new Trudeau government of 1968. Jean Marchand and Tom Kent, to be minister and deputy minister respectively of the new department, had expansive ideas of folding regional development into a restructured Department of Manpower and Immigration to form a Department of Development. Thought was given to the creation of a super-ministry that would have both federal coordinating authority for regional development and a programming capability. These options were shot down at both the political and bureaucratic levels in Ottawa, where fear of such a powerful department was extreme.[3] Other variations of the theme were explored. Kent said much later that "there were those who thought that the department should have been a purely planning, negotiating and coordinating agency with programming remaining with line departments."[4]

The end-result of the deliberation and internal negotiation (the Treasury Board in those days still carried a lot of clout) was a new department of government with an assigned regional development mandate. It carried some responsibility, but not enough authority, for interdepartmental coordination, and it had full planning and programming capability. For a time it also had two powerful ministers (that Jean Marchand, the first DREE minister, had the ear of the prime minister, is without dispute; Don Jamieson earned Trudeau's confidence by his demonstrated policial acumen).

From 1969 through 1973, the new department continued to deliver the programs it had inherited from other departments at the time of its formation, adding a new industrial incentives program, the Regional Development Incentives Program, and initiating a series of federal-provincial Special Area Agreements. During this period, however, the department was also carrying out one of the most comprehensive reviews of regional development policy ever conducted in Canada. The

35

new policy that emerged from that review, and that was put in place in remarkably short order, was to have a profound influence on regional economic development programming and federal-provincial relations. As a consequence of the policy intentions, a federal bureaucratic reorganization of a kind not before seen in Ottawa also took place. In a period measured in months, DREE was converted to a decentralized operational mode. Significant numbers of public servants were transferred out of Ottawa to the regions, with no level in the bureaucratic hierarchy being exempt. The result was senior officials in the field at the assistant deputy minister level, perhaps for the first time in federal government experience.[5]

A further dimension of the decentralized approach was the make-up of regional staff complements. It had by this time been conceded that made-in-Ottawa policies—and even more so, Ottawa-based implementation decision making—were not conducive to region-sensitive programming. Although the 1973–74 DREE decentralization did see large numbers of officials moved to the regions, the largest proportion of the DREE regional staff, across the country, was from those regions. This blend of knowledge and experience both of regional conditions and of the Ottawa network made a valuable complement to provincial government expertise in the field of regional development.[6]

These actions gave form to the government's committment to regional development as expressed in the Speech from the Throne for the 29th Parliament of Canada, January 4, 1973. One of four main objectives in the area of economic policy was to ensure that all regions of the country would benefit from the prosperity brought about by the expanding economy. One of the measures to be taken to obtain this objective was to decentralize the Department of Regional Economic Expansion to a greater degree so that it would be in a better position to identify opportunities for economic development.

Richard Phidd and Bruce Doern observe that the renewed federal approach to regional development had a political motivation. They attribute the policy changes that took DREE regional development programming into each Canadian province to the 1972 election results, which revealed weak political support in the West and in the Maritimes, and to continued post-election pressures. They further attribute the earlier DREE expenditure policy to strong political pressures that forced ad hoc program activity ahead of the later, more comprehensive policy development of the department.[7] David Milne reads into the creation of DREE the federal desire to extend its control over economic policy in Canada.[8]

The new federal policy was described to the Standing Committee on Regional Development in April 1973 by Donald Jamieson, by then the minister of the still-fledgling department: "This is what has led me to speak publicly in recent weeks about the possibilities inherent in a 'multi-dimensional approach' — an approach that would call for the identification and pursuit of major development opportunities by means of the coordinated application of public policies and programs, federal and provincial, in cooperation where appropriate with elements of the private sector."[9] Jamieson also saw the implications for federal-provincial relations when he pointed out that his suggested approach could bring about important improvements in federal-provincial cooperation in economic development.[10]

All the right ingredients were present to make the DREE approach work. In policy terms this was the most exhaustively developed concept of regional economic development yet advanced in Canada. Yet, in announcing DREE's death knell in 1982, Prime Minister Trudeau enunciated a new federal policy that would place the responsibility for regional development with all departments of government: "Every economy-related department within Government will be more sensitive and responsive to regional economic development issues, concerns and opportunities. New and major regional economic opportunities now make it imperative that the regional perspective be brought to bear on the work of all economic development departments and in all economic decision-making by the Cabinet." In a passing reference to DREE, Trudeau credited the department with having laid the groundwork for the regional development effort, but he maintained that one department was no longer enough to carry that prime responsibility.[11]

Because of this remarkable reversal in policy, it is reasonable to examine what happened to DREE over its short life, most particularly in the period 1974–82. Hopefully a new dimension will be added to Canadians' understanding of this imaginative approach to regional development in Canada and some of the myths and inaccuracies that have grown up without repudiation will be dispelled.

The policy thrust that precipitated the DREE departmental reorganization was founded on the principle of joint federal-provincial economic development planning. The vehicle for this joint collaboration was the ten-year (1974–84) General Development Agreement, an umbrella concept statement tailored to the economic circumstances of each of the nine participating provinces. Prince Edward Island had already signed a fifteen-year Comprehensive Development Plan (CDP) with the federal government in 1969, which remained valid. Each GDA permitted subsidiary agreements to be developed within its framework, to define project activities, and to describe their source of funding.

The objectives of the GDAS were clearly articulated by their proponents, and they have been interpreted and assessed by many observers. In simple terms, the GDAS were intended to be effective federal-provincial instruments for the enhancement of provincial and regional economies, planned around the comparative advantages jointly identified as existing in those provinces and regions. The GDAS would meet their objectives by strengthening the existing economic base, removing impediments to growth, and creating new economic opportunity. Individual agreements stressed closing measurable disparity gaps, allowing people to remain in the area of their choice, and working towards other specially identified objectives. Long-term, reliable, employment opportunity was a fundamental goal of all agreements. Appendix 1 provides more detail on the individual General Development Agreements and the Prince Edward Island Comprehensive Development Plan.

Over time, some of the federal government's other objectives in putting forward the DREE/GDA concept were abandoned. As early as 1973 the federal government was aware that the programs of individual federal departments, some of which were implemented through federal-provincial agreements, were not seen to be connected to any coordinated federal regional development policy. The government recognized that this diminished the likelihood of its receiving due credit for its efforts. Hence, the new approach deliberately intended that DREE be a conduit for all federal regional economic development activity in Canada. It was expected that even DREE's financial assistance programs, at the time represented by the Regional Development Incentives Program (RDIP), would be slotted into the overall economic development policy for the regions. Anthony Careless writes: "DREE was a positive response to the new criteria of economic and financial efficiency developed by Finance and Treasury Board, which they found repeatedly frustrated by existing departmental programs for tackling regional disparities."[12]

The GDAS were to concentrate only on areas of need. Ontario, British Columbia, and Alberta were identified as areas of natural high growth not requiring priority DREE attention. The subsidiary agreements to the GDAS were initially designed to bring together a coordinated application of existing federal and provincial programs; new funding devices were to be employed only where existing programs were found to be inadequate or where programs did not exist to meet an identified opportunity. It is perhaps in this area more than in any other that program activity deviated from intent.

Much of this discussion on DREE centres on the four eastern-most provinces, although the principles and processes addressed obtained across all the provinces and regions under the department's jurisdiction. A larger number of subsidiary agreements were written in the

Atlantic region than elsewhere, they were put in place sooner, and they covered a wider range of activity. In the first years, almost half the departmental program funds were expended in this region, never falling below 40 percent until after 1979–80. During the GDA period to March 31, 1982 (the year of the DREE/ITC merger), 48 percent of all subsidiary agreements, including the PEI Comprehensive Development Plan, were written in the Atlantic region, comprising 45.9 percent of federal financial commitments. See Tables 2.1 and 2.2. The magnitude of the DREE program activity in Atlantic Canada comprised well over $2 billion federal dollars committed and some $1.8 billion expended in the period 1974–82. Close to three hundred federal DREE officials and scores of provincial officials were involved.

In such a departure from any previous practice of regional development in Canada, views will be held on what is being done, why, how, and what success is being achieved. The clientele—individuals, businesses, provincial and municipal governments, and special interest groups—generally exhibit the most intense interest. Objectives, expectations, and motives are different for all who are involved with or who feel the impact of the new policy thrust. Academics and other interested observers want to study the experiment from a clinical point of view. So it was with the DREE experience of 1973–82.

Donald Savoie has written extensively on the practice of regional development in New Brunswick, basing his work on his own experience and on interviews with a number of the participants in the process in that province. Using this information base, he reached a number of conclusions, one being that the GDAs should not be renewed upon their expiration.[13] At the same time, he concluded that "given its remarkable flexibility, from an administrative point of view the GDA approach is perhaps the most appropriate and expedient federal-provincial decision making approach yet introduced."[14]

Results obtained through the interview technique must be interpreted with care. It is likely that interviewees have a particular bias on the subject being discussed. Very often they will say what they believe the interviewer wants to hear. More important, their opinions will be shaped by the degree to which they are involved with the subject being researched. This is the source of many of the inaccuracies that have inadvertently found their way into some of the assessments of DREE, thereby colouring some of the conclusions reached.

Savoie acknowledged that his findings in New Brunswick may not have held in other provinces but suggested that his conclusions might be applied to the other Atlantic provinces.[15] It is instructive to examine the content of Savoie's interviews and his conclusions based on them with reference to the actual operational mode that existed across the

TABLE 2.1
GDA COMMITMENTS

To End of Fiscal Year	Atlantic ($ '000)			DREE Canada ($ '000)			Atlantic As % of Canada		
	Agreements[a]	Total[b] Commitment	Federal[c] Commitment	Agreements	Total Commitment	Federal Commitment	Agreements	Total Commitment	Federal Commitment
1975–76	24	632,513	485,460	51	1,320,653	888,118	47.0	47.9	54.7
1976–77	35	809,231	620,928	69	1,809,241	1,221,114	50.7	45.4	51.3
1977–78	41	1,142,656	884,631	81	3,138,010	1,987,161	50.6	36.4	44.5
1978–79	45	1,344,737	1,038,615	92	3,795,429	2,412,109	48.9	35.4	43.0
1979–80	49	1,475,217	1,147,701	109	4,622,185	2,885,722	45.0	32.0	40.0
1980–81	54	1,707,247	1,338,709	118	5,053,765	3,177,380	45.8	33.4	42.1
1981–82	61	2,062,343	1,628,159	128	5,616,293	3,550,821	47.6	36.7	45.9
1982–83	Year of the DREE/ITC merger—20 agreements transferred, 16 expired								

SOURCE: DREE annual reports 1975–76 through 1982–83.

NOTES

1. It is important to recognize that these expenditures did not represent all DREE regional development program activities during the period. They represent as little as 46.5 percent in 1975–76 and up to a peak of close to 71 percent in the period 1978–80.

2. By 1982–83, DREE direct expenditures had fallen sharply as a result of the transfer of twenty agreements to other departments and the expiration of sixteen others.

3. This table was constructed as faithfully as possible by adjusting for agreement amendments, additions, and deletions, thereby differing from many other macro-comparisons that have been quoted by other sources.

a Number of subsidiary agreements, with each of the three phases of the PEI CDP counted as one agreement

b Federal and provincial, but excluding private sector contributions

c All involved federal departments

TABLE 2.2

DREE EXPENDITURE PATTERNS, ALL PROGRAMS[a]

Year	DREE Atlantic[b]	DREE Canada[b] ($ '000)	Atlantic as a percentage of Canada
1969–70	111,654	208,828	53.5
1970–71	174,490	317,708	54.9
1971–72	141,419	328,060	43.1
1972–73	153,786	348,134	44.2
1973–74	163,460	404,235	40.4
1974–75	195,406	413,884	47.2
1975–76	207,785	458,472	45.3
1976–77	207,734	445,493	46.6
1977–78	198,645	497,778	39.9
1978–79	204,798	506,570	40.4
1979–80	226,759	561,298	40.4
1980–81	201,569	594,520	33.4
1981–82	183,338	573,578	32.0
1982–83	129,662	389,161	33.3

SOURCE: DREE annual reports 1975–76 through 1982–83.

[a] All programs include GDA subsidiary agreements, RDIA, ARDA, Special Areas, the PEI Comprehensive Development Plan, etc., on the basis that regional development is not any one program but a coordinated effort of all pertinent activities. By fiscal year 1975–76, subsidary agreement expenditures plus the PEI CDP comprised 46.5 percent of program expenditures. They rose to 53.5 percent in 1976–77, 68 percent in 1977–78, and peaked in the period 1978-80 at close to 71 percent, afterwards falling off to 60 percent in 1980–81 and 63 percent in 1981–82.

[b] These data minus an "other" category of headquarters, regional office, and related administrative costs give more accurate *program* activity level comparisons—some others have not made this distinction in quoting DREE performance over the years.

Atlantic region, including New Brunswick, during the DREE period. The conclusions reached by Savoie do not accord with the reality of the DREE Atlantic experience over the 1974–82 period.[16]

HOW DREE WORKED

At an early stage there was a perception in some federal circles that the GDA concept had completely reversed past practice, with DREE now reacting to provincially proposed initiatives in regional development. This view was fostered by some provincial participants, but they were a minority. A broad criticism was that each province was a veritable fiefdom shared by the federal DREE officials and provincial officials

41

CHART 2.1
TYPICAL DREE ORGANIZATION CHART

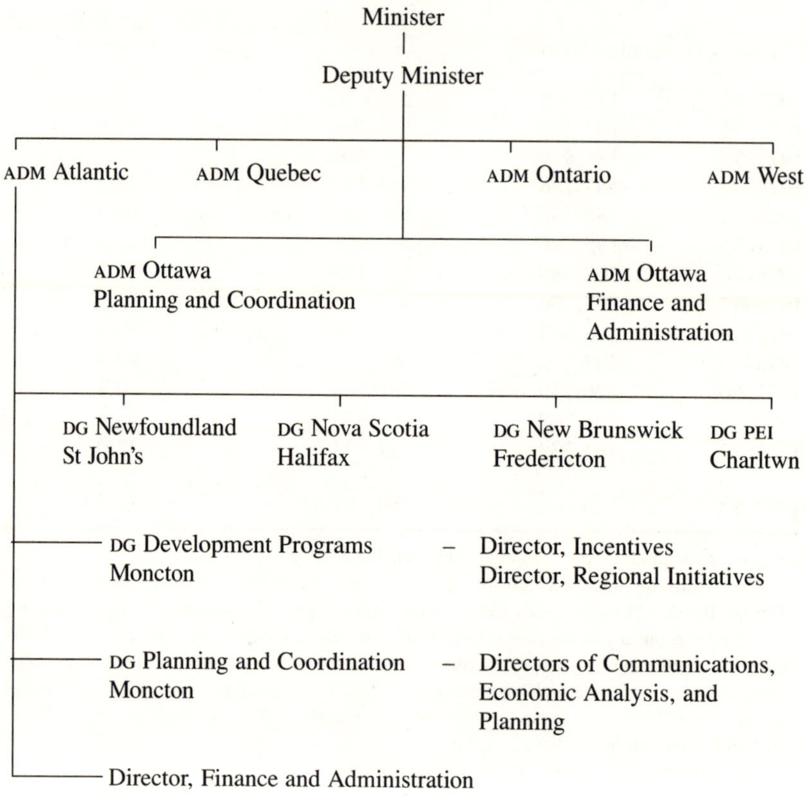

```
                          Minister
                             |
                       Deputy Minister


ADM Atlantic      ADM Quebec           ADM Ontario         ADM West

            ADM Ottawa                       ADM Ottawa
            Planning and Coordination        Finance and
                                             Administration


    DG Newfoundland    DG Nova Scotia    DG New Brunswick   DG PEI
    St John's          Halifax           Fredericton        Charltwn


        DG Development Programs      —    Director, Incentives
        Moncton                           Director, Regional Initiatives


        DG Planning and Coordination —    Directors of Communications,
        Moncton                           Economic Analysis, and
                                          Planning

        Director, Finance and Administration
```

to the exclusion of not only other federal departments but other DREE officials as well, and indeed even to the exclusion of ministers of both levels of government.[17] It was thought that such isolation resulted in inadequate consultation, competition between provinces, and unusual secrecy. All these perceptions amount to a myth that requires dispelling.

The bridge that provided the liaison and coordination within and between the regions and with Ottawa, other government departments, central agencies, and the minister was the director general (DG) of a particular province and the regional assistant deputy minister (ADM). These senior officers were best positioned to interpret all aspects of the policy, planning and decision-making processes that related to DREE regional development efforts. It was their responsibility to share that experience upwards to the minister and, to the degree possible, downwards to various levels in the DREE organization. The region was represented at regional and senior departmental management committees at these two senior levels. Regular attendance by the ADM at the committee meetings of the Ministry of State for Economic Development (MSED) and its successor, the Ministry of State for Economic and Regional Development (MSERD), gave the region full insight into the thinking of other government departments on proposed DREE initiatives and permitted explanation of those initiatives. The political opinion was secured through the ADM's attendance at meetings of the Treasury Board and meetings of the Cabinet Committee on Economic Development (CCED), and the Cabinet Committee on Economic and Regional Development (CCERD).

It is frequently forgotten that after an initial period during which DREE agreements were approved only by the Treasury Board Committee of Cabinet, the practice was changed so that the agreements first went to the Cabinet Committee on Economic Development (later Economic and Regional Development), were subsequently ratified by full cabinet, and were then reviewed by Treasury Board. This procedure dates from 1978.[18] There was, therefore, a process in place that provided complete opportunity for views on DREE intentions to be registered. Hugh Thorburn has said, in speaking of this cabinet committee process, "Instead of being judged purely by the criterion of economic efficiency, these are essentially economic decisions weighted by the political considerations of the ministers of the committee. It is they who must make the final tradeoffs and make the policies coherent in the political as well as the economic sense."[19]

With respect to the DREE minister, the author is not aware of the minister ever having expressed concern about being adequately informed. Meetings were held regularly with the minister on a one-on-one basis, in the presence of other federal ministers and members of Parliament, and with provincial ministers and premiers. Some of the most intense and meaningful sessions with the minister were held high over Canada, en route between Ottawa and provincial capitals.

The management regime in place in the Atlantic region, and this was not so very different across the department, was designed to ensure consultation, coordination, and sharing of information. The processes and management practices employed matured with time and experience. During the start-up period of late 1973 through mid-1976, a bold new attack on regional disparity was under way, the objective being to initiate important economic program activity as quickly as possible. In-depth analyses and research carried out by DREE and the provincial governments in the months prior to the signing of the federal-provincial GDAs had brought a number of significant initiatives to the point of consummation. In view of these predetermined priorities, it is not surprising that the impression existed that the DREE provincial offices were operating in a highly independent manner and in a fashion highly responsive to provincial proposals. As experience was gained, a more structured style of management was used in the Atlantic region, one that embraced more-integrated policy development, planning, coordination, and reporting. This was illustrative of what was going on throughout the department. It appears that many of the impressions formed by those interviewed and quoted by Donald Savoie were based on the earlier DREE operations during the start-up period.

The planning regime in the Atlantic region was led from, and coordinated by, the regional office under the direction of the assistant deputy minister. The budget determination process in the department was by region, not by province.[20] Funding was allocated to regional ADMs for accountability purposes and for subsequent reallocation within the region in accordance with negotiated and agreed-upon long-term planning horizons. The subregional (provincial) allocation was developed through collaborative sessions between the regional office and provincial offices, on both a collective and one-on-one basis. Within that process, however, heavy weight was accorded to the DREE director general's reading of economic circumstances in his or her province, provincial priorities, ministerial-level discussions and commitments, and budgetary constraints. Funds were also reserved for region-wide initiatives. Trade-offs between provincial budgets and priorities were made by the ADM, who took the aforementioned factors into account. Final regional budget allocations were confirmed in a country-wide exercise involving the complete senior departmental management and the minister.[21] The minister would be highly cognizant of representations from other ministers, members of Parliament, and a variety of interest groups, and, of course, of provincial priorities.

Within the context of decision making at the officials level, much has been made of the new-found influence and authority of provincial officials.[22] It would be expected that federal and provincial analyses of economic circumstances would usually be in accord and would form the basis of specific economic development initiatives. This was what was intended by the minister at the time, Donald Jamieson, in his description of the new GDA approach to regional development. Nevertheless, inclusion of a provincial priority within the decision-making process was not a guarantee of its acceptance. This is where the region-wide balancing of development effort came in, along with a testing against national policy thrusts. As Donald Savoie says, "The provinces have no assurance whatsoever that all programs and projects under a subsidiary agreement will be approved until the agreement is actually signed."[23]

Atlantic region management worked to set priorities, carry out the federal responsibilities for agreement negotiation and implementation, establish budgets, and ensure effective consultation and coordination of regional development activities. It also established objectives for DREE personnel.

Executive Committee meetings were held every five weeks somewhere in the region, usually in provincial capitals, on a rotational basis. This permitted committee members to view on-site development activities firsthand and to meet as a group with provincial officials and others interested in regional development in the province in question. These meetings were one device by which provincial officials had the opportunity to relate to all of the DREE senior regional management. The Executive Committee comprised the assistant deputy minister, the four provincial directors general, and the directors general of regional development and of policy, planning, and coordination. From time to time the group was supplemented by others of particular areas of expertise. The rotational approach to committee meetings was also employed by the departmental Senior Management Board, which met on a regular basis in all regions of the country for much the same reasons. This senior-level committee was made up of the deputy minister, the assistant deputy ministers, and the senior heads of certain staff functions, such as legal services. The system provided an excellent opportunity for interaction and discussion between senior managers at both the departmental and regional levels.

The Atlantic Executive Committee meetings provided the forum in which upcoming or planned initiatives were reviewed, progress reports were made on programs, projects, and agreements in place, and the budgetary situation was discussed. The committee addressed all aspects of the management of the region. All members of the committee had input to the agenda and helped determine the order of agenda priorities. It was also in this forum, not normally attended by what is euphemistically referred to as the working-level officer, that views were exchanged and subcommittees struck to examine issues common to the region as a whole. Although there may have been a healthy competitiveness between directors general, it was in the spirit of a shared concern for the economic well-being of their particular jurisdictions, and did not in any sense signify attempted secrecy or the withholding of information, which would hardly have been possible, given that the ADM was not only privy to all regional initiatives, but had to approve them.

The cross-fertilization within a region and between regions permitted useful and usable practices and initiatives to be shared and adopted, with modifications as necessary, in other DREE provinces and regions. The Atlantic region made it a practice to invite colleagues from Ottawa and the other regions of the department to attend its Executive Committee meetings to describe their plans, problems, and operations and to discuss matters of mutual interest. A standard agenda item was a debriefing from Senior Management Board. The idea that officials of provincial governments would be displeased at such sharing of information is rather naive, at best.[24] The provinces had their own network of information exchange, particularly within their region, and it was not uncommon for one province to raise with DREE the possibility of having an agreement along the lines of a neighbouring or other province. Senior provincial officials also made it a point of speaking regularly with the regional ADM, particularly if they had a specific problem. Sharing views and experiences was an essential part of the regional economic development process. The minister was similarly kept informed and consulted so that he could make the decisions on which agreement initiative proposals would go forward for Treasury Board and cabinet approval. The minister was never faced with a *fait accompli*.[25] Staff conferences, which brought together officers from every level and every discipline, were held regularly on both a regional and departmental basis to further strengthen contact and discussion.

The DREE administrative and decision-making apparatus was a well-developed process of opportunity identification, planning, consultation, and coordination, in harmony as appropriate with provincial officials. It was sometimes criticized as being too slow. Provincial administrations, on the other hand, because of fewer people to be consulted and ease of access to their ministers, were held up as models of simplicity in decision making. It is hardly surprising that the federal side performed differently, given the greater number of touch points that had to be taken into account, but something must have been working for forty-one agreements to be put in place in the Atlantic in the first four years of the new, and essentially untried, policy thrust.

The federal side was also compared unfavourably with provincial administrations in terms of numbers of people, the idea being that the federal bureaucracy was overstaffed.[26] It is fashionable to believe that bureaucrats seek to enlarge their sphere of influence in order to increase their power and personal status. However, the evidence does not show that empire building is a trait unique to the public sector. If it is an organizational trait, then it is a function of size rather than of discipline or vocation, and exists equally in large, private sector organizations. The downsizing that took place in private industry in North

America as the economy closed down in the late 1970s and early 1980s attests to this, demonstrating the excess that had been permitted to exist in companies to that time. Governments too were cutting back. The federal government has been practising what is essentially a no-growth policy since the early 1970s. DREE was allocated no additional person-years from 1973 onwards. (A person-year is the equivalent of one person's full year of employment.) DREE Atlantic had a person-year complement of 269 in 1982, nine fewer than five years earlier, despite the significantly increasing complexity of initiatives and program activity. The prime reason for growth in the bureaucracy of governments has been the political response to the perceived desires of the electorate for more and more new programs.

What is significant is not so much the style of the two levels of government, but rather that each in its own way pursued the objectives of the respective agreements towards a common goal that represented what continues to be the most innovative, and to date the most successful, attack on regional development in Canada. The federal objective in management terms was to ensure that good development opportunities were identified, evaluated, and put in place, with due regard to region-wide impact, pertinent national policies, and the budgetary framework. No apology was made for the time taken to ensure the consultation required in a federal system. The ten provincial governments, on the other hand, did not face the need for such extensive and complex consultation.

FEDERAL-PROVINCIAL NEGOTIATIONS

The federal operational intention behind the decentralized GDA approach was to place very senior managers and highly skilled officers in the regions of Canada, give them the on-site authority to develop initiatives tailored to the province or region in question, grant them the on-ground decision-making authority to implement the agreements, and hold them fully accountable for their actions.[27] It is said that officials advise, ministers decide, and officials execute.[28] Officials also take decisions and do so through delegated authority at levels commensurate with their experience and rank. In DREE, the significant authority accorded officials in the field to negotiate and subsequently implement federal-provincial agreements circumscribed the parameters within which operations were carried out.

Two contradictory perceptions have been held regarding the nature of federal-provincial negotiations conducted under the DREE subsidiary agreement approach, neither of which is accurate. On the one hand, there was the perception that the provinces simply presented proposals that were automatically accepted and put in motion by DREE. The other was that DREE and provincial officials met together in some incestuous way to fashion initiatives that somehow would be detrimental to at least the political will of the federal government. The facts are rather different.

It is reasonable to assume that professionals—whether federal or provincial—who are engaged in opportunity identification aimed at economic development in a particular region of the country will reach similar conclusions about the directions to take. Harvey Lithwick had said that "the genius of the GDA approach is that each step required full cooperation of the province, from planning to funding and administration."[29] Initiatives were usually based on identified comparative advantage or the removal of impediments to growth. The subject matter of the subsidiary agreements derived its broad direction from the analytical studies undertaken by both levels of government. On the federal side these included a series of DREE analyses known as the "yellow books" and the "blue books," as well as other, usually public, documents. Many of the provinces had also done their homework. The negotiations often focused on how best to translate these ideas into feasible programs and on the ordering of priorities.

Through to the approval stage, two things were paramount in assessing subsidiary agreement program proposals or initiatives. First, it was necessary that the proposal did, or would, fit into some broad policy framework. For both governments that framework was the annex to the General Development Agreement for that province (see Appendix 1). Both governments had their own ideas about what the priorities should be. The federal side carried the additional responsibility of testing the proposal, originated by one party or the other, against region-wide DREE activities and national policy frameworks. Second, the proposal had to be of high quality and well developed in terms of program detail and mode of implementation. These two factors determined the negotiating and decision timeframe.

Donald Savoie says that DREE officials in provincial offices and their provincial government counterparts were free to come up with practically anything they considered appropriate to stimulate development—they probably were—to some degree that is what they were charged to do.[30] The question is whether their proposals would be accepted by more senior decision makers. Doug Love, DREE deputy minister, points out that departmental officials in provincial offices could hold discussions with provincial government counterparts at any time, but he adds, "Once it went beyond discussion, however, and required the commitment of significant analytical resources, the approval of the ADM was required."[31]

That the GDAS were intended to be flexible, framework instruments has been acknowledged by most observers. The degree to which agreements subsidiary to the GDAS should also have had a degree of flexibility, has been more widely debated. The general thrust has been that it was dangerous to allow officials too much discretion, even if they were professionals in their field. Donald Savoie suggests that the subsidiary agreements represented a collection of ad hoc initiatives, unconnected in any discernible way to an overall strategy.[32] On the other hand, one-time New Brunswick premier Richard Hatfield, a long-time participant in the pursuit of regional development, in briefing new prime minister Joe Clark in 1979, said of a number of New Brunswick GDA initiatives: "These activities are not isolated and separate achievements. They are all part of a comprehensive program with the purpose of realizing the economic objectives of the province."[33] One may presume that those objectives were shared between the two levels of government.

Another practical reason for flexibility within categories of activities in the agreements was the need for legitimate experimentation in this still-fledging stage of the new regional development thrust. It was logical that there should be the opportunity to fine-tune initiatives through on-site experience, which was one of the reasons for having decentralized operations. All agreement objectives, however, clearly delineated the operating parameters for project-specific activity, and there were clear lines of authority to be followed on policy change and financial signing authorities. No auditor general observations were recorded in this regard for the Atlantic region during over eight years of intense regional development programming. Furthermore, if agreements had been written in a rigid, project-specific fashion within categories, numerous amendments would undoubtedly have been precipitated as new information came to light, thus slowing a process that some already found too slow.

What, then, was the practice in terms of the bargaining process? The overall management of the negotiating process at the provincial office level was the responsibility of a Development Committee. This committee drew its authority from the governing GDA and was headed on the DREE side by the DG and on the provincial side by a senior official. It was at this level that the development strategy for a province was first conceived. Within any identified category of development opportunity (or constraint removal), one side or the other brought forward an initiative for consideration. It may have surfaced as a possibility in any number of discussions or meetings, either between officials or at a political level, perhaps at annual and more frequent federal-provincial meetings of ministers. This was normally the first formal stage of the negotiating process—when the clock started running. Donald Savoie alleges that "the GDA approach operates in such a fasion that new initiatives are never submitted to a federal-provincial political-level meeting—rather they are submitted independently for approval through the federal and provincial political-administrative organization. Thus, political-level consultation under the GDA approach is sporadic and rarely involves politicians other than the Minister of DREE and the provincial minister designated."[34]

Savoie's allegation is quite wrong. In the Atlantic region more than 90 percent of all GDA subsidiary agreement proposals (and PEI CDP initiatives) received their first review at an annual federal-provincial political-level meeting. At such meetings the province was frequently represented by almost the whole cabinet, and as a minimum, by those ministers involved directly with DREE initiatives. On the federal side, the DREE minister carried the proxy of federal ministers if they were not present. If an initiative was on the agenda for the second or even third time, federal interdepartmental consultation would have taken place prior to the annual meeting.[35] Once it was agreed that an initiative was to be placed or retained on the agenda for further study and its priority ranking decided, the quality of the proposal dictated the pace that followed.

The next (second) step in the process of negotiation leading to decision on a proposed initiative consisted of technical evaluation and further federal-provincial discussion for clarification purposes. On the federal side this included consultation with other departments that could contribute technical and policy expertise. When officials at the proposal-evaluation level were satisfied, departmental discussion was launched and more senior level approvals sought. Call this step three of the federal process. The approval levels included the provincial director general concerned, the regional ADM, and the deputy minister. These kinds of discussions formed a continuum of ongoing departmental management. Depending on the nature of the initiative, a further step could be a sign-off from another department at either the officials or ministerial level. Sign-offs were also required from legal and financial officers. Final approvals were required by the minister, Treasury Board, and, in the later stages of DREE, cabinet.

It was reported that because subsidiary-agreement proposals made their way through the federal system in package form, there was a reluctance to make changes to them, even by Treasury Board, for fear of slowing the initiative or incurring political wrath.[36] Such a view overlooks the degree to which the details of proposals received scrutiny prior to being packaged. If, however, the political will to execute an agreement was present and it had been agreed to in a federal-provincial context by the minister charged with that responsibility, then the overall policy direction of the initiative was not open to further discussion, other than at cabinet committee.

For agreements reaching the final review stages, the role of Treasury Board was to assure conformity to budgetary limitations and the general policy of the government on regional development, the avoidance of interregional conflict, and the following of accepted operating practice. The Treasury Board frequently exercised its prerogative in dictating stringent regulation of eligibility criteria, program operating guidelines, and acceptable ceilings of financial assistance under incentives components of agreements. For example, the Treasury Board deleted components from the New Brunswick North East Development Agreement.[37] The board also exercised ongoing control over the size of project dollar commitment that could be made in the department; a commitment above a certain amount had to be referred to Treasury Board.

One could count as many as twenty steps in the process outlined above if each were taken sequentially, but this was not the case.[38] Most of the procedural steps, the majority of which also took place in the provincial government process, took place concurrently, with only the final approvals secured on a sequential basis. The preoccupation with numbers of steps in the process has meant that too often administrative requirements have been mixed with the important decision-taking stages, the latter being the key to the speed of completion of an agreement.

Federal officials will acknowledge that on initiatives already agreed upon between the two levels of government and brought to a point of completion that can stand the scruting of central agencies, a province can generally secure its respective authorities faster than the federal side. So it may have been in the DREE period. Nothing, however, could be more unproductive than to try to move an incomplete proposal through the federal system, as more than one minister found out. During the negotiating stage, however, it was easy for a province, or, for that matter, the federal government, to suggest that it was ready to complete an agreement on its own terms—not an unusual ploy in bargaining. What counted was the content of the proposal: Did it fit within a mutually agreed-upon framework? Had its priority ranking been determined within a recognized fiscal limit over a specified period of time? These and a score of other considerations contingent on the expenditure of public funds took priority over a desire for speed. Given that the DREE initiatives were intended for long-term benefit and were usually targeted for start-up the following fiscal year, the alleged slow decision making pales against the importance of having an initiative in place for maximum economic benefit for the region in question.

There is no denying that a high level of cooperation existed between the federal and provincial partners in most areas where regional development was critical to regional economies. Differences of opinion did occur, however, if the province thought that DREE funding represented simply another form of transfer mechanism, if the provincial and federal socio-political approaches conflicted or if the provincial and federal partners disagreed about the socio-economic direction for the province. Many of the proposals from either side that came forward for initial discussion never made it onto the formal negotiating agenda; many of those that did never made it through the gauntlet of scrutiny that followed.

Joint-agreement planning was usually projected over periods of up to five years. Projects would sometimes find their way onto a long-term list only to be deleted in subsequent year negotiations. In the Atlantic region, as time progressed, the DREE intention to move away from general infrastructure support and resource enhancement to more innovative initiatives sometimes conflicted with the wishes of the provinces. Although overall funding levels did not become critical to the pursuit of good developmental opportunities until late in the DREE period, particularly in the five eastern provinces, the immediate availability of resources influenced negotiations over the ordering of priorities for federal-provincial action. For these reasons, it is impossible to precisely quantify the number of proposals that made it onto the table and through the negotiating process. In the Atlantic region, it would be fair to say that less than half the ideas that came forward from either level of government ever came to agreement fruition.[39]

DREE brought forward and insisted upon priority attention for many initiatives, almost always taking the lead in the spatial agreements, an area in which it was particularly good at mustering federal action across departments. Spatial programming did not always accord with provincial priorities and occasionally caused a province discomfort, since it feared being perceived as favouring one part of a province over another. Many of the initiatives in Atlantic Canada, described in more detail later in this chapter and in chapter 3, were initiated by DREE.

DREE's comparatively modest budget for targeted regional development represented discretionary spending in the regions in which it operated, sometimes the only discretionary funding available. The suggestion that during negotiation provinces slipped projects and even programs into subsidiary agreements that should have been part of ongoing provincial line department activities makes an artificial distinction. If the provinces had had the discretionary funding, they may well have carried out a number of the program activities independently, but generally they did not have such funding. One could analyse provincial line department expenditures to assess the degree of increased effort brought about by DREE programs. This approach, if feasible, could not be taken at face value to measure provincial government effort, priorities, acceleration of intentions, diversification into new areas of programming, or attempts to strengthen support services. Given that DREE jointly approved every project executed under the subsidiary agreements, it had a good idea of what the provinces were intending within their own departmental budgets and could react accordingly. Quite obviously, a large amount of the DREE cost-shared activity was complementary to provincial planning frameworks.

All nine General Development Agreements, that is, all but that involving Prince Edward Island, were signed in 1974, the first with Newfoundland, the last with Nova Scotia. By design, development effort was concentrated in the Atlantic region in the earlier years because of the recognition of need and the considerable preplanning on both sides. Newfoundland, for example, conducted an extensive sectoral-based review of its economy immediately prior to signing its GDA and was fast off the mark. An examination of expenditures across the country from 1974 onwards reveals a pattern of earlier expenditure against fiscal capacity in Atlantic Canada, moving westward as commitments were honoured in the four most easterly provinces. By March 31, 1976, twenty-four federal-provincial agreements (including two under the PEI CDP) were in effect in the four Atlantic provinces compared to twenty-seven for all the rest of Canada. Although the number of agreements in the Atlantic region never fell below 45 percent of the national total in any one year, the federal cumulative dollar commitment fell from 54.7 percent at March 31, 1976, to 45.9 percent by 1981–82. See Table 2.1.

In recognition of the different fiscal capacities of the provinces, the maximum cost-sharing ceilings under the subsidiary agreements ranged from a high of 90 percent federal share in Newfoundland (and in PEI under the CDP), 80 percent in Nova Scotia and New Brunswick, 60 percent in Quebec, Manitoba, and Saskatchewan, to a low of 50 percent in the then wealthier provinces of Ontario, Alberta, and British Columbia. Another myth to be laid to rest is the assumption that all agreements were signed at the ceiling levels. On the contrary, agreements were regularly signed at lower federal participation levels, particularly where federal and provincial priorities differed in ranking.[40] DREE's bargaining strength was quite different in the wealthier provinces, where its funding was at best marginal and very incremental.

It was different, as well, in Quebec, despite DREE's proportionately high expenditure levels in that province.

The federal-provincial harmony created at the outset of the GDA approach continued until 1980, despite the changing political affiliations of provincial governments. Prior to and during the 1972–73 policy review period, there were no Liberal governments west of Quebec, yet General Development Agreements were signed in 1974 with all the provinces west of Quebec. In the first and highly active 1974–79 period of DREE, the federal Liberals had political kin in Nova Scotia (to 1978), Prince Edward Island, and Quebec (until 1976). By 1980, there were no Liberal provincial governments in power in Canada; other than the Parti Québécois in Quebec, the New Democrats in Saskatchewan, and the Social Credit in British Columbia, all were Conservative.

Ironically, the brief federal Conservative sojourn of 1979–80 did not produce unusual closeness between the two levels of government in the negotiation of regional development initiatives: fewer subsidiary agreements were signed then than in any equivalent previous period. Understandably, the new government wanted to evaluate the process. Rather than being evaluated, if suffered more from benign neglect, although DREE Minister Elmer MacKay from Nova Scotia did maintain the personalized nature of DREE's contact in Atlantic Canada set by his Liberal predecessors. Another exception to this lack of overall attention was Treasury Board President Sinclair Stevens, who continually questioned those initiatives put forward by his colleagues, more often than not with the intention of blocking them, even those of the powerful minister of finance, John Crosbie.

On resuming the stewardship of the country in 1980, the Liberals still faced an array of opposite political numbers in the provinces. David Milne, in reminding us of the underlying centralist tendencies that prevailed through the Trudeau regime and were manifested in both national and regional economic policy, says of early centralist motives (DREE, for example, was very centralized in the 1969–73 period), "Although these strong centralist measures were later relaxed in 1973 following the near defeat of the Trudeau government in 1972, the same spirit returned in the post-1980 period."[41] The federal political aggressiveness became very evident in the practice of regional development.

An expression of federal hawkishness was the introduction of direct program delivery. This action proved to be inefficient and expensive, and it failed to bring the extra credit federal politicians were seeking. Nevertheless, the practice swept across all four provinces of the Atlantic region. As contradictory as it might seem, all such activity was carried out under the negotiated arrangements with the province in question, albeit with the considerable displeasure of the province. The GDA was still the agreed-upon mechanism for regional development programming, and the subsidiary agreement still the instrument for effecting program activity. Section 6.4 of each GDA provided for "initiatives to be undertaken by Canada or the Province individually or jointly." Each government would identify what it would do and pay for, and this was incorporated into a subsidiary agreement that was jointly managed on an overall basis by the federal-provincial management committee of officials. In the Atlantic region, agreements of this nature included coastal fisheries development in Newfoundland, ocean industries development in Nova Scotia, and a development initiative in southeast New Brunswick. The most significant departure from past practice was in Prince Edward Island, where a comprehensive $92-million package across a range of sectors and activities was shared between the two governments, with $39 million of direct activity under the responsibility of six federal departments and the remaining $53 million jointly handled, as before, between the two governments. The traditional 90 percent cost sharing of the Comprehensive Development Plan, however, was changed to approximately 77 percent federal and 23 percent provincial.

Negotiations during this period were more difficult, with effective regional development slowing. At the same time, regional development planning was reaching a new level of maturity and sophistication. The trend in Atlantic Canada moved away from infrastructure and basic resource agreements towards ocean industry technology, more advanced industrial development initiatives, and support systems.

No review of federal regional development policy and the ensuing federal-provincial negotiation to put it into practice would be complete without comment on the Prince Edward Island Comprehensive Development Plan. The Plan, as it was called, was signed in 1969 with a fifteen-year horizon, with specified renewal periods each five years. Renewals actually took place in 1975, 1981, and 1984. It remains one of the most innovative vehicles for regional development planning and programming ever devised. It comprised what was, in effect, eighteen separate program elements, each equivalent to a subsidiary agreement. The subject matter, in recognition of the economic and social circumstances prevailing in PEI in 1969 and thereafter, covered industrial, municipal, urban, transportation, and social infrastructure, resources planning and exploitation, tourism and agriculture, skills training, and even educational support. As needs were seen to be fulfilled, the emphasis of programming changed.

The Plan was a collaborative effort from the beginning. It was jointly managed by officials of the two levels of government, with overall direction and priority setting determined by a senior Joint Advisory Board of both officials and ministers. In its earlier stages it was charged from time to time that the direction of the Plan was imposed by Ottawa bureaucrats. It is doubtful if this was the case, but in any event this possibility lessened with DREE decentralization and disappeared when the role of federal co-chair was assumed by the DREE ADM Atlantic. The provincial co-chair of the board was the premier. In mid-1981, the DREE minister assumed the federal co-chair, thereby ending an anomaly in terms of political-bureaucratic relations.

In summary, federal-provincial negotiation under the flexible and innovative GDA approach permitted ministers and bureaucrats of the two levels of government to come together for the common good in regional development planning and execution. If the process differed in any way from the past, it was in raising the practice of federal-provincial planning and negotiation to new levels of efficiency and effectiveness—undoubtedly one of the prime objectives of the architects of the concept.

Ministerial interest in and involvement with the process of regional development negotiation and programming was maintained through most of the period 1974–82. Successive federal ministers Jamieson, Lessard, MacKay, and De Bané regularly visited the regions to meet their counterparts and to consult with officials. Each new minister of DREE, almost as a command performance, visited the regional DREE offices to meet staff. Each of these ministers represented regions of unfulfilled economic opportunity, and they were very familiar with the phenomenon of economic disadvantage. Even though a new federal stridency had emerged by 1980, the level of federal-provincial contact was maintained to 1982, even by then minister De Bané, the architect, in a sense, of DREE's subsequent downfall.

IMPLEMENTATION AND THE DECISION-MAKING PROCESS

Donald Savoie says that "the [subsidiary] agreements were little more than an uncommitted block of funds to be allocated after projects were identified and formulated" and "that management committees like the Canada-New Brunswick Development Committee merely grant formal approval to initiatives which have been discussed and approved beforehand."[42] These statements appear to take the conclusions of Savoie's New Brunswick enquiries outside those boundaries and apply them to the practice in all provinces.

The mandate of officials charged with the implementation responsibility was to give effect to the content of the signed subsidiary agreements. No agreement was written without a clearly defined objective within the economic sector selected as a priority. The specifics varied with the degree of complexity and the innovative or experimental nature of the initiative. Certain agreements, for example, in transportation and municipal infrastructure, were usually clear-cut, even though in these areas discretion could be exercised by officials. As an illustration, if it were discovered after more complete engineering calculations that a highway would cut across an environmentally sensitive terrain, officials could agree on significant, and different cost, alternatives. Usually, however, the actual piece of highway was described in the agreement. In the Atlantic region, DREE involvement in highways was normally restricted to roads to resources or non-trans-Canada routes. Later agreements written by Transport Canada deviated from these criteria. More innovative approaches to regional development or programs that depended on the response of the targeted clientele had to be flexible in their application, and this flexibility had to rest with officials.

The centre of implementation decision making was the federal-provincial joint management committee struck for each specific subsidiary agreement. Its designated role was to manage the implementation of already-signed agreements. In each province the committee operated in the mode best suited to the existing organizational structure, but most procedural elements were common across the country. The DREE director general or his or her designate co-chaired the committee with a senior provincial counterpart. In certain instances, such as the Nova Scotia Sydney Steel Corporation agreements, the chair was taken on the federal side by the regional assistant deputy minister. Certain region-wide agreements, not under the GDA mantle, were chaired by either the regional ADM or a senior regional officer. Subcommittees of the main management committee were frequently struck to provide technical support to the initiatives being undertaken.

Written operational procedures were employed by most, if not all, management committees. Although sometimes criticized as being bureaucratic, these procedures were invaluable for audit trail purposes, provided an important point of reference for the rationale behind various decisions, and were benchmarks for precedent-setting decisions. The joint signing requirement protected the integrity of the authority of both governments. The financial controls and specified levels of financial signing authorities ensured the integrity of the funds-disbursement process.

The joint signing approvals for every project launched under a subsidiary agreement gave the lie to the fiction that the provinces could dictate program content. No project could go ahead with federal funding without federal concurrence.[43] This requirement was occasionally an irritant at the provincial political level, where it was sometimes felt that federal politicians were trying to influence operational decisions considered to be in the provincial domain. In one instance concerning a west coast Newfoundland industrial development concept, approved under the Clark government and already partially executed, then premier Brian Peckford lashed out at the new Liberal DREE minister, Pierre De Bané, for what he took to be a politically motivated intervention on the selection of municipalities for infrastructure development.

In New Brunswick, federal-provincial relations were strained on the issue of hiring practices under the highways subsidiary agreements. A long simmering dispute between the province and DREE, at both the bureaucratic and political levels, surfaced in the provincial legislature in June 1979 and was accorded national attention by the *Globe and Mail*.[44] The premier declared that federal accusations of political interference in highways hiring, in contravention of the DREE agreements, were intended to embarrass provincial Tories during the just-completed federal election campaign. DREE withheld funding from cost-shared agreements pending resolution of the stand-off, and the province threatened to sue the federal government. Notwithstanding testimonials to support the federal claim, the province stood fast in denying the charges and continued to demand proof of the allegations. Under the new Conservative federal government, the withheld funding was released and programming continued.

These two incidents underline important aspects of the GDA concept. First, the federal government did not have to fund projects with which it took issue, and second, the provinces could stonewall a federal position. Both levels of government could become exercised in situations where they felt their authority was being challenged or undercut. The federal side did, however, have an important card in its deck — its losing on one front could be remembered when it negotiated new agreements on another, a point overlooked by those who suggest that under the GDAs the provincial tail wagged the federal dog.

The management committee was the last stop before actual program and project activity could commence. Its officials put flesh on concepts that required detailed study and design before reaching the stage where costs started to be incurred. With the support of technical subcommittees and with advice from other experts, including other federal and provincial departments and on occasion hired consultants, they described the kinds of projects and programs that could be implemented, costed, monitored, and subsequently evaluated. They developed the more detailed aspects of project and program design, the physical location of facilities, the eligibility criteria for sub-program elements, the evaluation of tenders against specifications, the design of marketing programs, and many other elements involved in getting programs off the ground. In the Atlantic region, officials of some federal departments were physically located in DREE offices and others were seconded to DREE provincial offices for long periods of time.

During the implementation process, it was necessary that the content of the agreement continue to be tested against the criteria employed during its formulation. This was accomplished where necessary by inviting officials of other departments to sit on the management committees. This practice occasionally led to the criticism that officials from other departments were employing national policies in a regional development context. DREE at no time intimated that it would abrogate its national policy responsibilities while practising regional development. The fact was that it was rare for regional and national policies to be in conflict, despite the accumulated writings to the contrary. Where necessary, national policies were adapted to reinforce regional initiatives. The intent of interdepartmental consultation during development of a subsidiary agreement was to reconcile national policy positions before the initiative reached the implementation stage.

The federal members of the management committee operated under precise and clearly understood written instruments of delegated authority.[45] In the Atlantic region, these instruments were delegations from the regional assistant deputy minister. The DREE provincial director general had authority over program approvals, financial signing, and restricted agreement amendments. These authorities permitted the director general to give federal approval to implement those projects specifically described in the subsidiary agreement and to initiate and approve individual projects within a given program element. He or she could change funding estimates for specific projects within the ceiling of a program element but not between program elements, but could not approve any change judged to be a significant deviation from program intent. The written delegated authority from which the DG operated also permitted him or her to refer even those things within his or her authority to the regional ADM or higher, if the DG considered them to have particular policy implications. This option was frequently exercised.

Provincial directors general exercised payment authority on approved projects within major program or agreement financial ceilings. In addition to auditor general scrutiny, the department employed its own audit team to review regional operating practice. In the Atlantic, the ADM also had a regional audit unit reporting directly to him. Directors general could effect minor agreement amendments to project descriptions and cost changes within program elements. All substantive amendments required the minister's signature.

The ability of officials to move money between agreements has been greatly misunderstood.[46] Neither officials nor ministers could move money between agreements. Officials could accelerate or decelerate cash flow within an agreement over its life to optimize program implementation across a number of agreements in one province, but always within the overall agreement ceiling. Ministers could agree to change the overall level of funding in an agreement, upward or downward, but required Treasury Board and later cabinet approval before consummating an amendment to that effect. Departments, meaning ministers, could move funds between activities (the reference here is to the department's Estimates structure, not activities in subsidiary agreements) only with Treasury Board approval. Only Parliament could approve shifting funds between votes, in other words, approve increasing or decreasing vote funding.

Because of the day-to-day nature of the implementation function, which in one province alone could involve up to a dozen or more subsidiary agreements with several times that number of major program elements and dozens of projects per element, the burden of responsibility for implementation and the accountability that went with it rested with DREE provincial office officials and their provincial counterparts. It was not necessary for the detailed level of implementation to be further shared within the department. Reporting systems were in place, however, to track progress against objectives and to closely monitor cash-flow expenditures. (For an insight into the breadth of project coverage encompassed in DREE subsidiary agreements, see Appendix 2.)

DREE-OGD RELATIONS

The relationship DREE had with other (federal) government departments (OGDs) has been at the centre of much of the debate on the degree of success of the department in effecting economic improvements across a range of sectors. On the one hand, it has been claimed that DREE had little success in enlisting the aid of other federal departments in the battle to reduce or eliminate regional disparity; on the other, DREE has been criticized for engaging the involvement of departments said to be insensitive to regional concerns and too rigid in the application of national policies.

DREE's legislative authority to coordinate the activities of other federal departments was not as strong as officials might have wished, even though the expectation was there.[47] It did have, however, spending authority in almost all areas and acknowledged federal government signing authority for subsidiary agreements in any economic sector or activity. In addition, the intention that DREE lead all federal regional development efforts was very much evident in the statements of the day by both the prime minister and the DREE minister. Even when announcing DREE's dismantlement in January of 1982, the prime minister did not deny his earlier statement of 1969, saying only that all economic departments now had to play a more direct role in regional development.

Notwithstanding the views that may have prevailed, DREE was the acknowledged federal agency responsible for regional development in Canada in the period 1969–1982. During the years 1974–82, in particular, DREE's relationships with other federal departments had their highs and lows, not unlike those which existed, and still exist between various departments of the federal government. With DREE, the relationships were coloured to some degree by the vagueness of its responsibility in accountability terms and by the fact that, at the time, the department controlled the purse strings of regional development. As is so often the case, however, the disharmony that may have been present has been magnified a great deal more than the steady cooperation that existed between officials at all levels and, more often than not, between ministers. Most of the time the relationships worked, even in the most contentious areas, and at no time were the agreements written or programs undertaken of detriment to the economy of the regions or of the nation.

The degree of cooperation and collaboration between DREE and other departments can best be illustrated by example. In the Atlantic region, the level of continuous consultation between officials and ministers of DREE and of the Department of Fisheries and Oceans (DFO) was unmatched in any other sector, notwithstanding frequent public rumours and statements to the contrary. It is true that Fisheries Minister Roméo LeBlanc was frustrated by the consequences of the GDA approach, which denied his department direct federal-provincial agreement capability in favour of DREE in an area crying out for region-wide coordination. However, it was the GDA policy that received his public criticism.

Virtually all of the very substantial DREE program activity in the fisheries sector in the Atlantic provinces was subject to extensive DREE-DFO consultation and DFO sign-off. This included four fisheries subsidiary agreements in Newfoundland and fisheries components in the PEI CDP. It was in New Brunswick and Nova Scotia that LeBlanc declined to agree to a DREE subsidiary agreement. It is nonetheless true that even in the instances where he did agree to initiatives in the other two Atlantic provinces, LeBlanc would have preferred to write his own agreements and to administer them through his own department. In fact, the option was open to him through DFO legislative authority to implement federal fisheries programs, and he announced just such a $41-million program for the Atlantic provinces on April 20, 1977. As a consequence, DREE and the Province of Newfoundland agreed to discontinue the negotiation of a new fisheries subsidiary agreement covering fish-handling facilities, ice-making equipment and other elements included in the DFO program.[48]

Under the DREE-administered Regional Development Incentives Program (RDIP), DFO input on resource availability was standard procedure. Although it was within the DREE mandate under the RDI Act to evaluate the overall viability of a fish-processing project and to make the final decision on an offer of financial assistance, rarely would a positive decision be taken without DFO concurrence. Indeed, the RDI Act stipulated that resource availability, which DREE had little capability to assess, was one criterion to be taken into account when evaluating a project. A 1982 review of forty-seven RDIP-assisted fish-processing projects, involving total capital costs exceeding $100 million, revealed that forty-six of them had received written DFO concurrence. The one exception was approved by the DREE minister after the economic benefit was weighed against the resource implications.

On March 20, 1981, Fisheries Minister Roméo LeBlanc and DREE Minister Pierre De Bané signed a memorandum of understanding (MOU) that acknowledged DFO's jurisdictional authority in fisheries management and DREE's onshore economic development mandate in the sector. The MOU expressed a joint interest in improving the efficiency and effectiveness of federal expenditures and actions related to fisheries development. It also envisaged the joint development of a comprehensive development plan for the East Coast fisheries, joint management of development initiatives, a study of resource-processing capacity, and the imposition of a moratorium on RDIP assistance for the establishment of new plant capacity or expansion of existing plant capacity in fish processing. The two departments agreed to pursue "primarily federal implementation," one of the earliest expressions of this desire of the federal government to operate in a direct delivery mode. One outcome was the development of a major $17-million fisheries component in a new Canada-Newfoundland Coastal Labrador Community Development Agreement, with direct federal delivery by the DFO and joint DREE-DFO management of the undertaking. This was the first example of direct federal program delivery in the Atlantic, where the idea came to be most aggressively applied.

The close collaboration between DREE and DFO on fish-processing capacity and the use of the RDI was well illustrated in a standing committee exchange in 1982. Roméo LeBlanc was incorrectly quoted in the Halifax *Chronicle-Herald* as saying that 1981 fish-processing capacity in the Atlantic region was often aided by DREE financial assistance against the advice of DFO. What the fisheries minister actually said was, "There are cases where expansion took place against the advice of my department, with a refusal of DREE."[49]

Because of the region-wide nature of the fisheries, these initiatives were led on the DREE side from the regional office, under the supervision of the ADM, who in turn was receiving policy advice directly from the minister. By this time, all Atlantic DREE fisheries activities took policy direction from the regional office, including the input to the Kirby Task Force exercise on the East Coast fisheries.[50] Needless to say, this exercise could only be managed with the fullest cooperation and input from each of the four provincial offices.

The fisheries is but one example among many of the kind of interaction that took place between DREE and sister departments. Before 1978 subsidiary agreements were approved by Treasury Board within a given fiscal framework, but after that year agreements required cabinet committee approval. This procedure gave all ministers, including those who on occasion spoke out publicly on certain initiatives, the opportunity to register their point of view with their colleagues. The Bureau of Economic Development Ministers (BEDM), the Ministry of State for Economic Development, and the Ministry of State for Economic and Regional Development each provided the opportunity for bringing together various departmental opinions on proposed DREE initiatives.

At the operational level the cooperation between DREE and OGDS grew as time went on, leading to a further sharing of responsibilities. In the forest sector, DREE Atlantic designated the Canadian Forest Service to co-chair the management committees of a new generation of agreements with Newfoundland and New Brunswick scheduled for 1981–82 start-up. In Nova Scotia, DREE was co-managing a $24,875,000 Energy Conservation Agreement, the first of its kind in Canada. An important element of that agreement was a $10,875,000 Industrial Retrofit Program, which became the model for a national Energy, Mines and Resources program. DREE negotiated with the province the transfer of that agreement component to EMR in 1981, along with the unspent $6 million. DREE highway agreements gave way to Transport Canada agreements well before 1982. Second-generation minerals agreements with Newfoundland, Nova Scotia, and New Brunswick, to commence in fiscal year 1982–83, were predicated on equal cost-sharing and joint federal co-managing between DREE and EMR. DREE cooperated with Employment and Immigration Canada on the introduction and management of the Local Economic Development Assistance Program and with ITC on the Industry and Labour Adjustment Program.

In every one of the nine provinces in which a GDA had been signed, there were shared financial commitments between federal departments. One review showed commitments in excess of $150 million from ten federal departments.[51] These departments were all involved in the implementation process. In 1978, DREE Minister Marcel Lessard told the House of Commons that even then 57 of 88 subsidiary agreements involved other departments.[52] The DREE annual report of 1981–82 revealed that from inception to March 31, 1982, 76 of 126 subsidiary agreements were co-managed with other departments and 32 were cost-shared. Officials of other government departments were represented on a wide range of DREE federal-provincial management committees and subcommittees. One snapshot taken in the Atlantic region in 1980 counted no fewer than 77 different federal officers representing 12 federal departments, on these committees.[53]

Interdepartmental meetings provided a mechanism for OGD consultation. In the Atlantic, major gatherings of senior officials from across the region and from Ottawa, including central agencies representatives, were regularly convened. Five such meetings took place in the period 1975–81—in Moncton (twice), Halifax (twice), and Prince Edward Island—to review broad regional development strategies. These two-day sessions were especially conducive to an exchange of views on the role of all federal departments in regional development. They were not intended to deal with project-specific issues or the particulars of individual subsidiary agreements, something better left to bilateral discussions with specific departments.

In respect of regional development in Atlantic Canada, the interaction between departments at both the officials and political levels was pervasive and continuous. There was no possibility that points of view would not be registered, heard, and acted upon. There is no reason to believe that it was not the same in other regions of the country.[54]

THE "REGIONAL" CONTEXT OF REGIONAL DEVELOPMENT

The benefits of blending regional economies with the national economy are extolled by several writers on the subject.[55] The corollary of that belief, then, is surely that the component parts of those regions also exhibit harmonization of development policy within their own boundaries. The way that this can be achieved from a national government point of view is to ensure coordination of its actions within and between regions through the management regime. This was the operational mode of the Department of Regional Economic Expansion. Four regional assistant deputy ministers, operating from regional headquarters, oversaw all operations in the regions and ensured interregional liaison and coordination.

Earlier in this chapter, we noted that Donald Savoie has fostered the impression that DREE provincial offices operated independent of any external control and that both the regional headquarters and Ottawa were impotent bystanders to the process. Yet in comparing provincial and regional approachs to regional development, he says that "the federal government has consistently established, in the allocative process of its economic development schemes, a mechanism to look at the Maritimes or Atlantic Provinces, not simply on a province by province basis, but also from a regional perspective."[56] And so it did in the case of the decentralized DREE. Savoie acknowledges that in those instances where only Ottawa had such a perspective, this mechanism led to divisive federal-provincial relations.[57] Savoie unfortunately misconstrues the DREE regional operational mode in the two multi-provincial regions of DREE, the West and the Atlantic, when he concludes that the GDA approach did not provide a forum for review of proposed initiatives from a regional point of view and that the federal government was not capable of providing regional leadership in the field of economic development. On the apparent assumption that only Ottawa was capable of providing such leadership, notwithstanding the quality, he concludes that Ottawa was left to oversee the work of ten self-contained and relatively autonomous provincial offices.[58]

The DREE regional organizational structure not only permitted the review of proposed initiatives from a regional point of view and provided leadership, it raised coordinated regional development policy, planning, and implementation to a new level of sophistication. Previous sections described how the DREE regional management concept provided the coordination of and leadership for both provincial and region-wide initiatives and their integration into departmental and governmental policy positions. A separate section reviewed the role played by the regional offices in DREE relations with other federal departments.

The governmental process as it related to regional development policy and programming became more orderly over the life of DREE. By late 1978 the Board of Economic Development Ministers, later the Cabinet Committee on Economic Development (CCED), supported by MSED, introduced new discipline into the procedure for approving

65

DREE subsidiary agreement initiatives. Cabinet committee scrutiny was part of the regional development review process from 1978, and ministers of all the economic departments had full opportunity to make their views on program intentions known. It was the responsibility of DREE regional management to ensure that proposals going forward for cabinet committee review and approval did not carry interregional contradictions and that the necessary interdepartmental consultation had taken place. The operational mode of the Atlantic region is illustrative of how regional management exercised its role.

The responsibilities of Atlantic regional office headquarters were fivefold:

- to be concerned with precedent and the possible national implications of provincial/regional initiatives;
- to ensure a regional point of view where appropriate or necessary, including mustering opinions of other departments and avoiding unintended overlap;
- to provide large-project expertise in terms of economic and financial analysis;
- to represent the region as a whole in a variety of forums, including at intra- and interdepartmental meetings, in dealings with central agencies, and at cabinet committee meetings; and
- with regard to region-wide policy development, to prepare an ongoing series of analytical pieces on the region, analyses of economic performance, mobility studies, and evaluation methods and their application.

Almost every project in the Atlantic region that had clearly cross-regional significance or was of such a magnitude as to require dedicated analytical resources was managed either directly by the regional office or co-managed with a provincial office. A number of the larger industrial development projects were led by the regional office to facilitate interdepartmental and interregional coordination, since the dedicated resources and necessary skills to pursue them were available there. Expertise from other federal departments were also seconded in support of these initiatives. In early 1977 the departmental responsibility for a proposed world-scale, Nova Scotia–based, greenfield steel mill facility was repatriated to the Moncton regional office from Ottawa, where much of the analytical modelling had been done. The mill was to have been built by a partnership of the provincial government (under the name Canstel, later Cansteel), the German firm Thyssen, a company called Estel, and Dofasco. Its realization foundered when the world steel industry collapsed. All further Cape Breton steel projects, including the major $100-million Sydney Steel Corporation modernization agreement of 1980, were negotiated and managed from Moncton.

The $400-million Michelin Tire project for Waterville, Nova Scotia, which secured some 1,850 new jobs in the province and made the company the largest single private sector employer in Nova Scotia, was negotiated by senior regional staff. The project was a particularly good example of what big project bidding is all about. The bidding for that project was on an international scale and revolved around the degree to which Canada wanted a world-scale tire manufacturer. There was no question of the plant going elsewhere in Canada, but rather whether it would go to another country. History shows that the Michelin decision was a good one. After a worldwide shake-out in the tire industry that left only three multinationals, Michelin emerged the leader. The $52-million Halifax Panamax Drydock project and the Nova Scotia Ocean Industries initiative were both piloted through the bureaucratic process and cabinet committee by region-based officials.

Other regions of DREE and other federal departments were fundamental to the success of several of these projects. The Panamax project was closely coordinated with the Quebec region, which arranged for Quebec government financial participation and for some of the work to be done in that province. Industry, Trade and Commerce was involved on a partnership basis with steel and shipbuilding projects. At the time DREE was scheduled to be merged with ITC, the Atlantic region was developing a region-wide approach to industrial development rather than a provincial approach. Provincial initiatives had worked in their time but were in danger of becoming repetitive if they were not placed within a broader industrial development framework.

A far-ranging initiative on Cape Breton was led from the regional office under the aegis of the Cape Breton Task Force, which was chaired by the DREE Atlantic ADM. In addition to DREE personnel, the task force included senior officials from the Canada Employment and Immigration Commission, Energy, Mines and Resources, Environment Canada, Finance, the Federal-Provincial Relations Office (FPRO), Industry, Trade and Commerce, the Ministry of State for Economic Development, the Privy Council Office (PCO), and the Treasury Board Secretariat. The chair reported to an ad hoc committee which included the deputy prime minister, the Honourable Allan J. MacEachen, the minister of labour (former Nova Scotia Premier Gerald Regan), the minister of DREE, and selected senior (deputy minister level) officials from Finance, MSED, FPRO, and PCO. This committee examined and made recommendations on a variety of difficult economic development situations existing in Cape Breton at the time.

Sectoral policy issues took their lead from the region. Twelve of the fifteen initiatives identified for future attention in the DREE Atlantic 1980 and 1981 policy papers were compatible with the policy declarations that were to guide the Department of Regional Industrial Expansion, which followed DREE. The change in program direction away from the resource sectors and infrastructure, which predated by two years the thrust intended by the 1982 reorganization, originated with regional management. The DREE Atlantic approach to tourism was coordinated on a regional basis, given the efforts of provincial tourism ministers to thwart established provincial channels in dealing with the department by going directly to DREE officials and, where possible, to ministers. The planning agreements in the four provinces also had a common base of intent and application.

The DREE assistance for the forest complex that was eventually built in Fredericton, NB, was negotiated through the ADM Atlantic, based on meetings first held with the Council of Maritime Premiers in 1976. At that time the Council had approached the department and the minister with a request for funds to replace the Maritime Forest Ranger School. It was the DREE regional office that persisted through two changes of government and three ministers to support the establishment of a more broadly based forest complex in Fredericton. This continuing support was maintained in the face of apathy from time to time from other federal departments and of strident attempts by New Brunswick members of Parliament to fragment its component parts across the province to favoured constituencies. It is ironic that at the May 6, 1988, official opening of the Hugh John Flemming Forest Centre in Fredericton, no apparent reference to DREE (or DRIE) was made. It may not be inaccurate to suggest that the complex might never have been built, or at least would not have been realized as soon, without the ongoing efforts of DREE regional office and DREE NB office officials. Notwithstanding the New Brunswick location, the complex was to serve a regional function.

The federal assistance in setting up a $5-million endowment fund to establish the Canadian Institute for Research on Regional Development in Moncton, NB, was negotiated with the University of Moncton and the federal Treasury Board by the DREE ADM Atlantic at the request of the minister. When the Liberal government moved to direct program delivery under the subsidiary agreements of the GDAS, the approach to be taken across all four of the Atlantic provinces was developed on a regional basis, and it was the region, in support of the DREE minister, that made the presentations on the approach to cabinet committee.

As evidence that the "regional" dimension was ineffective, it was reported that there was no provision under the GDAS for region-wide agreements, nor was funding allocated to the regional office for such purposes.[59] In fact, the GDA subsidiary agreement was but one instrument, albeit a most important one, in regional economic development programming. The DREE Act itself was the authority for other forms of regional development programs. Under the DREE Act, several programs of region-wide application were put in place, including those in which more than one province participated. Examples of multiprovincial programs included the Physical Distribution Advisory Service (PDAS), the major Land Registration and Information Service (LRIS), and the Atlantic Provinces Management Training Agreement. This latter was negotiated by the regional office and signed by all four provincial governments. It was managed on the federal side by a regional official and on the provincial side by provincial officials on a rotating basis. All these programs were managed out of the regional office and the funding was allocated to a regional budget. The practice of identifying most program-funding allocations by province was primarily an administrative convenience and continued to be followed even after the creation of the Department of Regional Industrial Expansion.

The DREE regional office structure had other advantages. It was from here that government policies on official languages, equal access to opportunity, and similar personnel-related issues were made effective, where a uniform public information policy was made workable, and where resources in financial management, audit, and computer services were brought together. The Atlantic region developed and possessed the only working on-line computer program inventory in the department.

One of the most telling examples of the loss of region-wide coordination after the disbandment of DREE regional headquarters offices in 1982 was the degree to which so much of the coordinating role landed on the desk of the assistant deputy ministers in Ottawa responsible for sectoral policy. Even though not charged with any regional coordination responsibility, except to ensure harmony between national and regional development programs and policies, these ADMs assumed a de facto role in a range of regional issues. The Atlantic fisheries issue followed the former DREE Atlantic ADM to Ottawa, where he also held the DRIE national sectoral responsibility for the fisheries sector. In this capacity he represented the department and the Atlantic region in discussions relating to the Kirby Task Force work on the East Coast fishery, in interdepartmental meetings, at related MSERD meetings, and at meetings of the ad hoc committee of cabinet dealing with the issue. The policy relating to financial incentives assistance for the Atlantic fishery, which would in all likelihood have been the responsibility of the regional ADM if there had been one, was developed in Ottawa. A national policy on financial assistance to the forest products industry, developed in Ottawa, had particular relevance to regional projects in the sector, and most of the major forest products projects were led by the Ottawa-based sectoral ADM. In several other policy areas, such as petrochemicals, which carried both intra- and interregional implications, the lead role was carried by an Ottawa-based sectoral ADM. Fortunately, and contrary to popular belief, this worked because of the close working relationships between Ottawa and regional officials.

This section has dwelled at length on the role of the DREE regional headquarters structure. It is important that the implications for regional development of the loss of that function be recognized. The absence of a regional responsibility centre was one significant reason for the less than effective regional development programming that followed 1982. It was a recognizable reason for the creation in 1987 of regionally based development agencies. On the other hand, it is in no way suggested that regional office entities were solely responsible for successful DREE regional development efforts in Canada. The DREE provincial offices were largely responsible for direct programming activities and were essential components of DREE's successful regional development efforts. Even in those instances of aforementioned regional office leadership, the work took full account of DREE provincial office input. Regional and provincial office activities were both aired in the Regional Management Committee forum so that both received the benefit of senior regional management consideration.

DREE Ottawa played an important supporting role vis-à-vis the regions. Ottawa-based officials organized meetings, represented the regions at interdepartmental meetings if requested, and supplied economic and financial analysis on major projects if asked. Some of the criticism of "Ottawa" by officers in the regional and provincial offices stemmed from a lack of understanding of how to best utilize Ottawa expertise. Regionally based officials were encouraged to work with their Ottawa-based colleagues and to negotiate personally with or otherwise consult with Ottawa-based officials of other departments. Because the senior decision-making levels in OGDs were usually in Ottawa, senior DREE regional officials spent a lot of their time in that city in order to find someone who could match their authority for reaching agreement on matters of mutual interest.

This litany of regional office leadership and involvement in DREE regional development activity attests only to the obvious—that it was carrying out its intended function in an organizational structure designed for a high degree of senior on-site management. In the pre-decentralized structure, which had existed prior to 1973–74, these roles would have been discharged from an Ottawa base, with one very significant difference: the range and level of involvement would never have been as great as it was.

INTERPROVINCIAL COMPETITION

The potential for interprovincial competition is the corollary of region-wide regional development. The idea that interprovincial and interregional competition flourished because of DREE, provincial, or federal-provincial programs has been implanted in the history of DREE by more than one writer.[60] From an analytical point of view, George Nader, using intercensal migration data, did some work on provinces as meaningful units for regional economic planning; he concluded that "the results of the nodal regionalizations strongly support the use of provinces for the implementation of federal regional policy."[61] The study also concluded that for the full range of regional planning programs to be implemented, both sub-provincial and supra-provincial regions would have to be designated.

It is logical that provinces within regions should not be in competition with one another. There is litte benefit to individual provinces in mindless competition leading to overcapacity and lowered productivity. To understand the flexibility of the GDA in terms of its ability to permit non-conflicting province-by-province initiatives, but at the same time recognize the significance of a region-wide perspective, one may look at the GDAs of Newfoundland, New Brunswick, and Nova Scotia and the PEI Comprehensive Plan. The lessons to be learned apply equally to the other multi-provincial region of DREE, the West. The four federal-provincial umbrella agreements prevailing in the Atlantic region contained a number of common areas for attention, even if of different importance and priority in any given jurisdiction. It is instructive to look at them with a critical eye. They are as follows:

- Infrastructure – industrial, municipal, social, and transportation
- Resource exploitation, including renewable and non-renewable resources of the forests and oceans, minerals, and agriculture
- Industrial development and diversification
- Recreation/tourism
- Horizontal activities such as planning and support services
- Technology
- Spatial or geographic-specific initiatives

Federal-provincial agreements had the objective of enhancing provincial economies, based on comparative advantage and, to the degree possible, without playing favourites. A review of these more or less common themes reveals the following facts.

Infrastructure, of whatever kind, aimed at upgrading the ability of a province to develop its comparative economic advantages in the most efficient and effective way, does not precipitate interprovincial conflict. Better social infrastructure, through improved structures and facilities, encourages skills upgrading, higher levels of education, and better services. Hopefully it will be recognized that this is to the benefit of a region and the country as a whole. Roads to resources permit resource exploitation in a more efficient and competitive manner, but efforts towards this sort of improvement cannot be categorized as interprovincial competition.

It is also very unlikely that reasonable resource enhancement, much of it aimed at the long term, will create damaging competition between the provinces. In forest industries, mining, and the fishery, the competition is between Canada and other countries of the world, not between provinces, and it behooves us to do whatever possible to ensure the enhancement and best use of those resources.[62] Even in the resource areas, certain provinces have comparative advantages, such as the different species of fish and different minerals. In the Atlantic region, much of the activity in agriculture was directed at self-sufficiency. Competitive overexploitation of the fishery is an international problem, and federal fisheries management exercises control over domestic harvesting.[63] DREE development work in the fishery was aimed at onshore efficiency and quality improvements, not at harvesting.

Industrial development and diversification efforts by DREE concentrated on small- and medium-sized firms and on selected large projects. Most of the comment on interprovincial competition relates to industrial activity and usually focuses on the financial incentives given to attract, or otherwise encourage, specific kinds of such activity.[64] The small- and medium-sized firm activities are unlikely to generate interprovincial conflict by their very nature. Indeed, most current program efforts of both the federal and provincial governments continue the emphasis on the small- and medium-sized business component of regional economies.[65]

The GDA was one of the most useful instruments available for concluding large, one-of-a-kind, company-specific deals and for consummating the participation of the two levels of government usually involved.[66] Critical comment has not been lacking with regard to the location of, or locating of, the larger firm in any one of Canada's ten provinces and the role of government in the process. It has been alleged that the process led to interprovincial and interregional bidding wars. DREE may have encouraged the location of new industry in a particular province or region, but did not foster provincial bidding wars—it was the last thing the department wanted. Such bidding that did take place, most particularly between Ontario and Quebec, was at the initiative of provincial governments. DREE was sometimes caught in the middle but did not use its money to play the role of broker between the bidders.[67] In the overall scheme of things, however, few large, company-specific projects come the way of regional development practitioners, desirable as they may be.

Under the Regional Development Incentives Program, three factors militated against interregional and intraregional competition. The size of projects, at least in the Atlantic region, was such that interprovincial bidding was simply not a factor. Secondly, much of the program activity was in sectors indigenous to the region and could only take place in a given province. Finally, and something that is frequently overlooked, the program legislation obliged officials to look at the injury factor and forbade them from assisting one firm at the expense of another. There was a departmental sensitive industry list to guide program officers against recommending projects that would add unneeded capacity in a given sector. The Atlantic region had its own sensitive industry list, in recognition of the average size of business in that region. Thus the DREE GDA and RDIP activities had minimum, if any, impact on interregional or interprovincial competition (see chapter 6 for a detailed examination of DREE's incentives program performance).

In the tourism sector there was provincial competition for the tourist dollar long before the advent of DREE. DREE involvement centred on enhancing region-wide tourism attractions and physical plant, such as accommodation, and did not change the balance of competition between the provinces of the Atlantic region. Indeed, DREE was likely a factor in bringing some order into the Atlantic tourism industry. Other special situations that were unlikely to spawn competition and would have been discouraged by officials in any case included horizontal and non-competitive planning agreements and spatial initiatives, to name but two.

BUREAUCRATIC-POLITICAL RELATIONSHIPS

A discussion of the DREE GDA approach to regional development would be incomplete without reference to the role of politicians in the process and to their relationship with officials of both levels of government.

It has been suggested that officials held unusual, if not unhealthy, authority in the determination of initiatives and their implementation.[68] This suggests a lack of confidence in the motives of officials exercising their delegated authorities and, more tellingly, a lack of confidence by the politicians in themselves. Sufficient checks and balances surrounded the DREE subsidiary agreement negotiation and implementation processes to ensure the integrity of the system. Confident ministers never lacked for avenues of access, for information, or for input. This obtained at both the federal and provincial levels of government.

The level of authority delegated to regional DREE officials was no accident. It was determined at the outset that for the GDA to work, regional officials needed an authority level sufficient to match anything that the provinces could offer and, equally important, to match most of the senior levels of other federal departments, usually located in Ottawa. Thus was created a shuttle service of senior DREE personnel between the regions and Ottawa, arguing regional positions firsthand with departments and central agencies and supporting the minister at cabinet committee. And thus was created the structure whereby virtually all GDA subsidiary agreement implementation decisions and 90 percent of financial assistance decisions were taken on-site. Consequently, provincial officials and ministers knew that senior DREE officials negotiated with the confidence of ministerial backing. This was the essence of the GDA concept.

Notwithstanding its operational mode, DREE did not subvert the political process or political involvement at either the federal or provincial level. The very high expectations that existed during the DREE period may have been generated by the very objectives associated with a high degree of operational flexibility, on-site decision making, a negotiating device (the GDA) that permitted a range of economic initiatives to be considered, and the perception of almost unlimited amounts of money to make it all happen. These high expectations were held by federal and provincial politicians alike, along with municipalities, businesses and business organizations, special interest groups, and individuals. These expectations, particularly in the Atlantic region, were to resurface more than ten years later with the introduction of a new round of regional development programming.[69] In retrospect, the GDA went a long way towards fulfilling many of the expectations held for it.

The expectations of economic improvement were matched at the political level by expectations of political gain. This is evident in that the demise of DREE as a department was partially due to flawed perceptions, on the part of many who should have known better, of the political mileage accruing from the approach. "Political gain" was attempted in less savory ways than by just taking credit for program activities. There were those who sought to score debating points in the public forum by besting the other side on whatever point of procedure or project or agreement content they could seize upon, with the best economic benefit of secondary importance.

As quoted by Donald Savoie, federal and provincial elected officials in New Brunswick complained that they only saw the end-result of subsidiary agreement negotiations and that the positions taken by the two levels of government were never publicly revealed. Then member of Parliament, now senator, Eymard Corbin is quoted as saying, "If the province has a plan to deal with development, it's about time it was clearly spelled out so that people could know who's in and who's out." Member of Parliament Herb Breau suggested that the federal government should engage the provincial cabinet in a public debate in order to reveal to what extent the province was committed to alleviating economic disparities in the northeast of the province. A question in the House of Commons concerning a specific project met with the response that the decision was made by a joint federal-provincial management committee; this reply did not reveal whether DREE, the province, or both recommended that the request for financial assistance be denied.[70]

These examples suggest an adversarial dimension to the joint planning and execution of economic development initiatives for a particular region or province and even an adversarial dimension to the determination of eligibility of individual projects within established program components. In the development of new proposals, the mutual exploration of ideas and concepts, their acceptance or rejection either mutually or by one side or the other, and the negotiation of funding levels were all stages in a process envisaged from DREE's beginning. This process then led ministers and governments to decide the course of action to follow, often after further negotiation at the political level, additional input from various sources, and sometimes public debate. It was not a process conducted in secrecy for the sake of secrecy; neither was it a process intended to generate public confrontation for political gain. Above all, it was an approach intended to enhance the economic well-being of the regions in which it was practised.[71]

The effort to make political points is only one aspect of public debate and should not detract from the benefit of legitimate public discussion, including among non-politicians, on matters relating to the economy of a region. In retrospect, there was not enough public discussion on DREE initiatives and intentions, nor sufficient more-formal input to the development process. It would be easy from a federal point of view to lay the blame with provincial governments. DREE, however, could have facilitated more such involvement than it did. The many daily contacts between DREE officials and a wide variety of interested parties, initiated by either side, did, nevertheless, provide an invaluable source of information on the thinking in the regions and made an impact on the content of subsidiary agreements.

Provincial ministers involved with the subsidiary agreement process (the designated DREE liaison minister and those responsible for DREE-related activities) were expected to play an even greater role than federal ministers, given their relatively narrower range of responsibilities. This view is supported with regard to the Atlantic provinces, particularly New Brunswick, by Donald Savoie in his book on the Canada–New Brunswick GDA. In commenting on the capabilities of the provincial civil service and its strengthening over the years, Savoie concludes, "There is no doubt that the Provincial Cabinet and individual Cabinet Ministers dominate the decision making in the New Brunswick government, in that they decide not only when and which proposals should be implemented, but also, in fairly specific terms, how they should be implemented." He adds that the cabinet and the premier were very close to all aspects of policy making.[72] In commenting on federal officials' purported difficulties in gaining access to their ministers, Savoie states:

> New Brunswick officials have no such complaints. On the contrary, the great majority of them charged that ministers are far too preoccupied with what they themselves regard as administrative matters ... the provincial Cabinet ministers are much more a part of their departmental management team than are their federal counterparts. They participate, at times in a very direct fashion, in preparing their departmental budgets and in developing new initiatives. Furthermore, they are likely to know on a first name basis ... most of their departmental officials. Accordingly, ministers and officials interact frequently, not just on politically sensitive issues and when formulating new policies and programs, but also on program implementation and administrative matters.[73]

Savoie also reported that provincial cabinet ministers felt that the GDA process took away their ability to influence policies of even their own departments. They suggested they were deceived by provincial officials who sought to dilute ministerial authority. In reference to subsidiary agreement subject matter, ministers said they had no avenue of appeal over their own officials. Provincial bureaucrats added to the perception with statements to the effect that one of the benefits of the GDA was that it helped keep politicians under control. They said that to provide background information to ministers on GDA initiatives, as the federal officials did, would confuse the ministers, get them into difficulty, and perhaps lead them to add or delete program elements. In a more positive vein, provincial officials applauded one interpretation of the GDA implementation process: from an administrative perspective, they felt it afforded the opportunity to promote soundly developed measures for economic development.[74] Such an attitude by officials should have allayed some of the fears held concerning the motives of officials involved with the GDA process.

The attitude of self-importance on the part of some provincial officials puts in question much of the validity of the conclusions based on interviews with these same officials. These expressed opinions of both officials and ministers are at odds with the operating practice of New Brunswick government ministers that was revealed in earlier quotations; they must therefore be treated with considerable skepticism. They are even more at odds with the experience of senior DREE officials who dealt with these same ministers during federal-provincial negotiation.

Strong ministers in any government can dictate the nature of the activity of their department, and they will not be thwarted by systems or processes. For those who were unable to do so, the fault did not lie with the GDAs. Notwithstanding the existence or creation of central planning and coordinating authorities, such as the Community Improvement Corporation in New Brunswick, line departments played a strong role under the GDA approach. Almost every subsidiary agreement initiative, whether it concerned industrial development, resource development, tourism, or infrastructure, had to rely on departmental expertise for agreement formulation and implementation. In New Brunswick, where the premier was his own minister of regional development, each minister had a clearly identified avenue of appeal on issues relating to the GDA.

Project-specific implementation decisions were taken by the joint management committee. The provincial minister had every right to know the projects under discussion and to direct the departmental position to be taken. Donald Savoie lends support to this view: "All GDA initiatives are implemented through provincial government departments and agencies which, if nothing else, enables provincial Cabinet ministers to be far more familiar with specific projects than the Minister of DREE."[75] Could anyone seriously believe that then veteran New Brunswick premier Richard Hatfield was hoodwinked by officials? It was he who attended every GDA annual meeting, negotiated subsidiary agreement priorities, met successively and frequently with DREE ministers, and represented the province at First Ministers' Conferences, where regional development was a regular agenda item. If New Brunswick ministers were hoodwinked, it may have been by their own premier—hardly the fault of officials. By the same token, one could hardly envisage Minister Gerald Merrithew not playing a decisive role on the position to be taken by the various departments he headed in the New Brunswick government over the years.

The situation was not very different in the other Atlantic provinces. Premier Gerald Regan of Nova Scotia and his successor, John Buchanan, played a strong role in the GDA in that province, along with their ministers of development. In Newfoundland, ministers of the calibre of John Crosbie led the provincial negotiations. Successive premiers Alex Campbell, Bennett Campbell, Angus MacLean, and James Lee of Prince Edward Island were in the forefront of Comprehensive Development Plan discussions, as well as being co-chairmen of the Joint Advisory Board overseeing the Plan. Across the country, those ministers and premiers who wished to do so had no difficulty directing officials on provincial bargaining positions and, where necessary, influencing the provincial views on implementation. In retrospect, the GDA may have been used by some provincial premiers to bypass or otherwise diminish the provincial cabinet process, but the GDA cannot be held responsible for that.

In the federal system, due in part to its size, complexity, and the importance of continuity in policy and program development, officials have enjoyed a large measure of autonomy and influence. This is recognized by Donald Savoie with reference to federal-provincial collaboration under the GDA concept when he comments that, over a period of forty-three or more years, "the federal public service has traditionally held considerable influence over policy issues and almost unrestricted authority over administrative matters."[76] He appears to deny the applicability of this premise to the DREE experience, however, in saying that "federal departments are ... highly centralized administrative structures. The GDA approach radically departs from this tradition—it delegates authority to provincial DREE offices to develop initiatives in most policy fields." Savoie reinforces his view that regionally based authorities are less efficient: "At the policy level, decentralization leads to reduced national consistency in program delivery and raises new problems of control and accountability in program formulation and decision making."[77] Does this suggest that regionally based officials are less capable than those based in Ottawa, or that they have less access to the department's administrative structure? It clearly purports that national consistency is reduced, notwithstanding the hierarchal organizational structure that DREE continued to maintain. We have shown that at both the bureaucratic and political levels, policy and program initiatives ran a gauntlet of review, always with the intimate involvement of the DREE minister, other ministers, Treasury Board, and cabinet committee. Officials, then, did not insist on their own way in any irresponsible or unaccountable fashion—they did provide the continuity of program direction in the DREE GDA period across two changes of government, six DREE ministers, and countless other changes of political leadership.

From time to time members of Parliament did voice concern about activities under subsidiary agreements and complained about their access to information. Short of making MPs part of the bureaucratic process, however, it was not possible, in terms of workload alone, to impart all the information in the system to members or other interested parties. In terms of the negotiation process, there is little doubt that the regular and formal presence of members of Parliament, and axiomatically, members of provincial legislatures, would have resulted in a different character to the development of economic initiatives. Ministers of both levels of government, not officials, took the decision that this was not to be the case. Most General Development Agreements specified the make-up of the development committees, and the subsidiary agreements specified the make-up of the joint management committees. As described earlier in this chapter, however, politicians were frequently involved in initiatives in which they had a special interest or to which they had a special contribution to make.

What might the outcome have been if elected officials, including ministers, had been primary participants in formulating subsidiary agreements, or if they had had the option to exercise detailed revisions to proposals of officials? Savoie says, "While politicians can easily identify other highway projects to replace those they have discarded (as developed by officials), they are not able to do the same with, for example, a proposed agricultural agreement containing expertly designed proposals to promote economic development in selected agricultural industries." He identifies federal ministers, among others, as not having the expertise to critique proposals put forth by officials.[78] These two observations speak volumes about how difficult it would be for elected politicians to intrude into the domain of officials. One can not reasonably expect elected politicians to be expert in their own right in every economic aspect of the Canadian economy. Even regional ministers cannot be expected to know, in technical detail, all facets of the economy of their region. In the example of highways, it makes little sense to expend public dollars according to political criteria alone, with no regard to economic need, highway condition, usage rates, and safety considerations.

What has been overlooked in the debates over the secrecy in the agreement negotiation process and input opportunities is this: almost all the initiatives under discussion were actually in the public domain. One side or the other would have mentioned them, or they might have been made public in the news conferences and press releases following the annual federal-provincial GDA meetings. Even the ranking of priorities was frequently revealed. Ministers and members of Parliament had a standing invitation to be briefed by DREE officials. Some took up the offer, the majority did not.[79]

In the final analysis, there was too much preoccupation with the idea that the GDA was a process, rather than a concept. There was too much the perception that the GDA was somehow separated from all the other normal avenues of information and dialogue available to anyone who wanted to be informed on government activities or to register a particular point of view.

THE IMAGE ERROR

Notwithstanding all the evidence to the contrary, no notion was so erroneously perceived as that of the DREE image in the regions. George Baker, Newfoundland member of Parliament, said in 1978: "DREE is, as you know, if you look at the newspaper clippings, a very high-profile department in the Atlantic region. It is more high-profile there than it is in any other part of Canada, I am sure of that. It is extremely high-profile; it is high-profile in the news, with government, in conversations with the people."[80]

How did this misperception arise and persist when comments such as the above were common place? It was probably founded on the arm's-length experience of Ottawa-based bureaucrats and politicians alike. MPs and occasionally ministers, disenchanted because they felt they, or the government, had not received due credit for their regional development efforts, reacted predictably. Perceptions are frequently based on exceptions to the rule, as politicians are acutely aware, and the scores of examples where DREE and the federal government did very well in terms of visibility were frequently eclipsed by less fond recollections. DREE's image within the regions and the perception of that image outside the regions were markedly different.

Several reasons have been cited for DREE's perceived lack of image and failure to receive appropriate credit for what it was doing. These include the following: direct delivery by the province of most (not all) of the cost-shared activities under the subsidiary agreements; federal politicians not being available for media events; late DREE press releases; and, sometimes, mischievous provincial one-upmanship.[81] It is instructive for us to examine each of these propositions as they relate to the reality of DREE Atlantic, recognizing that the DREE presence was represented differently in other regions of the country. In western Canada, for example, there were few government members to carry the federal message and be present at official DREE functions. Although officials represented the department, the media was more inclined to report provincial representation and participation. In Quebec, the ever-present federal-provincial tension diminished DREE's image, although the departmental information function was particularly well executed in that province. In Ontario, the modest expenditure levels as a proportion of provincial government wealth could not be expected to generate significant exposure.

The provinces did implement the majority of DREE projects and programs under the subsidiary agreements. DREE directly delivered the Regional Development Incentives Program across Canada, which afforded the opportunity for a heightened federal profile and image. Certain other DREE programs, such as the highly regarded Prairie Farm Rehabilitation Act in western Canada, were also directly delivered. Other federal departments delivering their programs under the auspices of the DREE subsidiary agreements had all the public information apparatus necessary to highlight their efforts.

The starting point of every project and every program was the joint management committee approval for those projects and programs. Every provincial project tender issued carried both the DREE and provincial identifier. DREE was present at the tender openings. All written program eligibility criteria, forms, and guidelines were issued under the joint auspices of DREE and the province. Project signs revealed joint project sponsorship and cost-sharing. All officials openings and other media events were joint, as specified in each subsidiary agreement. In 1978, when the prime minister personally acted on behalf of the federal government to consummate public awareness agreements with the provinces regarding federal-provincial agreements, the DREE subsidiary agreements were cited as models of how this might be done. Therefore, even though the province was seen as the prime implementor of program activities, DREE was still prominently involved and so identified.

What is the significance of being the prime agency for program implementation? It involves the contracting for and sometimes the direct provision of goods and services, the offering of programs to businesses, associations, and communities, and some provincial government in-department activities. Although the design of physical facilities and the planning of highways, buildings, and infrastructure may be partially or even totally carried out by a provincial line department, such technical requirements are usually contracted out. Marketing and incentive programs, if not jointly designed by the two levels of government, always received strong input from DREE and other federal officials. The public at large is rarely involved in this process. People see a road being built or some infrastructure work taking place, and there may be the presumption that it is a provincial government activity unless project signs correct this impression. Being the implementing agency does little for public exposure or image. Awareness, image, taking credit, visibility — whatever the terminology — all these are largely governed through the provision of information.

The information function in DREE was executed through official openings and ribbon-cutting ceremonies, interviews and speaking engagements, publications of both a specific and general nature, project and program news releases, and responses to enquiries from the media, associations, communities, chambers of commerce, and individuals. These enquiries in turn frequently led to news items. Particular attention was paid to any situation involving a federal minister.

It is widely held that DREE took two to three months to approve the issuance of written media news releases, by which time they would have little relevance. This is a red herring. Ninety percent or more of news releases in the Atlantic region were authorized on-site by the respective director general or the regional ADM. Joint announcements were released according to a schedule agreed upon with the province; uniquely federal releases were scheduled to coincide with a particular event or occurrence, such as a ministerial visit. The approval procedures did go through a number of changes over time. In 1977, then DREE minister Marcel Lessard, on learning of the department's somewhat erratic process of news release approvals, directed that thenceforth such authority rest in the regions. The long news release approval time became a thing of the past. This situation generally prevailed, other than at a change of regime (government and/or minister), when a re-examination usually took place. Late news releases, as such, were never the cause of a diminished DREE image, since all major events received dedicated attention and media coverage.

Donald Savoie says that the local press communicated with the relevant provincial minister rather than with the DREE minister whenever they had a question about a project or a program. According to Savoie, officials were not as sensitive to public opinion or as eager as politicians to gain public exposure; thus, in the frequent absence of federal politicians, provincial ministers were able to occupy the stage with little competition from federal officials.[82] DREE Atlantic officials played a unique role in federal public service history in the degree to which they were expected to represent the department and the government of Canada on regional development matters. It was to their credit that they were able to discharge this responsibility in a professional and non-partisan manner up to the 1982 DREE/ITC merger. DREE Minister Elmer MacKay of the Conservative Clark regime had no problem in maintaining these same high expectations of regional DREE officials in the Atlantic and in building upon them. Because DREE officials were very sensitive to public opinion, they were able to explain the departmental and federal position on regional development issues without attributing a political context to it. Interestingly enough, even with ministers present at media events, the atmosphere was remarkably non-partisan, attesting again to the uniqueness of the DREE federal-provincial relationship.

What pervaded the DREE regional development program experience in the Atlantic provinces, as noted by George Baker above, was the incredible profile the department had. It is not possible to say how many enquiries were made of provincial ministers, but it is possible to record DREE's involvement in the public information domain over the DREE years. DREE owed its remarkable profile to the fact that most of the subsidiary agreement activities, notwithstanding provincial implementation, were just about always referred to as "DREE" projects; DREE schools, DREE highways, DREE industrial parks, and so on. These references were made by speakers at ceremonies and ribbon cuttings, in media coverage of such events, and in media usage of DREE news releases. It was not uncommon for provincial politicians to make reference to "DREE" projects, even when they were discussing jointly shared activities. DREE officials fielded hundreds of enquiries from all quarters, and enquiries of the DREE minister numbered in the hundreds.

Federal politicians were not as consistent as their provincial counterparts in attending media events, and some were habitual no-shows. But federal ministers did participate, some of them frequently, on such occasions. Successive ministers Jamieson, Lessard, MacKay, and De Bané were often present at Atlantic region functions, and elsewhere, and not only in their "own" province.[83] Atlantic regional ministers MacEachen, LeBlanc, Regan, Crosbie, and Campbell all played a role in the public information aspects of DREE projects, and the record was the same in other parts of the country. That the political profile was enhanced under the GDA, rather than diminished, is well put by Donald Savoie when he cites a number of GDA activities, province by province:

"All these initiatives provided both federal and provincial politicians with countless opportunities to be seen in public supporting Canadian regional development efforts and bringing development projects to their local communities."[84]

The following data demonstrate the kind and consistency of DREE media coverage in the Atlantic region over the several years of its GDA existence. As early as 1976, a DREE-commissioned national survey of newspaper stories mentioning DREE revealed that 531 references out of a total of 1,129, or 47 percent, related to the Atlantic region. In one quarter of 1979, the Atlantic regional office tracked 39 news releases to find that they had been used a total of 93 times. In 1981 a study of DREE media coverage in Newfoundland in the last quarter of the year showed that 29 media events (signings, official openings, press conferences) had been covered, and that there were, in total, 100 DREE media references during the period. In the third quarter of 1982, across the four Atlantic provinces, DREE received coverage for 19 media events; in addition, there were 57 speaking engagements, 35 news releases, 106 media enquiries, and 334 unsolicited media mentions.[85] Much, but by no means all, of the media coverage in 1982 would have included items relating to the 1982 DREE/ITC merger.

During a six-month period in 1980 (July 1980–January 1981, a period during which such information was recorded), the DREE ADM Atlantic was interviewed twenty-three times, for periods of up to one hour, by radio, TV, and the press, on both a regional and national basis. The agencies included CBC radio and television in several cities in the region, ATV television, radio stations CJCB Sydney, News Radio Halifax, CKCW Moncton, *Canadian Business Magazine*, the *Financial Post*, the Halifax *Chronicle-Herald*, the *Cape Breton Post*, and *Atlantic Insight*.

DREE maintained its own regional communications functions, through which it communicated with the media in all regions of Canada. In the Atlantic region, this permitted the dissemination of newsworthy stories of interest to the public in the region. Even without political involvement, what DREE was doing and saying in the Atlantic region was considered news. In 1981, for example, a senior DREE Atlantic official gave the keynote address at the September Atlantic Provinces Economic Council conference in Saint John, New Brunswick. The address received front-page or second-page write-ups in every major newspaper in the region and in the *Globe and Mail*; CBC and ATV television coverage in all four provinces in English and CBC French-language coverage in three provinces; and direct radio coverage from eight stations, with double that number taking a feed from "Broadcast News." Of particular significance was the large number of approaches made to DREE officials at the conference by business-people interested in economic prospects in Atlantic Canada and in DREE programs.

These randomly selected details on DREE media coverage in the Atlantic provinces serve to indicate, not that individual DREE officials had any particular profile, but that the department, DREE, was very well known and respected. That respect was held by provincial governments and federal MPs alike. Then premier Richard Hatfield was a well-known supporter of DREE. As early as 1977, he said that he had always been supportive of the DREE concept, and he told the provincial legislature that if DREE ever disappeared or was swallowed up by other federal departments, New Brunswick could suffer and would have to compete with other provinces for help from individual Ottawa line departments.[86] Hatfield never changed that opinion. Just a year before the announced merger of DREE with another federal department, which signified the loss of DREE's distinct role and mandate, the business community in the Atlantic provinces expressed its opinion of DREE through the Board of the Atlantic Provinces Economic Council (APEC) as follows: "APEC and DREE have a very good understanding and respect for each other, and APEC wants to see DREE strengthened in the Atlantic Region."[87]

Profile, then, entails more than taking credit for a particular project or besting the partner province in media coverage—it means an enduring reputation, based on a continuing presence and activity level. That reputation was acknowledged by federal representatives of both parties. Robert Howie, Conservative member of Parliament, York-Sunbury, and minister of state, transportation, in the 1979 Clark government, spoke in 1978 at the Standing Committee on Regional Development: "I have the feeling that this aspect of transportation is holding back regional development despite the very good work that DREE is doing."[88] Mr Howie spoke again on DREE in 1981, after having received further insight into the department through his experience serving with the Clark government: "Our DREE program has tried very hard to reverse these trends and these situations and we have embarked upon the Regional Development Incentives Act, which I think has been an excellent thrust, and I am particuarly pleased about the General Development Agreements and the subsidiaries, which I feel also are excellent thrusts. It is my view that DREE has to be empowered to take a lead in focussing a development dimension on the part of all branches of government."[89] It is interesting to note Howie's use of the word "we" in reference to DREE, implying a regional, rather than a political, connotation.

Maurice Harquail, Liberal member of Parliament from New Brunswick, also had words of support for DREE in 1981: "I want to begin

... by once again putting on the record how much importance I attach to DREE, and make in quite obvious in the same breath to say that I support the concept of DREE. I want to underline the importance of the continuance of DREE in all its important work that it will do in the four Atlantic provinces."[90]

The DREE profile in the Atlantic and in certain of the western provinces was very high and carried a positive connotation. Criticism from within the regions was usually directed at the size of the budget and its allocation rather than at DREE's performance. Of course, there was frustration from time to time with perceived delays in the signing of agreements, differences of opinion on priorities, and so on, but this rarely inhibited regional development efforts. When rumours about a possible disbandment of the department arose, supporters rallied to its defence. Not long after DREE ceased to be a separate entity, any disenchantment with its performance changed to fond recollections of the "DREE days," and new rumours about its possible reincarnation abounded.

What do image and taking credit contribute to an effective regional development effort? Not very much. It is important for accountability purposes and public knowledge to have a clear understanding of the roles of the various levels of government in regional economic development, as in any other area of expenditure of public funds. Above all, it is important that the public, as represented by businesses, communities, and individuals, have confidence in governmental efforts in this regard. This confidence is not enhanced by different sides competing to take credit for what is being done, particularly if it is done on a shared basis. At the same time, a sufficient public profile can be ensured if the effort is properly executed. Clearly, then, as demonstrated here, any belief that lack of credit accorded federal participation in regional development was a legitimate reason to effect the demise of DREE is misplaced.

Throughout this period of DREE regional development activity in the Atlantic provinces, the support expressed by MP George Baker never wavered. In welcoming officials from the Atlantic region to the 1981 Standing Committee on Regional Development he said, "I would like to as well welcome the officials here today from probably the most positive federal government department that we have in Atlantic Canada."[91]

Chapter Three

DREE in Retrospect

IN 1978 RICHARD PHIDD and Bruce Doern, after reviewing various policies and approaches to regional development practised to that time, said, "Thus the management of regional economic development policy is a complex activity. It would appear that neither a pure market system with its bias in favour of moving people to jobs nor an exclusive public sector strategy designed to create jobs in the lagging areas regardless of cost can solve the dilemmas in regional development policies which we have outlined."[1] The dilemmas were many—the coordination of federal efforts, the perceived conflict of regional development policy with national economic industrial policy, the respective roles of the federal and the provincial governments, political orientations, centralized versus decentralized planning and implementation, and the exercise of overall control of policy.

In referring to DREE's origins, Phidd and Doern noted that "public policies, although significantly influenced by economic considerations, are not formulated exclusively on economic values. The Department of REE was established therefore to formulate policies with multiple goals and objectives; hence the difficulties encountered with the evaluation of regional economic development policies."[2]

These authors recognized that DREE's wide range of activities need not be seen as a series of ad hoc programs, but rather as parts of a whole, a series of complementary moves to uplift the well-being of the regions in specific terms and to lay the groundwork for and otherwise support sustainable economic growth. There may not have been a master plan at the beginning, or even in 1973–74, that encompassed these component parts and scheduled them for execution. Things were moving too fast for that. Policy and strategy documents of the day, however, identified all the areas for attention as either areas of developmental opportunity of areas for removal of constraints. Such a mosaic also revealed a role for other federal departments and provincial administrations.

The observations by Phidd and Doern were made when DREE had little more than three years of decentralized operational experience to its credit, and they cannot be taken as a *carte blanche* endorsement of the federal government's regional development policy as represented by DREE. Phidd and Doern remained concerned about the integration of federal departments in the regions, the appropriate degree of decentralization with accompanying authorities, and the discretionary powers that should fall to provinces and municipalities. They concluded that the critical problem for the 1980s would involve the search for an appropriate mix between a centralized and a decentralized regional development strategy; they characterized this problem as an issue that had plagued economic policy formulation in all federal systems.[3] How accurate were Phidd and Doern in their 1978 assessment of federal development policy and DREE? To what degree did their views and predictions for the 1980s hold true for the remaining years of DREE's life? What messages did they hold for the post-DREE period of regional development programming?

In 1982 the Senate Standing Committee on National Finance, in looking back at the DREE era, said, "At the time of its creation, DREE's role was unique within the federal government. It was a 'horizontal' department, cutting across the policy fields occupied by other departments."[4] According to the report of the Federal-Provincial Task Force on Regional Development Assessment, issued almost ten years after the Phidd and Doern comments above, the principal reason for some success in regional development in the 1970s was that the majority of the funding was spent on programming designed to fit the specific needs of the areas in which it was applied.[5] Two of the pillars of DREE's regional development philosophy, across-the-board program coverage and on-the-ground matching of programs to identified need, had thus received endorsement from very different sources. It is now time to look at DREE's programs and associated activities in retrospect.

Explicit DREE programming was of three kinds: the occupation of unclaimed territory, sharing of jurisdiction with other federal departments, and sharing of provincial jurisdictions. DREE's ability to work with and influence the actions of other federal departments was fundamental to its success. As time went on, DREE regionally based expertise was sought by other departments, or offered up by DREE, on a range of issues. From time to time, DREE topped up the budget of another department to secure an action judged beneficial for regional purposes. (DREE/OGD collaboration was more fully discussed in chapter 2.) We know that DREE influenced the priorities of provincial governments and their departments. DREE had no more success than the MSERD, which followed it, in influencing Department of Finance macroeconomic policy making in Canada. DREE did bring about regionally differentiated tax credits in Canada, a practice carried further by its successor, DRIE.

THE GENERAL DEVELOPMENT AGREEMENT CONCEPT

DREE practised three phases of program development through the 1974–82 period: Phase I, the removal of constraints (infrastructure and related programming); Phase II, exploitation and enhancement of the existing economic base (resources and associated industries development); and Phase III, economic diversification.

By 1977, little more than three years after the signing of GDAS with all provinces but PEI, DREE planning was reaching beyond infrastructure and the resource base. In the Atlantic region, attention turned to the development potential of resources value added, hydroelectric energy, manufactured-goods import replacement, spatial development based on the natural advantages of deep-water ports, light industry corridors to take advantage of transportation linkages, community-level small-business programs, and region-wide tourism development. Ocean- and marine-related activities also surfaced in the region at this stage. By 1978 a DREE Atlantic staff paper had already identified keener competition at home and abroad, as the 1980s brought closer the dawn of a freer trade era.

In 1979 the Atlantic region described its move into Phase III programming in the following way:

> The complexity of the areas in which we are now developing or intending to develop proposals for the economic enhancement of the Atlantic Region overshadows anything to date. This complexity is interwoven with the more and more frequent regional implications for our development thrust. We are now preoccupied with such important and complex issues as ocean-related activities ... energy, both bilaterally with individual provinces and regionally; projects of such size and consequence ... that cannot be divorced from regional development implications, activities which relate to national policies such as shipbuilding and repair ... second generation agreements in areas in which we are already programming will become more complex because of the level of maturity being reached.[6]

In that same year Joe Clark's Conservatives wrested power away from the Liberals. A major policy paper, "Federal Regional Economic Development Policy—Implementing the Approach," was making the rounds in DREE, and in December the department published another series of papers (the blue books—the Conservatives were still in power) titled "Major Development Opportunities and Issues in Canada's Regions."

Evidence of the 1979 policy intentions and of the policy directions that followed can be seen in an examination of the subsidiary agreements, written or intended, over four periods of regional development activity in Canada: from 1974 (inception) to 1979; 1979–82; planned agreements at the time of merger in 1982; and post-1982 GDA/ERDA agreements. For analytical purposes, eight program categories were selected: resources, infrastructure, industrial, tourism, spatial, urban, planning, and technology. Each category is explained in footnotes to the following tables or in the narrative discussion.

Inception to March 31, 1979

In the first five years of the GDA, inception to March 31, 1979, for all of Canada exclusive of Prince Edward Island, 61.2 percent of DREE commitments fell in the resources and infrastructure categories; only 9.2 percent in industrial development support. Technology showed up at 1 percent (Table 3.1). There are a number of qualifications to the data shown in the distribution tables, and it is unlikely that any two analysts would make the same distribution of DREE commitments among the eight categories chosen. Some of the qualifications are shown with the tables themselves; several require repeating here.

Two categories in which legitimate differences of opinion may emerge are infrastructure and spatial/community. Other categories of resources, industrial and tourism, for example, are more easily categorized. Infrastructure is usually, if not always, put in place in support of something else, whether it be industrial, social, education, transportation, or municipal. For the purposes of this discussion, readily identifiable infrastructure is shown as a separate category. It includes highways, most municipal infrastructure, and agreements totally directed to industrial parks. The latter allocation can be legitimately disputed, but the reasons for so treating industrial parks will become clear for comparative purposes.

An even more difficult allocation decision comes with the spatial/community category. So much can fall into this grouping, which by design may cover infrastructure, resource exploitation, community economic and industrial diversification, skills upgrading and training, and many other activities, that to sort them out would require a detailed

TABLE 3.1
DISTRIBUTION OF FEDERAL GDA COMMITMENTS:
INCEPTION TO MARCH 31, 1979 (MILLIONS OF DOLLARS)

Sector	Atlantic	%	Quebec	%	Ontario	%	West	%	Canada	%
Resources	287.7	31.4	162.2	22.9	41.1	38.8	28.6	5.0	519.6	22.6
Infrast.	312.4	34.0	430.9	60.9	51.7	48.8	91.5	16.1	886.5	38.6
Indust.	39.2	4.3	68.0	9.6	–	–	104.9	18.5	212.1	9.2
Tourism	58.8	6.4	45.6	6.4	–	–	43.0	7.6	147.4	6.4
Spatial	106.1	11.6	–	–	5.0	4.7	287.4	50.6	398.5	17.3
Urban	80.0	8.7	–	–	8.2	7.7	3.0	0.5	91.2	4.0
Planning	8.9	1.0	–	–	–	–	9.1	1.6	18.0	0.8
Technol.	23.4	2.5	1.0	0.2	–	–	–	–	24.4	1.0
Totals	916.5		707.7		106.6		567.5		2,297.7	

SOURCE: DREE annual reports, 1975–76 through 1978–79.
NOTES
Federal commitments include all involved federal departments.
Resources include agriculture, fisheries, forestry, and mining.
Infrastructure includes highways and clearly identifiable industrial and municipal infrastructure.
Spatial includes community-oriented initiatives. This category will, by definition, also include some resource exploitation, business and industrial development, and infrastructure not otherwise categorized.
These tables exclude PEI Comprehensive Development Plan activities.
The second figure in each column is the percentage of the total for each region and Canada.

study of every subsidiary agreement component, something not encompassed in this book. Some selection was, however, made. Large and easily identifiable highway elements of some of the western northlands agreements and substantial municipal infrastructure elements of certain of the Ontario spatial agreements were placed under infrastructure. Similarly, industrial parks and municipal infrastructure in certain Atlantic agreements were also moved to the infrastructure category. Every effort was made to apply an even hand across the country. Spatial and industrial agreements also include legitimate planning and technology-related efforts, but these simply could not be extracted for separate placement purposes, which accounts for the low readings for these two activities. The PEI Comprehensive Development Plan provides for activities under all of the categories used for this distribution analysis. Breaking them all out for such allocation, a particularly difficult assignment, would not materially affect the percentages by category.

Table 3.1 shows that the percentage of commitments towards infrastructure was highest in Quebec, at 60.9 percent, in the five-year review period. Resource exploitation was highest in Ontario and the Atlantic. The western region heavily weights the spatial/community category for all years studied up to the disbandment of DREE. For the five-year period covered in Table 3.1, 50.6 percent of western region commitments were in this category.

Period April 1, 1979, to March 31, 1982

Table 3.2 shows the distribution of new federal commitments under the GDAS for the period April 1, 1979, to March 31, 1982, the year of the DREE/ITC merger. Note that in both tables 3.1 and 3.2, the data are for all federal government commitments, not just DREE's. Resources and infrastructure now show 28.3 percent of commitments, of which only 4.3 percent was for infrastructure.[7] The industrial category soared to 52.8 percent from its earlier 9.2 percent. The strongest industrial surge was in the three regions comprising central and eastern Canada, with the Atlantic region being the largest in absolute terms. By this time the industrial development category went far beyond the misunderstood industrial parks phase, covering such things as opportunity identification, the managing and financing of research, community industrial and business diversification, small-business assistance, support of industrial commissions, industrial malls and advanced factory space, and the application of new manufacturing technologies. Technology remained a disappointing 2.1 percent, even though there were considerable technological initiatives under the industrial category activities being pursued.

Planned DREE GDA Initiatives at February 1982

A further analysis, which must be treated with great care, concerns the planned DREE initiatives that were at various stages in the pipeline when the DREE/ITC merger was announced. Table 3.3 shows a breakout of this information by region, and Table 3.4 shows it on a consolidated national basis. In Table 3.4, the number of planned initiatives may be accepted as accurate, as they were extracted from the long-term DREE multi-year operational plan. The estimated funding for the agreements can be considered suspect, as the dollars attached to the proposals were estimates, carrying no approved status. Nevertheless, the table reveals some interesting things. Resources and infrastructure combined represented only between 9 and 16 percent of the DREE thinking in 1982 (based on either dollars or number of agreements).

TABLE 3.2

Distribution of New Federal GDA Commitments,
April 1, 1979 – March 31, 1982 (Millions of Dollars)

Sector	Atlantic	%	Quebec	%	Ontario	%	West	%	Canada	%
Resources	86.9	18.0	110.4	36.2	–	–	60.3	40.3	257.6	24.0
Infrast.	24.0	5.0	4.1	1.3	–	–	18.1	12.1	46.2	4.3
Indust.	286.0	59.0	166.1	54.5	100.0	74.0	14.0	9.4	566.1	52.8
Tourism	–	–	24.0	7.9	–	–	17.1	11.4	41.4	3.9
Spatial	54.2	11.2	–	–	35.2	26.0	7.0	4.7	96.4	9.0
Urban	8.0	1.7	–	–	–	–	32.0	21.4	40.0	3.7
Planning	–	–	–	–	–	–	0.75	0.7	0.75	–
Technol.	23.0	4.8	–	–	–	–	–	–	23.0	2.1
Totals	482.1		304.6		135.2		149.5		1,071.7	

SOURCE: DREE annual reports, 1979–80 through 1981–82.
NOTES: See Table 3.1.

The industrial category remained relatively high, at approximately 21 percent. The spatial grouping re-emerged at 34–37 percent, which included a soon-to-be-signed large Manitoba agreement. Technology had risen to 21 percent on a dollar basis with the Atlantic region planning five initiatives totalling over $200 million. It is evident that the policy was now deliberately shifting to another stage in the DREE multi-dimensional approach. Technology and skills-upgrading components were more and more finding their way into the subsidiary agreements. As well, the proposed new agreements envisaged a very high level of involvement of other government departments because of the expertise they could contribute in technology, human skills, and the like.

Post-1982

Without tracking the forty-four DREE agreements that were in the planning stage in early 1982, we can make one more comment on subsidiary agreement activity. During 1982 and into 1983, twenty or more DREE subsidiary agreements were transferred to other departments for management and implementation purposes. New agreements were henceforth to be developed and negotiated by the appropriate federal line department. For comparative purposes we can look at those subsidiary agreements signed after the 1982 period by DREE's

TABLE 3.3

DISTRIBUTION OF PLANNED DREE FEDERAL GDA COMMITMENTS AT FEBRUARY 1982, BY REGION (MILLIONS OF DOLLARS)

Sector	Atlantic		Ontario		West		Canada	
Resources	–	–	2	15	3	69	5	84
Infrast.	–	–	1	8	1	25	2	33
Industrial	5	85	1	100	3	84	9	269
Tourism	–	–	2	30	1	12	3	42
Spatial	3	40	2	40	10	377	15	457
Urban	1	50	–	–	1	40	2	90
Planning	1	4	–	–	1	5	2	9
Technol.	5	209	–	–	1	50	6	259

SOURCE: Task Force on Program Integration, DREE/ITC, March 1982.
NOTES
Source document did not reveal any planned initiatives for Quebec.
The first figure in each column is the number of proposed agreements. The second figure is the estimated cost.

successor, DRIE, that remained active in 1986–87. Table 3.5 shows $945 million of commitments in force across Canada, this time including PEI. Of these commitments, 43.7 percent were in the industrial category, although a significant component of a Quebec industrial development agreement was assigned for infrastructure purposes. Tourism reached a new high of 25 percent, and technology comprised 16.4 percent of country-wide commitments and 29.8 percent of Atlantic region commitments.

It is not the prime purpose of this review to analyse the project/ program-specific activities of DREE to determine where the dollar commitments went. This important piece of work must be left for another commentator on regional development in Canada; every one of the some 127 agreements would require detailed scrutiny, and if one were to go this far, a much more difficult complementary step would be to track the outcome or impact of each project and each program element. This review does, however, illuminate the thinking prevailing in DREE during the years 1974–82. It confirms DREE's three-phase policy approach: the putting in place of the wherewithal to assist various forms of economic development to mature; the enhancement of the existing economic base; and the intervention at more precise levels to make things happen.

Further sector-by-sector studies provide an insight into why the program activities undertaken by DREE and its provincial partners are

TABLE 3.4

DISTRIBUTION OF PLANNED DREE FEDERAL GDA COMMITMENTS AT FEBRUARY 1982, NATIONAL

Sector	Number	Estimated Funding ($ Millions)	Percentage Number	Dollars
Resources	5	84	11.4	6.8
Infrastructure	2	33	4.5	2.6
Industrial	9	269	20.5	21.6
Tourism	3	42	6.8	3.4
Spatial	15	457	34.0	36.7
Urban	2	90	4.5	7.2
Planning	2	8.5	4.5	0.7
Technology	6	259	13.6	20.8
	44	1,243		

SOURCE: Task Force on Program Integration, DREE/ITC, March 1982.

NOTES

The first percentage column is based on the total number of agreements in the planning stage.
The second percentage column is based on the estimated total cost of the planned initiatives.

considered by many observers to have been worthwhile and cost-effective. If history is any judge, these observers are not far off the mark, considering that every regional development effort since 1982 has either replicated the DREE programs or has built upon them. The less charitable could suggest there has been complete sterility of innovative thinking since that time. Appendix 2 provides a collage of randomly selected agreement projects and programs that exhibits the range of activities pursued by DREE during the 1974–82 period.

Infrastructure

There can be no disputing the role played by infrastructure in the removal of constraints to economic development and in the pursuit of economic opportunity. The Senate Standing Committee on National Finance said that infrastructure development was an essential component of economic development and if wisely employed would lead and focus economic growth. The committee concluded that the development strategy for the less-developed regions of Canada had to include infrastructure.[8] In recognition that the Atlantic region lagged behind the rest of Canada in essential infrastructure in support of economic development, DREE assigned it a high priority. This priority

TABLE 3.5

DISTRIBUTION OF DRIE GDA/ERDA COMMITMENTS, SIGNED AFTER
1982 MERGER: 1986–87 (MILLIONS OF DOLLARS)

Sector	Atlantic ($) (%)	Quebec ($) (%)	Ontario ($) (%)	West ($) (%)	Canada ($) (%)
Infrast.	None	None	None	None	None
Industrial	238.4 51.3	175.0 78.0	– –	– –	413.4 43.7
Tourism	73.9 15.9	50.0 22.0	22.0 100	90.9 40.0	236.8 25.0
Spatial	9.1 2.0	– –	– –	100.8 43.2	109.9 11.6
Urban	– –	– –	– –	25.0 10.7	25.0 2.6
Technology	138.3 29.8	– –	– –	16.6 7.1	154.9 16.4
Marketing	5.0 1.0				5.0 0.5
	464.7	225.0	22.0	233.3	945.0

SOURCE: DRIE, annual report, 1986–87.

NOTES

A resource category is no longer carried in the table, given the transfer of these activities to other departments.

The Quebec Industrial item includes a large infrastructure component, not readily quantified.

Table includes Prince Edward Island.

Table includes only agreements signed after merger and none of those still active but signed prior to merger.

Planning has been dropped in favour of marketing.

was, however, selectively applied within the region. In Newfoundland, for example, highway agreements formed a larger part of development programming than in Nova Scotia, where the need was not as great. DREE-supported transportation infrastructure made accessible previously inaccessible natural resource riches and brought about improvements to remote regional airports. It provided the means of getting goods to market and made it possible for citizens to have access to essential health, education, and social amenities. Municipal and industrial infrastructure established the bases upon which industrial diversification could take place. Infrastructure provided water-supply systems for fish plants, permitting them to operate with longer production runs and higher-quality levels. Marine service centres ringing the coast of Newfoundland meant that boats could stay out of the water for shorter periods of time and be better serviced. Infrastructure provided the educational facilities that led to longer student retention rates for higher average schooling levels and it also provided the vocational and technical facilities that furnished specific technical and other needed skills. The Federal-Provincial Task Force on Regional Development Assessment had this to say of infrastructure: "While the link between infrastructure and economic development has to be forged with some care, it is apparent that during the 1960s and 1970s major strides were made with limited funds to ensure that the regions' economic infrastructure would be supportive and attractive for private investment."[9]

While the provision of infrastructure in itself may not generate economic activity, there is little doubt that economic activity will not exist without it.[10] Until more recent times, infrastructure was usually thought of in such physical terms as roads, schools, industrial parks, water-supply and sewer systems, and power. It now carries a more elaborate definition — it comprises whatever kinds of physical facilities or services are needed to support a burgeoning service economy, including different educational inputs, new technologies, research and development, communications systems, and the like. The old needs may also remain, but they must take their place beside the new.

Natural Resources

Natural resources have formed the foundation of the economies of almost every region of Canada. The natural resource base of the Atlantic economy, notwithstanding its predicted decline of importance in relative terms, remained an important element in DREE regional programming. By 1981, even though DREE still carried significant resource-based commitments, the move away from the primary resources was well advanced, partly because resources were within the jurisdiction of federal and/or provincial departments which had the mandates for their exploitation, and partly because DREE intended to shift its emphasis from the supply side to the demand side. Future programming was to be restricted to improving the productivity and value added in those sectors. Resource-based processing industries were recognized as yielding excellent returns to public financial support in terms of incremental employment in rural areas, increased value added in the region, and in foreign exchange earnings. Selective support, particularly to the small- and medium-sized elements, was still envisaged in area-specific development plans and programs. It was intended that DREE involvement with resource industries would be found more under the industrial development category than under resource industries. DREE cost-shared program activity in agriculture, forestry and forest industries, mining, and minerals significantly influenced provincial government policy in these sectors to the extent, in some instances, of effecting long-lasting legislative change. Land-use and land-ownership policy in agriculture and forest areas changed the management approach for these provincial resources.

Project-specific activities in the resource sectors were aimed at resources identification, inventorying and protection, improved management practices, higher utilization rates, and the supply of more efficiently produced, higher-quality raw materials for the processing and manufacturing operations that followed.

Tourism

Tourism was the focus of DREE-related programming in almost every province in Canada. Some of it was experimental, some of it was based on unrealized optimism, and some of it failed. There were no claims that everything carried out under the innovative GDA approach worked perfectly or all the time. Experimentation was part of the process. In tourism, a lot of things worked. DREE/provincial government programming combined to provide better accommodations and more and better attractions (the historic villages of King's Landing and Le Village Acadien in New Brunswick, to name but two, were, and continue to be, highly successful) in Canada's regions. The infrastructure essential to making Gros Morne such a major national park attraction in Newfoundland, computerized reservation systems, hospitality training programs, impressive and functional reception centres at provincial points of entry each added to the strength of tourism as a generator of jobs and income. Comprehensive tourism programming in western Canada was epitomized in the Saskatchewan Qu'Appelle Valley agreement, with its emphasis on cultural and historic sites and the better management and utilization of the area's resource base. Coupled with support for the development of the travel industry, DREE program efforts left a legacy of better tourism practice across the country.

Industrial and Business Development

Business development was central to DREE programming in Canada's regions. In the Atlantic region, industrial and business development had long been recognized as having the potential of moving the region beyond its mainstay reliance on its natural resources, which were usually sold (generally exported) in a low state of value added. Industry and business were seen as providing the diversification of the economy that would permit a legitimate service sector industry to flourish. Each element comprising the industrial sector—capital investment, labour force skills, institutional infrastructure, and modern technology—was tied to the others. DREE maintained a strong commitment to industrial development under industrial development agreements in force across the regions it served and under the federal RDI incentives program. In the Atlantic region, specific-purpose industry-related programming on the scale of pulp and paper modernization, Michelin Tire, the Nova Scotia Panamax Drydock, other shipbuilding and repair, and manufacturing and processing opportunities in steel, coal, zinc, aluminum, and potash was seen as providing an anchor in the region for employment of a skilled labour force and the adaptation of new technologies. Pulp and paper modernization agreements in Ontario and Quebec made contributions to those provinces' peripheral regions of equal if not greater value than in the Atlantic region. The role for DREE and the federal government was to identify opportunity, attract capital investment, and offer flexible financial support.

Industrial development went far beyond infrastructure, industrial parks, and company-specific incentives. DREE established the Bureau of Business and Economic Development to identify growth potential opportunities in the regions and to make the business community at large aware of such opportunities. DREE successfully initiated the special 50 percent investment tax credit for seriously disadvantaged regions. Assistance was provided to industrial and rural development commissions as an early expression of concern for economic well-being at the community level. The infrastructure that was supported, whether industrial, transportation, or municipal, was tied to economic opportunity, with the emphasis shifting over time only to that which could be directly related to identified opportunity.

Substantial program and project-specific effort was directed to increasing value added to the resources, complementing the work going on in resources enhancement. The use and diffusion of technology was encouraged, and in the small-business sector competitive service companies in support of manufacturing and processing were promoted. In other words, there was a dovetailing of cross-sectoral activities within and across different subsidiary agreements. The contribution of technology to industry and business translated into ocean industries initiatives, and efforts in the energy sector were directed to making Atlantic industry and business more competitive.

Industrial Parks

Industrial parks merit special attention in a discussion on industrial development. They provide the nucleus for light industrial and service industries, for physical concentration, and for business diversification.

They substantially reduce the cost to municipalities of providing common services because of the close proximity of businesses. Industrial parks are equally beneficial for businesses because of this same proximity of goods and services. Industrial parks facilitate the transportation of goods, particularly in conjunction with transportation infrastructure development. They thus become logical focal points for regional economic development and industrial diversification efforts.

In 1979, DREE Atlantic completed an economic impact analysis, for the years 1969 to 1976, of industrial park development in the four provinces in the region. Over this period, the provinces had received federal (mainly DREE) financial assistance totalling $31 million.[11] Forty-three active parks in the four provinces contained 769 operating companies representing 18,000 person-years of employment, payrolls totalling $178 million, and personal taxes of $26.6 million. Of the 769 companies, 42 percent were in trade; 26 percent in manufacturing and processing; 11 percent in transportation, communications, and utilities; 8 percent in construction; and 12 percent in other.

It was found that industrial park occupants tended to be more diversified in their production, with a higher level of value added, than businesses in the region as a whole. The analysis also estimated that a high percentage of the firms in the parks represented activity incremental to the region. As part of the study, a data bank containing information on every firm in the forty-three parks was established. The intention was to update the study in 1982 with new information on materials sourcing, municipal taxes paid, and other important indicators of economic impact. The only real way of assessing the impact of financial assistance to companies, whether direct or through infrastructure such as industrial parks, is to track those companies over a period of time, measuring every quantifiable indicator that is considered significant.

In assessment terms, it is legitimate to ask whether the parks would have been created by the private sector if governments had not been involved. There was no evidence of that in 1976 or thereafter. Would the companies have had the same economic impact without the industrial parks or any direct incentives assistance? This, together with other aspects of government support to the business sector, is discussed in chapter 6.

A one-community industrial park study was conducted for the city of Moncton, New Brunswick. This city had seen the closing of one of its two major employers, the T. Eaton Company, which had employed over 1,000 workers, as well as a continuing deterioration of employment at its other major employer, the C.N. Rail Yards (eventually closed in the mid-1980s). As of 1977, in the greater Moncton area there were four DREE-assisted industrial parks, containing 180 companies that employed 3,750 people. Forty-six of the companies were in manufacturing and processing, of which 32 had received DREE RDIP assistance ($7 million offered to these 32 companies generated $28 million of investment, 1,000 jobs, and a $36-million payroll). Connected to the Trans-Canada Highway by DREE-assisted arterial highways and located in the self-styled hub city of the Maritimes, these industrial park companies had excellent transportation connections to the three provinces and outside the region.

The Burnside Industrial Park in Dartmouth, Nova Scotia, became so successful by 1989 that in adjoining Halifax, also a beneficiary of DREE programming, there was concern that business would be drawn away from the capital because of the benefits provided in Dartmouth. Burnside was originally established to be the industrial centre of the Halifax/Dartmouth partnership, with Halifax concentrating on commerce and the service sectors. Burnside is now the largest industrial complex east of Montreal. It covers over 400 hectares and, of particular significance, has attracted a range of other economic activity around its perimeter. Since 1982, park expansion has been paid for out of revenues, and in 1989 Burnside was contributing 20 percent of the budget of the city of Dartmouth.[12]

DREE Atlantic, with its provincial partners, was an early promoter of the use of industrial and incubator malls for light industrial and business development. In these malls, companies in a start-up mode could rent ready-made facilities and equipment, completely serviced; when they became established, they could move on to the more traditional type of industrial park. The industrial park/incubator mall concept was deliberately employed to foster particular kinds of economic development in centres across the four provinces. The concept could be employed in other ways as well. For example, funding was provided in Nova Scotia for the development of a light industrial corridor, running from Amherst through Truro, to encourage diversification outside the Halifax/Dartmouth centre.

Technology

Technology has long been a byword for success in economic endeavour, and insufficient levels of research and development (R&D) in Canada have been decried as inhibiting a level of economic progress and international competitiveness that might otherwise be obtainable. This was the thinking as well in the DREE years. Clearly, in the country's peripheral regions, a better understanding and use of technology was critical to upgrading the resources base, enhancing the competitiveness

101

of existing and envisaged new industrial opportunities, and making successful forays into new areas, such as service industries, or into areas where comparative advantage might be exploited.

In Atlantic Canada, several federal departments, the provinces, research organizations, universities, and the private sector were involved in the pursuit of technology. DREE envisaged a framework for a more deliberate approach to research, so that the R&D would be applicable to the manufacturing, processing, businesses, and services of the region. This approach would be coupled with a more orderly strategy for the use and distribution of technologies essential to the competitiveness of regional firms. DREE was also building technology components into certain of its subsidiary agreements, and some agreements, such as those concerning the ocean industries, were largely based on the exploitation of technology.

Ocean-related activities were seen as a natural comparative advantage for the Atlantic region—one in which a reputation for excellence could be established. Ocean industries technology and development came to the Atlantic as early as 1976 with DREE's support for the establishment of the Newfoundland Ocean Research and Development Corporation (NORDCO). Sadly, NORDCO was disbanded in 1991. A region-wide ocean industries initiative, encompassing ocean-related activities in all four Atlantic provinces, was presented to the Conservative government in late 1979. A component of the initiative was the establishment of the Interdepartmental Committee on Ocean Industries, chaired by the DREE ADM Atlantic, to coordinate all federal (Atlantic) ocean industry–related activities. Because of the pending February 1980 election, the committee met only once and the government postponed decision on the initiative. On its return to power, the Liberal government reviewed a similar ocean-related proposal (March 1981), but decided to restrict programming to Nova Scotia. A Canada–Nova Scotia subsidiary agreement on ocean industries development was signed July 24, 1981. It was only in 1984 that Newfoundland secured an agreement in that sector.[13] The federal government continued to struggle with oceans policy for several years after the demise of DREE.[14]

Energy

Energy was high on the economic agenda throughout the DREE era, and its development and use rated a high priority for regional development purposes. The department, recognizing the importance of energy in keeping regional businesses competitive, was widely involved, on its own and in collaboration with federal and provincial agencies, in seeking ways to use energy to enhance regional economies. Then, as now, the Atlantic region was rich in natural energy resources, from recognized sources such as coal and hydroelectric power to the more conceptual possibilities of tidal, and even wind, power. DREE was interested in three aspects of Atlantic region energy development: (1) that it not proceed so fast as to vitiate any reasonable opportunity of the regional economy to participate in its development; (2) that the region be assured of energy security through its own resources; and (3) that related manufacturing and service industries be afforded the opportunity to grow or be established in the region.

Energy projects that appeared possible at the time included hydroelectric power in Labrador (a still-viable energy resource today), gas findings on the Scotia Shelf, a trans-Maritime natural gas pipeline, and, more distant, Fundy tidal power. Also energy-related was energy conservation through retrofit and off-peak usage experiments, improved technology, and alternate energy systems. As early as 1977, DREE joined with Energy, Mines and Resources and Prince Edward Island in funding the energy cable connection between PEI and New Brunswick. In 1978 DREE introduced, with Nova Scotia, Canada's first energy conservation agreement.

Given the regional/national context of energy, many of the energy-related activities in the Atlantic provinces were executed by the regional development branch of regional headquarters. DREE Atlantic executed the first major study of the potential for export of Atlantic-generated power, particularly hydroelectric power from Newfoundland. DREE Atlantic conducted the department's early discussions on the development of Labrador hydroelectric power and of coal-generated energy in the region. DREE was represented on the federal working group of the Maritime Energy Corporation by the ADM Atlantic, who was also the departmental member of the board of directors of the Lower Churchill Development Corporation, which studied the feasibility of Lower Churchill power development. The region also assumed departmental responsibility relating to the Cape Breton Development Corporation (Devco); this responsibility had earlier rested in Ottawa.

Urban Development

Urban development—a sometimes no-man's-land, yet by no means unclaimed territory—played an important part in regional development. Even without the presence of the one-time Ministry of State for Urban Development, some federal departments played a role in this predominately provincial/municipal arena. The jurisdiction has been jealously guarded by the provinces, although all of them have bent the rules if it meant that federal monies might flow through provincial agencies.

DREE, if not a pioneer in urban development and renewal, was nevertheless prominent in recognizing its importance in rounding out regional economies and carried out extensive programming in the field throughout its life. Urban growth and development are seen as prerequisites to economic progress through the development and application of new technologies. It is widely held that rural–urban migration will accelerate as younger, better-educated Canadians, together with firms, are attracted to areas of economic opportunity. Centres of technology and the generally more available social amenities in urban areas will reinforce the agglomeration syndrome.

In its earliest days, DREE adhered to the growth-pole concept, which was based largely on assumptions surrounding industrial growth. This approach led to considerable underpinning of the infrastructure of a number of cities in peripheral areas of the country. With the advent of the GDA concept and the continued use of the PEI Comprehensive Development Plan in that province, urban development entered a new phase, with urban redevelopment linked more specifically to economic potential. Although business activity could not be guaranteed prior to the commitment of funds or even at the launching of major community improvements and redevelopment projects, a look across the country reveals that the gamble largely paid off.

In a score or more locations, from Winnipeg through Dartmouth, Halifax, Quebec City, Saint John, Charlottetown, Summerside, St John's, and even lesser-known locations such as Bathurst, New Brunswick, things happened. Most of the programs introduced contained significant business-related elements, and funding was frequently shared by three levels of government and the private sector. DREE participation in innovative urban development was aimed at making these centres more hospitable to businesses and to the people with the skills to run them.[15] Given the coastal location of most Atlantic urban centres, it is not surprising that the DREE activity in that region had a waterfront redevelopment bias.

Education

Every jurisdiction claims an interest in and acknowledges the importance of education and training to competitiveness and economic progress. Education jurisdictional lines are well drawn; those for training less so. DREE was conscious of the need to upgrade human resource skills in the regions to a point well beyond the department's early involvement with educational facilities in some of the provinces. Management capability, most particularly at the small-firm level, was a special concern. In the earliers days in the Atlantic region, DREE supported the Newfoundland Institute of Management Training and the Atlantic Management Institute based in Halifax, Nova Scotia. In 1977, DREE brought a common basis to its shared management training commitments with the four Atlantic Provinces, by signing of the multi-million-dollar Atlantic Provinces Management Training Agreement, to which each province was a signator. This agreement encouraged the more pertinent design and improved delivery of management courses and wider business owner/manager course attendance.

Other human resource skills in the region were improved through direct or indirect DREE and provincial government programming. Province-specific land surveying and mapping agreements and the region-wide Land Registration and Information Service agreement created an aerial photography/mapping capability in the Atlantic region that until then was only in its infancy. DREE funded the Atlantic Region Labour Education Centre (ARLEC), which provided labour/management training, before voluntarily turning responsibility for the centre over to the Federal Department of Labour.

The skills question came in for special attention. In 1981 Employment and Immigration (CEIC) and a parliamentary task force carried out a review of federal activities in the fields of training, income supplements, labour markets, and skills shortages; this review led to recommendations for action by CEIC within the jurisdiction assigned to it. DREE was supporting region-wide management training and teaching, as well as research institutions in the forest- and marine-related sectors. Four provincial jurisdictions of education and at least three other federal departments had some responsibility for management training. DREE effort had to be sensitive to these jurisdictions, concentrating primarily on gap-filling across those areas considered as essential to competitive business development in Atlantic Canada.

Community Development

In 1973–74, DREE Atlantic undertook to examine the potential for the costs of, and the issues surrounding specific initiatives designed to strengthen the capability of the regional economic support system. In other words, DREE sought to grasp the fundamentals of the region's economy. Three areas selected for study were local communities development, services to entrepreneurship, and computer and communication industry development.[16] Even at this early stage, it was recognized that the resource base was declining as a contributor to regional economies and that the large, one-of-a-kind industrial projects, while desirable in terms of direct and multiplier employment, could not on their own be relied upon to provide the necessary conditions for economic improvement and stability. A consultant report prepared for the department concluded: "Without deliberate action to gradually improve the inherent capability of the regional economic support system ... much of the real potential for economic development generated by large projects will remain unrealized."[17] The consultants made the equally significant observation that even where resource value added did comprise a viable component of a regional development strategy (which was the case throughout the 1980s), resource rationalization would lead to decreased employment and the spin-off potential of major projects would not be realized without the emergence of many small-scale, linked economic activities.

These instructive comments remain valid today. The consultants' mandate was to explore ways to provide federal-provincial assistance in initiating and maintaining a locally managed development process in groups of communities throughout the Atlantic region. The ojective was to foster locally based economic growth and local capability to influence the course and quality of development. A leadership structure was required to identify local assets, opportunities, and aspirations, to establish directions of development, and to assess and initiate investment activities consistent with realistic directions of development. It was envisaged that governments would assume the role of helping local areas to organize a structure and to acquire the expertise to pursue these goals, with financial support, as necessary, at the outset. This somewhat sophisticated approach was ahead of its time at this early stage of governments' decentralized attack on regional disparity, but the early identification of the importance of community-level and community-led regional development was not lost on DREE and led to a number of initiatives across the Atlantic region.

During the DREE GDA era, local participation was widely secured in a number of areas, although not enough in terms of broad strategic planning and implementation. DREE supported the formation and ongoing operational costs of a variety of institutional arrangements in small-business, industrial, and rural development. It assisted sector-specific approaches, producers' associations, and spatial or area-specific initiatives (Labrador, NENB, Kent County, New Brunswick, etc., in the Atlantic region alone; community development was also a major component of development programming in the western region). DREE funding permitted the hiring and training of full-time staff, association counselling and opportunity identification, and assistance to community businesses and small entrepreneurs in their search for help under the many government programs available to them. Mini-incentives programs were also funded, usually in cooperation with the provinces and sometimes in cooperation with other federal departments. The support included programs for skills upgrading and management and technical training for small entrepreneurs, as well as programs for project-specific start-up, expansion, and modernization.

As early as 1974, DREE cooperated with Memorial University in Newfoundland in establishing the Community Learning Centres Project, whereby rural people, via an animator, received project- and business-specific tapes, videos, and instructional material prepared by experts in their respective fields for on-site training purposes. It was a successful pilot project over its 1974–78 lifespan but was regrettably terminated, partly owing to its lack of political visibility. Other DREE involvement in the Atlantic region included long-term financing for rural development associations in Newfoundland (numbering forty-eight in 1981), industrial development commissions in Nova Scotia and New Brunswick, and the Strait of Canso Industrial Development Authority in Cape Breton. Funding was provided for woodlot owners, craft producers, and agricultural and tourism associations.

In 1976, 45 percent of the population in the Atlantic region lived in rural areas, compared to 24 percent for all of Canada. This pattern would have been accentuated if many of the economic development prospects identified for the region, particularly the service industries and technology-related activities, had been acted upon under free-market forces alone. However, it was considered possible, without neglecting the most logical location for economic development in the Atlantic, to take measures to equip the less urban areas to share in economic improvement. Particular emphasis was given to strengthening management and labour force skills so that all residents could better participate in opportunities as they arose.

Community and area development was assigned a priority in DREE Atlantic 1981 strategy papers aimed at the balance of the decade. All areas of the region were to share in development. DREE's objective was to improve, with heavy local participation, rural and small-community life. DREE planned on continuing the emphasis on spatial programming through a two-pronged approach: (1) area-specific, multi-sectoral programming and (2) community economic development programming. Community development would build upon small-business, rural development, and community initiatives that had been practised and refined by DREE in the 1974–81 period. DREE intended to develop regional support systems to provide local development institutions in Atlantic Canada with technical expertise, training, organizational skills, opportunity identification, and research. It also envisaged funding the establishment of an Atlantic Institute for Community Development Resources and Research.

The community development thrust was lost with the termination of DREE. Little coordinated effort was possible in the new DRIE, and the introduction of the Atlantic Canada Opportunities Agency (ACOA) in 1987 did not foster a dedicated effort towards community development across the region.

Spatial Development

Spatial, or area development, which generally concerns large, subprovincial regions requiring development attention, goes hand in hand with community development. Spatial development activities were especially prominent in the DREE western region, encompassing two of three broad program groupings: western northlands and rural areas. Northlands agreements across the western provinces emphasized resources and community economic development, human development, community services and facilities, and, in recognition of the distances involved, transportation and communications. Programs aimed at rural development targeted agricultural and industrial diversification in secondary and rural communities. Certain programs, such as Special Agriculture Rural Development Agreements, were designed to encourage commercial enterprises and development opportunities. All programs had the underlying objective of increasing income and employment opportunities and the participation of the residents in the areas selected. The Northwest Territories and Yukon were not left out of the region's plans.

In Ontario, spatial development was also a priority, with community and resource development, northern rural development, and single-industry resource communities development targeted for expansion and diversification of the economic base.

In New Brunswick, DREE invited the province to assign a high priority to a northeast development initiative, and held public hearings in that subregion so that the needs of the residents could be better understood. This effort culminated in a $95-million subsidiary agreement involving almost every aspect of the region's economic and social make-up. In coastal Labrador, DREE, with the cooperation of Health and Welfare Canada, mounted a gratifying attack on the conditions that existed there. When the US Air Force pulled its Strategic Air Command establishment out of Happy Valley/Goose Bay, Labrador,

DREE took the lead in establishing an economic development commission, persuaded DND, Transport Canada, and Public Works Canada to maintain and make available base housing and related facilities, cooperated with the province in putting in place upgraded infrastructure for the community, and persuaded the US Air Force to turn over important assets, including the hospital, to the community. This did not replace the loss of the economic value of the air base to Happy Valley/Goose Bay, but it did provide a breathing space and a base upon which the town could try to build.

Spatial and community development program efforts too often represent desperation moves of government in the face of emerging or arrived economic crises in the more vulnerable parts of the country. Some, such as the Labrador initiatives, work better than others—but still not well enough.[18] Coordinated forward-looking development planning and sustained effort over time would go a long way to obviating the crisis solutions that have too often been the norm in Canada.

Concluding Thoughts on the DREE Retrospective

The Department of Regional Economic Expansion had reached an advanced level of program maturity by 1981, which events dictated would be its last year under its own direction. Policy papers proliferated across the regions as the department prepared for the decade just commenced. DREE Atlantic positioned itself for the 1980s in a strategy paper entitled "Atlantic Canada Regional Strategy" (November 3, 1981). It defined its principles and objectives, and proposed priorities and their translation into program form as follows:

• the development and expansion of the industrial, processing, and service capacity of Atlantic industry;
• the establishment of business enterprises capable of taking advantage of new markets, products, and technologies;
• strengthened management and an upgraded labour force;
• the improved viability of rural and small-community life;
• and the active participation of the people of the region in the economic development process.

These priorities required a number of changes to effect the transition from existing federal region development efforts to the new base for the 1980s. The strategy paper recognized the essential contribution that an integrative federal effort could make to the regional economy in the natural resources sectors and called for renewed coordination among federal departments. In response to the intended sharper

109

focusing of effort, the strategy paper declared that the trend of declining expenditure on general infrastructure was to continue, with rigorous selectivity towards infrastructure directly supportive of economic development potential.

In program terms, DREE Atlantic recognized that the shift in priority to the areas of technology, marketing, and human resources would require an improved and more direct relationship with the business sector. Federal assistance was to be comprehensive and appropriate to the growth needs of firms at their particular stage of development. Programming would be linked to capital assistance for expansion or modernization, support for product development and research, adaptation of new technologies, improved management, labour force skill development, and market development.

The economic development thrust proposed by DREE in the strategy paper was summarized in these words: "The application of these priorities during the transition period to planning and program development will change the focus of the federal development effort towards improved productivity and marketing in the resource sectors; reduced emphasis on infrastructure; increased emphasis on private sector cooperation; more direct community development support; and emphasis on support activities such as labour force development, management skills, technology and marketing to improve productivity."

These intentions of DREE were to be converted to program-specific design when (if) the strategy received government approval. DREE was well positioned in 1981 to continue to lead the federal effort in regional economic development. The department was moving into areas that, in many instances, did not reappear for attention until 1987. Some initiatives relating to industrial activity were carried forward by DRIE. Others, already identified by DREE as ones to be pursued by other departments, also went ahead. But many did not, and the overall federal objectives DREE had proposed were not accomplished by the structures that followed.

DREE expected to receive a renewed mandate from government to strengthen its position in bringing together the efforts of other departments, something DREE saw as more essential than ever in the more complex world of the 1980s. Would DREE have been successful in this regard? The department had worked hard at building bridges with other departments, and the strategy was working. Suasion often works better than legislative dictum—there are many examples of the latter being thwarted despite the best of intentions. DREE knew what it wanted to do, had a cadre of experienced people across the country, the respect and cooperation of the provinces and the private sector, and well-established relations with other federal departments.[19]

THE END IN SIGHT

Background

By the year 1981, an accumulation of factors had come together to prompt a serious review of the government's regional development policy and of DREE's program direction. The spark for specific action has been identified as an exchange of letters between DREE Minister Pierre De Bané and Prime Minister Pierre Elliott Trudeau in the winter of 1981, but many views prevail on the weight of the different reasons for the review.

Rumblings about the continuing existence of DREE go back to 1977, scarcely three years after the GDA policy concept was translated to operational form. This was one of the first occasions when federal discontent with the credit it was receiving for its regional development efforts surfaced in a public forum. In mid-November 1977 a rumour spread that cabinet ministers were disgruntled with the apparent lack of federal profile associated with DREE regional development programming. Some thought the rumour might have been a trial balloon to measure the support that DREE carried in the regions. DREE Atlantic staff handled a flurry of media enquiries about the rumour, discounting the story as a non-event and rejecting the trial balloon premise. After a two-hour meeting with Prime Minister Trudeau on November 10, New Brunswick Premier Richard Hatfield moved quickly to issue a public statement expressing concern over reports that DREE might be disbanded. DREE Minister Marcel Lessard rejected the premise in the House of Commons.

In December 1978, in a House of Commons debate on the proposed establishment of the Ministry of State for Economic Development, Marcel Lessard revealed that sometime earlier he had written the prime minister to suggest the need for better federal coordination of regional development activities across all federal departments.[20] The exchange had actually taken place in the summer of 1976. Lessard intended to bring forward proposals for better interdepartmental coordination, one of the perceived problems of the DREE model, and to propose the means by which cabinet could be kept more systematically informed of regional development activities.[21] Program and policy changes were also envisaged. Treasury Board was asked to devise ways for tracking and assessing the spending plans of departments and determining their impact on regional economies, but the board never took this task.

It was also in 1978 that the ambivalence of first ministers towards regional development first became apparent. At the November 27–29, 1978 First Ministers' Conference (FMC), first ministers reaffirmed their commitment to a strongly coordinated federal-provincial approach to the reduction of regional disparities and stressed that regional development should be based on viable economic opportunity afforded by such natural strengths as fisheries, forestry, agriculture, and tourism. All governments agreed that federal-provincial initiatives under the General Development Agreement system, combined with a range of federal and provincial initiatives, provided a good basis on which to build.[22] First ministers also indicated that regional development should have a high priority in Canadian industrial development, with industrial growth predicated on the resource base and skills of each region of the country.[23] Yet in a February FMC of the same year, Premier Bennett of British Columbia had attacked DREE, and even at the November meeting Premier Davis of Ontario expressed less than enthusiasm for regional development spending.

The fact remained that in DREE's tenth year the economic environment in which regional development was taking place was significantly different from that existing at DREE's inception. Of equal importance, the relative economic strengths of the regions of the country had either changed or were anticipated to do so. Since the mid-1970s, modest growth and high levels of unemployment and inflation had arrived. Energy production and distribution were significantly altering relative growth rates and shares of economic activity among the regions. Industrial adjustment was predicted in Canada's central region, as its manufacturing base became vulnerable to international competition. Ontario was signalled as having a soft economy. There were predictions of a continuing shift of economic balance away from industrialized regions towards resource-rich regions, particularly those endowed with energy resources. It is now easy to see how short-lived some of these events were. We are reminded how difficult it is to predict the future for regional development or any other kind of economic performance.

By the beginning of 1979, the stage was set for an intensified review of regional development policy in Canada. The time had come to assess the effort to date under the GDAs. The review was accelerated by the political pressures that were emerging as economic circumstances changed across the country and by pressure from federal politicians who felt that there was insufficient gratitude for the federal effort. It was interrupted and redirected as a result of two federal elections within the ten-month span of May 1979–February 1980 and the different attitudes the new governments carried with them. DREE engaged in a policy review aimed towards its receiving a renewed mandate and being granted increased authority by government and Parliament under more specific legislation.

In the summer and fall of 1979, shortly after the Conservative government of Prime Minister Joe Clark assumed power in Canada, the premier of New Brunswick, Richard Hatfield, and the Council of Maritime Premiers (CMP) wrote to Mr Clark on the question of regional development in the Atlantic region. The message on both counts was clear and unequivocal. Concerned about recurring rumours of structural changes within DREE or affecting DREE, Premier Hatfield and the CMP expressed strong support for the policies and programs of regional development and for DREE as the instrument of the federal government for this purpose. They were concerned, however, that the spread of DREE's activities across the country carried the danger of dilution of effort and of reduced resources for the Atlantic region. The prime minister quickly responded to put the Maritime premiers' minds at ease, referring to the Speech from the Throne, October 9, 1979, which revealed that legislation was to be placed before Parliament to strengthen DREE's mandate. The Clark government also advised the premiers that it intended to introduce legislation to improve coordination among federal departments and to focus DREE's activities in terms of geographic impact. The government, however, did not survive long enough to act on its intentions. It was in the October Speech from the Throne, as well, that the new government signalled its intention to repair federal-provincial relations: "It is a primary goal of my government to bring about a new era in federal-provincial relations. Consultation and co-operation will be the hallmarks of that new era."[24] After the short-lived Clark regime, the federal-provincial picture reverted to a position of particularly strained relations.

In early 1981, Pierre De Bané, only a few months into his term as DREE minister, wrote to Prime Minister Trudeau expressing his disenchantment with the federal government's approach to regional inequalities in Canada. During his years in Parliament as a member and latterly as a minister, De Bané was preoccupied with both social and economic inequalities in the country.[25] He strenuously lobbied for larger DREE budgets, more effort by other federal departments, and a complete recasting of DREE policies and programs. Several things militated against his getting his way—his stridency, his relatively junior status in cabinet, and a growing, if uninformed, swell of opposition to DREE.

Officials who worked closely with De Bané during his tenure at DREE were well aware of his frustration with regional development effort and accomplishment in Canada. They were familiar as well with his intellectual and philosophical concern with regional disparities in the more remote parts of the country. De Bané feared that too many Canadians came into contact with their federal government only in unemployment offices or in filling out their income tax forms. In his first DREE Atlantic briefing on becoming minister of the department, De Bané asked how many DREE offices there were in the four Atlantic provinces. On learning that there were seven, he immediately enquired about the logistics of establishing a network of up to thirty offices across the region.[26] These two concerns—with opportunities for contact and with public awareness of the federal presence in the country— were at the root of De Bané's promotion of more direct federal program delivery. In letters to the provincial premiers, he insisted on greater public recognition of DREE's involvement in regional development in the provinces.[27] Many late-night briefing sessions with Pierre De Bané were devoted to philosophical discussion of the regional development dilemma in Canada.

De Bané's early 1981 letter forced the government to come to grips with its policy on regional development and with the structures and instruments to give it effect. The letter also marked the point at which De Bané lost control of the process. Prime Minister Trudeau's March 1981 reply to De Bané's letter touched on all the right points. The prime minister acknowledged that De Bané had both the mandate and the obligation to examine the regional development problem in Canada, and he endorsed a review of policies and programs to that end. Trudeau pointed out, however, that it would be premature to suggest new organizational structures before considering available options, and he outlined a Privy Council–led exercise to study policies, programs, and options for regional development in Canada. He also made the significant statement that regional development objectives should be defined in terms of their contribution to national economic objectives.

Pierre De Bané's 1981 letter may not have been prompted by De Bané's opinions alone. In November 1980, Donald Johnston, minister responsible for the Ministry of State for Economic Development, had advised De Bané that before MSED could consider further federal-provincial cost-shared initiatives, De Bané would be required to bring forward and up-to-date policy on regional development and proposals for the role and mandate of DREE. At this stage the Liberals had only been back in power for a scant few months and the DREE portfolio was still new to De Bané. In any event, De Bané's letter to the prime minister triggered a series of irreversible events that, coupled with other activities during the same period, led to a major government reorganization in January 1982 that was to bring the DREE era to an end. Although De Bané may have been initially pleased with the intended centralizing of regional development policy in MSERD and the objective of sensitizing all departments to regional economic circumstances in Canada, he must have been disappointed with the ultimate outcome.

The process of review triggered by De Bané's letter, a review that might well have come in any event, involved the establishment of working groups centred in the Privy Council Office and a role for the Coordinating Committee of Deputy Ministers. The process and the part played in it by certain key senior deputies have been accurately described by Bruce Doern.[28]

Reasons for DREE's Demise

One of the most frequently cited and, in the author's view, least valid reasons for DREE's dismantlement (ironically, the GDA approach was not done away with and still flourished at the end of the decade) was that the federal government believed that it received insufficient credit for the funding and associated efforts it was contributing to the regional development effort. Given that the department was only the instrument of implementation for the GDA policy approach, killing the department did nothing to change the credit accruing to the federal side. Even the introduction of direct federal program delivery in 1981, still under the GDAS, and the subsequent writing of subsidiary agreements by a number of federal departments after 1982 did little for federal image-making. Although the federal government was having its problems in Quebec with the visibility factor, the reasons for that went far beyond DREE.

The claim that the provinces took all the credit for DREE-type program activities was never valid in Atlantic Canada, was a non-issue in Ontario, and likely had minimum validity in the West. The federal government had much larger problems in the West than its DREE image. Even if there was some merit to the federal concern about visibility, one would like to think that the government had the maturity to put the good of the economy of the regions ahead of its hurt feelings—perhaps a naive hope at best.[29]

A Macdonald Commission assessment of the 1982 reorganization of economic departments was categorical on the federal visibility question: "It is ironic that one of the primary objectives of the reorganization—the enhanced visibility of federal government activities in the eyes of Canadians—was also the one that has come closest to remaining unfulfilled."[30] Yet the federal government never heard or understood the message.[31] Federal (and, for that matter, other) politicians have never properly understood that assigning credit for regional development effort is not uppermost in most people's minds and that the federal (or any) government can have its share of credit if it performs properly. This, then, is the least acceptable of all the reasons for doing away with DREE or changing regional development policies in Canada.

There is some credibility to the theory of interdepartmental rivalry in the federal system, at both the political and bureaucratic level, notwithstanding the considerable progress that had been made up to the time of DREE's demise. This rivalry was accentuated by budgetary restraint, concern about receiving credit at the political level, federal hawkishness in federal-provincial relations after 1980, and the central agencies' not surprising suspicions about anything that could run as well as DREE did without their constant attention. It was a question of more than just rivalry. Many Ottawa-based officials, sometimes despite their origins or professional backgrounds, had no particular affinity for regional economic development nor understanding of its roots. In 1982 one observer of the regional development issue had this to say: "There's never been a bureaucratic commitment to regional development and basically, the bureaucrats won and the politicians lost."[32] The politicians, however, did play a role in the loss, but clearly DREE bureaucrats, who argued, some thought persuasively, for the retention of its better features, did not.

In addition to the central agencies suspicions cited above, many departmental bureaucrats and ministers were uneasy with, if not jealous of, DREE's extraordinary delegated decision-making authority.[33] Some actions prompted by ministerial jealousy, or at least the desire to be part of the action, became rampant after the 1982 merger, to the great exasperation of provincial governments. Interestingly enough, this ministerial intervention in decisions involving small and large grants and in program elements under the subsidiary agreements brought them exactly the opposite kind of attention that they had so wanted in the DREE days. Ministerial involvement in what in the majority of cases was the day-to-day business of project authorization and expenditure, executed within clear guidelines and already-approved program parameters, significantly slowed the process of regional economic development, to no one's credit.

The DREE/ITC difference of opinion on the best location for a new Volkswagen plant in Canada (referred to earlier), which boiled over in public statements by the ministers involved, was not a reason in itself for major organizational change, nor was it even the straw that broke the camel's back.[34] Coming, however, in the middle of a stream of other activity and a national economic and regional development policy review, it gained a lot of attention, politically, bureaucratically, and publicly.

DREE officials, although optimistic about progress in interdepartmental relations, would have preferred to see other departments make a more determined effort to use their policies and programs in more direct support of improving regional economies. DREE officials did not accept the automatic assumption that regional policy conflicted with sectoral policy, and their position was substantiated by the many examples of DREE/OGDS' collaboration under subsidiary agreement cover. Conversely, the suspicion remained, even after 1982, that regional programming by departments other than DREE and later DRIE in fact attempted to draw on other than their own budgetary reference levels, including the somewhat imaginary Regional Fund. DREE officials, however, did not expect to be able to officially coordinate other departmental programs and budgets, and would not have proposed DREE's demise as a solution. They knew that a MSERD model would not work unless it were embraced by line departments, and as it turned out, that basically did not happen.

The Economic Environment Other theories advanced for regional development policy change were based more on perceptions of economic conditions and prospects, less on personalities and political expediency. There was a growing view held by economists, the Department of Finance, and some officials of DREE that things were getting better in overall regional development terms. Although measurable economic indicators did not reveal much closing of the gaps between the regions and national averages, neither did they reveal a widening, signalling some gain in absolute terms. The Atlantic region was seen by some to be on the edge of an energy-rich resurgence, but this was not a view held by DREE Atlantic officials, certainly not in the short term. There was also visible evidence in the Atlantic and elsewhere of a significant upgrading of personal well-being. While none of this was necessarily or solely attributed to DREE, it was felt that transfer and equalization payments were having an effect.

Coupled with the above was the spectre of general economic downturn. The April 14, 1980, Speech from the Throne of the restored Liberal regime struck a sober note on Canadian economic prospects. The Speech pronounced an aggressive approach "to promote a national development policy that will provide jobs, stimulate growth, build upon regional strengths, and increase Canadian ownership and control of the economy." It spoke of renewed federalism but also dwelled on restraint, saying that Canadians understood that difficult economic times prevailed throughout the world, recognized the need to live within their national means, and would accept sacrifices in order to meet the economic challenges of the 1980s. Of significance for development in the peripheral regions, there was a specific reference to the economic strength of Ontario slipping away. Some of the regions would no doubt have liked to have been so blessed. The Speech closed with words to the effect that ministers would continue to pursue policies of expenditure restraint.

In mid-1981, Finance Minister Allan MacEachen headed a task force whose mandate was to develop the new industrial strategy for Canada that was promised in the 1980 Speech from the Throne. The results of this work were expressed in the November 1981 budget paper "Economic Development for Canada in the 1980s." The paper made optimistic predictions for Canada's economic future, concluding on a positive note: "Seldom in this century has it been possible to identify genuine prospects for growth in every region. But this is the prospect today." It said that the Atlantic region was entering the 1980s well positioned for a decade of solid growth. However, by this time, Canada's economic reality was being read in various ways. Governments of the Atlantic provinces were of the view that federal DREE funding for the region was insufficient and on the decline. The country had seen a softening of the strong central Canadian economy, particularly Ontario, and international economies were experiencing serious disruptions. In Canada, a mood of restraint had set in, which did not bode well for regional development.[35]

The paper "Economic Development for Canada in the 1980s" touched on five priority areas (down from the eight put forward by MSED in 1980): industrial development, resource development, transportation, export promotion, and human resources. It also identified service industries, matching skills to needs, and being competitive in the manufacture of those products in which Canada could aspire to be best. And the government again disclaimed the idea of supporting uncompetitive industries for which "all Canadians must bear the cost." The federal government staked out its own territory in the economic development field in the following way: "The Government of Canada must assume a leadership role in the field of economic development. Harnessing the resources of the economy is a national enterprise which includes but extends beyond the interests of particular regions or sectors." One could read an ominous sign in this phrase for dedicated regional development programming.

The government did say, however, that it would place new emphasis on economic development in all the regions of Canada, with regional economic development being central to public policy planning at the federal level. What exactly did this mean? If all regions of the country were to receive new emphasis and be central to federal public policy planning, was that anything more than a Canadian economic development policy? Such a policy would be neutral in the traditional sense of regional development policy by which peripheral regions, or those

118

otherwise defined as being economically disadvantaged, had received special attention. In reciting its various priority policy areas, which also included direct reference to innovation and adjustment, the paper said that all of the policies and programs would be developed and implemented on the basis of the government's regional development objectives. The paper also gave an insight into government attitudes with the statement "There is need to recognize that both the federal and provincial governments have economic development responsibilities ... although joint implementation of economic development programming may not always be desirable, joint planning and coordination of such programming is critical." The government intended to give priority to economic development within its own areas of jurisdiction.

The objectives expounded in the 1981 budget paper can only be interpreted in the light of subsequent actions by the government. Taken at face value, the paper added up to a reasonable statement of coordinated economic development across the country—one might even presume some particular attention to the regions. Performance from 1982 onwards, as discussed elsewhere, leads to the conclusion that something was lost in the translation.

DREE *Operating Practices*

Suspicions about certain operating practices of DREE collapse under scrutiny, as shown in chapter 2. The provinces did not dictate either the pace or the content of subsidiary agreements during the DREE years. Economic planning and opportunity identification was a forte of DREE. Agreement content was negotiated between two (or more) governments, and every agreement project and program was authorized by accredited officials of the participating governments. The subsidiary agreements contained sensible activities aimed at removing constraints to development and increasing the opportunity for regional economies to improve. Projects and programs were designed against sectoral strategies—they did not emerge from ad hoc wisps of imagination, indiscriminately concocted on the spur of the moment by officials. The agreements were intentionally flexible to permit program innovation and response to implementation experience, not for purposes of collusion by officials or some other mischievous reason.

DREE was not out of control. It had one of the tightest management regimes in the federal system. Accountability was complete, from the provincial offices right through to the minister. There was no collusion by officials to the detriment of other government departments, regional development programs, or ministers. Both federal and provincial politicians had access to the system. Ministers participated in determining agreement content and exercised the final decision-making role. Cabinet Committee authorized every DREE subsidiary agreement entered into.

There was remarkably little political interference (as opposed to involvement) during the DREE GDA period. Ministers were involved and were generally guided by the economic and viability analyses conducted by officials. Ministers exercised the right to order priorities, which also meant they led federal-provincial negotiations. Regional development programming was never seriously in conflict with national sectoral policies and didn't have the opportunity to contradict other major national policies.

There was little or no company-specific interprovincial or interregional competition practised by DREE. Large projects were few and far between, and the truth was that DREE did not have any great success in influencing their location. From time to time DREE did, nevertheless, provide financial assistance to such projects. This may have been the exception to the rule of no political interference in programming. Because large projects do bring very significant benefits to regional economies, the differences of opinion between ministers and officials concerning them usually related to the need for government assistance rather than to the desirability of the project itself.

The reasons given for DREE's demise were basically invalid. The department was making progress in enhancing regional circumstances; a downturn in the national economy was not a reason to discontinue a winning formula for regional development; the perceived softness of central Canada's economy was short-lived; and the federal government received as much credit for its efforts as it could expect, and more than it received thereafter.

The Outcome

Despite all of the theories, opinions, perceptions, and misperceptions, and despite the deliberations of individuals and task forces alike, it still cannot be said that in 1982 a rational argument had emerged for the option selected to solve Canada's regional development conundrum. Nevertheless, Prime Minister Trudeau was persuaded that DREE as it existed should end, giving way to a new Department of Regional Industrial Expansion that would combine the regional objectives of DREE and the national economic development objectives of Industry, Trade and Commerce. The trade function was moved from ITC to External Affairs to bring together the trade and political dimensions of Canada's foreign affairs endeavours. The decision was announced on January 12, 1982.

120

Regional economic development policy was to be centralized in the revamped Ministry of State for Economic and Regional Development (MSED became MSERD). MSERD's operations were decentralized so that it would stay on top of regional economic circumstances, much as DREE had done. MSERD's strengthened mandate also gave it the authority to coordinate all economic development activities in Canada. All economic departments of government were authorized to deal directly with provincial governments in the pursuit of economic development within their jurisdiction. According to Aucoin and Bakvis, "The death of DREE was to signal the emulation of its organizational structure by all those departments with which it had interacted in its efforts to produce regional economic development policy. Its spirit was to live after its departure!"[36]

During the final stages of the deliberations on the reorganization of economic departments, De Bané and the DREE officials were left out of the action. Bruce Doern says: "As to further consultation with the affected DREE and ITC ministers and their deputies, it was felt that the Senior Deputies Committee already had persons with a detailed knowledge of industrial and regional policy concerns."[37] There was, in fact, no person in the various groups studying the question who had senior regional development policy or practitioner experience. Further, Bert Laframboise had to carry out his difficult and sometimes thankless task relating to the resource-integration aspects of the merger with the knowledge that much of the organizational form had already been preordained by PCO, particularly the elimination of the DREE regional headquarters management systems.[38] Regional development in Canada did not recover from that mistake.

The public and political reaction to the newly announced reorganization of economic departments was mixed, ranging from cautious optimism to outright opposition. The opinions of bureaucrats directly affected by the changes came later. John Crosbie, then an opposition member of Parliament, voiced his clear opposition: "I am completely opposed to this reorganization of January 12. I consider it to be a disaster to the region — to any program to overcome regional disparities in this country ... we will have the department DREE finished off and put under the Department of Regional Industrial Expansion, DRIE; 'E' has been changed to 'I' and it is going to be a disastrous one-letter change for the people of the Atlantic provinces."[39]

Liberal Brian Tobin of Newfoundland, on the same occasion, said, "I would just like to comment that I, for one, am not entirely overjoyed with the changes we have seen in DREE ... and the subsequent delegation of responsibilities that were normally envisaged to operate under one department being split into so many ... I suspect there is going to be real danger that this kind of focus and effort such as we have seen in the past from DREE—I think it has been an excellent department and I mourn its passing into something else—may slip away. That will be a real tragedy for Atlantic Canada and for other underdeveloped parts of this country."[40]

New Brunswick was fast off the mark with its opinion of the newly announced reorganization. At a meeting in Fredericton on January 28, 1982, with the DREE/ITC Minister Herb Gray, Premier Hatfield expressed his concern about the apparent demise of DREE, saying that it had been a highly successful instrument of both federal-provincial cooperation and economic development activity. Later that same day he publicly expressed his skepticism of the federal intentions in a speech in Moncton. The echoes of the opinions of provincial governments and others, particularly the Atlantic provinces, remain to this day. In researching the establishment of the Atlantic Canada Opportunities Agency (ACOA), Donald Savoie describes Atlantic Canada opinion in 1986–87 in the following way: "The criticism voiced from all four provinces at the 1982 federal government re-organization for economic development which saw the disassembling of DREE remains particularly strong and intense," and, "DREE was perceived as having been far more effective and relevant to the Atlantic region than its successor, DRIE."[41]

It did not take long before there were second thoughts even within the government in power. Bruce Doern reports that "there were also growing vestiges of political doubt among some Ministers as to just what the new policy meant in practice."[42] Ministers and MPs alike were already starting to miss the one-stop shopping that DREE provided them in terms of regional development projects in their constituencies and the opportunity, when they wished to avail themselves of it, of being part of media events.

At its close, DREE was not only on the threshold of new program directions but was actively engaged in their realization. Just about everything that subsequently took place in regional development thinking following 1982, up to and including agency programming in 1990, had been envisaged by DREE in 1981. The short-term political perspective held by governments caught up with the longer-term outlook of DREE regional development policy. The policy process in DREE, rather than consisting of distinct and relatively infrequent events in the department's history, was a continuum, from 1972 through 1981. Superimposed on that continuum was the political necessity to review regional development policy to ensure that it matched government-wide thinking on economic policy—in itself, a logical imperative. DREE's regional development policy did not come apart because it contradicted national economic policy, but because it did not meet other political criteria, which included federal visibility.

The First Ministers' Conference of February 2, 1982, provided a fitting closing to the DREE era. At that conference, Prime Minister Pierre Trudeau described the federal reasoning behind the just-announced reorganization of economic departments in the following way:

A dozen years ago, we were conscious of the need to work towards more balanced regional growth across Canada. We established the department we have all come to know as DREE — a department which was intended to concentrate on regional development. The problem was — as we came to recognize slowly — that one department alone could never do the task. We had to find some means of ensuring that the needs of each region for development would permeate every decision taken by the federal government concerning national economic or fiscal policies, or concerning specific programs for industrial expansion. This, we believe, the new organization will achieve.

The federal government has responsibilities in regional economic development and we plan to meet those responsibilities — and be held accountable for them — by dealing more directly with the problems and opportunities of Canadians.

In his opening remarks to the FMC, Premier Richard Hatfield of New Brunswick provided a rebuttal to the prime minister on the question of DREE and regional development. Hatfield said he was surprised to hear the prime minister say that he had slowly come to the conclusion that DREE was not working, taking that to mean that the prime minister had concluded that really cooperative economic development could not take place. The premier repeated the prime minister's statement that the federal government had responsibilities in regional economic development and expected to be held accountable for them, then went on to outline what he described as very significant investments in New Brunswick — investments totalling $3 billion in pulp and paper, mining, industrial infrastructure, natural gas, real estate, and manufacturing and processing. He said that this was, to him, pretty substantial and significant evidence of the success that the provincial government and the federal government working through DREE had had, and that it had meant both the creation and maintenance of thousands of jobs in New Brunswick. He added, "Now, despite this record of real achievements, the federal government now talks, and we have seen evidence of it in New Brunswick, of abandoning co-operation. I don't think that a more serious mistake could be made in dealing with our economy at this particular time."

It was in 1982 that the Constitution Act of 1982, section 36(1), repeated the commitment of the federal government and the provincial governments to the promotion of equal opportunities for the well-being of Canadians and to the furthering of economic development to reduce disparity in opportunities. DREE could have played its part in helping the federal government honour its share of that commitment. Instead, it gave way to DRIE.

Chapter Four

After DREE: DRIE and MSERD

THE MANDATE ANNOUNCED for the new Department of Regional Industrial Expansion included the enhancement of the administration of regional programs and an improvement in the government's capacity to pursue balanced industrial growth on a national basis. The department was to focus the government's industrial policies and programs in support of regional development strategies. DRIE would concentrate on deriving industrial benefits from major projects, engaging the private sector in dialogue focused on development opportunities, and facilitating industrial adjustment.[1]

THE MECHANICS OF CHANGE

Public sector reorganizations, particularly of the magnitude of the DREE/ITC merger and related MSERD and External Affairs changes, involve an array of activities in addition to the expected development or redeployment of program instruments that normally accompany a policy change. The consequent legal and administrative actions required can very well make or break the best of policy intentions. Legislative authority, personnel relations, administrative logistics, and a gauntlet of controls, guidelines, and procedures all come into play. Teams were established in the new department to address all these aspects of the reorganization. Programs and resources were the subjects of two of the task forces put in place. A number of working groups addressed the specifics of organizational structures and the logistics of merging the two departments. Management wrestled with reporting relationships, span of control, and regional and central authorities delegation.

Organizationally, people continued to do their jobs. Senior officers, whether officially appointed or not, took responsibility for broad areas of activity encompassing their existing duties, assigned "merger" tasks, and the preparation of eventual new jurisdictions of responsibility to which they were expected to be appointed. The DRIE senior management committee grew in size to include officials from both departments. By the summer of 1982, most senior appointments had been made, whether confirmed (to level) by Treasury Board or not, and people got on with the job. The DREE provincial directors general became regional executive directors (REXDS). The senior position in Ontario was filled from ITC, the senior Quebec position from DREE, both as ADM-level REXDS. The DREE western region and Atlantic region ADMS assumed responsibilities in Ottawa. ADM-level positions in Ottawa were filled by officials of both departments, with former DREE regional ADMS bringing much-needed regional experience into the Ottawa enclave. As time went on, the interchange of former senior DREE and ITC people between Ottawa and the regions continued, representing one of the most positive aspects of the merger.

The formalizing of middle-management-level positions in the new DRIE, as well as appointments at levels in both the officer and support categories, was somewhat more traumatic, given the numbers involved (over 3,000 excluding transfers out) and the requirement to reduce the departmental staff complement by approximately 250.[2] A core of ADMS and the associate deputy minister, supported by the personnel department, met regularly, sometimes daily, to review what was in many ways the most critical part of the reorganization. Getting the right people in the right jobs and keeping morale at some reasonable level of operational efficiency was not an easy task. The attempt was not always successful, and it was publicly rumoured that morale was not good. Perhaps it was naive to expect anything different, given the nature of the overall exercise. Tom Kent reported that the government reorganization that created DREE in 1969 also had its share of publicly revealed staff morale problems.[3] It is likely that no reorganization, no matter how well executed, can escape disenchantment by some of those involved.

The reduction in people (or person-years, in bureaucratic jargon) brought about by consolidation struck at all levels in the organization. ADMS and directors general, middle-level managers and support-level staff, all experienced reduction in numbers. When it was all over, very few people actually lost their jobs. Nevertheless, the lengthy duration of the merger, attributed to Treasury Board recalcitrance over confirming position levels, the painstaking exercise of brokering positions in other departments for surplus employees, and changes at both the minister and deputy minister levels at critical times during the process all took their toll on staff morale. If the senior officer complement held up through it all, it may well have been because they were working so hard that they did not have time to think about anything else. From the day the merger was announced, departmental policy was business as usual and all of the aspects of organizational change were added to that undertaking.

Underpinning the reorganization was the drawn-out process of confirming new policies and programs, approving the concomitant legislation, handling the rather horrendous administrative logistics in moving people across the country, finding adequate headquarters and regional accommodations, melding two different financial and administrative regimes, and blending two different departmental cultures. Until DRIE was formally approved by Parliament near the end of 1983, the DREE and ITC names and their various program authorities continued to be in force and in use.

After the reorganization of 1982, the protocol for federal-provincial relations changed at the polical level, less so at the officials level. DRIE ministers Herb Grey, Ed Lumley, and Sinclair Stevens (the new Conservative head of the department in 1984) did not give the same dedicated attention to the regional development culture that their DREE predecessors had. There were reasons for this, not the least of which were the dual mandates of the department and, until 1984, increasing federal-provincial friction as the Atlantic provinces, in particular, brought forward evidence of declining explicit federal spending on economic development in that region. The character of the General Development Agreement and its very existence was put in doubt during the program review carried out in the new Department of Regional Industrial Expansion and the Ministry of State for Economic and Regional Development. While subsidiary agreement negotiations continued to be conducted, DRIE was restricted to agreements with industrial development and spatial themes, with other activity areas subsumed by the appropriate federal line department. The GDAS expired in 1984, giving way to a new generation of Economic and Regional Development Agreements (ERDAS).

The new series of ERDAS turned out to be neither different from nor "simpler" than its predecessor. What was different, however, was that provinces now had to deal with a score of different organizations rather than simply with DREE, which had been the focal point for all programs prior to the change.[4] Individual departments, while nominally coordinated by MSERD, no longer had DREE subsidiary agreement expertise available in the federal-provincial negotiating process. Furthermore, MSERD was playing both a developmental role in the regions and a central agency role in Ottawa. One further important difference was the loss of a multi-provincial coordinating capability in the Atlantic provinces and the West. Within DRIE and MSERD, the policy and implementation role that had been exercised by DREE regional ADMS was lost. The effort to coordinate and provide management direction from Ottawa for the diverse activities represented by DRIE and MSERD in the regions was never quite successful.

When the Conservative government of Prime Minister Brian Mulroney came to power in September 1984, it embraced all the policies and programs of its Liberal predecessor for regional economic development. The main federal-provincial instrument for joint collaboration in regional development planning, the ERDA, remained in force. Within three months of coming into office, the new government had signed the remaining three outstanding ERDAS with Quebec, Ontario, and British Columbia. The seven agreements already in place had been signed by the Liberal government in 1984 upon the expiration of the GDAS. In addition to approving the ERDAS as enabling documents under which more program specific initiatives could be launched, the new government signed forty-two subsidiary agreements in the period September 1984 to March 1987.

The new government also accepted, for the time being, existing industrial development instruments, the two main ones being the Industrial and Regional Development Program (IRDP) and the Defence Industry Productivity Program (DIPP). Although used for regional development, both these programs had a strong industrial bias. They had their greatest impact in Canada's manufacturing regions notwithstanding the IRDP formula, which favoured the less-developed regions. The government also moved to enhance regional economies, particularly in the Atlantic provinces, by introducing the Atlantic Enterprise Program (AEP), Entreprise Cape Breton (ECB), and differentiated investment tax credits for the Cape Breton region of Nova Scotia.

The Conservatives' acceptance of existing regional development programs did not signal an act of faith, but rather the pragmatic recognition that something had to be maintained while the government developed its own policies and positions. In fact, the Mulroney government moved almost immediately to launch a review of the ERDA concept, and DRIE was already reconsidering the still-new IRDP program. IRDP was also under evaluation by the Nielsen Task Force on Program Review (set up by the Conservatives under Deputy Prime Minister Erik Nielsen to review over 300 existing federal programs), but little came of that. In addition, the government, along with others, questioned the wisdom of having industrial and regional development mandates in the same department, DRIE.

The government's early attention to the health of regional economies confirmed the importance placed on the subject by successive political administrations in Canada. By 1984 there was a growing dissatisfaction in Ottawa and in the regions with the apparent lack of success of regional development efforts in the country, despite the attention and the financial support directed to them. Conventional economic indicators of unemployment, earned income, and fiscal capacity had not shown appreciable improvement over time. The report of the Royal Commission on the Economic Union and Development Prospects for Canada, the Macdonald Commission, commissioned by the previous Liberal government, reported its extensive findings in 1985. While giving minimum attention to regional development, the commission did offer views on the causes of, and solutions for, regional disparities and assigned specific roles to respective levels of government. The commission report said that "regional economic well-being is the responsibility of all levels of government. ... The justification for including the federal government lies in Canadians' concept of what it means to be a citizen of this country and the practical need to integrate regional development with national development."[5] It went on to say that the federal government should not involve itself directly in regional job creation but rather commit itself to overcoming regional productivity gaps and labour market imperfections. It commented that the government should set regional policy in a national framework.[6] The commissioners' specific recommendations that followed from these views had some advice for the governments of the day and bear repeating:

The federal government should direct regional development programs toward improving regional productivity and the efficiency of the labour market.

Provinces should take full responsibility for place-specific employment measures ... provinces receiving equalization payments should also receive Regional Economic Development Grants from the federal government.

A sustained federal commitment to regional development requires that a single central agency be responsible for injecting regional concerns into the programs of individual federal departments and for coordinating federal efforts.[7]

The commissioners translated some of these ideas into program terms in suggesting that programs include measures to improve worker and management skills, enhance research and development efforts, ensure a high level of infrastructure support, and supply assistance for intra- and interregional mobility. They opted for the elimination of employment-creation programs and regionally differentiated subsidies, tax breaks, and tax credits.[8] In assigning a prime role to provincial governments in the regional development field, the commissioners recommended that the federally funded development grants be used by the provinces as they saw fit, subject to a code of economic conduct.[9]

Some of the Macdonald Commission's recommendations made sense in terms of the role of federal and provincial governments, the activity-specific areas for attention, and even the general discontinuance of various forms of incentives assistance. Given the record of the provinces in the use of non-tied funding, however, one would have to be very skeptical of the suggestion that the federal government provide unconditional development grants to the provinces.[10] This recommendation also overlooks, or dismisses, federal government responsibility for national consistency and avoidance of injurious provincial competition in an area not assigned constitutionally to the provinces. It also ignores the political aspects surrounding who receives credit for expenditure of the taxpayers' money, a point on which the federal government has exhibited considerable paranoia.[11] It is interesting to see the Macdonald Commission return to a theme advanced by the Economic Council of Canada in its annual review of 1966, that regional development in Canada required a centralized coordinating responsibility that rested in a central agency charged with injecting regional concerns into all departments of government. This implies that the commission did not consider MSERD a success; otherwise it would have commented on its status vis-à-vis DRIE in 1985 and made some suggestion as to whether it should have been returned to an independent central agency status.

In addition to the new government's internal review of the ERDA concept (the results of which were never publicly revealed), an ambitious federal-provincial initiative on regional development was launched in 1984 under the auspices of the later defunct Federal-Provincial Committee of Regional Development Ministers. On January 21, 1985, that committee enunciated nine principles for regional economic development, which were subsequently endorsed by first ministers at the Regina conference of February 14–15, 1985. The principles were published in an intergovernmental position paper in June of that year.[12]

Certain of the 1985 principles are revealing in light of what was to follow for regional development in Canada. Principle 3 stressed the importance of effective consultation between governments to ensure complementary policies and programming. Principle 4 spoke of harmonizing all regional economic development efforts to reduce duplication, to include all programs, services, promotions, training, and human development policies. The harmonization principle referred also to the need to eliminate wasteful competition between provinces and entreated that "multilateral discussions among regions" be pursued. Principle 5 addressed major federal policies relating to fiscal and monetary practice, procurement, transportation, trade and sectoral policies, and their impact on regional economies. Principle 8 addressed the desirability of enhancing interregional trade through the reduction of barriers to such trade. The position paper concluded by stating that the principles reflected the joint commitment of governments "to implement a truly effective regional economic development policy within the country."

By this time the Conservative government had accepted the de facto presence of the ERDAS as the means of pursuing regional development jointly with the provinces in support of its declared intentions to improve federal-provincial relations. Sinclair Stevens, although not adopting the approach of his predecessors, took a keen interest in the ERDA process and personally participated in determining development priorities. Indeed, he was quickly identified as the guardian of Cape Breton, probably to the surprise and perhaps amusement of now senator Allan MacEachen.

DRIE did achieve some of its strategic intentions. Over its life, sectoral and regional policy collaboration steadily improved within the department. In close cooperation with the regions, DRIE developed policies, which became de facto federal government policies, that involved financial incentives in forest industries, the Atlantic fish-processing sector, petrochemicals, biotechnology, automotive parts, the aerospace industry, the red meat sector, and a number of others. In the important service industries sector, the Ottawa-based Service Industries Branch developed program guidelines common to the department on appropriate levels of assistance to firms in the sector, which the regional operations of the department could then tailor to the specific needs of the regions. Big-ticket items were always pursued jointly by Ottawa-based sector-area responsibility centres and regional operations, with the lead role assumed by one party or the other. This combination of technical expertise and knowledge forged economically sensible recommendations that were sometimes accepted, sometimes rejected, at the political level.

When DRIE lost its minister, Sinclair Stevens, one of the most powerful members of the Mulroney government, in 1986, it also lost much of its influence in the competitive world of Ottawa politics at both the political and bureaucratic levels. Political unrest, the disenchantment of less economically advantaged provinces with what they believed to be declining expenditures on regional development, criticism of slow DRIE-incentives-program turnaround times, and provincial unhappiness with decision making under the ERDAS combined to lead the government to contemplate other means of righting regional economic wrongs. The government also hoped to better prepare Canada to compete internationally in terms of productivity and technology. After Stevens's departure and a short interregnum under Donald Mazinkowski, DRIE lurched on to further embarrassments with Minister Michel Côté and Junior Minister André Bissonette, both of whom left government under a cloud. By the time Robert de Cotret took the helm four deputy ministers later, the stage was set for a further effort to redeem the department and the government's regional development policy. Through all this, DRIE staff in the regions and in Ottawa soldiered on, keeping things going as best they could. The short-lived DRIE was thus destined to become Industry, Science and Technology, passing off some regional development responsibilities while retaining others.

MINISTRY OF STATE FOR ECONOMIC AND REGIONAL DEVELOPMENT

If DREE was not successful in pursuing a regional development strategy that embraced every aspect of government policy and action, neither was the new Ministry of State for Economic and Regional Development. MSERD was a result of the reorganization of economic departments in 1982, which saw the addition of the regional dimension to the existing MSED. MSERD was to feed regional considerations into the cabinet committee decision-making process, develop regional economic policies, and coordinate the activities of other government departments.[13] However, no government-wide policy was ever put in place and no master plan existed to permit such an experiment to be successful. What MSERD attempted to do was to test the policies and initiatives that one department might wish to bring to cabinet against the policies and initiatives of other departments, with particular reference to their regional impact. It was a responsive mechanism. MSERD did have a major projects branch in Ottawa that reviewed large-project proposals in steel, coal, energy, and other areas, but its influence in these areas was not great. Until 1984 MSERD managed the deputy minister mirror committee, which passed carefully worded views of departmental intentions to the ministers of the Cabinet Committee on Economic and Regional Development (CCERD).

MSERD was expected to develop a plan for economic development for each region in which it operated, and these plans were to be the basis of federal-provincial negotiations. In some regions, MSERD officials did try to bring a focus to the federal actions that were being contemplated and to harmonize them with provincial government intentions. The MSERD person on the ground, the federal economic development coordinator (FEDC), also chaired a federal coordinating committee in his or her province, but the situation in this regard was no different than before, with the main decision-making levels of most other departments still residing in Ottawa. Unlike DREE, which had regional ADMs in place to ensure complementarity across more than one province, MSERD had no such authoritative presence; a "region" in its terminology equated one province. Although the MSERD headquarters organization (note that supreme decision-making authority now resided only in Ottawa) carried out cross-regional examination and coordination, it was not as effective as the DREE regional ADMs had been. MSERD had no effective mandate to operate in several of the areas in which DREE also had been unable to operate (macroeconomic, fiscal, and monetary policy, for example), although it might well have monitored such areas more closely.

MSERD had the mandate and the responsibility to promote greater regional sensitivity within federal departments in the exercising of their policies and the implementation of their programs. It presumably recognized that administrative and structural decentralization such as DREE had enjoyed was one means of furthering that objective. Former Nova Scotia FEDC J. D. Love has said, however, in speaking of MSERD, "When the chips were down, it tended to back away from any intervention on organizational matters."[14]

The Cabinet Committee on Economic and Regional Development that was served by MSERD had the same opportunity as the cabinet economic development committees of the DREE days had had to view economic activities horizontally, granted with a higher level of identification of competing initiatives. However, MSERD was more restricted in the degree to which each proposal was evaluated in regional development terms. The practice that flourished for several years, including in the DREE days, of each memorandum to cabinet requiring a paragraph on regional development impact was never particularly effective.[15] As a matter of note, Tom Kent reports that in 1963 a paragraph on federal-provincial relations was required in all cabinet documents. This requirement was the result of certain unpleasant experiences involving federal decisions (the particular case cited was a crown corporation) that were unfavourable to regional economies.[16]

It has been generally accepted that the 1982 reorganization of economic departments did not work. Yet the idea had some merit in theory and at its inception had strong political backing. Aucoin and Bakvis attribute a lot of MSERD's problems to the perennial conflict between headquarters and the regions. Culling out motives of self-interest from a series of interviews they conducted, they conclude that "there were serious problems in meshing the operations of the FEDCS with those of Headquarters in Ottawa."[17] The problems referred to were said to stem from "a) the inherent difficulty of reconciling and integrating ten different regional views with each other and the national view; b) the complexity of the decision making machinery ... and c) a lack of commitment to the concept of regional responsiveness on the part of crucial segments of the headquarters' staff."[18] MSERD was experiencing some of the growing pains of DREE in its early days, but there was a significant difference. Whereas MSERD was clearly controlled from Ottawa, with major policy directions dictated from headquarters, the DREE regions were full partners in the management of the department, had ready access to the political level, and had no trouble being taken seriously—a complaint reported by Aucoin and Bakvis with regard to MSERD regional operations. Aucoin and Bakvis point out that despite sometimes heroic efforts, the FEDCS and MSERD had little success in coordinating the activities of government departments and virtually no success in influencing departmental "A" base program intentions and expenditure plans.[19] DREE was clearly not exempt from similar problems, but the recognized authority that senior regional officials carried within the department and the coordination of DREE regional positions in four responsibility centres rather than ten significantly eased the negotiations with other government departments.

The internal difficulties of MSERD and the replacement of DREE with DRIE did little to enhance federal-provincial relations. The provinces were already apprehensive about the loss of the generally well-liked DREE and the announced intentions of the federal government to pursue direct program delivery.[20] Federal-provincial relations as exercised by MSERD were found to be confusing, due partly to unclear lines of authority and more complicated, yet perceived less efficient, interface between the two levels of government. Federal politicians and many bureaucrats had found the previous relationships between DREE and the provinces too cozy for their liking, an opinion that led the senior government to search for a different kind of arrangement that would produce more direct contact with the clientele and a higher level of visibility. Aucoin and Bakvis summarize this situation by concluding that "on the whole, the general effects of MSERD and the 1982 reorganization of federal-provincial relations can best be described as confusion and unhappiness."[21] On the question of the general public, they conclude that the experiment had not accomplished its objectives: "The lasting impression of the 1982 reorganization in the minds of the general public, particularly those in the outlying provinces, will be that DREE was abolished and simply replaced with a watered-down and much less responsive entity called DRIE."[22] Aucoin and Bakvis had earlier predicted the potential for problems to occur in all the foregoing areas—lack of department-wide coordination without strong cabinet and prime ministerial support, lack of a coherent and respected regional development strategy by MSERD to prevent system overload, and conflict and lack of cohesive working relations within MSERD, particularly with regard to the Ottawa-regional interface and intergovernmental relations. At that time, they were prepared to give the benefit of the doubt.[23]

In July 1984, just two and one-half years after its optimistic creation, MSERD was demoted to being an adjunct of DRIE for reasons that had nothing to do with its effectiveness. John Turner, new head of the Liberal Party and now prime minister, had decided to streamline the political decision-making process and reduce the influence of the bureaucracy. By September of the same year, with the Conservatives in power, the MSERD role was represented in the Cabinet Committee on Economic and Regional Development by that committee's chairman, Sinclair Stevens, minister of DRIE. With Stevens's fall from power in the winter of 1986, the CCERD chair was assumed by the deputy prime minister, Erik Nielsen. It subsequently moved to the president of the Treasury Board. Internal briefings became confused, with PCO now briefing the chairman of CCERD, not wanting to share information with DRIE officials, even though the former MSERD now resided in that department. After joining DRIE, the one-time MSERD organization disbanded or otherwise scattered much of its central (Ottawa-based) analytical and coordinating capabilities, and the regional FEDCS reported to a DRIE associate deputy minister in Ottawa.

PROGRAMS

In regional development, program instruments represent the translation of policy into action in the attempt to achieve the objectives set in the policy declaration. The new Department of Regional Industrial Expansion was to carry an impressive array of program instruments to promote industrial and business development in Canada, and it set about aggressively to develop its policies, objectives, and operational mode.

DRIE would continue to employ the GDA subsidiary agreement as its major program instrument in the furthering of regional economic development, restricted only in its use as circumscribed by business and industrial nomenclature. The department made good use of the flexibility provided by the broadness of the business/industrial label, and although some twenty existing agreements were transferred to other departments, DRIE retained a number of agreements falling into its newly defined mandate, including the spatial agreements. The GDAS became the means by which all departments of government would now consummate subsidiary agreements to further federal regional development aims.

DREE and ITC were running a number of assistance programs outside the GDA framework. DRIE moved quickly to study these programs, establishing the Marshall Task Force on Program Review on January 18, only six days after the reorganization was announced. Comprised of officials of the two departments, the task force reported its findings and recommendations barely two months later. Even before the department's mandate was refined at the policial level (that is, before legislation regarding its mandate was reviewed by cabinet or introduced into the House), the task force (to its credit, in many ways) already assumed what the department's programs should be all about. It concluded "that the mandate of the Department of Regional Industrial Expansion should be to increase the economic prosperity of Canadians in all regions."

The task force suggested that the objectives of the department would be accomplished by encouraging the establishment, expansion, and upgrading of industrial facilities, enhancing regional industrial benefits from major projects, and promoting domestic and international marketing development. It proposed a program concept that would apply to all phases of the development cycle, from conception to commercial exploitation, with financial assistance, as necessary, provided by a range of instruments, including loan guarantees and contributions. The regional dimension would be handled by skewing the levels of assistance available according to regional economic circumstances, to be measured by a "regional index" that had been earlier developed by DREE. The new ideal program was to have a simplified program structure and be highly decentralized for operational purposes. Large projects would be considered by a central public sector review board.

The task force took its lead in developing a mandate statement from the government's November 1981 budget paper "Economic Development for Canada in the 1980s" and from the prime minister's January 12, 1982, statement on the reorganization of economic departments. As far as the task force was concerned, the new department would not give up its capability and its right to address and influence trade policies and programs and policies on macroeconomic stabilization, taxation, competition, manpower and employment, procurement, and, above all, regional economic strategies and sectoral strategies.

The Marshall Task Force on Program Review inventoried a startling number of programs before recommending what was to become the Industrial and Regional Development Program. At merger, Industry, Trade and Commerce was operating eleven major general-purpose incentives programs and close to a score of other, end-use-specific (usually small) financial assistance programs. There were, as well, a dozen or more non-financial programs, which included duty remission, an import analysis service, management training and counselling, and industrial regional benefits. The task force decided to concentrate primarily on the RDIP, the Montreal Special Area Program, the special ARDA programs of DREE, the Enterprise Development Program (EDP), Defence Industry Productivity Program (DIPP), and certain other trade and community development programs of Industry, Trade and Commerce. Other programs were continued, at least for the time being, or left to wither on the vine.

The main DRIE incentives assistance program that emerged for business and industry, the IRDP, fell considerably short of the expectations of the Marshall Task Force in both content and objectives. The program had to be somewhat hastily constructed, which did not permit sufficient consultation with experienced incentives officers within the department. Many of the issues that DREE had been addressing on regional incentives programming were ignored. Rather than being simplified, the new IRDP became more complex for both the client body and program administrators. The unwieldy four-tier program structure, partially imposed at the policial level, was confusing to everyone who encountered the program.

Notwithstanding its regionally biased tier structure, the program was seen as being of limited value to the peripheral regions of the country (see, however, the analysis of the program in chapter 6). The kiss of death was the denial of the level of delegated decision-making authority to officials, particularly in the regions, on which the Marshall Task Force had predicated the program structure. The good elements of the program included the consolidation of some program instruments and the fact that it covered the development cycle from conception to commercialization. Because of the inadequate decision-making structure, however, it was difficult for program officers to use the IRDP in a truly proactive, developmental way, and it remained a largely passive or responsive program. With the 1984 change of government, certain key elements of the program were stripped away and overall assistance levels further tightened and reduced. The program's success was questionable, depending on the view of the observer, and it was blissfully permitted to expire in June 1988.

A full understanding of the DRIE program years from 1982 through 1987 can only be appreciated through examination of the departmental project approval structure that was employed during that period of time. The three senior programs of the department, represented by the Industrial and Regional Development Program, the Defence Industries Productivity Program, and the GDA subsidiary agreements, will suffice for illustrative purposes.

Delegated regional authorities during the life of the IRDP were at an all-time low of only $100,000 of crown assistance. Projects between that level and $1 million passed through an officials screening committee and then generally went to one of the junior ministers, acting under authority delegated from the senior minister. Sometimes the task was divided geographically and/or by political jurisdiction. Regional officials had some latitude on project revisions and rejections. It would be unkind to call the process a disaster, but it seriously retarded progress in furthering small-business industrial development in all regions of the country. Busy ministers kept small-project proposals on their desks for inordinately long periods of time, and when deciding on the merits of projects before them, they may have imputed more political overlay than a straight viability test would suggest.

IRDP projects over $1 million came to the Ottawa-based DRIE Internal Board for further review. This board was comprised of senior officials responsible for the sector branches, tourism, finance, and—under different names at different times—special projects. It met biweekly or more often, as the need arose. Proponents of projects, whether from the regions or headquarters, were available in person or through telephone conference call to speak to written proposals before the board. The board did not take decisions, but made recommendations to ministers.[24]

The DIPP, aimed, as its name implies, at defence-related projects in aerospace, electronics, and some of the other more sophisticated sectors, was administered centrally in Ottawa. An interdepartmental committee that had previously approved projects now recommended them to the DRIE Internal Board, where they were exposed to the same kind of scrutiny as the IRDP.

One of the most fundamental differences between DREE and DRIE involved the administration of program and project activities under the subsidiary agreements. Under DREE administration, virtually all implementation decisions under signed subsidiary agreements were taken in the region, and the only financial ceilings were the project and program levels written into the agreements. Shortly after merger, projects over $1 million were submitted to the DRIE Internal Board. The recommendations of the board were dealt with at various ministerial briefing sessions and ad hoc meetings. After 1984, under a scheme introduced by Sinclair Stevens, a minister-level committee was constituted to make final decisions on projects over $1 million. It usually met every third Wednesday evening, often going on to after midnight. Its members included the DRIE ministers (senior and junior minister of state), the ministers of state for science and technology and of finance, and the minister of international trade. This committee fell into disuse sometime after the departure of Stevens. The DRIE Internal Board review process continued into 1989.

Securing approval for the provision of incentives to enhance Canadian industrial competitiveness and to improve regional economies was not easy. It was little better for other forms of regional development expenditures. Donald Savoie quotes one federal official: "DRIE has been constrained, controlled, proceduralized, and systematized to death."[25] This is the nature of a centralized, highly complex organization that generates its own insatiable desire for information in every conceivable form. A consequence is an erosion in accountability as responsibility and control is held tightly at the centre. The regional aspects of the department suffered the greatest in this regard. Regional officers were all required to report to only one Ottawa responsibility centre, creating an unrealistic span of management control. The evidence suggests that the decisions taken through these involved procedures was not any better, only slower.

Regional development policy and program revision continued almost unabated throughout DRIE's lifespan. A substantial effort was put into identifying candidate members for an intended national advisory body to advise the department on economic and industrial development, but such a group was never realized. Although not structured specifically for regional development purposes, several sectoral advisory committees were formed through the initiative of Minister Ed Lumley in sectors of the economy having significant regional implications. These included committees on the aerospace, automotive, textile and clothing, petrochemical, and forest industries. The latter committee remained constituted as a permanent advisory committee. Sinclair Stevens, after becoming DRIE minister, gave a considerable amount of his time to those committees that still existed, particularly the forest industries and textiles and clothing committees. The Conservative government revised the IRDP to make it more selective in its application, at the same time introducing a series of new programs, especially in the Atlantic provinces. An abortive attempt to "devolve" the lower

139

end of the IRDP to the provinces for administration was also tried under Stevens's tutorship.[26]

THE ERDAS

Within the programs context, it is instructive to look at what was to have been a major program instrument change in 1982. By this time the GDA concept was falling into disrepute in some quarters. It was felt to be too general in content, too complicated to administer, and to leave too much control in the hands of the provinces. At its expiration in 1984, it was to be replaced by Economic and Regional Development Agreements, which were to be simpler, more precise, and which would facilitate direct federal program delivery. Reference to Appendix 1 reveals little evidence to support that rationale. Aucoin and Bakvis put it this way: "Nonetheless it is clear that, in contrast to the early DREE period, the ERDAS lacked clear policy objectives and certainly any kind of long-term strategy. It is also clear that the various subsidiary agreements under the ERDAS received much less critical scrutiny and evaluation than that formerly provided by DREE officials."[27]

The federal-provincial regional development agreement concept remained in use throughout the 1980s, still criticized to some extent as too provincially oriented, but yet to be replaced by anything better.[28] The reason for this is quite simple. It is not the instrument itself that determines success, only the way it is used. The content can be good or bad, precise or vague. The objectives sought can encompass whatever purposes the politicians want, including the visibility question, but finally it rests with the agreement architects and implementors, politicians and bureaucrats, to make the instrument work. It has no soul of its own. Aucoin and Bakvis observe of the ERDAS that "political expediency tended to dominate the setting of priorities more than under DREE, while in economic terms, there was very little in the ERDAS that were either new or innovative."[29]

The use of the ERDA for unilateral programming by the federal government merits attention. A review of seventeen randomly selected subsidiary agreements entered into after the ERDA came into being in 1984, selected primarily for their availability, was carried out with particular emphasis on the direct delivery question. The seventeen agreements were located in seven provinces and covered eight major activity areas or economic sectors, including resources, industrial development and advanced technology, spatial programming, and tourism. The agreements represented total funding of $637 million, with 41 percent being direct federal delivery, 34 percent provincial-only delivery, and 25 percent falling in the more conventional shared category. Certain agreements, for example, the Ontario and British Columbia forestry agreements totalling $450 million, were excluded due to their unusual skewing effect on the data. These agreements both had direct delivery components, but 80 percent of the activity was in the shared category.

It was hard to discern any logical pattern in the distribution of activities for direct (unilateral) program delivery. In the resource sectors in particular, areas of technical expertise fell primarily, but not exclusively, to the federal side. In forestry, the provinces were heavy on reforestation backlog, harvesting, and renewal resource development. In industrial development and advanced technology, the federal leaning was towards diversification, grants and contributions, research and development, innovation and productivity, assistance to development associations, development funds and marketing. The provinces were not excluded from these areas, but tended to be involved in promotion, domestic marketing, risk reduction, and access to employment. The federal side was also heavy on economic development studies and planning. Both governments were involved in opportunity identification.

There seemed to be no particular rationale for many of the other areas of regional development programming. Under the agreements, both levels of government carried responsibilities for human resource development, program management, business and community development, technology transfer, and development analysis. Even in areas where there was a leaning one way or the other, program descriptions were remarkably alike. In tourism, for example, both governments listed incentives, travel generators, reception centres, and marketing under program responsibilities, although probing revealed some separation of concentration for domestic and foreign markets. Some agreements seemed to leave the decision on which government would be the implementor to the management committee, a not illogical approach to determining respective roles, based on jurisdiction and expertise.

The overall conclusion, perhaps unfairly reached without further research, was that there were somewhat arbitrary assignments of respective roles, more of form than substance, dictated in large measure by the federal government's desire to attract the still-elusive credit for its efforts in regional development.[30] If that was the case, the ERDAS also failed the test. Aucoin and Bakvis report, "One of the political needs that was ostensibly to be met by the ERDAS was that of visibility, and this was the second failing in the ERDA process."[31]

The federal government continued to agonize over the ERDA instrument. Following Harvie Andre's complaint that the federal government was not getting the credit it deserved under the ERDAS and the subsequent reduction in its use and in the cost-sharing formulas (see chapter 3, note 31, and chapter 5, note 46), the federal government again attacked the provinces by accusing them of skimming funding from the cost-shared agreements to supplement provincial departmental budgets and to pursue high-profile province-only projects by which they would gain the full credit.[32] The claim was made that ERDA funds were being built into provincial operating budgets, which in itself is hardly surprising, given that government estimates and budgets usually identify sources of revenue.

Federal ministers also accused the provinces of tailoring programs to fit agreement criteria (one would hope so!), overlooking the obvious fact that no project under a subsidiary agreement should be approved unless federal members of the management committees were satisfied with its validity. The federal claims would seem to substantiate the above observation by Aucoin and Bakvis that agreement content was no longer getting the scrutiny it had received in the DREE days from officials well-schooled in the practice of federal-provincial agreement management. It appeared as if the federal government had given up control of the instrument when the minister of the Department of Western Diversification, expressly formed to pursue regional development in the West, said that the agreements had become a form of transfer payment.[33] It is hard to believe that federal officials let the negotiating process with provincial governments degenerate to such an extent.

THE 1982 REORGANIZATION OF ECONOMIC DEPARTMENTS IN RETROSPECT

According to Aucoin and Bakvis, "The manner in which the government is organized affects the distribution of authority, power and influence in ways that are not politically or policy neutral. A particular structure will give certain ideas and interests an edge over other ideas and interests by virtue of the way it distributes authority, power and influence, politically and in the bureaucracy."[34]

Public sector policy changes frequently lead to organizational reform aimed at better implementation of policy intentions. Sometimes the converse is true: cosmetic organizational change takes place to mask the fact that there has been no real redirection in policy terms. Confusion frequently reigns in either case. In regional development, organizational form has always played an important, sometimes decisive role in the achievement of regional economic development objectives.

Most pre- and early DREE federal regional development policies and programs were hatched in Ottawa, and their implementation was highly regulated from Ottawa, even when actual program delivery was effected through provincial governments. Anthony Careless writes that federal autocracy reached a zenith in the early years of DREE, with the senior level of government reserving the right to ensure efficiency and effectiveness of spending and the provinces more or less relegated to a take-it-or-leave-it status.[35] DREE changed all that in 1973 by deliberately putting implementation decisions and a high degree of policy determination in the regions. Aucoin and Bakvis say of DREE, "It deconcentrated its structure, it decentralized its decision-making process; and it reoriented its approach to more effectively focus its efforts on the regional or spatial dimensions of its policies and programs. Its reorganization marked a turning point in federal departmental organization."[36]

After the 1982 reorganization of economic departments, the apparatus existed for regionally based operational autonomy. MSERD was decentralized but was not greatly effective. DRIE, the only remaining vestige of a department dedicated at least in part to regional development, maintained its regional structure, but real decision-making authority in the regions was essentially emasculated. Aucoin and Bakvis pinpoint the DRIE problem: "DRIE represented a compromise between the concentrated/centralized design of ITC and the deconcentrated/decentralized design of DREE. Moreover, DRIE was in operation for some time before its regional [that is, provincial] executive directors were included in the central management committee of the department."[37] And DRIE lacked the essential coordinating device of regional ADMs that had given DREE its more focused form. Aucoin and Bakvis elaborate their view of the importance of real regional involvement in departmental affairs by declaring that regional structures and authorities form an integral part of departmental structures and management. They say that delegated authority should be exercised within a framework of departmental goals, plans, objectives, and policies developed with the participation of those who exercise delegated authority.[38] This was the secret of the DREE management framework; it separated DREE from its contemporaries of the time and from most federal structures thereafter.

Most regional development program practitioners believe that there must be a tangible organization with a high degree of resident decision making in the region to which the policy objectives apply and in which the programming is to take place.[39] Organizational form in itself, however, is incomplete in terms of having an effect on policy and programs. The key rests with the centres of authority within the organization in question. Regional officials had little impact on policy or programs in the pre- and early DREE days. From 1973–74 through 1982, the picture was reversed, with DREE regional officials (who carried a much higher rank in the organization) having a dominant policy and programming influence at both the bureaucratic and political levels. The regional offices of DRIE, even while maintaining a substantial operation in the period 1982–88, had considerably less influence on policy and programs, even within the department.

In 1984, in examining the merits of a shift away from gap closing through transfer payments towards developing the economic potential of slow-growth regions, Donald Savoie said, "The question that now presents itself is whether such an effort is better sustained by a government-wide focus on regional development or by a dedicated department with a specific regional mandate? It is suggested in this paper that a dedicated department is preferable."[40] In criticizing the 1982 reorganization of federal economic departments, which was designed to make regional development central to federal economic planning, Savoie commented, "The reorganization has left no department or agency with the capacity on its own or in cooperation with provincial governments to go beyond sectoral mandates to bring together and promote small-scale and multi-dimensional initiatives capable of responding to problems and opportunities at the local or sub-provincial level." He added that if DREE was unclear in its objective and was employing dated instruments, an appropriate solution would have been to reorient the department.[41] The instrument (the GDA federal-provincial multidisciplinary approach) was hardly dated. It continued to be the major regional development device employed to the end of the 1980s. The statements by Savoie imply an endorsement of the DREE model and of DREE itself. Savoie twice said that to do away with DREE, which had the potential to be sensitive to regional circumstances, in the belief that it would make federal economic departments more sensitive to them, appeared to be naive and to constitute a step backward.[42] He further observed that the 1982 reorganization no longer left anyone in cabinet specifically charged with the responsibility of speaking on behalf of the regions or bringing regional considerations into the discussions whenever new economic activities were proposed.[43] By this time Savoie was also disenamoured with the possibility of meaningful multidimensional initiatives (as DREE was capable of), beyond sectoral mandates.[44]

The importance of having a minister at the cabinet table is well known to officials who understand the process of moving initiatives through the review process to ultimate ministerial decision. When an item, no matter how important to some, is but one of may issues on a crowded cabinet committee agenda, it is essential that one minister play an ownership role for an agenda item if it is to have any chance to survive. Cabinet committee represents a competitive process and all of a minister's most persuasive powers are usually needed to have his or her initiative receive approval. If there is no one present to play that specific role, the chances of approval are distinctly diminished. In 1978 Phidd and Doern saw the importance of the establishment of DREE in this light: "The creation of DREE places in the federal cabinet a political minister whose task is explicitly to help reduce regional economic and social disparities."[45] The Senate Standing Committee on National Finance, in its lengthy hearings on government policy and regional development, quickly discerned a pending problem with the reorganization. After noting that "as a department of the federal government, with ministerial representation in Cabinet and in Parliament, DREE was able to act as the conscience of the more developed and voice of the least developed regions of Canada," the Senate committee asked who would champion in cabinet the cause of the least-developed regions. It concluded that with the demise of DREE there was no longer a federal department with the sole mandate of promoting development in the least-developed regions of the country.[46]

The effectiveness of a minister at cabinet committee is proportional to his or her seniority and influence with the prime minister. How good is the record of ministers who have held the regional development portfolio or that of those regional ministers who have had an influence on them? In chapter 2 we recorded the effectiveness of both the late Jean Marchand and the late Donald Jamieson. Each had the ear of the prime minister and each was more or less successful in getting what he wanted when minister of DREE. Interdepartmental collaboration may have left something to be desired in the early stages, but federal-provincial relations certainly flourished under Jamieson. Successive DREE ministers Marcel Lessard, Elmer MacKay, and Pierre De Bané, all junior in their time to Jamieson and Marchand, gave generally credible performances and maintained federal-provincial relations until the 1980–82 relapse, which occurred during De Bané's tenure. All three succeeded in increasing the level of interdepartmental cooperation. The junior minister status was revealed from time to time, most notably in De Bané's exclusion from meaningful involvement in the 1982 reorganization of economic departments.

Other ministers without a direct responsibility for regional development were sometimes more influential than the DREE minister in supporting or thwarting departmental initiatives. Allan MacEachen, who had reached a high level of influence in the Trudeau government as the years progressed, could usually count on being listened to whenever the subject of regional development came up. Other ministers

145

with influence on regional development matters included Lloyd Axworthy in the West and a number of ministers in Quebec.

In the 1982–84 period, Herb Gray, in his short tenure at DRIE (technically both Gray and Lumley held the dual portfolios of DREE and ITC until late in 1983) and Ed Lumley, who held the portfolio until the Liberal loss of power in September 1984, were influential ministers, but their attention was divided between regional and national policies, with the latter frequently commanding the majority of attention. Nevertheless, many of the national issues handled by Lumley and by the following DRIE ministers had strong regional significance. Unfortunately, the record of Conservative DRIE ministers was spotty, with one or two being especially ineffective.

Harvey Lithwick, in discussing the federal quest for visibility, insecurity in the face of provincial assertiveness, and preference for policy [and program] independence, coupled with shifting views on economic development strategy, says of the 1982 reorganization, "It would appear that those who planned the reorganization of regional policy were not as concerned about the latent contradictions and the need for sophisticated institutional design to cope with them." He continues: "The best that can be expected, therefore is some improvement in federal sectoral coordination. What has been overlooked is the cost for regional policy of this approach. In directly challenging the provinces, both by trying to weaken them fiscally and by downgrading their involvement in regional policy within their own borders, Ottawa has misread the very essence of the federal system and how it affects regional policy. It is improbable that any regional economic goals can be achieved without provincial (and local) cooperation."[47]

A somewhat less public but more ominous reason for the new regional development policy direction reflected a concern for the provincial role that went well beyond the visibility question. One consequence was the entrenchment of the direct program delivery mode, which had emerged in selective form in 1980, in the new federal policy. The Senate Standing Committee on National Finance was equally apprehensive about this added federal aggressiveness.[48]

By 1987, Savoie had changed his mind and no longer believed that a dedicated department was preferable for the practice of regional development in Canada. In a specific reference to both DREE and DRIE, he said, "The regional development efforts of a single line department are unlikely to amount to little more than the delivery of a handful of programs to designated regions. It will never result in a multidisciplinary and comprehensive approach simply because they do not have the capacity to cut across jurisdictional lines ... Experience has shown

146

that the most effective approach to regional development is multidisciplinary."[49] DREE introduced multidisciplinary regional development programming into the lexicon of regional development terminology in 1973 and practised it widely until 1982. From 1982 on, MSERD did not extend this approach even though separate departments individually practised regional development, with MSERD providing the overview.

By this time, Savoie's 1982 optimism for the reorganization of that year had evaporated.[50] He concluded, "With the aid of hindsight, we recognize that the premise underpinning Ottawa's 1981 policy shift in regional development was false and has had far-reaching implications for Atlantic Canada and for the allocation of federal funds earmarked for regional development."[51] The premise to which Savoie referred included the assumption that a (national) economic development policy for Canada could include the objective of bringing improvements to all areas of the country. Regional DREE officials repeatedly reported that any dramatic improvement in the national economy could not play out evenly across the country.

The legislation that put DRIE in place was also credited with contributing to some of its problems. In the summer of 1987 and after a change in federal regional development policy had already been announced, Donald Savoie said, "The new legislation, however, does not limit the government to certain sectors, regions, or activities, nor does it give any kind of policy direction. More important, it does not in any way limit the flexibility and the free-wheeling range the government has in developing regional development initiatives, nor does it tie the programming to the regional comparative advantage approach. No program criteria and no targets to be achieved have been laid out."[52]

Savoie gave his own prescription for regional development legislation: "New legislation should be introduced in support of Ottawa's regional development efforts, which would be directly tied to the theoretical framework that gave rise to the policy. The new legislation should be much more specific about the theory from which the policy is formulated, and about the type of initiatives that should be supported. It should also spell out more clearly the regions [to] which efforts should be directed."[53]

The enunciation of political policy intentions should be as precise and explicit as possible, in legislation and elsewhere. That legislation also convey the expectations of its architects is an added advantage. The difficulty arises with regard to the operating principles required to translate policy into programs and into action. Determining the best way to put forward these principles is no easy task. The application

147

of legislation rests largely with the goodwill and integrity of those charged with that responsibility. While abuses can be cited, it is nevertheless true that to write legislation so restrictive that there is no room for innovation is counter-productive to its intent and may be taken as a significant vote of non-confidence in elected and non-elected officials alike.

One now rarely finds legislation that spells out the kind of precise details usually left for later specification through regulation and order-in-council. The spatial coverage of regionally differentiated programs, disparity indices, and like tools have always been dealt with in such a manner. Acts of Parliament, much like the GDAs, are basically enabling documents, declaring the intent of government but leaving enough latitude to accommodate lessons that can only be learned with experience.[54] Even though the DREE Act was weak, for example, it did not retard effective regional development programming or inhibit further policy determination. The legislation creating DRIE could not have counteracted the government's ambivalence on regional development policy or slow the political interference in program delivery that helped bring about its downfall.[55] There is no reason to believe that the end-result of program activity issuing from any of these acts, from the DREE Act in 1969 to the ACOA Act in 1988, would have been any different with an attempt to write everything into the legislation.

There is no single, patently obvious reason that explains the ending of an idea—there are many. However, in the case of the 1982 reorganization of economic departments, the government's initial objective of gaining greater control over economic and regional development in Canada was inadequately thought out in policy and implementation terms, with insufficient regard to the consequences for regional economies. This must, therefore, rank high on the list of reasons explaining DRIE's perceived inadequacies. The organizational form, too often experimented with in attempts to find a panacea for regional development programming, cannot by itself solve regional development problems. Organizational structures only reflect policy intentions, designating the location of decision making and responsibility. If properly developed, they can facilitate the efficient and effective translation of policy into action. The reorganization of economic departments in 1982 went down as another uncertain attempt by the federal government to remedy regional economic inequalities. It also proved again that structural change, without a clearly determined and enunciated policy intent to accompany it, is probably bound to fail.

Chapter Five

New Directions?

A REDIRECTION OF REGIONAL DEVELOPMENT EFFORT

By 1986 it was important for the Conservative government to put its stamp on the regional disparity problem in Canada. Notwithstanding an upsurge in economic activity and employment in the mid-1980s, prosperity reigned unevenly across the country. It was easy for the government to criticize past regional development policies, more difficult to devise new ones. On June 4, 1986, regional development ministers, building on their statement of principles for regional economic development of a year earlier, commissioned a study on regional development assessment. The study was to be conducted jointly by federal and provincial officials for submission the following year to the first ministers.[1] Without awaiting the recommendations of that study the government, in the Speech from the Throne of October 1, 1986 (33rd Parliament, 2nd Session), made clear its intentions for regional development for the remainder of its first term in office, as well as its second, ensured by a convincing election win on November 21, 1988:

> For many years, successive governments have sought to provide measures intended to promote regional development. Their efforts have not been as effective as hoped. Regional disparity remains an unacceptable reality of Canadian life. Our experience has shown that spending more money, by itself, has not solved the problem. It is time to consider new approaches, to examine how our considerable and growing support for Canada's regions can be used more efficiently, more effectively and with greater sensitivity to local conditions and opportunities. In renewing their efforts to come to grips with this longstanding problem, my Ministers are

convinced many positive proposals for new policy initiatives will come from those who live and work in the regions concerned.

Building on the human and natural resource strengths of the regions, a renewed cooperative effort will lead to a new development agenda. Special emphasis will be given to diversifying the economic base of Western Canada.

As a first step in achieving improved results from this sustained national approach, an Atlantic Canada Opportunities Agency will be constituted to facilitate and coordinate all federal development initiatives in the area. This agency will make fuller use of the expertise available in the Atlantic region and invite the maximum participation of other governments and organizations in the area.

The commitment to the Atlantic region was reinforced in a speech delivered by Prime Minister Brian Mulroney in Moncton, New Brunswick, in the fall of 1986. His office commissioned Donald Savoie, of the Canadian Institute for Research on Regional Development, to conduct interviews and subsequently bring forward recommendations on what form an agency should take and how it should function. This 1986 initiative led to more than two years of organizational upheaval and regional development program change in Canada.

The report of the Federal-Provincial Task Force on Regional Development Assessment, which became available in May 1987, was refreshing in its breadth of treatment of the subject matter, both in its retrospective and forward-looking dimensions.[2] The report went beyond many of the conventional limitations of regional development thinking to embrace broad principles bearing on regional economies. It did not, however, present a blueprint for regional development programming. The task force concluded (1) that the critical factor in international competitiveness would be the application of technology, (2) that the emergence of the small-business service sectors held the key to trends in output and employment, (3) that a shift of income and employment from rural to urban areas was inevitable, (4) that regional competition and comparative advantage in Canada would be based increasingly on economic competition and specialization among urban centres, and (5) that effective regional development policies needed to emphasize measures that promote flexibility and adaptability in regional economies. The task force made suggestions relating to the transfer system (that it should be designed to encourage productive employment), the education and training system, innovation and technology, entrepreneurial development, and urban specialization. The report also recognized the importance of consultation, of joint planning and programming, and of matching of national sectoral policies with regional policy objectives, and the necessity for delegated authorities and program flexibility.

The government put its regional development policy into action in the three-month span of June–August 1987. For the fourth time in almost twenty years, federal policies and programs on regional development were undergoing change. The 1987 policy was regionally differentiated; the approaches, systems, structures, and priorities emerged independently by region as this loose framework was applied across the country. Public announcements revealed the character of the new approach. DRIE would be relieved of its regional development responsibilities in eight of the ten provinces and would be combined with the Ministry of State for Science and Technology to form a new department, Industry, Science and Technology Canada (ISTC). Responsibility for regional development would be assumed by a mix of organizational entities, a mix that would differ depending on the region involved. Already announced, the Atlantic Canada Opportunities Agency, carrying responsibility for the four Atlantic provinces, was first off the mark. The Department of Western Economic Diversification was assigned the responsibility for the four western provinces. In northern Ontario, a small staff of officials would operate FEDNOR, the Northern Ontario Development Corporation, which remained attached to DRIE/ISTC. The arrangement employed in Quebec, which emerged a year after those applicable in other parts of the country, remained embodied within the concept of the Canada-Quebec Economic and Regional Development Agreement of 1984. A further organizational shuffle, which took place in 1991, removed responsibility for Quebec from ISTC.

THE ATLANTIC CANADA OPPORTUNITIES AGENCY

The Atlantic Canada Opportunities Agency, or ACOA, as it came to be called, was formally unveiled on June 6, 1987. It was to be a separate agency with its own legislation.[3] The bill authorizing its existence was passed in the House of Commons on May 10, 1988, almost a year later, but the agency had been up and running since early summer the year before, using the staff and programs of DRIE Atlantic regional offices. The Senate gave the bill a rough ride, under the leadership of Senator Allan MacEachen, who wanted to see it split so as to separate the Cape Breton regional development initiatives from the direct control of ACOA. The Senate finally relented, however, and royal assent was granted August 18, 1988.

In the Speech from the Throne the government said that experience had shown that spending more money, by itself, had not solved the regional development problem. In an earlier statement, Prime Minister Mulroney had said, "Our top priority is to work towards a more effective use of the generous funds already set aside for the development of the Atlantic region."[4] In the eventual announcement of its establishment, however, $1.05 billion of new money was dedicated for the use of ACOA, over and above all other federal commitments and expenditure levels in the region. This intended incrementality was strongly stressed in statements by the prime minister,[5] and the Honourable John Crosbie reinforced the message in the House of Commons.[6] It may well be that the lure of being seen to do something soon (too often mistaken to mean spending dollars) was too great to overcome the good intentions expressed in the Throne Speech and other statements.

The mandate of ACOA is based on a four-pronged platform of activity. *Action* is intended to provide a direct stimulation of economic activity through risk sharing in partnership with the private sector. *Cooperation* represents the federal-provincial collaboration first embodied in the GDAS, later in the cooperation agreements under ACOA. *Coordination* focuses federal economic programs on opportunities in Atlantic Canada. And finally, *advocacy* promotes and defends the interests of Atlantic Canada in a national context.[7] The mandate manifests itself in terms of enhancing growth in earned incomes and employment opportunities, creating an environment conducive to economic growth, encouraging small- and medium-sized businesses, and helping the people of the region to help themselves. In its first year of operation, the agency's president said that "ACOA is not intended to eliminate economic disparity in the region ... [but was designed to stimulate entrepreneurs, not to] promote or assist development in this or that sector or community as such."[8]

From the beginning, the agency was structured to be independent of any other department of government. Its strength was to be based on its physical location in the Atlantic region and on-the-ground decision making. Its mandate suggests that no activity that might benefit the economy of the Atlantic region is exempt from its consideration.

Operationally, ACOA took over from DRIE a number of the ERDA subsidiary agreements in the region, along with the Enterprise Cape Breton and Atlantic Enterprise programs and the administration of the IRDP during the remainder of its life. Enterprise Cape Breton, as an entity, was disbanded in the budget of February 25, 1992, its role folded completely into ACOA. As early as 1980, DREE suggested taking over the Industrial Development Division of the Cape Breton Development corporation; that division was the forerunner of Entreprise Cape Breton. The agency was also empowered to develop new program activities for the enhancement of the regional economy. ACOA may collaborate with other levels of government, establish designated areas, and transfer funds to other departments. The range of the agency's program devices includes support to enterprises; development of entrepreneurial talent; support of business associations, conferences, studies, trade shows, and market research; the development of data banks; and the identification of business opportunities. ACOA may use grants, contributions, loans, and loan guarantees, take stock options, and enter into contracts in the pursuit of its objectives.

On February 15, 1988, ACOA announced an enhanced and expanded Action Program in support of medium and small business. The program would draw on features of the Atlantic Enterprise Program and the IRDP.[9] Activities of businesses, non-profit organizations, provincial crown corporations, and specialized services in support of small- and medium-sized businesses were all eligible for consideration. Financial assistance levels were raised to 50 percent for eligible capital costs for new establishments, to 40 percent for product expansion, and to 30 percent for facility modernization and expansion. The differentiated four-tier granting system employed under IRDP was effectively removed. Favourable features of predecessor programs were retained, including interest buy-down (a means whereby financial assistance will be provided to "buy-down" the interest on a term loan for an eligible project) to a maximum of six percentage points and loan guarantees. The Atlantic agency stressed the one-stop shopping concept of account managers, where responsibility for a client and the project rests with one person from beginning to end.

Organizationally, the agency is headquartered in Moncton, as were the DREE Atlantic operations during the years 1973–82. Each province in the region has a substantial ACOA office presence, which is based on the offices of the previous federal economic development coordinators and supplemented by transfers of DRIE staff and other recruitment. In 1989 the total regional staff complement was announced to be in the order of 300 persons.[10] The agency started out with an advisory board comprised of both private sector and government representatives, attesting to the commitment—most strongly made in the Atlantic—to ensure local input to the process. After the federal election of November 21, 1988, the board was reconstituted with a private sector membership only.

ACOA's political leadership started out with Senator Lowell Murray as minister responsible, with the Honourable John Crosbie answering in the House on agency matters. This was in keeping with the declared intention of having the agency report to a senior minister, as recommended by Savoie in his report on the setting up of the agency.

According to Savoie, the premiers of the Atlantic provinces were adamant on this point.[11] This resolve subsequently evaporated with the transfer of the responsibility for ACOA to the minister of veterans affairs, hardly a senior portfolio in federal government terms. However, the incumbent in the last half of 1988, Gerald Merrithew, who had held senior portfolios in the New Brunswick Hatfield government, did carry significant credentials for the role. A major cabinet shuffle of January 30, 1989, saw Merrithew replaced by the minister of public works, Nova Scotian Elmer MacKay, who had been minister of DREE in the 1979 Clark government. Turning full circle, the responsibility for ACOA reverted directly to John Crosbie in yet another cabinet shuffle of April 21, 1991, with his assumption of the portfolio of Fisheries and Oceans.

In the beginning Atlantic Canada was said to be under the gun. In fact, both of its responsible ministers suggested that ACOA was the last kick at the can for the region.[12] The Atlantic provinces have a long history of federal and provincial financial assistance and encouragement in the promotion of their economies. There was a high degree of concern and skepticism when the well-regarded DREE, with its dedicated mandate to promote regional development, was merged with Industry, Trade and Commerce in 1982.[13] Much of the disenchantment that prevailed in the Atlantic region in the immediate post-DREE period translated itself into either further skepticism or unusually high expectations with the announcement of ACOA. Dissatisfaction prevailed well into 1988 with the perceived slow start-up of the agency.[14] The criticism came from all quarters. The chairman of the Atlantic Provinces Chambers of Commerce, Rick DesBrisay, called ACOA's advisory board, which was touted as an essential ingredient in bringing regional opinions and guidance to the operations of the agency, a "toothless tiger." One of the board members described it as ineffectual.[15] Even the Atlantic premiers, who effusively endorsed ACOA on its announcement, were having second thoughts by January 1988 when they learned of the range of projects not considered eligible for ACOA funding.[16]

Over these start-up months the agency patiently explained the necessity for front-end consultation and long term horizons, emphasizing at the same time the direct support intended for small- and medium-sized business. Criticism of slow program start-up can be expected with the introduction of any new program organization. In ACOA's case it may not have been deserved. It did, however, create another up-hill-climb problem for the agency. Not surprisingly, the concern with ACOA re-emerged from time to time. In May 1989 Premier Frank McKenna of New Brunswick said he wanted to discuss the "lack of policy direction in the Atlantic Canada Opportunities Agency" with the other Atlantic premiers.[17] Not content to leave industrial development to the federal government, McKenna announced provincial plans to attract investment to the province and spark entrepreneurship through a range of incentives.[18] In 1990, over $3 million of assistance was provided to 383 small businesses through a package of programs for business start-up, management and technical assistance, planning, training, software acquisition, and quality improvements – all areas eligible for assistance under ACOA programs.

Although ACOA was foretold in the fall of 1986 and studied until its announcement in June 1987, little operational planning was focused on the means by which the agency would open its doors for business or on the legislative changes required to give effect to the agency. Information provided by PCO to DRIE just prior to the public announcement of ACOA's creation was not only sketchy but inaccurate on more than one point regarding the practice of regional development in the Atlantic provinces at the time. DRIE was asked for suggestions on how ACOA might work, something that should have been meticulously planned before it was declared operational on June 6. Although Savoie had made general statements on the ACOA structure and its operations in his report to the prime minister, he was not in a position to lay out an organizational and operational blueprint. One impediment to effective pre-planning for the agency was the lack of a chief executive officer until just before its announcement. Such a person should have been in place to lead the planning well before ACOA became operational. As it was, an onerous burden was placed on the agency head, who was simultaneously required to design an organizational and operational mode, determine policy, and manage an agency declared to be operational.

When legislation finally reached the House of Commons, debate centred on the incrementality of ACOA funding over and above those expenditures and commitments represented by ERDAS, IRDP, DRIE, and other federal departments operating in the region. There was a concern that even with increased spending, the overall level in the region might only return to what it was in the 1970s.

The Atlantic Canada Opportunities Agency developed some impressive numbers in its first two years of operation. Close to 500 applications had been approved by March 31, 1988, involving total project costs of some $338 million. By year end 1988, activity in the Atlantic region had ballooned to over 5,000 approved projects involving some $500 million of federal commitments. Agency officials reported a level of Action Program activity to September 29, 1989, of over 6,000 approved projects, $630 million of federal commitments triggering $1.8 billion of investment, creation of 18,000 jobs and the maintenance

155

of another 20,000. Actual Action Program expenditures to the end of fiscal year 1988–89 were reported as $112.373 million.[19]

Examples of projects meriting financial support illustrate ACOA's small-business bias.[20] Projects receiving assistance included pizza food processing, furniture and woodworking operations, tourist accommodations and attractions, sea cage culture operations, contract logging, a stone-crushing plant, computer-assisted drafting services and sign making, heavy equipment repair and manufacture, desk-top publishing, and silk-screen printing. Feasibility studies and business plans were also supported.[21] In the larger project category, ACOA provided aid for a major real estate project in Fredericton, NB, pulp and paper and mining operations, and fish-processing plants. The agency committed financing to the Telemedicine and Educational Technology Resource Agency project in Newfoundland, and support for the Newfoundland and Labrador Institute of Fisheries and Marine Technology and for the Centre for Marine Communications in that province. The support of technical institutions was reinforced with financing for the revitalization of the New Brunswick Research and Productivity Council. Of particular note was ACOA's collaboration with regional universities, represented by funding for the establishment of a chair in management technology and entrepreneurship and an industrial outreach program at the University of New Brunswick and a chair in regional development at the University of Moncton.

Numbers alone do not reveal the quality of projects supported under financial assistance programs. Activities in support of business and technical infrastructure to enhance the environment for viable economic activity are laudable. The value of the thousands of small-business projects can only be determined when their survival rates and other assessment measures are evaluated in the future. A review of how many projects are indigenous to the region, as opposed to being imported, will be particularly interesting.[22] The nature of the financial assistance provided in the Atlantic region reveals that the region appears to favour the interest buy-down feature, coupled with an outright contribution to eligible projects. The contribution level was restricted to projects under $100 thousand after the February 20, 1990, budget decision to make federal incentives grants repayable.

WESTERN ECONOMIC DIVERSIFICATION

The government could not stop its new regional development strategy at the eastern border of Quebec, but it did leap-frog that province to reach next into western Canada. On August 4, 1987, the government announced the creation of the Department of Western Economic Diversification.[23] First known as the Western Diversification Office, it became WD in shorthand (also D-WED). The bill formalizing the new department was passed by the House the following spring, on May 10, 1988. It received royal assent June 8, 1988.

"The Western Diversification Initiative builds on the Government's action to implement the 1984 Prince Albert Declaration which set out the fundamental principles that should underlie Western Canadian economic development policies."[24] These principles included strong western representation in cabinet, understanding between the federal government and the West, and recognition of the importance of providing opportunities that allow young people to remain in the West.[25] WD's mandate is founded on economic diversification. The agency claims rigorous adherence to this policy to the extent that it excludes assistance to already-competitive firms; it does not, however, shield firms from the competition of market forces. The mandate includes the coordination of federal economic activities in the West and works in conjunction with existing programs of other federal departments. WD encourages the development of new businesses and industries and related business infrastructure. The department has the fundamental objective of creating additional job opportunities.

Operationally, WD took over responsibility for the administration of IRDP in the western provinces from DRIE, along with the Western Transportation Industrial Development Program (WTIDP) and certain ERDA agreements. It operates its own Western Diversification Program, which encompasses a mix of flexible operating instruments, including contributions and interest buy-down. Its program application covers studies, all phases of technological identification, development and exploitation, productivity improvement, market development, and assistance for new, expanded, or modernized establishments. The western program is categorical in demanding that projects meet the test of contributing to diversification in the four western provinces and that priority sectors are identified against which projects can be tested.

Headquartered in Edmonton, WD has a presence in each of the four western provinces that is based on the former FEDC offices, with staff intake from DRIE and other sources. Its first five-year budget was set at $1.2 billion. The department was originally organized operationally on a sectoral basis. Each of approximately eleven major sectors of the western economy, including agriculture, forestry, mining, manufacturing and processing, energy, and transportation, was assigned to a senior officer in the region, who held the prime responsibility for programming in the assigned sector. Subsequently, it was found through experience that some sectors were more active than others, and staff assignments and priorities were realigned accordingly. Each of the four (provincial) regions in the West also has resident sectoral expertise. These experts have the responsibility of ensuring adequate consultation with appropriate federal line departments and presumably provincial government agencies as well. In terms of program and project priorities, WD prefers to be involved in more horizontal or systemic activity areas, such as trade support for an industry grouping or sector, developing assistance policies for an entire sector of the economy or providing a pathfinder service through the bureaucracy. In cooperation with provincial governments, WD mutually identifies priority areas for attention.

WD's first minister was Bill McKnight, though he was soon moved to the more senior Defence portfolio. He was replaced by Charles Mayer, minister of state, grains and oilseeds, not a significant ranking in the cabinet pecking order (although in the West, the WD minister acted in many ways as the surrogate for Deputy Prime Minister and Minister of Finance Donald Mazankowski, who called the important shots for that region). Ministers Jake Epp (Manitoba), Bill McKnight (Saskatchewan), and Kim Campbell (British Columbia) each have a say on issues of particular importance to their respective province. WD has no advisory board.

Although the announcement of Western Diversification was embraced with enthusiasm at the provincial political level in most of the western provinces, a familiar chord of skepticism was exhibited by business and the public in western Canada.[26] The some $240 million annually earmarked for the four provinces, even if completely incremental, was seen to pale beside massive federal agricultural payments and other federal expenditures in that region. Not surprisingly, criticism of the program direction for western Canada also found a voice in the opposition parties of the House of Commons.[27] Skepticism about the true incrementality of the funding was aggressively expressed, and the overall magnitude of the financial assistance was compared unfavourably with previous federal regimes.

From the outset the WD initiative seemed directed towards building on the activities of other federal departments and to looking for ways to strengthen the basic support infrastructure of the region. Early-announced financial assistance included support for the Potash Institute of Canada, the Centre for Frontier Engineering Research, a marketing program for British Columbia's shingle-and-shake industry, a structural testing facility at the University of Manitoba, the development of an electronic data interchange (EDI) system in Vancouver, and support for a 1990 Vancouver trade conference on business and the environment. On May 9, 1988, $13.5 million of WD funding towards the construction of a $30-million forest research centre to be built in Vancouver was announced. This was a proposal that had been under discussion with governments prior to the creation of WD and would likely have received support in any event.

Project assistance announcements that followed in subsequent months included support of $9.6 million for a Manitoba health products development centre (the Aging and Rehabilitation Product Development Centre), in support of a Canada-Manitoba health industry development strategy, and up to $50 million of shared government funding for the National Agriculture Biotechnology Initiative. On WD's second anniversary, August 4, 1989, Canada, Alberta, and Sherritt Gordon Limited announced the establishment of WESTAIM, a $140-million advanced industrial materials initiative directed to the commercialization of applied research and development projects in this new field of international interest. Industry committed itself to a contribution of $70 million over five years, with each government coming in for $30 million. At least half of the federal involvement is through WD.

On the other hand, by its second anniversary WD was boasting of $618 million of support for 1,134 projects, with the small- and medium-sized business segment heavily represented. A year later approved projects approached the 2,000 level, with a corresponding increase in federal commitments. These individual projects ranged from as low as a few thousand dollars for companies making kitchen cabinets, appliances, packaging, staircases, control panels, and sawmill products up to several hundred thousand dollars and higher for projects in the field of protocol analyzers, polyvinyl chloride production, farm equipment production, logging skidders, fibreglass storage tanks, a dioxin-testing laboratory, and the only computerized lumber grader and optimizer in the world.

In addition to the establishment, modernization, and expansion of facilities, projects involved research and development, design, marketing, and consultant studies. Service industries were not neglected, and assistance was offered for a number of computer applications for software and control systems for manufacturing operations. Exciting projects in legal information systems and in CAD/CAM and data security systems pointed to a high level of program interest from the information technology business community. By March 31, 1991, 18 percent of WD support was being directed to the services sector.

Although the WD guidelines state that the Western Diversification Program is not an entitlement program and that applications are to be assessed for their contribution to diversification of the western economy, the range of assistance provided by the department reveals little in the way of a coherent economic development approach. In the West many offers are made on the basis of their being repayable, "conditionally" repayable, or interest-free repayable. Twenty-nine percent of projects approved to March 31, 1991, were to be repayable. A study of all project offers would likely reveal a pattern of assistance packages designed to match the needs of the client, although the evidence suggests that the Atlantic region and the West have different ideas about incentives assistance.

The Department of Western Diversification's 1990–91 annual report reported some $685 million being administered against 2,192 projects approved since the department's inception in 1987. Seventy-eight percent of the projects were urban located, with 39 percent falling in the manufacturing category. The reported continuing support for horizontal activities such as international marketing, supplier identification and information seminars, and targeted assistance for the commercial development of new technologies can only be viewed as positive.

NORTHERN ONTARIO

Well before the creation of DREE, a myriad of federal programs, including PFRA, ARDA, Special ARDA, FRED, and the Special Areas and Highways Program found application in most provinces other than Ontario. Programs such as the Atlantic Development Board, Maritime Marshlands Rehabilitation Act (MMRA), and Newstart were region-specific. Only ARDA was operative in Ontario. It was with the advent of DREE that arrangements were made for more sophisticated area-specific programming in Ontario through the Canada/Ontario General Development Agreement signed in February 1974. That agreement targeted areas of northern and eastern Ontario for attention. The federal ability to cooperate on such initiatives with Ontario was extended with the signing of a ten-year ERDA on November 2, 1984. The ERDA again emphasized the need to sustain the resource potential of northern Ontario and to capture as much value added activity as possible. Direct business incentives programs such as DREE's RDIP, ITC's EDP, and DRIE's IRDP also had application in certain designated areas of Ontario, based on criteria of unemployment and earned income.

The Conservative government did give attention to northern Ontario between the ACOA and WD announcements, but on a much-reduced scale. On July 13, 1987, the federal government announced a five-year, $55-million program for the region, under the name FEDNOR, headquartered in Sault Ste Marie, Ontario. At the time, the role of the Northern Ontario Advisory Board to FEDNOR was highlighted in the announcement made jointly by then solicitor general James Kelleher, who represented the riding, and then minister of regional industrial expansion Michel Côté. With Kelleher's election defeat, the board reported to the minister of state for small business and tourism, Tom Hockin. Unlike ACOA in the Atlantic and WD in the west, FEDNOR remained within DRIE and assumed responsibility for the DRIE Thunder Bay and Sudbury offices. Its total staff complement would not exceed twenty-four people.

FEDNOR operates on a much more modest scale than the independent ACOA and WD. The initial federal commitment comprised $40 million of direct contributions and a $15-million reserve against $60 million of loan insurance. The accompanying news release suggested that this package represented $100 million of backing for business and predicted that it would stimulate twice that amount of business activity. The target for such assistance was identified as the small- and medium-sized business community and it is unlikely that the programs stray far from this target group. In April 1990 an additional $14 million of funding was announced for FEDNOR.

The main program instruments of FEDNOR are the Core Industrial Program, a replacement program for IRDP, a special rural, small-business program, both of which have a higher enrichment level and more flexibility than the IRDP and a tourism assistance program.[28] From FEDNOR's inception in July 1987 to December 31, 1991, some $34 million of funding had been committed to approximately 440 businesses, generating $118 million of additional private sector capital. Employment creation is estimated at 1958 jobs, with another 607 being maintained.

FEDNOR's involvement with regional development in northern Ontario expanded beyond its primary small-business bias as it gained experience, as evidenced by substantial $600,000 assistance to Science North in Sudbury and its involvement in the consummation of a $95-million Canada-Ontario Northern Ontario Development Agreement (NODA) for the enhancement of the forestry, minerals, and tourism sectors. FEDNOR has also aggressively promoted its Market Access Program, in cooperation with Supply and Services Canada, to assist northern businesses to participate in public sector contracts.

An important aspect of the federal venture in northern Ontario is the degree to which it complements or otherwise relates to provincial government commitments to the North. The two governments already had an ERDA instrument to permit them to work together in the province. The province placed very senior decision-making authority in the northern region across several of its departments, and in the budget of April 20, 1988, announced the $30-million Northern Heritage Fund. A board of nineteen was set up to manage the fund, with a mandate to help single-industry towns disrupted by layoffs, encourage the use of new technology in the natural resource businesses, and aid small-business start-ups. Given that there is only so much that can be done at any given time, the importance of close working relations between the two governments at the regional level is evident. By remaining within the jurisdiction of the ISTC, the federal northern operations have the backing of the full departmental apparatus of planning, policy, sectoral expertise, and administration at their disposal. FEDNOR remained the only regional development responsibility of ISTC as 1991 came to a close. With its original five-year sunset provision set at March 31, 1992, the agency sought public sector input on its future as 1992 began. On April 2, 1992, Tom Hockin, minister responsible for FEDNOR, announced a $60-million, five-year extension of the agency and the appointment of a full-time chair of its advisory board.

QUEBEC

Next was the problem faced by the federal government in Quebec. In one form or another the federal government had carried on regional development programming in that province for a number of years, even during the height of the strained relations of the early 1980s. The most formal and most significant arrangement used was the DREE federal-provincial GDA signed in March 1974, followed in December 1984 by a new ten-year ERDA. This arrangement ensured that the government of Quebec would have at least an equal say in determining the use of federal dollars for regional economic development programming, an influence it was to use to full effect.

With the national coordination of regional development activities disintegrating along with plans for separate initiatives in each region, the announcement of federal intentions for Quebec was anxiously awaited. Given the amounts of funding involved, it seemed unlikely that Quebec would be denied its share. Conversely, as was quickly made known on November 25, 1987, by Gil Rémillard, the minister designate for federal-provincial relations, Quebec would not acknowledge any federal jurisdiction in regional development in that province.[29] The debate between the two governments on how to effect regional development without disadvantage to either of them continued over the winter of 1988. Quebec ministers, in rejecting direct federal programming in the province, indicated their preference for essentially strings-free "block funding" transfers to the province. DRIE Minister Robert de Cotret had rejected such a suggestion in November 1987.

What was the nature of the federal plan for Quebec that it should precipitate this public debate between November 1987 and May 1988? In keeping with its new policy of targeted regional activity, the federal government had proposed carrying the concept even further in Quebec by the creation of four distinct regions; l'Est du Québec (Gaspésie-Bas-St Laurent), la Côte Nord, le Saguenay-Lac-St-Jean, and le Nord-Ouest du Québec. These were areas in which Canada and Quebec had collaborated in the past for regional development purposes. It would also have been difficult for the federal government to ignore a fifth area, Montreal. In December 1987, DRIE Minister de Cotret had revealed that the federal government agreed with sixty-three of the seventy-six recommendations put forward in the federally sponsored Picard report on the economic situation in the Montreal area.[30] He had further announced, on February 24, 1988, federal assistance totalling $275 million of new and existing money for the Montreal east end, but it was not well received. Despite protestations that the province and the federal government were working together, there was no joint announcement on Montreal East and city officials were unaware that the announcement was to take place. The province, while criticizing the federal government for dragging its feet, also announced $105 million of assistance for the area.[31]

What alarmed Quebec was the presumed federal intention to operate in the regions with federal officials, with funding allocated against a set of federally determined policy parameters. Quebec, if not to receive block funding, which it knew was not realistic, proposed including the regional development initiative under the Canada-Quebec Economic and Regional Development Agreement, with funding to match. The solution to the impasse had still not been reached by the end of May 1988, underlining the serious difference of views between the two levels of government on their respective rights and obligations in regional development terms. This is noteworthy, given that the Canada-Quebec ERDA signed December 14, 1984, states as a consideration, "The Government of Canada and the Government of Quebec agree that it is in the public interest to undertake and implement coordinated measures by their respective departments and agencies to improve the economic and regional development of Quebec." One stated objective of the ERDA was to facilitate cooperation between the two governments in implementing measures for economic and regional development through procedures of consultation and coordination.

By the following month, however, both governments had made sufficient concessions to allow an agreement to be reached. On June 9,

1988, the announcement of a $970-million financial package for Quebec signalled a reconciliation of views between the two governments. Reinforcing the significance of the event, Prime Minister Brian Mulroney and Premier Robert Bourassa were both present for the occasion. Canada and Quebec agreed to augment existing Quebec ERDA subsidiary agreements by $150 million, to be shared equally, and signed the new Canada-Quebec Subsidiary Agreement on the Economic Development of the Regions of Quebec. Until this time, Canada had steadfastly refused to consider extending the life of existing subsidiary agreements. It was generally perceived that the additional $75 million of federal funding for existing agreements was the price extracted by Quebec for agreeing to federal direct regional development programming in Quebec. For its part, however, Canada had made it clear that it was going ahead with some sort of plan, with or without the province. By its consent, Quebec had astutely ensured that the federal side would now have to recognize many of the same kinds of program elements in the new Canada-Quebec agreement that were present in the subsidiary agreements being extended by the two governments.

The new agreement provided a total of $820 million, with $440 million to be supplied by the federal government and $380 million by Quebec. The funding and activity was directed to two regional development blocks: Resource Regions and Central Regions. The Resource Regions grouping was further divided into five areas: Eastern Quebec, the North Shore, the North-Centre Region, Western Quebec, and Northern Quebec. Activity is concentrated on resource development, technology, business development, human resource development, and economic infrastructure support. The Central Regions block covers those areas of the province not included in the Resource Regions. Programming is targeted on business development for those areas embracing the Montreal–Quebec City axis along the St Lawrence River, which contains 84 percent of the province's population, and Hull-Gatineau to the West.

At the June signing, Gil Rémillard, Quebec minister responsible for intergovernmental affairs, reinforced both the collaborative significance of the event and the preservation of respective jurisdictions: "More significant than the dollar value of this agreement, is the importance of the collaboration framework that the two governments have established. The Agreement entered into by the government of Canada and the government of Quebec will ensure cooperation based on a real partnership with the utmost respect for the jurisdiction of both governments."[32] The Canada-Quebec Subsidiary Agreement on the Economic Development of the Regions of Quebec is an example of what two levels of government can accomplish when they put their minds to constructive examination of the economic development needs of a region and the means by which to achieve agreed-upon objectives. Quebec probably had its own way in much of the design and intended implementation of the agreement content, but that is of little matter. Although meticulous care was taken to ensure adequate credit and public exposure for the efforts of both governments under the agreement, there is no guarantee that such will necessarily be the case. No matter, again, unless the federal government were to become sufficiently picayune on the issue to try and delay or withdraw some of its involvement. This is not likely to happen, given the almost certain political backlash that would accompany such a move.

The Agreement

The structure of the Quebec agreement in terms of program content and delivery and underlying policy is a model that could be followed in other regions of the country. Though complex, it preserves the intent of federal-provincial collaboration and coordination to a greater degree than structures employed in other regions, while at the same time accomplishing meaningful regional economic development.

The objectives of the agreement are designed to strengthen the intent of the 1984 Canada-Quebec ERDA to enhance the province's comparative advantages and develop and strengthen productive businesses. They include mobilizing local entrepreneurs, fostering excellence and technological development, stimulating the development and processing of natural resources, diversifying the regional economic structure, improving market exploitation, and facilitating adaptation to change in the international economy (including the consequences of the Canada-US Free Trade Agreement). The organization and management of the agreement is complicated. Under the five Resource Regions listed above are five development frameworks: business development, research and technology development, natural resources development, economic infrastructure reinforcement, and human resource development. Each framework has specific objectives, instruments of programming, and assigned roles for each government.

Business development, which is aimed at small- and medium-sized businesses, is intended to encourage the entrepreneurial spirit. Goals include the stimulation of investment in the establishment, expansion, or modernization of businesses; improved productivity, product quality, and management capability; the development of marketing and opportunity identification skills, and the development of consulting services to businesses. Canada accepted the obligation to operate a

165

dedicated incentives program, comprising an industrial component and a tourism component, to support small- and medium-sized regional entrepreneurship and industrial diversification. Quebec assumed the obligation to deliver a program aimed at the diversification and expansion of business.

The research and technology development framework is aimed at including the regions in technology trends, strengthening the comparative advantage of certain sectors, and fostering the establishment of new activities based on advanced technology. Measures to accomplish these objectives include innovation and technology transfer, new product development and industrial design, improved production methods, marketing, consultant services, and networking. Under this element, Canada agreed to implement a program of testing and experimentation for the agri-food, fisheries, and aquaculture sectors.

Under the natural resource development framework, the emphasis is on resource management, conservation, and enhancement measures. Economic infrastructure reinforcement is directed at basic facilities and services for industrial and tourism purposes, including industrial technical centres and specialized training and research, chiefly benefiting small businesses and groups pursuing regional development objectives. Normal municipal infrastructure – roads, water and sewer systems, and municipal buildings – it not eligible under this program. Human resource development focuses on facilitating labour adjustment through teaching new production and marketing methods, upgrading technical and professional skills, and aiding the acquisition of skills in specialized fields.

The Central Regions grouping essentially comprises all regions not included in the Resource Regions category. Business development assistance is highlighted in the Central Regions and is aimed at strengthening productivity in the manufacturing sector, revitalizing the economy of disadvantaged regions, and developing the Montreal area. In the Montreal region programming is focused on high technology, international finance and trade, design, cultural industries, tourism, and transportation. Canada and Quebec both operate their own programs in the Central Regions. Canada delivers the Manufacturing Productivity Improvement Program (MPIP) to strengthen productivity in the small-business manufacturing sector. The province is responsible for industrial adjustment, an area that includes a businesses and business groups component, providing assistance for asset acquisition and technology and software packages and systems for projects targeting diversification of production, modernization, automation, application of new technologies, and market prospecting and diagnosis.

The elaborate organizational and management structure of the regional development approach in Quebec may be seen as either a sophisticated and highly professional system or the Achilles' heel of the billion-dollar venture. Program activity under the Quebec agreement can be one of four kinds, providing for a mix of unilateral, joint, or third-party project and program design and delivery. The important thing is that provision exists for the two governments to work independently of one another, together, or with a third party. There is also no doubt that the activities are structured to ensure that each government receives due credit for its efforts and financial commitments. For example, under economic infrastructure reinforcement, municipalities in the Resource Regions are eligible to participate in the program but must submit an application proposal to a management subcommittee. It is the provincial representative who rules on eligibility and so informs the federal member and the municipality. For an approved project, funds are conveyed by bank transfer. It seems clear from this procedure that the province controls what is to be considered for assistance and both governments try to ensure, through the means of payment, that they receive credit for their support. The agreement also has a schedule addressing the public information procedures to be followed by each party.

The management of the agreement is under an umbrella management committee, with one subcommittee for the Resource Regions and one for the Central Regions. For each of the five Resource Regions there is a consultative committee to advise ministers and a regional committee for the "concertation and coordination" of the actions of the two governments. There is a provision in the agreement by which the appropriate sector departments of the two governments are given the responsibility for developing and implementing programs and projects falling within their particular jurisdiction and area of expertise. Either the agreement is receiving some of the best and most efficient management ever accomplished under a federal-provincial arrangement or it is a bureaucratic nightmare. It is likely that as time has passed and program content has become settled, some of these advisory and consultative devices have fallen into disuse.

A review of the program coverage of the Quebec agreement suggests that the resources are spread too thin to accomplish all of its stated objectives. A more realistic approach would have been to more carefully and selectively concentrate on those areas of economic activity that would make the greatest difference to the provincial economy. Experience after two years of operation indicated a preoccupation with a myriad of programs and projects, each perhaps valid in an individual sense, but not contributing in a more complete way to a gain in regional economic development for the province.

The two governments had now reached a level of satisfaction on their respective obligations for regional development in Quebec, confirmed their commitment to the ERDA process for the period 1988–94, and agreed to undertake negotiations from January 1989 onwards to set the terms and conditions of the ERDA and related subsidiary agreements for its remaining four years. For its part, the agreement fitted plans that Quebec had been developing since at least 1986 for a more structured approach to regional development in the province.

For economic and social reasons the government of Quebec, by December 1987, had divided the province into sixteen regions. A year earlier it had instituted a series of conferences with the regions and had signed agreements with them on the government's regional development policies and programs. Quebec also undertook to place regional development concerns at the heart of government policies and actions, not unlike the intentions of the federal government in its 1982 reorganization of economic departments. Quebec carried its philosophy of regional development into its negotiations with Canada. It would seem from Quebec's own Plan d'action en matière de développement régional that it was able to dictate many of the terms relating to the signing of the June 1988 agreement.[33]

INDUSTRY, SCIENCE AND TECHNOLOGY CANADA

DRIE had its own ideas about regional development in Canada, even as final arrangements were being put in place for the agency approach. IRDP was to be abolished. The department's minister, Michel Côté, spoke of federal funds being used to assist regions in developing their natural strengths rather than to attract companies to improbable locations. He said, "We cannot afford to spend millions of dollars on projects that have no chance of being economically viable just for the sake of appearing to do something about regional disparity."[34] (Côté may have been out of touch with what the department had been doing in its short life, unless he was concentrating on Sinclair Stevens's efforts to coax companies to Cape Breton). The department was thinking of building the soft infrastructures of regions—research and development, training capabilities, and better government-wide cohesion of effort. Michel Côté stepped down under a cloud, the agency concept was launched, and Industry, Science and Technology Canada was born. The ideas being tossed around in DRIE were incarnated in ACOA and WD.

Bill C-128, the act to establish the new Department of Industry, Science and Technology, was introduced for first reading in the House on May 12, 1988. It provided a clear legislative basis for the department to practise regional development in Ontario and Quebec. Clause 6(2) under Powers, Duties and Functions of the Minister granted that "the powers, duties and functions of the Minister extend to and include all matters over which Parliament has jurisdiction (not otherwise assigned) ... relating to regional economic development in Ontario and Quebec." The bill also provided wide programming latitude to the new department in Ontario and Quebec equal to that of ACOA and WD. The bill left no doubt about federal intentions for these two provinces. Bill C-128 died on the order paper when Parliament was dissolved prior to the November 21, 1988, election but reappeared as Bill C-3 on April 12, 1989. It moved rapidly through committee and debate in the House, was passed on June 22, and received royal assent on January 30, 1990. All of its essential ingredients remained intact.

The federal government's emphasis on entrepreneurship, technology, skills upgrading, international marketing, and service industries was retained in the ISTC mandate. The department was also to be much more selective in the application of financial assistance programs. The IRDP was terminated in June 1988 in favour of more regionally tailored programs. The new department would collaborate with private business, the science community, other federal departments, and other levels of government to promote international competitiveness and industrial excellence in Canada.[35] ISTC aims to renew and expand the scientific, technological, managerial, and production base in Canada and to develop its own intelligence-gathering system. It has staked out an advocacy role for itself in support of sound industrial and technological development; in this capacity, it hopes to influence the policies of other government departments and agencies. ISTC acknowledges that these policies should have a greater impact on the economic climate in the country than do the financial incentives programs, but it has nevertheless incorporated the authority in its legislation for an array of incentives schemes to be deployed, as appropriate, to further the above-stated objectives.

The somewhat forgotten regional operations of ISTC still hold many good ideas for economic improvement in Canada's peripheral areas, anchored by sector strategies that continue to form part of the department's mandate. By accessing ISTC-sector expertise, ACOA and WD could avoid costly duplication in the agencies, an important consideration given that so many ideas for regional development are built on industry, science, and technology. ACOA and WD both stress broader infrastructure support to small- and medium-sized business through technology diffusion, skills upgrading, and the like, and ISTC collaboration would be a valuable addition.

ISTC continued to play its direct role in northern Ontario and Quebec until April 21, 1991, when another reordering of ministerial responsibilities again eroded its already narrow regional development base. In a major cabinet shuffle, the responsibilities for regional development in Quebec followed then minister Benoît Bouchard to his new portfolio of National Health and Welfare. The new agency, the Federal Office of Regional Development (Quebec), based in that province and in Ottawa, was put in place with order-in-council authority, thus creating a fourth regional development organization in the country. The tightening of the ISTC mandate to a more centralist, nationalist focus removes the department from any genuinely effective role in regional development in Canada. Its new minister, former finance minister Michael Wilson, is also charged with the responsibility for International Trade, returning the relationship between industry and trade to the position that existed prior to the 1982 reorganization of economic departments that sent trade to External Affairs. In announcing the new super-ministry assignment for Wilson, the prime minister said that the change would create the best possible circumstances for assisting Canadian industry to respond to the challenges of globalization and competitiveness. The two departments continue as separate entities, however, although the logistics of this, from the private sector point of view, will be tested. Wilson also chairs the new Cabinet Committee on Economic and Trade Policy. On October 29, 1991, the department issued a discussion paper, *Prosperity through Competitiveness*, in which it identified learning, science and technology, financing investment, a competitive domestic market, and international trade as priority areas for attention. This further emphasizes the department's preoccupation with national/international competitiveness and the move away from all but marginal involvement with direct regional development. Nevertheless, ISTC's degree of success in reaching its objectives will be of great significance to regional economies.

An Assessment of Performance

The Conservatives had now closed the loop in their regional development intentions for the country. Two distinct agencies led the attack in the Atlantic and western provinces. From 1988 until 1991, Industry, Science and Technology Canada, with a supporting cast of other federal departments, took the lead in executing the Quebec initiative. In 1991 the Quebec initiative, too, received its own distinct identity. An ISTC adjunct, FEDNOR, held sway in northern Ontario. Even with this array of organizations and instruments dedicated to regional development, the government continued to employ ad hoc measures of procurement, locate federal facilities in the regions, and support public and private projects as they came to mind or were lobbied for by provincial governments and special interest groups.

As the decade of the 1990s began, more than three years had elapsed since the federal government announced a revitalized attack on regional economic inequalities. To what extent did the creation of ACOA, WD, and FEDNOR in 1987 and the Economic Development of the Regions of Quebec Agreement in 1988 reflect a deliberate regional development policy of the 1984 Conservative government? What were the implications for the allocation of federal and provincial responsibilities in the field? To what degree did the extensive consultative process and the recommendations of the different groups studying regional development in Canada influence government policy?

Although the Macdonald Commission had been established by a Liberal regime, the Conservative government took what it wanted from its report but did not publicly subscribe to its regional development recommendations. The evidence is slight that the report was a building block for Conservative regional development policy, especially since the government discarded the commission's recommendations on the relative roles for the federal and the provincial governments, including the suggestion that the federal government vacate the field of direct company incentives.

Given the broadness of the federal policy objectives, it is difficult to deny that some of the commitments made by the government in the 1985 "Intergovernmental Position Paper on the Principles and Framework for Regional Economic Development" may be found in the actions taken in 1987 and 1988. By 1989, fewer than one-third of the original signatories to the position paper remained in their portfolio or even in the government – there had been five changes of government at the provincial level. It is equally difficult to say how much influence the report of the Federal-Provincial Task Force on Regional Development Assessment, dated May 1987, had on the government's thinking as revealed in the summer of 1987. Certain of its suggestions are found in some of the operational parameters developed by the agencies themselves. The government selected only parts of the recommendations of the Savoie report, which had been specifically commissioned by the Prime Minister's Office to present views on the Atlantic Canada Opportunities Agency.

Incrementality

Questions raised as to the true incrementality of the original $1.05 billion allocated in the Atlantic region and the $1.2 billion in the West were valid, not because of any intentional deception on the part of the government, but simply because of the accounting and coordination difficulties associated with the identification and recording of agreed-upon regional development expenditures. The Ontario and Quebec programs fall into a somewhat different discipline. At any one time, under the ERDA agreements alone, hundreds of millions of dollars of commitments are outstanding, both in total agreement terms and in annual cash flows.[36] The agreements are individually managed across a dozen different federal departments, with a number of them expiring each year. There are the grants, contributions, loans and loan guarantees, interest buy-down schemes, differentiated investment tax credits, and other program expenditures designed for regional development purposes. There are those federal expenditures that are not made in the name of regional development, but which dwarf the dedicated funding of ACOA, WD, and the Quebec agreement and have enormous impact on regional economies. This poses real problems for the calculation of the historical average annual expenditure level for comparative purposes.

The prime minister, quoted in the editorial of the *Financial Times* of June 15, 1987, spoke of $1.05 billion of new money for ACOA and went on to stress, "We will maintain the present level of spending on regional development and in addition we are committing $1.05 billion to the region over the next five years. This is not a 'topping-up.' It is not old money in a different guise. It is a commitment of new resources to a new agency for new programs in the Atlantic Region." In introducing the ACOA legislation in the House on January 18, 1988, John Crosbie was equally clear: "We will continue spending on these programs [ERDAS] or similar programs and will add to that level another $1.05 billion over the next five years. Our commitment is for an additional $200 million yearly for five years."[37]

In simple terms, the comparative base could be calculated by averaging expenditure levels of explicit regional development programs over a chosen period of time. The interval selected would have to be the 1985–87 three-year period during which the Conservative government was in power to the time of announcement. Indeed, in his January 18, 1988, speech in the House, Crosbie dwelled on the increased level of ERDA expenditures in Atlantic Canada since the Conservatives had been in power, quoting $198.5 million as the annual average over three years. In direct incentives to business, annual DRIE Industrial and Regional Development Program commitments in the four Atlantic provinces averaged $53.9 million over the three fiscal years 1984–85 to 1986–87, but this amount has to be discounted to reach the actual

172

expenditure figure. If the unusually high commitment level in New Brunswick in 1985–86 is removed, the average is closer to $40 million. In the five-year period 1978–79 to 1982–83, average annual (DREE) Regional Development Incentives Program commitments were $32.8 million. Average annual expenditures were $23.3 million.[38] Similar data could be developed nationally on these two high-profile programs and on other more directed programs such as the Atlantic Enterprise Program, the Enterprise Cape Breton Program, and WTIDP in the West. The match of the DREE and DRIE program activities to ACOA and WD programs would have to be carefully developed to ensure accuracy of comparison.

These programs represent the ones that are easy to cost because of their visibility and methods of data recording. Other activities would be more difficult to handle. Whatever the comparative base finally calculated, an additional $200 million per year in Atlantic Canada puts annual expenditures within the reach of a half billion dollars. The president of ACOA, in discouraging the idea that ACOA funding would be used for infrastructure, had said that "it is fair to say that the thrust is towards improving the competitive circumstances of the individual entrepreneurs."[39] Is it realistic to expect such annual expenditure levels in Atlantic Canada if the ACOA programs concentrate on small- and medium-sized business to the exclusion of infrastructure and all the other kinds of things that would find their place under subsidiary agreements?[40]

ACOA writes subsidiary agreements in its own name, but it is impossible to say if the activity is incremental compared to what would have taken place without its presence. Even with the flexibility inherent in the ACOA mandate, the danger exists of indiscriminate action in order to meet relatively arbitrary dollar targets.[41] Given the way the $1.02 billion was announced, it would be reasonable to conclude that the spending was to be by ACOA, exclusive of other federal subsidiary agreement activity, but there is little doubt that the funding has been used to top up the programs of other departments. Under the guise of maintaining existing spending levels in the regions, other federal departments may concoct schemes within their mandates to share in ERDA base-line budgets. Within a region, each province may expect to be guaranteed the same base spending level that it had in 1987, for example, as well as some guaranteed percentage of announced incremental funding for the region as a whole.[42] Newfoundland devoted over half of a discussion paper on ACOA to the funding question, belabouring the point that funding percentages should return to those of the DREE days, recommending specific funding levels by province for the ACOA budget, and insisting that the budgets of other federal government departments not be incorporated into ACOA so as to avoid blurring the incremental effort.[43]

The difficulty in determining accurate base lines for comparative purposes and the real commitment of the Mulroney government to regional development in Canada were starkly exposed in the April 27, 1989, budget. It had become increasingly clear that the government was backing away from many of the promises it had made during the fall 1988 election campaign, and even from what the government itself had described as pre-election commitments. By March of 1989, fears were surfacing that regional development funding was going to be cut. It was rumoured that the $300-million B.C. Forest Resource Development Agreement would be axed before its 1990 termination date, despite the province's request to negotiate a $700-million renewal.[44] Manitoba, Saskatchewan, and the four Atlantic provinces said that no progress was being made on the negotiation of new agreements despite the scheduled expiration of existing agreements on March 31. It was predicted that $6 billion of activity was in jeopardy and that skilled people across all economic sectors might leave the area. New Brunswick even offered to carry the federal government financially for a year in that province.[45] Credibility was lent to the fears being expressed when Minister of Industry, Science and Technology, Harvie Andre was quoted as saying that fewer deals might be made and at different cost-sharing ratios.[46]

Confusion continued to reign after the April 27 budget. On May 1, Hyman Solomon of the *Financial Post* said that the scare headlines of previous weeks had been disproved by the budget's earmarking $1.1 billion annually for the following five years for regional development instead of the $832 million per year dispensed over the previous five years. However, on May 8, he said "Even regional development, which was cleverly portrayed in the budget papers as a 35% increase in funding over the next five years, ... is really a sharp cut of several hundred million dollars from the past two years."[47] The budget papers drew a distinction between explicit regional development efforts, described as a more narrowly defined set of programs and policies, and the large number and variety of federal activities that could also be viewed as supporting regional development. Regional development expenditure patterns and intentions were expressed in these terms:

Total spending over the 1984–85 to 1988–89 period is estimated at $4.2 billion. This compares to $2.8 billion over the previous five-year period. On an annual basis, spending has increased from

$0.6 billion in 1984–85 to an estimated $1.3 billion in 1988–89 ... the current all-time high levels of spending under regional development programs are not fiscally sustainable. The budget therefore provides for a consolidation of the federal commitment to regional development ... Although overall funding will be higher over the next five years as a whole, adjusting from peak year expenditure levels to the more fiscally sustainable funding levels now established will result in short-term constraints on regional agency budgets.

Federal expenditures on these regional development program activities over the 1989–90 to 1993–94 period are established at an estimated $5.6 billion—a figure some 35 per cent higher than estimated actual expenditures over the past five years. On a year-to-year basis, following a projected peaking of expenditures at close to $1.4 billion in 1989–90, annual funding provisions will be stabilized at somewhat over $1 billion a year. This compares with an annual average spending level of some $830 million over the past five years. While constraints will be experienced over the short term, over the next five years as a whole funding in each region, with the exception of Ontario, will exceed estimated spending levels over the past five years.[48]

It is not too surprising that the budget papers led to varying interpretations. The situation was further aggravated a short three weeks later when it was learned that the reduction from the peak spending levels was to be achieved through the "re-profiling" (a favourite expression of bureaucrats for spreading out expenditures over longer periods of time) of some expenditure commitments and absolute reductions in others. ACOA's budget was to be spread over seven years, not five, and the Western Diversification budget was to cover six and one-half years. Senior federal officials were quoted as saying that the regional development budget was to be cut 25 percent after inflation and that cuts averaging 6 percent per year would follow in each of the next three years, for a total reduction approaching $2 billion by 1994. The cuts were to hit the federal-provincial ERDA agreements most heavily. The prime minister continued to say that spending would be up 51 percent over the previous five-year period, but he was immediately challenged in the media by a counter-claim that spending on a year-over-year basis would be in fact off by 7 percent.[49] The budget imposed a ceiling on ACOA projects of $200,000 for many of the Action Program elements, further reducing the flexibility of the agency.[50]

Without a detailed explanation of the composition of the projected regional development expenditures to 1993–94, information not forth-coming from the federal government, it is difficult to determine how realistic the 1989 budget statement was. It is more than likely that the totals arrived at included ongoing commitments from previous ACOA and WD budgets and other commitments already made, but not expended, of countless other federal programs. The level of new money actually available for new, or uncommitted, initiatives for the period ending in 1993–94 could very well be substantially less than the amounts announced in the budget.

By the summer of 1989 the federal government's intentions relating to the ERDA subsidiary agreements started to emerge, giving some credibility to earlier provincial concerns. In June a spokesperson for federal Tourism Minister Thomas Hockin revealed the abandonment of tourism subsidiary agreements across the country, a decision said to cost the four Atlantic provinces the federal share of $90 million of planned activity.[51] In late June, Newfoundland signed subsidiary agree-ments worth $83.3 million, the province's share being 30 percent. The indication that Newfoundland's contribution was to stay at 30 percent was reflected in subsequent agreements signed at that level—for example, a $64.3-million 1991 forestry agreement consummated on the same terms. On August 3, 1989, New Brunswick struck a five-year, $174.6-million deal with Canada by which the province would contribute 44 percent of the cost, considerably higher than the 20 percent frequently employed in earlier agreements. Nova Scotia came on board on September 22, 1989, agreeing in principle to three pacts valued at $62 million, but with federal cost sharing down from 70 percent to 55 percent on two of them and 60 percent on the other. In 1988 the province had signed $269 million worth of agreements in agriculture and urban development. The contest continued into 1991 with an angry British Columbia signing a forestry agreement con-taining a reduction of federal funding from $150 million to $100 million over five years and with forestry negotiations stalled with Ontario as Canada proposed reducing its five-year funding from $75 million to $25 million.

What does incrementality really represent? The report of the (ACOA) minister for the fiscal year 1988–89 claimed that federal funding for regional development in Atlantic Canada rose from an average annual level of $185 million in the period 1979–84 to $287 million in 1984–89 and would average $425 million in 1989–94. It reported expendi-tures of $479 million for the year 1988–89 and predicted a level of $500 million for 1989–90.[52] The definition of federal expenditures includes the ACOA Action Program, funds for the Cooperation Program federal-provincial agreements, and funds specifically dedicated to regional development spending by other federal departments.[53] The calculation of the base line is not given.

The only conclusion that can be reached is that the summation of all federal activities that one wishes to include in the calculation of regional development expenditure is impressive. In the Atlantic, DREE annual expenditures exceeded $200 million per year from 1974 onwards and, with the addition of many other kinds of federal expenditures, such as the financial support to the Cape Breton Development Corporation (Devco), could probably be levered up to a half billion dollars per year with little difficulty. The most important remaining consideration is the nature and quality of the activities supported.

Continuing Programming

In addition to their direct action programs, ACOA and WD continued to be involved with Cooperation Program agreements, in their own name and in cooperation with other federal departments. One result of this was that ACOA and WD made joint announcements with the provinces of projects under subsidiary agreements that had been, and in many cases continued to be, the responsibility of other federal line departments. In the West, for example, WD jointly announced loan assistance to sixty-nine companies to mid-January 1988 under cost-shared small-business incentives programs. Over $25 million of government assistance was announced by WD under the Canada–British Columbia Industrial Development Subsidiary Agreement. To the end of 1988, assistance of over $3 million to twenty-nine companies was committed under the Canada-Alberta Agriculture Processing and Marketing Agreement (APMA). By June 1989 the APMA had been fully subscribed at 324 projects and $27 million and the receipt of applications was discontinued. Well into 1988, WD was announcing funding under the former DRIE IRDP. In the Atlantic region, ACOA continued to jointly announce project assistance under the Canada–New Brunswick Industrial Innovation and Technology Development Agreement.

Neither the subsidiary agreement projects being announced on behalf of the federal government nor those announced under then existing incentives programs such as the IRDP could be considered incremental to the level of assistance existing at the time of the formation of ACOA and WD. The majority, if not all, of the company-specific projects assisted by the agencies would have been eligible under IRDP, WTIDP, AEP, ECB, and like programs that were taken over by ACOA and WD. Although not widely known, DRIE's Industrial and Regional Development Program contained authority to provide financial incentives for the service industries sector. Regulations to permit this feature to become operational were being developed in DRIE but were put on hold until a major study of the service industries was completed. There was a legitimate concern that there would be a proliferation of service industry projects before some understanding of the true economic benefit of that sector had been discovered in regional economic development terms. The study was completed in late 1988 and is dealt with more completely in chapter 7.

A review of the range and nature of the announced ACOA and WD incentives program projects confirms little of a proactive development strategy — rather, the projects appear to be a client response to a passive program, one of the earlier criticisms of both RDIP and IRDP.[54] The business infrastructure and similar kinds of generally larger-projects assistance pursued by ACOA and WD encourage one to believe that the regional agencies are striving to meet their mandates of upgrading the underpinning of business and technology. At the same time, these kinds of things would also have been possible under an existing (probably DRIE) subsidiary agreement of one form or another. Incrementality in funding is less significant than incrementality in activity. The evidence indicates little of the latter, but the question is one that can be neither proved nor disproved easily.

Coordination of Regional Development Effort and Advocacy

The coordination of federal government activity in the name of regional development is a component of the acts that established ACOA and WD. It is one of the four planks of the Atlantic agency's mandate. Little is heard, however, of the role the agencies play in the ongoing administration of subsidiary agreements and the negotiation of new agreements. A critical question persists on the degree to which the agencies are able to influence the subsidiary-agreement intentions of other federal departments. National and interregional coordination of economic activities affecting the regions was lost with the disbandment of MSERD. Even the coordination and review mechanisms that did exist experienced difficulty in influencing the activities of individual federal departments. To suggest that coordination can take place at cabinet committee is unrealistic. Ministers can make decisions among alternatives, but they cannot be expected to collectively develop those alternatives when considering individual program initiatives.

As a First Ministers' Conference agenda item, the broad principles of regional development policy could be further debated and agreed upon. Individual actions by region, however, would not merit this kind of attention, nor would it be possible to deal with them in such a forum. Subcommittees of FMCs could examine individual situations.

An example is the subcommittee struck to look at interprovincial trade, an item referred to first ministers for special attention by the 1985 Committee of Regional Development Ministers. The Intergovernmental Committee of Ministers on Internal Trade was formed to identify barriers, receive representations, and take such other actions as may be required to reduce barriers to interregional trade.[55] The committee established two working panels to address liquor board marketing practices and procurement, but progress was slow. Five years later, no agreements had actualy been signed between the provinces, although agreement in principle was received at successive FMCs. As 1990 began, hope was expressed that by August of that year an agreement on procurement would be in effect and that recommendations would be made on a dispute resolution mechanism. Yet more than a year later, little real progress had been reported and the Canadian Manufacturers' Association called for a Canadian common market for interprovincial trade, which it estimated would produce savings of over $6 billion.[56]

In its September 24, 1991, constitutional paper *Shaping Canada's Future Together*, the federal government renewed its plea for the dismantlement of interprovincial trade barriers—a component of its proposal for economic union in Canada—and proposed amending section 121 of the Constitution to this effect. Exemption from the provision would still be permitted, however, for regional development purposes. The report of the Special Joint Committee on a Renewed Canada (the Beaudoin-Dobbie report), released February 29, 1992, in its recommendations for the free movement of goods, services, people, and capital in Canada, retained the idea of still permitting domestic trade restrictions in the interests of regional development.

The sharing of direct responsibility for regional development among ministers (there were five of them at the outset—ministers Murray, Crosbie, Kelleher, de Cotret, and McKnight before the November 21, 1988, election) and the practice of having "regional" ministers advise those carrying the direct responsibility provide one forum for decision taking among options, but this approach does little for overall operational coordination. Competition among ministers may even aggravate the coordination problem. The required spadework to develop policy and program options no longer rests with any one federal organization.

Just as important as the coordination of the policies and actions of dedicated regional development departments and agencies are the identification, coordination, and development of policy alternatives for those activities not ordinarily thought of in terms of their impact on regional economies. The controversy that surrounded federal decisions on the Canadian Patrol Frigate Program, the CF18, and the Polar 8 icebreaker (subsequently cancelled in the February 20, 1990, federal budget), to name but three, illustrates the specific contradictions that can arise for federal decision makers. An important question in regard to these large, one-of-a-kind project decisions is the degree to which the agency people are part of the process that defines regional development consequences.

Section 5(2) of Bill C-103, the act establishing ACOA, states that "the Minister [of ACOA] shall coordinate the policies and programs of the Government of Canada in relation to opportunity for economic development in Atlantic Canada." Bill C-113, section 5(2) makes a similar statement respecting "development and diversification of the economy of Western Canada." In speaking to this in the House, then transport minister John Crosbie went even further in his interpretation of the bill when he said, "No federal department will be able to operate in Atlantic Canada without input from this agency" and "The Minister is given unprecedented authority to coordinate all policies and programs of the government of Canada in relation to opportunity for economic development in Atlantic Canada."[57] Crosbie spoke of agency input, but not veto, leaving in doubt the real authority of the agency to have a final say in the plans of federal departments. Given the impact that a large project can have on a subregional economy, it is critical that the agencies have a real voice on the large initiatives unfolding in their regions. There is the danger, however, that such a role may lead to interregional competition or advocacy for projects that may be less than viable over the long run. The agencies have had some success in talking their way onto interdepartmental committees that exist to consider major procurement projects (usually defined as over $100 million), selectively attending those of particular interest to their region or on which they might have an influence. This does not alleviate interregional rivalry, since representatives from the different agencies/regions compete with one another at such meetings. Some of the most sensitive decisions, such as that concerning the Space Agency, were taken only at the cabinet committee level.[58] These mechanisms still do not accommodate the need for formalized collaboration between the various entities charged with the responsibility of economic development in Canada's regions. Sporadic instances have come to light that indicate a less than satisfactory arrangement for dealing with interregional issues.

In July 1988 the *Financial Post* highlighted a disagreement between ACOA and WD on a national procurement policy for projects over $100 million, saying that the differing views held by the two agencies had defeated an attempt to bring some order in the federal decision-making process vis-à-vis such significant influences on regional economies. Even cabinet was apparently unable to resolve the issue.[59] Another example of interregional oversight relates to land registration systems in the Maritimes and the West. During the 1970s, DREE put millions of dollars into the cost-shared, sophisticated Land Registration and Information Service in New Brunswick, Nova Scotia, and Prince Edward Island, which was turned over to the provinces in 1978. It was developed to provide the basis for land registration and management and resource management and exploitation. The technology was to have a high potential for export sale. On January 26, 1989, Western Diversification announced $400,000 of assistance to a company that planned to develop a Land Related Information System to assist in land titles and assessment, water resources, transportation planning, utility management, and resource and land management in Western Canada. Once in operation, the system was to have "significant potential for export sales." On March 17, 1989, the *Globe and Mail* reported that the Maritime LRIS was to be disbanded and that each province would take over responsibility in its own jurisdiction. The same article indicated that NB was again asking the federal government to assist it in developing a mapping industry in that province. It is hard to believe that DREE would not have brought some coherence into the federal approach to such a situation.

Still unresolved is the question of how coordination can be effected in a meaningful way without slowing the entire decision-making process of government. The deputy minister of western economic diversification originally chaired an interdepartmental committee of deputies that provided a forum for discussion for that region, but the committee fell into disuse after a period of time. When the heads of ACOA and WD meet together or with other senior department heads, it is on an ad hoc basis only.

The most serious conclusion to be reached on the government's 1987 policy redirection is that there is no forum for overall, national reflection on regional development policy, no place where sectoral policies are reconciled with regional development intentions, and no mechanism to even ensure coordination between the regional development organizations themselves. By November 1988, questions were being asked around Ottawa along these same lines. An ad hoc committee of deputy ministers involving ACOA, WD, ISTC, and certain other departments was put together to look at the situation. It reported to Privy Council the opinion that the existing approach was working satisfactorily, consultation practices were adequate, and issues of common interest to the three prime agencies were best dealt with on

181

an ad hoc basis. One might legitimately ask what constitutes an issue of "common interest" and what happens in those cases not perceived as being of common interest.

The ad hoc committee reiterated a commitment to the principles of differentiated regional development approaches, autonomous delivery agencies under separate ministers, and collective decision making by ministers on sectoral and regional development priority setting. The deputies also reached a consensus on consulting on the preparation of memoranda to cabinet, periodic meetings on policy, early consultation between sectoral departments and regional development agencies, and the importance of a departmental lead role being assigned on major projects. Committees of deputy ministers do provide one forum for discussion, but there is no indication of how successful the forum is in influencing the policies and actions of other departments or in effecting cooperation between regions. It is possible that discussions dwell more frequently on what the agencies are up to or whether they are in conflict with other government departments, rather than the reverse. They are no substitute for a recognized focal point for policy reflection.

A report written for ACOA by Donald Savoie, titled *ACOA: Transition to Maturity*, confirms the fears expressed herein as to the application of incentives programs in the region and the degree of success achieved in program and policy coordination, cooperation, and advocacy. Savoie concluded that the agency had adopted a reactive approach to applications under the Action Program and that a continuation of the emphasis on establishment and expansion of Atlantic firms under the program could not be judged as successful as it might have been. He summed up ACOA's advocacy and coordination mandate elements by saying that few, even inside the agency, would argue that ACOA had been successful. Significantly, he emphasized the danger mentioned above, that advocacy was a one-way street to Ottawa, with scant interest paid to the agency's views and calling for a more formal mechanism of ACOA input to policy memoranda and presence at policy briefings. Throughout the report he identified the lack of a strategic framework and overall regional game plan as a fundamental weakness of the agency.[60]

National Policy Versus Ad Hoc Intervention

In the name of regional development, the Conservative government continued to announce assistance to large, firm-specific projects in Canada both within and outside the context of the agencies, despite earlier statements to the contrary.[61] The breach of any non-intervention

182

policy took place in September 1984, the new government's first month in office, with a commitment of $15 million to the Pétromont petrochemical operation in the Montreal/Varennes area of Quebec. The outgoing Liberal government had made one $15-million commitment in 1983, but Minister Ed Lumley had adamantly refused further such assistance in June of 1984. In April 1985, the damage became irreparable when the government bowed to pressure to provide assistance, against the advice of officials, to a billion-dollar Domtar pulp mill renewal at Windsor Mills, Quebec. The DRIE minister, Sinclair Stevens, had refused to participate in the project but was overruled by the prime minister. Domtar became the rallying point for those who opposed government intervention in the economy and the precedent for a flood of applications from other companies for similar assistance. It was still being cited in 1989 as a capitulation by the government to big business.[62] The Domtar mistake was followed in December of the same year by a further $55.8 million of federal assistance to Pétromont.[63] The irony was that the Pétromont announcement was completely overshadowed by the announced shutdown of the Montreal Gulf Oil refinery, which led to the resignation of besieged Environment Minister Suzanne Blais-Grenier.

An analysis of government intervention in private sector projects is a study in itself and would not be restricted to the behaviour of the Mulroney Conservatives since 1984. The focus is on this period, however, because of what that party had said while in opposition. A quick review shows that Repap, a Canadian company that was in the process of becoming one of North America's largest catalogue/insert coated-paper producers and that had already received significant DRIE financial assistance in 1984–85, was offered another $32.5 million of federal funding for a New Brunswick mill expansion.[64] Daishowa, a Japanese company, was offered federal monies amounting to $9.5 million for infrastructure assistance (and $65.2 million for transportation and other infrastructure assistance from Alberta) towards a $500-million greenfield bleached-kraft pulp mill.[65] In September 1991, a year after coming into production, the mill was reported to be for sale. The Donohue company turned sod in 1988 in Matane, Quebec, for a new $287-million pulp mill while awaiting massive government assistance.[66] Still in the forest products sector, Millar Western asked for $50 million from the Western Diversification fund for a mill project in Saskatchewan, and Scott Paper said that "federal and provincial government assistance was expected" for a $110-million pulp mill in Quebec.[67]

Perhaps one of the saddest cases of misplaced funding in the forest industries sector was the ITT-Rayonnier mill at Port Cartier, Quebec. Found to be an expensive albatross to the company from its inception and moth-balled in 1979 after losses estimated at $600 million, efforts continued to be made to have it start up again in that high-unemployment region of Quebec. In January 1986, after the pounding taken by the federal government for not interfering in the just recently closed Gulf Oil refinery in Montreal, discussions took place between Canada and Quebec to decide whether something could be done at Port Cartier. The mill was reopened with direct funding primarily from Quebec through its crown corporation Rexfor. The mill closed again in the summer of 1991. It was evident that federal financial assistance to large, regionally important projects, had become a foregone conclusion.

Such actions call into question the degree to which the federal government has had any national policy for regional development and whether it will ever be able to resist the temptation of large, firm-specific grants. The lesson to be learned from such experiences, which governments steadfastly refuse to learn, is that the political cost of providing funding to large private sector projects that should be viable in their own name is enormous, particularly in areas not favoured with such largesse. In the pulp and paper sector, in particular, the federal government has been plagued with controversy over the years. Criticism clung to grants to companies that could afford to do their own financing. The private sector attacked the government's inability to resist overtures to assist projects not considered viable by the industry itself. The companies involved in pulp and paper are large, they are usually multinationals, and they can raise financing in their own name. The high-quality and scarce forest resource in Canada will sooner or later have companies chasing it. Many of the problems associated with resource sector project financing are attribuable to ownership by large conglomerates that are able to earn a better return on their money elsewhere. These are not problems that governments should be asked to solve.

Unfortunately for the government, in the eyes of the voting public, its success rate in funding projects considered to be in the national interest or part of its ongoing federal responsibilities has been as controversial as its support of the private sector. The June 1989 debate that swirled around the relocation of the federal Space Agency to St-Hubert, Quebec, reached new heights of personal accusations and innuendo. The Mulroney government gained little credit for its decision, and an area that could have stimulated some sense of national pride became tainted with the suggestion of blatant political patronage.[68] The decisions on the geographic or economically most logical location of such major projects as the CF18, the CF18 maintenance program, and the Frigate program led to speculation about the government's motives for its actions. They caused vigorous, often acrimonious debate in the House of Commons, debate that rarely effected any decision reversals but that left the government alone in bearing the brunt of any criticism generated.[69] Given the evident political nature of some of the decisions, the government could hardly expect House support for some of the things it chose to do, even though the opposition would be cautious in its criticism of actions purporting to benefit a disadvantaged area of the country. The public comment that accompanied the federal government's decision of July 18, 1988, to proceed with the Hibernia energy project (rather than with other projects judged more viable at the time) suggested that the government had made a political decision that implied great cost to the Canadian taxpayer.[70]

The Hibernia story is another instance of optimism turning to pessimism. With over 1,000 people working on the project, Gulf Oil, one of the key consortium members, announced its pull-out in February 1992. The project was put on hold; layoffs followed immediately, along with predictions of cancellation if a new consortium member could not be found. Canada and Newfoundland tried not to be so negative but dispelled any hope that they would come to the rescue with additional monies. Once again the lives of residents of a peripheral part of the country were being toyed with.

And one other federal bail-out decision that won the government no friends outside of Quebec was its July 1991 injection of $263 million into the provincially owned MIL Group's shipyard at Lauzon, Quebec, to enable it to survive long enough to honour its obligations as a subcontractor to Saint John Shipbuilding in the building of navy frigates for the Canadian government. This was taking place at the time that Versatile Pacific of Vancouver, which was to have built the Polar-8 icebreaker for Canada, was on the verge of bankruptcy. Charges of sacrificing West Coast shipbuilding in favour of eastern Canadian yards were widespread.

Delegated Authorities

A key element in the operations of ACOA, WD, FEDNOR, and the Quebec undertaking is the level of decision-making authority delegated to the regions to complement the wide-ranging program flexibility inherent in the program instruments. It was said that 90 percent of the decisions under the ACOA Action Program were taken at the provincial level. Such was the case with the DREE RDIP years before. It can be misleading to judge decision-making authorities on percentages of projects approved in the regions. It is probably true that in the small- and medium-sized business segment, 90 percent of the projects would be picked up under the delegated authorities.[71] More important is the degree of regional decision-making authority for major activities under subsidiary agreements and the more generic program activities inherent in the mandates of ACOA and WD.

During the life of the DREE GDAs, officials had essentially unlimited project decision authority under the subsidiary agreements until the 1982 DREE/ITC merger. At the beginning of 1989, the Atlantic Canada Opportunities Agency held by far the highest levels of authority delegated to the regional development organizations. ACOA provincial vice-presidents held on-site decision-making authority up to $1 million of crown assistance, with projects between $1 million and $10 million going to the minister. In the West, the deputy minister of WD held decision-making authority over all projects up to $250 thousand of crown assistance, with those from that level to $10 million going to the minister. The deputy minister of WD's practice of approving virtually all western project offers, along with the minister, has been defended in terms of region-wide consistency, in itself an important consideration. With the experience time brings, field managers might have been accorded a share in the project decision making to facilitate project negotiation. On balance, however, the WD's is a lower-risk approach than that practised in Atlantic Canada, where criticism was not lacking over how ACOA was spending its money. The situation differed significantly with the ISTC-managed initiatives. Regional officials carried only $100,000 of delegated authority, with the junior minister responsible for decisions involving projects from that level to $1 million and the senior minister for those between $1 million and $10 million; in all cases the reference is to crown assistance. Projects over $10 million go to Treasury Board for approval, and those over $20 million to cabinet.

The delegation of authority will frequently change at the whim of the minister and his or her desire to exercise direct control over program operations, and the values of the authorities may or may not have held over time. With different levels for each region, there is the failing of no national coordination, inconsistent application of criteria, injurious competition, and—of real danger—inadequate budget control. Thus, the ACOA budget was seemingly out of control by early 1989, requiring expensive remedial action.[72]

CONCLUSIONS

In 1987 the government of Prime Minister Brian Mulroney put its own stamp on regional development in Canada. Economic policy, planning, programming, and decision making were distributed across the country in a series of unconnected organizational entities, two of which were accorded their own legislative base. Under that policy, each economically disadvantaged region of Canada, as defined by the federal government, was able to influence its own economic future, with federal financial and technical assistance. Such, of course, was the rationale for the introduction of the General Development Agreement concept in 1974 and its continuance under the ERDA mantle after 1984.

A premium was placed on resident expertise, whether individual, corporate, or governmental. Available funding was readily taken up, although dollars by themselves do not constitute a good proxy for regional development effort and are a poor predictor of success. Entrepreneurship, small- and medium-sized business, technological improvement, skills upgrading, and improvements in business infrastructure became the priority areas for attention. Program instruments of grants, contributions, loans, loan guarantees, and interest-rate relief were available for just about any end use. The mandates of the regional development organizations and the instruments available to them left little to be desired in terms of pursuing regional economic development.

Although the federal government is playing the regional development role region by region, it is still questionable whether there is a national policy of regional development in Canada in accordance with the 1985 commitment of the federal and the provincial governments. A collection of regional policies may be perceived as a national policy and may even satisfy the provinces if they receive due attention. Such a collection cannot meet the test of national coordination or harmonization of the regional development efforts so as to reduce duplication and minimize wasteful competition (Principle 4 of the 1985 position paper "Principles and Framework for Regional Economic Development"). What is left unanswered is who is playing the coordinating role and how are the flexible mandates and instruments of the agencies being used to support a national commitment.

Notwithstanding how successful the individual efforts of the agencies may be, they will fall short of full success if they are unable to influence the actions of other federal government departments in the respective regions. Even if the activities of any one federal department can be blended with the strategies and priorities of a given region, how can national policies in transportation, technology, resource exploitation, skills upgrading, or industrial effort be harmonized on a national basis—with regional differentiation—without a national focal point. Other federal departments may not be interested in applying their policies in a regionally differentiated fashion. There is little evidence that departments such as Finance have been successfully enlisted in a deliberate way so that broad-based federal policies are reconciled with regional development policy.

Have the provinces been brought into policy making and priority setting in a way that will have them thinking regionally, even nationally, instead of provincially? The provinces have had little success in influencing federal policies relating to interest rates or transportation or any number of other federal policies they feel have a detrimental impact on their regions. Indeed, the federal government does not hesitate to invoke the national interest to refute provincial points of view.[73] There is a partnership role for the provinces to play with regard to federal strategies and even with regard to federal projects of direct significance to their economies.

Whether these federal regional development policies, programs, and structures will be permitted to continue long enough in an untampered form to make possible a true evaluation of their achievements will be the test for this policy approach. In order for a real assessment of any regional development policy to be carried out, enough time has to elapse to measure its impact on regional economies.[74] History shows that the patience so demanded might not be forthcoming. If expectations are viewed as being unfulfilled and the pressures become too great, yet another change of direction may be precipitated. In the meantime, the four approaches now employed will be judged in large part on what they are seen to be doing, the degree of effective decision making that resides in the regions, and the true incrementality of the program expenditures.

Federal government policy statements have studiously avoided comparisons between current and DREE policy and programming, despite their many similarities. However, it was claimed that the new approach was better than DRIE, and some reference to DREE was made during committee and House of Commons debates on the establishment of the agencies. Is the separate agencies concept an improvement over previous efforts? The evidence is yet to come in. What can be recorded now, however, is that the DREE regions in the period 1973–82 had unlimited programming flexibility across all sectors and disciplines. The authorities existed to do any of the programming practised or contemplated by the agencies created in 1987. It will not be lost on the reader that what was designed in Quebec in 1988 was accomplished under the same program device first introduced by DREE in 1974.

It was not necessary to move to new organizational forms to better accomplish regional economic development objectives when all the instruments were either available or could have easily been put in place without the creation of new agencies. DRIE incentives programs and the ERDA subsidiary agreements, as the DREE incentives programs and

CHART 5.1

REGIONAL DEVELOPMENT: CHRONOLOGY OF FUNCTIONS, 1969–91

1969	DREE	First dedicated regional development department Centralized (RDIP, Special Areas, ADA)
1973	DREE	Federal-provincial collaboration through joint development agreements Decentralized (GDAS, RDIP)
1978	MSED	Created
1982	DRIE	Merged DREE/ITC minus trade. New policy—all departments playing regional development role Centralized/decentralized (IRDP, GDAS)
1982	MSERD	Created from MSED to oversee economic and regional development activities of all departments (GDAS) Centralized/decentralized
1984 MSERD		ERDAS replace GDAS Disbanded—regional development function moved to DRIE
1987	ISTC	Merged DRIE/MOSST—industrial development, science and technology—regional development diminished as a priority Centralized, with regional offices
1987	ACOA	Regional development agency for Atlantic (flexible program instruments)
1987	DWED	Regional development department for West (flexible program instruments)
1987	FEDNOR	Small regional development agency for northern Ontario (rural and small-business programs)
1988	ISTC	National science and industrial development mandate—IRDP terminated Targeted regional development—Quebec (ERDA)
1991	Federal Office of Regional Development (Quebec)	Separate regional development agency for Quebec
1991		No federal central responsibility for coordinated regional development in Canada

GDA subsidiary agreements had done before them, could have provided the umbrella for all the programming carried out by the agencies. It would have been logical, before moving to other systems, to at least try to identify the shortcomings of existing (and not very old) systems so as to determine if corrective action could be taken. Perhaps the Conservative government's own drive for recognition was too great for that to happen.[75] The section "Concluding Thoughts on the DREE Retrospective" in chapter 3 shows just how many of the intentions and objectives for the agencies in 1987 were present or envisaged by DREE in 1981.

The DREE, one-department, dedicated national responsibility for regional development is absent from the regional development strategy initiated in 1987. No national coordinating capability has existed since the demise of MSERD. The conclusion has to be that something has been taken away from overall regional development in Canada—the question still outstanding is what has been added.[76]

Chapter Six
Evaluation

EVALUATION MEANS DIFFERENT things to different people. It has been fashionable to base success or failure of a particular policy, program, or action of government on the degree to which it can influence quantifiable performance indicators. Latterly, influential authorities, including the Economic Council of Canada and the Macdonald Commission, have cautioned that judging economic and social performance on the basis of numbers alone is not sufficient.[1] Evaluation experts have long been aware of this. Draft evaluation guidelines circulated by the federal Treasury Board Secretariat (TBS) in 1978 observed that performance indicators were but one important element of a management information system and a useful adjunct to program evaluation. The TBS said that indicators "can contribute materially to evaluation and may expedite the conduct of evaluations. Indices are not, however, a substitute for evaluations." The guidelines reaffirmed that common-sense experience and good judgment played a central role in all aspects of program evaluation.[2]

The TBS was not alone in this line of thinking. DREE evaluation officers, in assessing DREE Atlantic evaluation efforts in mid-1978, reported, "In the mid-1970s, evaluation was regarded primarily as a strictly quantitative number-crunching exercise done by economist-technicians. Evaluation research is now regarded as a much broader multi-disciplinary exercise where quantitative analysis plays a role, but is not all there is to it. In this broader sense, evaluation research is still in its infancy."[3] This was an early expression of the difficulties DREE faced in demonstrating to others, and developing for forward-planning purposes, an evaluation framework for its activities. These sentiments also expressed the obvious—statistics may shed light on what may have happened, but are incapable of explaining why. This is the other important dimension of evaluation.

If indices are not a sufficient test of regional development policy, an analysis of subsets of the policy may provide an insight into program performance. What does one look for in regional development evaluation? One looks for the development, and comparison over a specified time frame, of economic and social performance indicators, which will be person-, project-, program-, and sector-specific. The information will be used for forward planning, benefit-cost analysis, backward justification of actions taken, and justification of abandonment or continuance of a particular program. In DREE, it was accepted that there should be an accounting of expenditures of public funds, but even more important, a record of performance that could be used for future economic development planning in Canada's regions. To the extent that current information could inform current decision making, evaluation held the potential of better project-specific decisions and more general program redirection decisions.

Evaluation of regional development effort cannot easily be separated from other influences that bear on economic and social performance in society. Targeted regional development expenditures are dwarfed by transfer payments. The DREE budget was never more than 2 percent of the federal budget and usually closer to 1 percent. The actions of other federal government departments have a significant impact on regional economies. Changing economic circumstances, externalities, and major decision points outside the hands of a regional development department combined to make it next to impossible, in comparative terms, to accurately assess the worth of regional development effort.

DREE Atlantic struggled with the evaluation problem throughout its existence, and it was a point of considerable frustration and disappointment for officials that progress had not been greater. By DREE's end in 1982, they thought they were starting to get it right. All along, however, DREE had faced the conundrum of trying to put together a short-term assessment on a long-term policy.

By 1978 DREE Atlantic had evaluation committees and a regular evaluation reporting system in place and was developing its own guidelines based on Treasury Board requirements. The approach was two-pronged, with evaluation carried out at both the provincial office and regional levels. In some cases, consultants were retained to perform the task. By August, 1978, eighteen final and eleven interim evaluations had been completed, but it was recognized that a number of them fell more into the category of activity report rather than that of evaluation. The problem included inadequate databases for tracking performance over the life of an agreement and the inevitable difficulty of determining meaningful indicators for some of the earlier infrastructure

192

and resource agreements. For an evaluation to be meaningful, data collection had to be continuous, and the provinces were generally in the best position to ensure that it was. At this somewhat early stage, however, provincial collection of data was irregular across the region.

By 1981 DREE Atlantic had engaged in an even more deliberate attack on the evaluation problem, bringing new methodologies to bear, being more deliberate in the design and execution of evaluation sections in subsidiary agreements, and collaborating with provincial governments on data collection. By this time the federal government was better positioned to become more directly involved in data collection, particularly with regard to direct program delivery. After January 1982 the department quickly lost interest in retrospective evaluation, and with the pending disbandment of the Atlantic and western regional offices, the focal point for the regional evaluation drive was lost. If the effort had been maintained, valuable information would have been available for use in the construction of subsidiary agreements under the next generation of ERDAS and as a guide in the determination of regional development policy directions.

Although it is comforting to do so, one should not blame the lack of adequate evaluation of DREE activities on the 1982 DREE/ITC merger exclusively. It remains legitimate to ask why the many efforts that were made were not more fruitful. The well-used "time-frame" argument was, in fact, very valid. The constant demand that DREE prove itself in evaluation terms worked to create an unreal environment for the practice of long-term regional development.[4] Because of the variables referred to earlier and the external factors bearing on the regional economies, it is not possible to determine with complete accuracy the degree to which DREE programming improved regional economic and social conditions. It is equally impossible to disprove the contention that things would have been a lot worse if DREE program activity had never taken place. There is no doubt, however, that almost every project and program executed by DREE and the provinces had a positive impact in the sector or area of activity in which it was employed. It was the contention of officials that the common-sense experience and good judgment referred to by the TBS ensured good projects with positive impact, even if not posthumously confirmed by evaluation exercises. On the other hand, benefit-cost and opportunity-cost techniques were also employed in DREE project and program development and analysis. It is also important to differentiate between evaluation and impact. Impact analysis attempts to determine what has been accomplished and what effect, frequently in a broad context, that accomplishment has had on regional circumstances. An evaluation,

193

usually employing techniques of quantitative analysis, attempts to judge in fairly precise terms the success of a project, program, or agreement in reaching stated objectives.

In the majority of cases, the GDA subsidiary agreements did lend themselves to evaluation, notwithstanding the difficulties cited above. These were the agreements DREE was attempting to evaluate. At the same time, much of the impact data required for individual agreement evaluation were not available until a number of years after completion of agreement projects and programs, even for very project-specific agreements. The time frame for many activities extended beyond 1982, when the disinterest in past performance evaluation set in. Before 1982 project indicators existed or were being developed for evaluation purposes in a number of sector and business agreements. For transportation infrastructure, quantifiable data related miles of highways constructed and passenger/freight miles travelled to economic growth. The placement in the workforce of graduates of DREE-supported institutional infrastructure, such as the technical schools and institutes, was being traced, albeit with some difficulty.

In the resource sectors, evaluation related kilometres of access roads built, hectares of forest land treated, and millions of tree seedlings planted to the value of the resource to be exploited. Evaluation compared consolidation data and management units formed for small tree-lot operators with improved performance and value of production. Acres of agricultural land irrigated, cultivated, or converted to alternate uses could be evaluated in economic and productivity terms. New and expanded livestock production facilities and the number of on- and off-farm storage facilities put in place could be quantified. The use made of marketing programs and technology transfer schemes by the farming community to improve farm productivity and efficiency led to measures of economic output. The identification and categorization of mineral deposits were related to their economic development potential. Offshore test-hole drilling for coal and experiments in the use of peat for power plants could be compared to the cost and value of their energy output.

Other techniques lent themselves to the evaluation of the resource sectors goods-produced stage. These included measuring quantities and values of goods produced, productivity per acre or per hectare of land, markets penetrated, and return on investment. Primary research revealed the capacity utilization of the marine service centres in Newfoundland, the value of improved turnaround time for the vessels, and consequent increased fish landings. Numbers of tourists visiting attractions and accommodation facilities, visit-days per province, and dollars left in the destination areas all permit economic measurement of tourism related programming.

In particular, business and industrial development activities under the GDAS could be readily evaluated. With time, tracking, and monitoring, very specific economic data can be, and were being developed on the performance of companies in high-tech parks, on surviving companies assisted under small-business programs, and on the number, nature, and impact of enterprises encouraged by industrial commissions and rural development associations. Rates of business formation could be compared to historical data to determine the impact of programming aimed at improving the climate for doing business. And even employment creation could be related to new business activity.

Much of the foregoing evaluation was being done, but even more remained to be done when DREE was brought to a close early in 1982. Activities associated with the General Development Agreements consumed upwards of 80 percent of the human and financial resources of DREE in the 1974–82 period; yet insufficient evaluation of a quantifiable nature was conducted in that period, or thereafter, to provide the basis for an unequivocal opinion on DREE's success. Chapter 3 does provide some evidence of the direction of DREE programming over its short life and strong evidence that agreement-specific activities were well directed.

FINANCIAL INCENTIVES TO BUSINESS AND INDUSTRY

Direct incentives to business have been evaluated by a number of observers. Because of the interest such incentives engendered over the DREE years and thereafter, the subject deserves particular attention in this review of regional development programming in Canada. In 1976 the Atlantic Provinces Economic Council listed 42 major federal and provincial industrial development schemes active in the four provinces and referred to a Federal Business Development Bank inventory of nearly 300 federal and provincial programs operating in the region across all areas of economic endeavour.[5] In 1982 the Task Force on Program Integration, established shortly after the DREE/ITC merger announcement, listed 39 programs (excluding those represented by subsidiary agreements to the GDA) active in the two departments and another 99 related provincial programs.[6] The Nielsen Task Force, which was established soon after the Conservatives came to power in 1984, reviewed over 200 federal incentives programs.

What is it that governments want companies to do to improve regional economies? Why are direct financial incentives to business the chosen instrument to reach these objectives? What is the basis for believing that the private sector will respond in the desired way? What is the opinion of private businesses on incentives? What factors do companies take into account in reaching plant establishment, expansion, or modernization decisions, and can incentives be tailored to match them? Can incentives overcome locational disadvantages, real or imaginary? This section addresses these issues within the evaluation context.

DREE's Regional Development Incentives Program became operative in early 1970, and for at least three reasons it received attention from that time onward: (1) data were available for public scrutiny, (2) the data could be manipulated in a mathematical way, and (3) everyone seems to hold an opinion on the usefulness of industrial incentives. DREE also participated with the provinces in a range of small-business, community, and urban-based incentives programs in addition to the RDIP. Under the guise of the subsidiary agreements, more sophisticated sector-specific programs were delivered by DREE, such as those aimed at the high-tech ocean industries sector. This analysis deals only with RDIP and its successor, IRDP.

The objectives of the Regional Development Incentives Act were stated as "an Act to provide incentives for the development of productive employment opportunities in regions of Canada determined to require special measures to facilitate economic expansion and social adjustment." The act indicated that a region could be designated if "a) existing opportunities for productive employment in the region are exceptionally inadequate, and b) the provision of development incentives ... will make a significant contribution to economic expansion and social adjustment within the region." There was no exhortation to attract industry from elsewhere, and the regulations governing the application of the program specifically precluded assistance to any firm in moving from one area to another if that action was deemed as detrimental to either region. In its 1972–73 Main Estimates, DREE translated the act's intent as being the "identification of industries that have potential for growth in designated regions and special areas; improvement of employment opportunities by inducements to the establishment, expansion and modernization of appropriate plants under (the Act) for the creation of continuing productive employment."[7] There was no suggestion that the inducements mentioned should be aimed specifically at firms outside a region, and the inclusion of modernization and expansion in the objective clearly delineates the generality of the statement.

In its application, the objective of the RDIP was basically to influence the business decision framework, with priority assigned to projects that introduced new technology, increased value added to the natural resource sectors, better utilized raw materials, or promoted industrial diversification, labour force stability, and the development of higher-level skills in the workforce. An increase in absolute and comparative employment levels was a fundamental objective of all DREE programming. The federal government, then, wanted companies to create jobs, create economic expansion, and facilitate social adjustment in the less-developed regions. How well did it do?

EVALUATION OF FINANCIAL INCENTIVES

An evaluation of incentives program performance can be derived from an analysis of investment and job creation over the respective lives of the DREE RDI and the DRIE IRD programs.

DREE *Regional Development Incentives Program*

From DREE's inception (taken as July 1969) to March 31, 1982, 7,292 RDIP projects had either been completed (4,706) or were still active (2,586). Offers of incentives that were at first accepted by companies but subsequently turned down or that were withdrawn by the department, as well as projects launched but discontinued, are excluded from the data. Incentives commitments against the 7,292 projects totalled some $1.2 billion and were predicted to generate some $6.2 billion of investments of eligible assets and to create 181,150 jobs. Atlantic Canada, with under 10 percent of the population (9.2 percent in 1981) represented 19 percent of accepted offers, 22.6 percent of dollar commitments, 19.5 percent of predicted investment, and 18.9 percent of predicted jobs.[8] In other words, the impact in the Atlantic provinces was twice what its population relationship would indicate. Quebec, with 26 percent of the population, had more than half of the accepted offers and expected jobs. The conclusion is that the RDIP, created primarily for eastern Canada, had its greatest impact there, despite its continually expanding geographic growth over its life.

DRIE *Industrial and Regional Development Program*

The IRDP, DRIE's combined answer to previous DREE and ITC financial incentives programs, came into force in 1983. It covered the development climate (non-profit centres, studies, specialized services, and some infrastructure), marketing, innovation, new establishments, modernization, expansion, and restructuring in four "tier" areas.

Tier I consisted of the most developed census divisions of the

TABLE 6.1

RDIP-ATLANTIC AS A PERCENTAGE OF NATIONAL PERFORMANCE
(JULY 1969–MARCH 31, 1982)

Element	National	Atlantic (% of National)
Projects	7,292	19.0
Commitments ($)	1.2 billion	22.6
Investments ($)	6.2 billion	19.5
Jobs	181,150	18.9

SOURCE: DREE, annual reports, 1975–76 through 1981–82.
NOTE: Number of projects completed (4,706) or active (2,586), excluding offers first accepted by firms but subsequently refused or withdrawn by the department, and discontinued projects.

country, embracing 50 percent of the population. Tier II accounted for about 30 percent of the population. Tier III covered relatively less-developed areas of the country and included approximately 15 percent of the population. Tier IV included the least-developed areas and contained about 5 percent of the population. Incentives levels were greatest in the least-developed areas (that is, tiers III and IV), declining to the least assistance in the developed areas (tiers I and II).

The IRDP analysis covers the period from its inception (established as July 1, 1983) to March 31, 1989, and may be considered representative of the program's performance, given that no applications were accepted under the program after June 30, 1988. Total applications received were 13,921, with 4,880 offers made and 92.7 percent (4,524) accepted. Of that number, 47.2 percent fell in the less-developed tiers III and IV, despite their comprising only 20 percent of total population. Tiers III and IV also accounted for 42 percent of total funding of $1.5 billion, 33 percent of the 90,529 jobs said to be created, and 41 percent of the 65,396 jobs said to be maintained. The greatest numbers of jobs created and jobs maintained were, not surprisingly, in the modernization and expansion categories.

In terms of activities, an encouraging 25 percent of the accepted applications and 26 percent of the funding was taken up by the development climate, marketing, and innovation categories. New establishments comprised 19 percent of the accepted offers and 26 percent of the funding. Modernization and expansion, which may be considered as building on strength, represented 55 percent of the accepted offers and consumed 47 percent of the funding. Other data reveal the significance of company size in the program. A full 64 percent of the

TABLE 6.2

IRDP EVALUATION: INCEPTION TO MARCH 31, 1989

Category	Tiers I and II % of total	Tiers III and IV % of total	Totals
Accepted offers	52.8	47.2	4,524
Funding	58.0	42.0	$1.5 B.
Jobs, created	67.0	33.0	90,529
Jobs, maint.	59.0	41.0	65,396
Program Elements	Accepted Offers % of total	Funding % of total	
Climate, Marketing, Innovation	25	26	
Establishment	19	26	
Modernization, Expansion	55	47	

SOURCE: Industrial and Regional Development Program annual reports, 1984–85 through 1988–89.

NOTE: Figures do not add to 100% due to omission of minor restructuring element.

accepted offers were for projects offered less than $100,000, but these offers represented only 9.8 percent of the total funding. Projects with authorized assistance under $1 million accounted for 95 percent of the accepted offers and 39 percent of the funding (see Table 6.2).

One of the important objectives of the IRDP was to increase investment leverage—the ratio of private sector dollars to federal dollars committed to a project. The data show a range, being highest for establishment (over 5:1) and lowest in the development climate, marketing, and innovation categories. Leverage was over 3:1 for all tier structures. Over the years, the leverage factor was appreciably different, up or down, but always significantly better than 1:1.[9]

It may be concluded that those projects calling out for assistance in the less-developed areas of the country were accommodated under the RDIP and IRDP. Given the population difference between the IRDP tiers, one would not expect the jobs created or maintained (33 percent and 41 percent in tiers III and IV) to match the 47.2 percent of accepted offers in those two areas. Funding, at 42 percent of the total, was within striking distance of the jobs-created projection of 33 percent.

For both the RDIP and IRDP, the concern for employment creation should centre on new jobs, with the "jobs maintained" category under the IRDP being more suspect.

THE DISTRIBUTION OF BENEFITS

How well were these investments and these jobs distributed by region? As indicated above, regions such as Atlantic Canada, falling primarily in tiers III and IV, were better served than generally realized. In 1979 the Atlantic Provinces Economic Council was pleased with the fact that the region, with 9.5 percent of Canada's population, had received 24.5 percent of RDIP monies in the period June 1969–December 1975.[10] In 1975–76, the Atlantic received 26.6 percent of RDIP industrial incentives assistance compared to 38 percent for Quebec and 16 percent for Ontario. In 1981–82 the figures were 14.6 percent for Atlantic Canada, 59 percent for Quebec, and 9 percent for Ontario.[11] The figures change from year to year, depending on the health of the economy and the rate of program take-up by private business. With the exception of the Montreal Special Area Program, which does have a distorting influence on the data, the application of the RDIP in Quebec and Ontario was also directed to areas designated as economically disadvantaged.

The RDIP was, in general, a responsive program, with its take-up dictated by the initiative of the private sector and, in gross dollar terms, by the size of projects that came forward. There was little to be gained in proposing an arbitrarily greater share of RDIP assistance for any given region. The Atlantic region was never denied funding for any worthwhile eligible projects that came forward. The only other way DREE could have changed the program's distribution across the country would have been to deliberately withhold funding in one region in favour of another, but this would not have promoted any more activity in the peripheral areas.

The perception has sometimes been fostered that the less economically wealthy regions of the country have not fared well under federal incentives programs. Data have been recited for programs and specific sectors showing the Atlantic region receiving only just over 2 percent of agricultural subsidies and only 11.4 percent of Industry, Trade and Commerce funding (mostly in shipbuilding) in 1980–81, with almost nothing under the DIPP, the Enterprise Development Program, and other ITC programs aimed at design, adjustment, and certain sector-specific programs, and little assistance under the community-directed Industrial and Labour Adjustment Program.[12]

Closer scrutiny reveals some of the reasons for these program distributions and apparent discrepancies by region. A directed regional development industrial incentives program such as the RDIP is, by definition, only applicable in the regions for which it is designated. The ITC programs cited above were designed for national application, with no regional bias. It is, therefore, somewhat misleading to quote the distributional aspects of programs such as the DIPP (defence), IDAP (design—Industrial Design Assistance Program), EDP (industrial development—Enterprise Development Program) and GAAP (adjustment—the General Adjustment Assistance Program) in regional development terms. To the degree that they were applicable in the regions, the regions could make use of them. The GAAP was aimed at companies judged to be disadvantaged by changing tariff structures; the design program was aimed at upgrading Canadian design capability (perhaps it could have been used more proactively for regional development purposes, but it was not so developed); the DIPP was, at the time, very much defence industry—oriented and that industry was located in central Canada. No regional politician or industrial development proponent would suggest deliberately injuring or disadvantaging central Canadian industry just because the regions had not yet reached a similar level of prosperity. To the degree that the "share" argument could be considered valid, it would be to the extent that all federal departments were not thinking regionally and that insufficient attention was being accorded coordination of federal actions.

INCREMENTAL ACTIVITY

Were the new jobs really new and was the additional investment really incremental—that is, would the company's intended plans, in the absence of the incentives, not achieve similar results? The requirement that DREE-sponsored projects be incremental in this sense caused problems for applicants and program administrators alike. Clause 7(1) of the RDI Act specified that "no development incentive may be authorized ... if a) it is probable that the facility would be established, expanded or modernized without the provision of such incentive; or b) the establishment, expansion or modernization would not make a significant contribution to economic expansion." Section 9(1) specified that "no development incentive may be authorized (under the Act) for the establishment, expansion or modernization of a facility for which a contractual commitment was made, whether or not the commitment remains in force, before b) the day on which an application ... is received by the Minister." The provisions of these two clauses placed an onerous responsibility on program officers. As legislated program elements, they allowed no discretion in intent but required interpretation in application. This was especially the case with section 9(1). The interpretation of these clauses in project-specific instances occasioned many references to departmental legal counsel.

The basic rationale for an incentives grant (actually a contribution— a grant has little or no strings attached to it in accountability terms) is to encourage economic activity. The incrementality requirement was to some degree artificial, particularly for activities indigenous to the region, as in the resource sectors. What was important was to make something happen. If the objectives of the program could be achieved as part of an intended business decision, especially if that decision could be shifted forward in the time schedule, its implementation was to the advantage of the region. If new location-neutral enterprises could be attracted, that was a bonus. This was the rationale for differentiated assistance levels.

There have been no conclusive studies conducted on the incrementality question and most of the studies that have been undertaken can be discounted. The Economic Council of Canada judged the DREE incentives as a modest success, estimating 25 to 59 percent incrementality.[13] The Atlantic Provinces Economic Council estimated a qualified 80 percent effectiveness in 1971, far too early in the life of the program to be significant. The department's own evaluation produced a 78 percent incrementality level and the Atlantic Development Council's evaluation weighed in at 60 percent.[14] The Economic Council's work was based on a historical births and deaths analysis for firms before and after DREE; there was no apparent factoring in of prevailing economic circumstances and only selected manufacturing firms were studied.

The sometimes quoted Harvard thesis study by David Springate is most suspect. It was based on interviews with personnel from eighteen large firms and thirteen small firms, representing twenty new establishment projects and eleven expansions.[15] Springate concluded that the DREE incentives had virtually no influence on the timing of project decisions and reported that two-thirds of the offers accepted by large companies and one-half of the offers accepted by smaller companies had no effect on investment decisions. He therefore saw the grants as windfall gains for the companies.[16] The fact that company decision makers admitted to such a relatively low rate of influence is no more reliable than the declaration they were required to make under the program that the incentive was a significant element in their decision to proceed—the only difference being that the earlier declaration, if not in fact true, was hardly ethical.

Two other 1970s studies examined, each from a very different perspective, government intervention that was intended to influence the business decision-making process. Philip Mathias investigated in detail five cases of primarily provincial government involvement, concluding that two were likely successful (Churchill Falls hydroelectric generation in Labrador and two pulp mills in Saskatchewan) and three were basically disasters (a NS heavy water plant, Churchill Forest Industries in Manitoba, and a fish-processing fiasco in PEI). He identified insufficient technical experience in the bureaucracy as a significant problem in the assessment of these projects, which at the time were each the single biggest economic development in the provinces involved. These were one-of-a-kind situations, not related to the performance of more broadly based programs such as the RDIP and IRDP. By the time these programs were in force, a cadre of officers with industrial experience were evaluating private sector applications. It was also Mathias who said of the DREE RDIP, "The most flexible and probably the most valuable federal assistance plan was launched in mid-1969, when the federal government introduced a new incentive grant scheme to combat regional disparity."[17]

The potential conflict between the joint objectives of employment creation and capital formation of the RDIP has garnered a number of comments, generally to the effect that the program contained an inherent capital bias. Woodward suggested that companies would deliberately substitute capital for labour to increase the size of grant they could expect from the program, even to the extent of obtaining more capital than was actually needed for the project. He concluded that where employment did increase as a result of a DREE contribution, it was because the production functions of most firms limited the substitution option.[18] Concern about a capital bias in incentives schemes does not recognize that companies are very unlikely to overload their capital plant over the long term for the benefit of a one-time incentives grant. The smaller companies may not be sophisticated enough to draw the capital/labour distinction in an incentives offer, and the larger companies will understand the limitations of such a determination over the long run. Much more important, however, and much more significant from an employment stability point of view, is the fact that the maintenance of reliable jobs is the most critical element of an employment strategy, and if this is to be accomplished by investment in capital, such investment is a worthwhile component of any industrial development program. This was recognized and acknowledged by many union leaders in the 1980s.

THE DRAWING POWER OF INCENTIVES: AN EVALUATION
OF THE RDIP AND IRDP (OR, TO WHAT DEGREE DO COMPANIES
RESPOND IN THE DESIRED WAY?)

Federal incentives programs did not, in fact, attract a great deal of new industry into any one region from elsewhere. Companies considering the establishment of new enterprises were at liberty to consider any area of Canada they wished for such an undertaking, as they would have been if the RDIP had not existed. Rarely was assistance given to a company that closed in one location to relocate in another. The attraction of foreign companies was considered legitimate. Even here DREE maintained a clearing-house function in Ottawa for the convenience of the regions, by which offshore enquiries were circulated to regional offices to determine levels of interest and avoid interregional conflict; follow-up was then determined on the basis of that interest. Some DREE regions also did direct foreign prospecting.

The skills needed for high productivity, market penetration, and competitiveness are judged as significantly lacking in the peripheral regions of the country as compared to central Canada and a number of other countries. If one of the best ways to obtain new technologies, manufacturing and management practices, and marketing expertise is to have a company exhibiting such skills locate in your region, then this is another reason to provide incentives for progressive companies to establish or upgrade themselves in the underdeveloped regions. To encourage companies to cooperate in the attainment of federal objectives, the motivation would need to complement the companies' own objective of improving profitability.

If the RDIP had been successful in attracting substantial new industry to designated regions, there would have been validity to the contention that regionally differentiated industrial incentives distorted the location of businesses within regions or within Canada. In an attempt to examine this premise, DREE RDIP incentives offers accepted by companies in the four Atlantic provinces for the last two years of DREE's life, 1981 and 1982, were analysed. So that the premise might also encompass the influence of financial incentives in general on company behaviour, the DRIE IRDP was also reviewed from its inception in 1983 to March 31, 1988.

Each of 746 company applications was categorized as either indigenous to the region or footloose, that is, location-neutral. For each application, the nature of the project and the sector involved were recorded, along with the program category under which it fell (establishment of a new facility, modernization or expansion, or new product expansion). Under the IRDP, innovation, marketing, and development climate (the latter terminated in 1984) were included. Sector categories included the resource sectors, metal fabricating and machinery, printing and publishing, and other, with the latter subdivided into plastics, chemicals, etc., depending on frequency of occurrence. For the IRDP the more detailed classification used in the source material was used. In each determination the benefit of the doubt was given to the footloose category.

The study revealed that 82.7 percent of the 746 company applications accepted fell in the "indigenous" category.[19] Several factors favour the indigenous classification. By definition, only new facilities establishment can be considered footloose. In 1981 only 30 percent of RDIP-accepted applications were for establishment, usually in the resource sectors. In metal fabrication and machinery, only one in ten was establishment, and that pattern repeated in subsequent years. Conversely, all modernization and expansion projects automatically become indigenous. Under the IRDP, thirty projects in 1984–85 were tourism, by definition indigenous, and only four of twenty-four projects in the food grouping were new. Similar kinds of relationships obtained in the three years that followed. These data indicate little in the way of attracting firms from outside the region.

Most resource-based projects were judged indigenous to the Atlantic region. Fish-processing operations, small sawmills, and certain agricultural further-processing activities, such as potato processing, are known to be indigenous to the region. Certain services (small metal fabrication and rebuild shops or small printing operations) and products (peat moss and bakery products) aimed at the local market either go forward in the region or not at all. It is obvious that these products and services could be obtained from outside the region, but the scale and nature of the projects were such that local entrepreneurs would not undertake them other than in the region. The most that could be said would be that they constituted import replacement activities. It appeared to be a case of local businesspeople perceiving a business opportunity and going after it; the role played by the incentive in the business decision remains open to question.

Despite the high percentage of accepted offers judged indigenous to the Atlantic region, there were 129 new projects, covering a wide variety of activities, that were judged to be location neutral. A few, such as a potato chip plant in the potato heartland of New Brunswick, would probably only have gone forward in the region, but on balance the activity would likely have occurred in one place or another. The projects that could be rated as having been attracted to the region included production and farm machinery, plastics and chemicals products, business forms, packaging and paper products, electrical projects, metal fabrication, and a considerable number of projects attracted to Cape Breton in Nova Scotia.

These data add more fuel to the debate on the degree to which incentives influence corporate locational decisions. One would expect the percentage of indigenous projects to remain high, as long as expansion and modernization projects continued to be eligible under incentives programs. These data must also be used with caution in any examination of incrementality, defined as a company doing something more than it might otherwise have done without a financial inducement. The incentives may well have been significant in influencing the footloose projects, and they may have changed the decision time frame of those projects deemed indigenous to the region. The data will not convince those who have concluded that the DREE (and DRIE) incentives placed low on the scale of factors influencing companies to do something they had not already decided to do.

No company would be expected to make a location, establishment, modernization, or expansion decision unless it conformed to good business practice, and therein lies the basis of the operational application of the RDIP. Financial incentives (including tax breaks), differentiated by geographical location, were intended to make it more attractive for firms to locate in areas where certain factors of market size, transportation, and perceived lower levels of skills would militate against their being a company's first choice. Programs prior to the RDIP were more deliberate in declaring the attraction of new firms as a prime objective. But the RDI Act spoke of "productive employment in Regions of Canada," and analysis shows that the majority of activity was in sectors indigenous to the region in question or quite sector-neutral.

Even though the RDIP comprised a relatively small percentage of DREE expenditures and activity, it has been assessed as having the capability of skewing industrial activity in the regions. Careless says that "the federal incentives in a poor province could very significantly affect the arrival and location of new industries and hence the overall mix of industries in the province."[20] Lithwick speaks of "dysfunctional competition for industry."[21] The evidence demonstrates that the ability of incentives to attract industry is less than generally presumed and that incentives are unlikely to have a significant influence on the industrial mix of a province. Only when indiscriminately used, as is reputed to have been the case in Smallwood's Newfoundland, can incentives be disruptive to the point of being detrimental.

In principle, however, account must be taken of the sector distortion or crowding-out effect of assistance to firms within a region. It may be generally concluded that a firm that has received financial incentives assistance is better off than one that has not, thus creating some distortion in competitive positions. The RDI Act was written to discourage the crowding-out effect. Officers were obliged to assess the market consequence of an incentives offer. Sometimes they concluded that more competition would be a good thing where a market was dominated by existing firms or was inadequately supplied. Of a more delicate nature was the question of import substitution of products from other parts of Canada. Even here, however, given the propensity of national firms to ship into the regions rather than produce there, it was often decided that a local entrepeneur should receive support.

What Did the rdi Program Cost?

Judging the success of industrial incentives on incrementality and the cost per job in creating employment, the two most common indicators used, misses the mark in assessing the contribution to regional economies of the assistance given to firms. What is important is the obtainment of the objectives set for the programs employed.[22] The most accurate way to evaluate the worth of an incentive made to a company is to conduct an economic impact analysis over time of what that firm means to the community and to the region—employment, payroll, personal and company taxes paid, sourcing of materials, markets developed outside the region, effects of the increased purchasing power, etc. On this basis, the actual cost of the incentive to the taxpayer and the even less valid cost-per-job indicator fade to insignificance. Dwelling on program administrative costs frequently results in misleading conclusions.[23] The administrative costs of incentives programs can easily be put in perspective. See Table 6.3.

RDIP grants, averaging approximately one-third of DREE program expenditures prior to the GDA era, fell to between one-fifth and one-quarter of program expenditures by the time the subsidiary agreements were in full swing (from 36.6 percent in 1971–72 down to 21.7 percent in 1974–75).[24] Personnel and supporting administrative costs for DREE RDIP incentives were always proportionately smaller than that in comparison with total departmental levels. In the three fiscal years prior to the introduction of the GDA (1971–72 through 1973–74), incentives program person-years represented 11, 12.5, and 14.4 percent, respectively, of departmental strength.[25] RDIP administrative costs for these three years were 12.5, 14.5, and 17.1 percent, respectively, of departmental administrative costs. If one applies the average 14.7 percent for these three years to 1981–82, DREE's last independent year of operation, RDIP administrative costs would have been $13.2 million, an undoubtedly inflated figure, given that the RDIP was by then an even smaller percentage of total operations.

By 1984–85, DRIE's grants and contributions category exceeded a billion dollars. The new IRDP was estimated at $651 million for that year, with predecessor programs, including the RDIP, reported at $253

TABLE 6.3

RDIP ADMINISTRATIVE COSTS AND PROGRAM EXPENDITURES

Year	RDIP Pys	Dept Pys	%	RDIP Admin.	Dept Admin.	%
				($000)		
71–72	209	1944	10.75	3,499	28,056	12.47
72–73	263	2093	12.56	5.337	36,742	14.53
73–74	325	2264	14.35	6,302	36,800	17.10
74–75	NA	2230		NA	43,295	
75–76	NA	2230		NA	53,156	
81–82	NA	2045		NA	89,823	

Year	RDIP G@Cs (thousands of dollars)	All G@Cs	RDIP as % of All G@Cs
71–72	101,950	277,958	36.67
72–73	86,160	262,216	32.85
73–74	90,132	319,208	28.24
74–75	70,229	323,841	21.68
75–76	86,537	384,493	22.50
81–82	127,014	513,940	24.71

NOTES:

G@Cs = Grants and Contributions.

RDIP = Regional Development Incentives Program.

Admin. = administration.

Pys = person-years.

Percentages represent RDIP pys and administration costs as a percentage of departmental pys and administration costs.

million.[26] In that year, *all* departmental administrative expenses totalled $231 million, covering all incentives, subsidiary agreement and other programs administration, economic analysis, planning and research, corporate overhead, and everything else carried on in an unusually complicated department of government. Administrative costs assigned to incentives program administration would have been no more than the average 14.7 percent figure derived above, or some $34 million, a far cry from Savoie's inference of excessive incentives program overhead costs.[27]

The quality of projects assisted by DREE incentives has come under scrutiny, with concern expressed over the fact that some companies receiving assistance subsequently went bankrupt or that DREE bailed out other projects that were doomed from the start. The record shows that the failure rate of firms receiving DREE incentives was no greater than that under conventional banking and similar financing of new projects. DREE, in fact, was sometimes criticized for not being adventurous enough. To the best of the ability of officials, money was not advanced on lost causes, but legitimate restructuring situations were eligible for consideration. Every application had to meet a viability test, a requirement of the legislation.

PROVINCIAL INCENTIVES PROGRAMS

Every province in Canada provides enticements to industry to locate within its boundaries, generally without regard to other provinces and frequently in competition with them. Allan Tupper has written an insightful piece on industrial policies and interprovincial conflict that elaborates the degree to which some provinces seek not only foreign firms, but firms located in other provinces.[28] Tupper suggests that it is hard to quantify the economic costs of cutthroat provincial competition and that such efforts to relocate industry within Canada may not be very significant in an economic sense.[29] Despite the uncertainty of success and attendant costs for provinces, he observes that "without approval from other members of the federation, provinces may subsidize firms, offer financial services to industry, own firms engaged in interprovincial commerce, and even enact purchasing codes which explicitly favour provincial firms."[30] The implication of Tupper's views is that there is confused and uncoordinated action on the part of the provinces and, by default, the federal government. The need for some discipline in the whole process is clearly voiced.

With respect to policy and program evaluation, Tupper comments that "those exercised about the economic atrocities routinely committed by Canadian governments are remarkably vague when delimiting the actual costs incurred ... few sophisticated studies have been undertaken on the economic effectiveness and consequences of federal and provincial industrial development schemes. Nor is much rigorous research available on such topics as the economics of preferential provincial purchasing, or even DREE programs."[31]

The federal government had its own concerns about the impact of provincial policies on the national economy. Quite apart from the influence that such policies might have had on industrial relocation, Industry, Trade and Commerce in 1977 voiced its view that programs to develop manufacturing industries within provincial boundaries could be at the expense of broader national interests, citing interprovincial trade barriers, preferential procurement policies, preferential access to provincial natural resources, and industrial incentives. The department noted that while such approaches may form optimal instruments to further provincial objectives, there was evidence to suggest that they tended to fragment the Canadian market, thereby depriving Canadians of the benefits of economic integration within the federation.[32] These same federal concerns surfaced fourteen years later in the constitutional proposals paper *Shaping Canada's Future Together*.

Whether federal or provincial incentives are involved, the danger of competition would seem to be of the same order, except that federal programs such as the RDIP and the IRDP had built-in provisions against interprovincial competition. More importantly, if the analysis of federal programs showing an extremely high bias towards indigenous industry applies as well to provincial programs, which is undoubtedly the case, then the interprovincial competitive influence is likely to be much less than some critics believe. This also suggests that provincial programs should be evaluated against the same criteria as federal programs in terms of their contribution to regional economies. One difference that does exist between federal and provincial approaches, and it is an important one, is the proclivity of provincial governments to bail out losing firms to the extent of taking ownership. Experience has shown that such firms are rarely turned around, never making the longer-term contribution to the economy that offsets the value of the incentives made to firms that survive.

LOCATIONAL OPTIONS

The factors that a multi-plant operation will consider in weighing the impact of locational incentives on their debt-equity structure and the availability of bank financing include the value of up-front grants, contributions, interest buy-down schemes, and conditionally repayable advances. Any conditions placed on the firm by the government or governments involved in the deal—guaranteed job creation, skills training, technology transfer, local company participation, or local sourcing of supplies—will make the incentives less attractive.

For most manufactured and service products (very much less so for semi-finished goods and initial-processed resources), a firm will like to be in, or have assured access to, the market to be served. Even if the market is elsewhere, firms are more comfortable when in familiar surroundings, with other firms, and where supplies, services, and repairs are readily available to keep the operation running. Secondly, although it may be technically and logistically possible to service a market from another country (or sometimes from another region in the same country), factors such as local purchasing preferences (interprovincial barriers), customs, duties, tariff and non-tariff barriers, and quotas may make it advisable for the firm to be located in the market it wishes to serve. An apparent contradiction has been the substantial share of the North American market taken by offshore companies, although some of them now consider it politic to locate in Canada and the United States and joint venturing is more and more common.

The degree to which these considerations enter into the locational question in regional development terms ranges from almost insignificant for the firm indigenous to the region (especially if the firm is small and the region is its market) to significant for the firm that has a high degree of freedom in the locational choice. In studying the corporate culture of national and multinational multi-plant operations, Bernard Bonin and Roger Verreault found that studies carried out on the locational preferences of multinational firms were inconclusive — some firms move to comfort-level zones of most familiarity (others were already there), others to areas of surplus labour. Some studies suggested that multinational enterprises (MNES) were attracted by incentives; others reached a contrary conclusion. Bonin and Verrealt also found that the real value of a financial incentive could be diluted by other actions of a host government (relaxing business controls) or by override devices employed by the firm, such as in-company transfer payment policies, which could be advantageous or detrimental to the subsidiary operation.[33]

In coming to Canada, MNES are probably influenced by our proximity to the US, Canadian markets, reliable energy supplies, and the relative stability of government. The benefits or drawbacks implied by the Canada-US Free Trade Agreement, which allows greater exemption from trade barriers for firms locating in either country, were under vigorous debate as Canada-US trade relations underwent considerable stress in 1992. Where to locate in Canada also comes into play, but even this decision will be influenced by these same factors. If there is some flexibility in location, however, incentives can be a factor, as has been seen from time to time in some of the very large multinational projects attracted to Canada.[34]

R. Keith Semple developed a more disquieting set of data that relates the degree of foreign ownership in major Canadian economic sectors to the location of decision making, whether in the regions or external to them.[35] Semple found that the average foreign ownership in 1984 was 57.5 percent in the resource sector, 66.7 percent in chemicals, 89.7 percent in machinery, and 16.5 percent in metal fabrication. Most of the transportation, communications, finance, cooperatives, and utilities sectors in Canada are domestic, with the latter usually provincially owned. No evidence relates these data to operations distribution.

Semple shows that in respect of the "Urban System," the largest cities dominate every sector and subsector of the economy, with Toronto well out in front. In 1984 the largest ownership in resources (52.9 percent), manufacturing (52.4 percent), and services (34.8 percent) resided in Toronto. Montreal was in second place, followed by a scattering of cities where a particular company might have been prominent in a particular sector. Atlantic Canada is scarcely mentioned, other than in terms of total revenue of resource and manufacturing corporations headquartered in Saint John, Halifax, Sydney, Florenceville, and St John's (out of a listing of sixty-two cities). In each case, as little as one company may have put a particular city on the list (McCains in Florenceville in the top sixty food companies grouping). St John's was also in the top sixty food companies group, on account of the fisheries subsector concentration in that city.

For service corporations, Halifax, New Glasgow, and Stellarton, NS, and Saint John and Moncton, NB, gained mention in the retail, communications, and cooperatives subsectors out of a list of thirty-two cities.[36] Of a listing of the top sixty-six Canadian cities controlling the non-financial sectors of the Canadian economy in 1984, in millions of dollars of revenue, Saint John was listed as number 14, Florenceville 19, Stellarton 22, Halifax 24, Sydney 30, Moncton 31, St John's 32, and New Glasgow 54. These cities are referred to as Eastern Region "fifth level" decision makers in Semple's urban decision-making hierarchy.[37] The story is much the same with the financial, utility, and real estate corporations, with Toronto far in front with control of 44 percent of national assets and Montreal with just over 35 percent. In Atlantic Canada, only Halifax (with Central Trust and Nova Scotia Power Corporation), Fredericton (New Brunswick Power) and St John's (Newfoundland Hydro) rated a mention. The latter two were included only because of their utilities' crown corporation ownership. Halifax was somewhat more diversified in the Diversified Finance, Utilities, Life Insurance, and Trust subsectors. Charlottetown also merited mention with a modest utility.[38]

Given Semple's evidence of a large foreign ownership presence in Toronto and two or three other major centres, it would be logical to extrapolate this influence to decision-making affecting regional economies. An interpretation of Semple's data leads to the conclusion that most of the major decisions on both financial and non-financial assets would likely be taken outside the control of those directly involved with regional operations. Semple proves this by use of a domestic and a composite index calculation that reveals negative domestic indices for almost all cities outside of Toronto and Montreal, based on revenues and assets controlled in the respective regions; he proves an even worse scenario by use of a composite index that includes the foreign control factor.[39]

What is the implication of this ownership pattern in terms of regional economies and regional economic development efforts? If the regional operations of large national and multinational firms contribute to their competitiveness and profitability, it should auger well for regional economies in terms of employment, value added, services supported, taxes paid, and the sharing and dissemination of new technology. Less pleasant is the thought that the geographic operations of the corporation, wherever located, are always vulnerable to consolidation and rationalization. Corporate power can also influence the price a corporation will pay for goods and services supplied to it and what it will charge for its product. In peripheral regions, local suppliers may be squeezed on their profit margins or simply bypassed through corporate national or bulk buying policies. This may be particularly harmful to technological development for regional companies.

The evidence suggests that large national and multinational companies that have decided to locate in Canada will place their headquarters in major centres, take their most important decisions there, and think more and more in terms of what is best for their global competitiveness. Their highest level of regional involvement will usually be in the resource sectors and in some financial services. They will restrict their non-resource–based involvement to those situations where government pressure (such as in the breweries), very specific attractions (labour force availability), or market niche or market dominance make it worth their while to do so.[40] In such an environment, financial incentives in themselves would be unlikely to outweigh other decision factors. For those companies operating in the world marketplace, the need to be competitive may well overshadow any attraction of locational financial incentives, other than in resources, unless there is some very specific reason to the contrary.[41] Semple concluded his 1985 analysis as follows:

> It appears that, at least in the short run, the unique position of Canada will lend itself toward fewer and more geographically concentrated corporate locations. This spatial concentration will occur in the largest centres and as a result, the existing corporate cities will play an even more dominant role in the affairs of the nation....
>
> A second trend will see foreign investment expand at an ever-greater rate, with investment taking place in the fastest-growing sectors and sub-sectors. The investment will be directed by corporations with headquarters locations in the largest and most visible Canadian corporate centres.[42]

213

Semple's sentiments were shared by the Task Force on Regional Development Assessment, which concluded that "regional competition and comparative advantage in Canada will be based increasingly upon economic competition and specialization among urban centres." The task force added the admonition that without special efforts to stimulate regionally based centres, there will be an increase in regional disparity in Canada.[43]

The theory that development efforts should be directed to helping regions help themselves in supported by Semple's work. Yet the impact of a major facility on a regional economy, directly and indirectly, cannot be overlooked. The presence of such a facility, ironically, provides an excellent impetus to the self-help approach, permitting all kinds of periphery manufacturing and service businesses to develop. The question that remains is the degree to which such large facilities should be pursued for regional development purposes. Almost certainly, a balanced approach should be pursued, with the greatest effort directed to building in the region, but an eye always on the lookout for the big-impact project (and sometimes a wary eye). It is also important to be reasonably entrepreneurial in searching out those middle-sized projects that hold considerable promise in terms of their being location-neutral and having the potential of bringing important new attributes to the region. In the past, a poor record in attracting new firms to the region may well have been due to the passive nature of the incentives programs and insufficient prospecting by government agencies. Despite the eloquence of the arguments for local development and the odds against attracting the big impact project, the lure of the latter appears irresistible. British Columbia Regional Development Minister Elwood Veitch, in lobbying for the construction of a Chinese steel mill in BC, predicted the mill would make the province "recession-proof."[44]

The private sector, despite protestations to the contrary, has been a regular user of government incentives programs, including the RDIP, IRDP, DIPP, EDB, and every other program mentioned up to this point in this book. At the same time, it professes discomfort in doing so. The influential Business Council on National Issues (BCNI) established a committee in 1989 to promote a better understanding of the danger of high national deficits. On its agenda was the question of subsidies to business. The council head admitted that businesses were under intense pressure to take advantage of programs, grants, and subsidies.[45] The Canadian Manufacturers' Association, in its 1989 recommendations to government on deficit reduction, said that the deficit-reduction effort should include a thorough review of all spending on business-related programs. At the same time, it asked for a variety of tax breaks to improve international competitiveness.[46] During the same period, which was a run-up to a pending budget, the Canadian Chamber of Commerce called for examination of handouts to industry or bailouts of failing businesses.[47] Small business, represented by the Canadian Federation of Independent Business, stated flatly that grants and handouts to business be eliminated.[48]

By January of 1990, the tone of these private sector groups had significantly toughened. The BCNI put business handouts at the top of its list of recommended government spending cuts. The Canadian Chamber of Commerce was almost disdainful of the government's budget reduction efforts and also put cuts in support to the private sector at the top of the list. Even the Economic Council of Canada, in concluding that the federal government could balance the budget by 1994 if it so wished, included capital assistance to business and subsidies to business in its list of five areas for government action.[49] The February 20, 1990, federal budget announced the government's intention to eliminate outright grants or subsidies to business and to replace these with repayable loans. By October 1990, with the country in recession, the BCNI, the Canadian Chamber of Commerce, and the Canadian Manufacturers' Association banded together in what was characterized as an unprecedented joint plea to governments, federal and provincial, to freeze spending and reduce interest rates. They said that "all of us, including business, must be prepared to reduce our demands on government ... The business community in Canada is willing to stand first in line to see spending programs and bailouts and subsidies cut."[50]

SOME ECONOMIC RESULTS

A 1979 DREE report on economic prospects for the Atlantic region of Canada commented that, in the period 1971–78, "had it not been for the spectacular growth of the Western Region, mainly caused by the oil boom, the Atlantic Region would have registered the highest growth rates in the country."[51] During that period, the gross domestic product of the Atlantic region increased by 120 percent, only marginally less than for Canada as a whole, and higher than for Ontario and Quebec. The growth of earned income per capita was marginally better than for Canada. Growth in output, measured by real domestic product, marginally lagged the national output, although the goods-producing sector matched the national growth. The value of manufacturing shipments for Atlantic Canada grew by 230 percent compared to 160 percent for Canada (census value added in goods-producing industries). With a net in-migration and participation rate increase in the period, the ranks of the employable increased, with the dual effect of increasing consumption patterns and aggravating the unemployment situation. The labour force in Atlantic Canada grew more rapidly than for Canada as a whole in this period. Employment creation was at 90 percent of the national rate, itself inflated by rapid growth in western Canada. The labour force growth pushed unemployment rates higher (and at a faster pace) than the Canadian rate of 2.2 percent, with unacceptably high levels being reached in Newfoundland and New Brunswick.[52]

For the period 1971–80, almost a decade, Atlantic region growth was slower than that of the resource-rich western region, but higher than growth in Quebec and Ontario in most respects; earned income per capita grew at the same rate as in Canada, and growth of the goods-producing sectors (rather than in the traditional service sectors) matched the Canadian performance.[53] Real domestic product in Atlantic Canada increased 34.8 percent in 1980 over 1971, compared to 39 percent for Canada as a whole. Employment growth over the period was 3.0 percent per year compared to 3.1 percent for Canada. In 1980 (in the middle of the international recession), Atlantic employment grew 3.9 percent compared to 2.8 percent for Canada. Unemployment fell slightly. Over the decade, the Atlantic labour force grew at 3.5 percent, outstripping that for Canada (3.2 percent) partially because of in-migration during the period. In spite of high unemployment rates, there were 499 persons employed for every 1,000 over fifteen years of age in 1980, compared to 463 in 1971.

Between 1970 and 1980, population, employment, and earned income per capita for the Atlantic region grew at a rate roughly equal to the national average despite unprecedented growth in western Canada. Manufacturing shipments and the labour force in the region grew at a faster rate, while real domestic product and investment growth were below the national average.[54] The favourable performance in the Atlantic region during the 1970s did not mask the reality of absolute regional disparities; the region lagged behind the rest of Canada in terms of personal income, earned income, participation rates, and employment. These cold statistics helped form the basis for intended continuing regional development efforts for the 1980s.

CONCLUDING THOUGHTS ON EVALUATION

Justification for federal government regional development policy in the 1970s cannot rest solely on the kind of program evaluation recorded in this chapter. Far too much is missing in concrete terms. Without a comprehensive analytical analysis, using some agreed-upon measurement criteria, of just about every element of every federal-provincial agreement and every assistance program, it will never be possible to accurately assess the success of DREE programming during the period.

The period 1982–88 passed with little constructive reporting on the federal government's attempt to have all federal departments direct their attention to regional economies. The problem of differentiating line department national mandate activites from those aimed more specifically at regional development, is too great. Dissecting those aspects of a national activity that could be credited with a regional benefit is a more daunting task than assessing the programs of a dedicated department such as DREE. If it can be proved that the ordinary policies and programs of a line department are not detrimental to regional economies, it could be argued that they are, then, beneficial to the regions.

To what degree are the positive aspects of the Atlantic region's economic performance during the 1970s attributable to DREE (and predecessor programs)? It is evident that the DREE contribution cannot be easily quantified. Given the multitude of positive and negative factors that bear on economic performance, it is not possible to precisely segregate the impact of any one factor. One can only say that if the DREE programs were sensibly conceived and efficiently executed, things would have been much worse in their absence. Others have passed qualitative opinions on the contribution of government efforts to improve regional circumstances, related in some degree at least to DREE and DREE/provincial efforts.

The Atlantic Provinces Economic Council, in its analysis of the 1982 reorganization of federal economic departments, touched on DREE's modest percentage of overall economic expenditures but added: "Nevertheless, DREE's programs and initiatives have contributed significantly to the development of poorer regions ... There is no doubt that these expenditures have enabled the Atlantic Provinces to progress in areas that would have been impossible if left to their own resources and limited revenue base."[55] The council's continued adherence to the measurable indices school of thought, however, was evident in its conclusion that the lack of any real success in improving quantitative measures of unemployment, participation rates, and per capita incomes had been damaging to DREE. However, APEC did say that DREE should not shoulder all the blame for the lack of substantive progress in improving the economy of the Atlantic region.

In 1987 the report of the Federal-Provincial Task Force on Regional Development Assessment again drew attention to some of the modest advances made in earned income, provincial gross domestic product, and employment growth in the regions (with specific reference to the Atlantic) and pointed out that there were stark measurable differences between these gains and the national performance.[56] The report also raised the spectre of the high level of performance that would be required by what are traditionally considered the economically disadvantaged regions of Canada (a contradiction in itself) to significantly close the gap with the rest of Canada. The task force suggested that holding their own was better for the regions than falling backwards and that measurable performance indicators, by themselves, represented an incomplete proxy for assessing regional well-being and regional economic development efforts. The task force concluded that regional development efforts in the 1970s were effective in the context of the amount of resources applied to them, and put this comment in perspective: "The resources applied specifically to regional development over the past 25 years have been small, in relative terms, less than 3% of total federal economic expenditures. Greater expenditures could well have had significantly greater results." It added that the principal reason for the success achieved was that the majority of the funding was spent on programming designed to meet the needs of the areas in which it was applied.[57]

A number of statements have been made on the improvement over the years in the circumstances of the Atlantic provinces, some related to DREE, others not. The preambles to the Prince Edward Island, New Brunswick, and Newfoundland ERDAs each referred to improved regional circumstances over the decade just concluded. Donald Savoie, in his report leading to the creation of the Atlantic Canada Opportunities Agency, wrote: "It is clear to anyone familiar with the history of Atlantic Canada that the region has made important progress in the past twenty-five years. Basic infrastructure facilities ... are now in place or beginning to take shape, as a result of federal regional development efforts. Schools, main arterial highways, tourism facilities, to list just a few, have been established," and, "it is evident, even to the most casual observer, that life in small Atlantic communities has improved and become modernized in many ways over the past twenty years or so."[58]

Other comments on the value of federal economic development policies fall somewhere between outright rejection and tentative support. The Macdonald Commission concluded that "the best that can be said is that we may have prevented the less-developed regions from falling further behind."[59]

Most of the DREE/provincial program activity had an immediately identifiable result in quantitative as well as qualitative terms; the DREE regions were starting to assemble such data before the merger. The data are a gold mine for researchers willing to undertake the substantial work required to seek them out, although this becomes more and more difficult with the passage of time. The longer-ranging impact of the programs, in quantifiable economic terms, is more difficult to determine. There can be little argument, however, with the conclusion that better transportation linkages, improved quality of forest stands, increased productivity and quality of all resource products, more modern and technically advanced processing and manufacturing facilities, the aggregation of industry and business in efficient industrial parks, a greater diversification of the economic base of the regions, increased management skills, awareness and use of new marketing techniques, and the score of other consequences of DREE programs have helped the regions to be better positioned in economic terms than before. Perhaps this begs the question of cost-effectiveness, but if it is presumed that every project and program was carefully constructed and executed (granted, this is a heroic assumption), then the sum of the parts should have made a positive contribution to regional economic circumstances.

Chapter Seven

Prescriptions

INTRODUCTION

Most of the prescriptions for improving regional economic circumstances in Canada's regions fall short of addressing the difficulties the implementor faces in translating these theories into practice. The widely quoted Economic Council of Canada study of 1977, *Living Together: A Study of Regional Disparities*, phrased its recommendations as framework policy statements, rather than as specific courses of action to be followed.

The Atlantic Development Council, in its 1978 report, "The Atlantic Region of Canada: Economic Development Strategy for the Eighties," listed at least seventy recommendations for action by governments and the private sector, but presented its report as a general thesis for study. It remains a valuable reference document, and many of its recommendations have been adopted over the years, while others have become outdated. In its report, the Federal-Provincial Task Force on Regional Development Assessment said of its work, "In the discussion of policy and program directions, we did not attempt to identify specific initiatives or program measures. It seemed to us more appropriate ... to take a longer-term perspective concerning the elements of a contemporary and forward-looking approach."[1] Some of its recommendations were nevertheless phrased in terms specific enough to be recorded here where appropriate.

Framework concepts embrace the broadest and most macro-oriented aspects of how the national and regional economies work. In the main they represent valid ideas for the attention of governments willing to address longer-term solutions for Canada's regional economies. They occur at a level of decision making and in areas requiring such coordination, however, that they test the ingenuity of those assigned the responsibility of developing programs based upon them. Such concepts are not easily connected to other policies and programs of government already recognized as being aimed at, or having an identifiable influence on, regional economies. Some are fraught with political danger and require deliberation and decision only at the cabinet level. Notwithstanding these reservations, it is generally acknowledged that they be taken into account.

Thomas Courchene is a leading exponent of the idea that governments should adopt a different approach to addressing the ills of lagging regional economies. Certain of his views have been discussed in previous chapters. He subscribes, as do others, to the theory of positive adjustment, given that adjustment is an irreversible process. On the social front he advocates that "our socio-economic assistance and insurance programs must be redesigned to facilitate adjustment and initiative."[2] Concern for social programming and adjustment prompted the Economic Council of Canada, in a study of the Newfoundland economy, to say, "The objective of new policies should not be to cut off transfers to Newfoundland but to reorganize them in a way that will compensate persons affected by the changes and reduce or eliminate the detrimental side effects that the current system of transfers has on economic efficiency, incentives and equity."[3] This premise applies equally well to other less economically advantaged areas of the country. In 1982 the Senate Standing Committee on National Finance said, "To the extent that transfers distort the functioning of natural economic adjustment mechanisms, they can also hinder development and lead to inappropriate social and economic policy decisions. The objective should be to retain those properties that facilitate development and efficiently implement social and other programs, while purging the system of those that block normal economic growth."[4]

The Federal-Provincial Task Force on Regional Development Assessment continued the theme in 1987: "There is no reason to believe that structural change will decelerate ... there is ample evidence that technological opportunity will accelerate the pace of change. ... This suggests that particular attention needs to be paid to the transfer and incentive system, to education and training and to the role of entrepreneurship ... in short, to the adaptability of human resources to changing market opportunities."[5]

These opinions strike hard at the inadequacies of the social support and transfer systems in Canada and embody an underlying theme of positive adjustment, economic efficiency, and human initiative and adaptability. They recognize the inevitability of change in a now-emerged technological world. They reveal a genuine concern for the well-being of individuals but reflect an understanding of the dependency syndrome by which people, rather than responding more positively to adjustment themselves, want governments to compensate for adjustment. All emphasize the importance of breaking away from the dependency psychology. It is this concept that forms the basis of the self-help theory of regional development. It is not enough to change systems, policies, and programs. Fundamentally, there must be a coincident change in people's attitudes—away from dependency to self-reliance.

The popularity of the adjustment theory, precipitated by international competition, technology, and the knowledge-based services, has generated demands from every quarter for greater efficiency and increased productivity in regional economies (each of the 1984 ERDA agreements contains this admonition). Courchene says of adjustment: "Restructuring-cum-restraint will tilt regional development towards efficiency and adjustment, towards decentralization and towards an increased reliance on private sector participation."[6]

There is little indication that governments are receptive to suggestions that would require substantive and courageous change to the social assistance program parameters that now exist at either the national or regional levels, notwithstanding the benefits that would accrue to all concerned with their consideration.[7] As well, these views are far from being universally subscribed to by all academics.[8] The steady reduction in the level of federal transfer payments and the tinkering with programs such as unemployment insurance, succeed only in shifting the burden of social support to the provinces. Most federal actions of this kind are driven by budget considerations, not by a fundamental rethinking of how to improve the support network and better equip individuals with the education and training they require to become productive members of a competitive economy. For this discussion, then, it is necessary to proceed on the assumption that specific regional development actions comprise the most realistic means of improving regional economic circumstances.

Moving from these more general framework concepts to slightly lower-order policy prescriptions, we still encounter a level of generality, but in a form sufficiently tangible to permit us to envisage possible courses of action to give them effect. Thus emerge the self-help theories in the more concrete terms of community development, small business, entrepreneurship, and service industries. The debate on incentives to business in reopened, but now with a service industries bias. The role of technology at the local level, the role of government in the provision of hard and soft infrastructure, and the role of people with skills and motivation become more definable. Practitioners may be more comfortable dealing with these issues, even though they carry significant policy dimensions, perhaps because once decisions are reached they can be given effect in program form. In the remainder of this chapter, we will examine some of the areas in which change is recommended and other areas where change is inevitable. It is the latter category that may demand the greatest attention of governments and decision makers.

COMMUNITY DEVELOPMENT

In the hierarchy of suggestions for improving regional economies, the concept of community-based self-help efforts stands high. In 1978 the Atlantic Development Council spoke of the "area community," a cluster of small communities and rural settlements focused on an urban centre within commuting distance of its supportive hinterland. In 1977 the Economic Council of Canada recommended that in provinces with lower than average national income levels, urban strategies should recognize that the tendency for people to drift from rural to urban areas and from smaller to medium-sized urban settlements can be used to advantage. Again, in its 1980 study of the Newfoundland economy, the council recommended a provincial government strategy aimed at providing services, infrastructure, and related employment opportunities in one or two urban centres in each of the province's peninsulas, centres that had access to the Trans-Canada Highway and were within commuting distance of the outports.[9] In 1981 Mario Polèse added, "Future regional development policies should put increasing emphasis on local development, on raising the educational and general knowledge level of the population and on encouraging local entrepreneurship."[10] Donald Savoie has endorsed variations on the concepts as a fundamental premise of regional development on more than one occasion.[11] The 1987 Federal-Provincial Task Force on Regional Development Assessment concluded that a strong case could be made for directing more resources to community development groups for their own training needs in developing and implementing local development strategies.[12]

Here we see two complementary streams of thought on the community development theme: (1) communities need some urban attributes to form an economically strong base and (2) initiatives for regional improvement should originate at the community level. Community development, embracing self-help initiatives, small business, entrepreneurship, local development associations, commissions, institutions, and corporations, has been in and out of favour for most of the period that regional development has been taken seriously by governments, dating particularly from the 1960s. Community-level development found favour with the Conservative Party before it formed the government in 1984. In that pre-election period, the party spoke of putting community opportunity development corporations in place, made up primarily of community-level representatives of business and other local organizations and elected members of governments. Their role would be to coordinate community resources, act as a planning focus, and promote training and education. They would have a strong financial management capacity but would rely upon the federal and provincial levels of government for actual funding. There would also be a Canada Opportunity Development Board for federal funding and project approvals. Small business was to play a prominent part in the community-level programming. The final manifestation of the Conservative philosophy turned out to be considerably different in form from these intentions, but it did retain the more significant principles of the policy approach. When in power the Conservatives resurrected community development as a new solution for regional disparities in the 1986–89 period, and ACOA incorporated the bootstraps concept into its new mandate in 1987. Local input, however, fell considerably short of the earlier proposals.

The community development approach by itself is not a panacea for all the problems of economic imbalance that exist across the country. Community development organizations cannot execute major resource-based strategies of resource identification and renewal in the forestry, fisheries, and minerals sectors, cannot deal with major transportation and communications issues, are unlikely to be able to handle the provision of major industry-specific infrastructure requirements, cannot deal on an interprovincial basis, and cannot provide the facilities and supporting infrastructure for skills upgrading, technological innovation, and research and development.

The community-oriented approach can provide the essential means by which local input is secured for any planned initiatives of direct or related impact on a community or collection of communities, can engender locally based development proposals, and can stimulate small business and entrepreneurship. Local development institutions (LDIs) can represent views to government, develop plans for the economic and social well-being of the areas they represent, be a full-time focal point to ensure continuous attention to economic and social improvement, and act as a contact point for all those that wish to get involved. They can also be the conscience of a community, never letting it forget its status or state of well-being, never hesitating to urge greater effort to improve a community's lot.

The popularity of the community-based regional development

concept is hardly surprising. Communities, as generally small concentrations of people and economic activity in incorporated or unincorporated villages, towns, and even small cities, comprise the majority of the geographic areas designated as economically disadvantaged. In Atlantic Canada, much of the West, many parts of Quebec, and northern Ontario, community life is the norm. The word community may also be used in its more collegial form, applying to any grouping of any size that holds a common interest and represents itself as a community for the purpose of forming associations, developing plans, negotiating with governments, or for other valid reasons.

Governments and communities have had a lot of experience with community development, none more so than DREE itself. The Canada Employment and Immigration Commission tried a number of local development and community employment strategies over the years, including the Local Economic Development Assistance program conducted jointly with DREE in 1980 and the Community Futures Program in 1985 and onwards. In 1980, Industry Trade and Commerce came along with ILAP, the Industry Labour Adjustment Program, in cooperation with CEIC and Labour Canada. Its community designation criteria had some people wondering, with such opposites as Windsor, Ontario, and McAdam, New Brunswick, both designated as ILAP communities. One major program of the Canadian Industrial Renewal Board (the CIRB was launched by ITC in 1981), the Business and Industrial Development Program, could be categorized as a community development program, given that it targeted seven designated communities (five in Quebec, two in Ontario). The program was very much government managed, however, with little coordinated development effort in each of the designated areas.

A number of lessons were learned from experience over the years, the most recurring being the importance of strong and dedicated institutional leadership at the community level, the fact that success breeds success and that areas with little in the way of natural attributes have not fared well. The importance of a significant local commitment to any project or undertaking, either as funding or contributions in kind, and the importance of longer-term planning horizons and expectations and of a concomitant pledge by governments to honour their part of the bargain over a similar time frame, also emerge as essential ingredients to successful community-level development. Many of the shortcomings of the community development approach reflect a mirror image of the foregoing, including a too high level of dependency on governments, the lack of any economic attributes on which to build, and a scarcity of planning, administrative, and management ability at the local level.

225

In many ways, DREE had seen it all. The first architects of DREE saw it as a natural vehicle for encouraging local community development. Tom Kent said that the department had the power to assist genuine community development, and he highlighted the importance of local involvement and local organization. Kent was thinking in terms of special areas that provided the authority "for the participation of persons, voluntary groups, agencies and bodies in those special areas."[13] The DREE experience confirmed some of the problem areas previously outlined. The level of community association management varied widely from one organization to another, and there was a general lack of forward planning, with much effort directed to short-term employment-generation projects. It was found that most success was achieved when there was a definite focus of activity or community interest, such as existed in the agricultural associations and group management for forest land associations in Nova Scotia. Industrial development commissions were not unlike other community-based structures. Their performance varied greatly, according to the quality of their management and the economic base from which they started.

Many of the government programs put in place to assist communities, such as the spatial programming and most of the activities of the community development associations and commissions, failed to recognize that the structural cause of regional disparity was an inadequate economic base on which to build. It was also clear that community development activities were severely inhibited in times of economic downturn. Tom Kent has said, "No sensible programs will diversify much economic growth to the more peripheral regions when little growth is taking place in the more prosperous areas. A cold economic climate will stunt even the best devised community development projects."[14] The new look for community development in the late 1980s and early 1990s is founded on a high degree of self-help, autonomy, and risk-taking (by governments). It is an approach that has much to commend it, but past experience suggests some particular areas for the attention of those who are going to provide the funding, as well as for the community associations or whatever instrument carries the implementation responsibility:

1 It is essential to ensure a high level of competence of association management in terms of organizational abilities, opportunity identification, planning, financial control, and entrepreneurial spirit.
2 Delegated funding and decision-making authority to the community development institutions should be commensurate with the qualifications indicated under (1).
3 Different community target groups, from the greatly disadvantaged

to those with a good threshold level for economic development, must be recognized, and all assistance, authorities, autonomy, and programming should be so differentiated. The CEIC Community Futures Initiatives started out on this premise.

4 Community development initiatives require some degree of longer-term planning, without ignoring immediate opportunities that present themselves.

5 Community development institutions should not overlook the possibility of merger or affiliation with neighbouring associations if they are too small to be viable on their own—cooperation between institutions should be strong so as to increase the learning-experience opportunities.

6 Communities will have a greater chance of success if they form part of a cluster that has access to urban-like services and amenities.

7 Governments can increase the likelihood of success if, in addition to subscribing to the foregoing, they
   a) recognize that economic and social development go together;
   b) encourage the local production of goods and services with local resources;
   c) tailor direct financial assistance for entrepreneurs to their particular needs;
   d) develop a system of small-scale technology diffusion; and
   e) develop a private sector support system, including university extension departments that can provide the financial, legal, technical, marketing, and other such expertise that may be needed for development institutional use.

One final condition must be met if the community self-help approach is to make its contribution to improving regional economies within a broader-based strategy of regional development: dedicated federal agencies, other federal departments, and the institutions themselves must submit to some degree of cooperation and coordination so that they can avoid working at cross-purposes, counter-productive actions, and ineffective use of funds. One problem that has plagued community development schemes has been that they have frequently become political pressure points—the objective of executing sensible developmental initiatives is overshadowed by the objective of spending public monies.

URBAN STRUCTURES

Notwithstanding the emphasis on self-help community development policies and programs, there is a growing acceptance of the undeniable fact of urban centre prominence in regional economies. The growth-pole concept may have come into favour and subsequently fallen into disfavour with theoreticians, but accumulated evidence supports the importance of some form of urban structure focus for economic advancement. And the importance of this focus has been accentuated with the advent of information technology. The advantages of clustering have not been overlooked when community-based approaches have been considered, as is evident in recommendations of the Atlantic Development Council and the Economic Council of Canada cited elsewhere.

The benefits of viable urban centres become self-evident in economic terms. They revolve around access to knowledge and the people who have it, educational and technical centres and other amenities to attract such people, the use of the latest technologies and business practices in manufacturing and service industries, and the overall supporting hard and soft infrastructure that maintains momentum. The Task Force on Regional Development Assessment suggested that past impediments to a more decentralized economic structure in Canada, such as market size and transportation, may be less important than they had been for the traditional goods-producing industries. It sounded the sombre warning, nevertheless, that without adequate knowledge-based infrastructure (most often found in urban centres) and social amenities in place, economic development is more likely to occur in existing urban centres, mainly outside the peripheral areas, further exacerbating regional disparities. The task force added that urban-centred growth needed to become a more explicit component of regional development policy in Canada.[15] Later we will see that decentralization to the smaller urban or to the community level is at the centre of the debate on the role that technology and service industries play in regional development. Despite the potential for community-based areas of new technology, communications advances, and service industries, the likelihood is that a hierarchy of three levels of urban-based structures will remain in Canada.

The Unconnected Community Although perhaps diminishing in numbers over time, the small, unconnected community, based on the coastal fishery of Newfoundland, the agricultural base of the West, or the forest resource of northern Ontario, will continue to be an important part of the Canadian mosaic. These usually resource-based communities have a somewhat predictable future, at lower levels of wealth, even though vulnerable to changes in world commodity prices in fish, agricultural, and forest products and minerals. The luckier ones may be those supporting a large pulp and paper or mining enterprise, which provides fairly high levels of economic well-being as long as the resource base continues, but they are very vulnerable to economic disaster if that base disappears. Even the communities at the lowest level of the hierarchy in economic (not social and cultural) terms will, however, benefit from communications technology, but as receivers, not generators, of these benefits.

The Area of Communities (or the Connected Community) From a community and lifestyle point of view, the community area concept, based upon access to urban service centres, may be the optimum. Within reason and depending upon the size and viability of the urban-like focal point, most modern services could be available to the individual communities making up the area. Consumer goods and services may be taken for granted in such a structure. Financial services, educational facilities, computer and telecommunications services, and access to the use of up-to-date technologies in resource processing, manufacturing, and service industries should all be available. The area's products should become more competitive in national and world markets as a result. These centres, however, with very few exceptions, will also be receivers, not generators, of the fast-moving technologies that will drive the Canadian economy.

The Urban Structure The highest level of urban structure is recognized in but a few Canadian cities—Toronto, Montreal, Vancouver—with a second-level tier in Ottawa, Winnipeg, Calgary, and Halifax, to name a few. As we saw in chapter 6 in the analysis of corporate locational choices, bigness begets growth—companies like to be where the services and the markets are, where the amenities exist to draw the people they want, where the business climate is familiar to them. It is necessary to acknowledge the exceptions to this rule. For many years, there has been a phenomenon of decentralization outside major cities. Major corporations are locating up to 160 kilometres from the core of cities like New York, but they remain essentially satellites of those cities and well within reach of all the cities offer in technical and economic terms. The disenchantment with the high cost of living in Toronto has meant that it is no longer the mecca for those seeking work at whatever level of professionalism, and companies and individuals are moving elsewhere. But the growth, the agglomeration of services, and the push for world competitiveness in all the new economic fields remain there.

The distribution of people, goods, services, wealth, and technology between these three levels of the hierarchy is an essential consideration for regional development policy makers. How much should they attempt to influence this distribution? Is it sufficient to ensure the dissemination of information and technology to the two lower levels of the hierarchy so that living standards and the competitiveness of their products are held at acceptable standards to maintain chosen ways of life? How are the cities comprising the highest level in the hierarchy to be categorized? Should governments be providing assistance to the second- or third-tier cities in the urban category so that they can catch up with the leaders—in other words, should governments seek to close the disparity gap? On a practical basis the answers to these questions may not be as difficult as they first seem. They may become more so with a political overlay.

One must be cautious in making recommendations pertaining to the unconnected community-level structure. Despite the number of analyses of the much-maligned Newfoundland Resettlement Program, no clear-cut conclusion has ever emerged on whether it was a fundamentally sound idea or what life would have been like in the areas affected if they had been left untouched. The Resettlement Program was one of the first attempts at implementing the community area concept which entailed bringing people into a more viable community entity for education, health care, and (to a lesser extent, as it turned out) economic prosperity purposes. The small and generally unconnected communities will remain in Canada, substantially resource based and declining in population and in numbers. Responsibility for their welfare and the support they require to avail themselves of modern services and technologies should rest primarily with provincial governments. The generally wealthier single-industry or single-sector community at this level in the hierarchy should similarly fall within the provincial government responsibility orbit, but the federal government will never be absolved of involvement when catastrophe strikes. This is interesting, given that the single-sector community is largely resource based, is within the provincial jurisdiction, and quite often has been established with provincial assistance and persistence.

The decisions taken when a crisis strikes the single-industry/single-sector community, are almost always taken within a much larger national and even international context. The federal government has never had any success in establishing a policy for dealing with such situations. DRIE tried, as did DREE before it, but the most realistic approach has been the one-at-a-time treatment, learning where possible from previous experiences. The sad truth is that it is difficult, if not impossible, to parachute a new economic activity, of the same significance as one that has been lost, into an area facing economic collapse. This is true for one very important reason: the previous activity was there for a purpose—whether because it was resource based, a once needed military installation, or logical for some other reason. The one-at-a-time treatment does have the advantage of allowing government to tailor the solution to prevailing circumstances. The model to be used from a federal point of view, if any chance of success is expected, is that of a full-time dedicated task force approach, the only way in which some redress might be accomplished. In the absence of a continuing centre of responsibility to focus collective efforts, it is a waste of time to urge either federal or provincial government departments to think about a crisis situation when exercising their assigned mandate.

The second-tier communities, located within an area configuration with access to urban amenities in whatever form that may exist, fall realistically within the ambit of both levels of government for development purposes. Here must be developed the soft infrastructure and services, in particular, that are usually beyond the fiscal capacity of the communities themselves, individually or collectively. This is where agencies such as ACOA and WD should legitimately be concentrating, along with other federal and of course provincial departments that have policies and program instruments that may be applicable.

Federal options relating to the highest-level community aggregation, the truly urban centre, are dealt with in the "Technology" and "Telecommunications and Service Industries" sections, which follow the "Small and Medium-Sized Enterprises" section below.

SMALL- AND MEDIUM-SIZED ENTERPRISES (SMES)

Small- and medium-sized businesses, entrepreneurship, and skills upgrading go hand in hand with the community self-help concept. Most of those who have written about regional development, whether in macroeconomic policy terms or with more specific suggestions for action, have emphasized the importance of translating the community self-help theme into the tangible expression of business enterprises, operated and managed by competent local entrepreneurs. Small- and medium-sized enterprises, the SMES, have received a lot of attention from governments over the years, directly and through the many government-supported economic development commissions and associations. The degree to which community-based sponsorship of local entrepreneurship has been successful was examined earlier in this chapter. Much of the effort of governments has been concentrated on direct financial assistance to the SMES in the form of preferred financing, grants and contributions, and modest levels of business counselling. Several federal agencies, including DREE, DRIE, FBDB

231

(Federal Business Development Bank), and CEIC, have provided training and formal business instruction for the smaller entrepreneur, directly or under federal-provincial collaborative arrangements. The provinces maintain an array of instruments designed to encourage local entrepreneurship. What has not been as coherent has been the attention to the infrastructure and service support linkages necessary for the SME sector to survive and flourish, even though many discrete attempts in this regard have also been made.

In 1974 DREE Atlantic studied services to entrepreneurship. Consultants examined measures that would encourage such an activity within the private sector itself, with possible public sector cost-sharing in the early stages. A business support system, operated by a venture formulation office, was designed to assess and evaluate the technical and commercial feasibility of new ventures, assist in the preparation of business plans, and identify the linkages necessary to carry ideas from the formulation through to the decision-taking stage. At this early concept stage, the operational form was viewed as being highly flexible. The essential premise was the assembling of the necessary expertise to identify a prospective business proposition and carry it through to decision point, with public-private collaboration. The goal was to create a sustainable private sector business support system. This was too complex to capture the attention of provincial governments just embarking on a new federal-provincial approach to regional development and with a range of important and identifiable development initiatives from which to choose. Although some progress was made on elements of the idea in individual situations, it never regained the interest it had generated at the outset.

It is much easier to propose the existence of a strong business community than to make it happen.[16] Donald Savoie recognized this when he explored new approaches to regional development in the Atlantic provinces.[17] We already know that the natural attributes of a region, its distance from markets and transportation systems, its educational and technological skills, its people migration patterns, and a host of other influences dictate the nature of its business community. We earlier discussed the obstacles to importing businesses to a region and the degree to which this was ever considered a viable development approach by practitioners. The alternative then becomes one of building on existing regional enterprises or developing new ones in the region. It is a short step from this line of reasoning to the realization that peripheral markets are not big enough to support a sustained effort in this direction; to succeed, the enterprise must expand beyond regional borders to national and international markets. Such a course of action raises the problem of competing with those who are either already occupying, or vying for, those same markets, and competing at their level of technical, marketing, manufacturing, and services competence. If a deficiency in these skills is one of the reasons the peripheral areas of the country are not as successful in business terms as they would like to be, the corollary becomes one of building these disciplines. This leads to a concentration on people strengths and on how they can be improved. As the Economic Council of Canada had said, the hope for the peripheral regions (here represented by Newfoundland) lies with the people; much depends on how they train and apply themselves, their skills, and ingenuity to improving their own lot.[18]

Views on what to do about raising the skills levels in the regions to permit entrepreneurship to thrive, to develop the efficiency, productivity, and competitiveness necessary for success in national and international markets, and to develop a diversified economic base in the regions range from the general to the specific.[19] When still Liberal Party leader in opposition in New Brunswick, Frank McKenna outlined six pillars for job creation: the development of small business and entrepreneurship, the exploitation of the potential for research and development, the greater involvement of educational institutions in economic growth, the modernization of traditional industries, the diversification of the provincial economy through service industries and tourism, and selective infrastructure investment.[20] These pillars are also found at the federal level and in the federal-provincial ERDAS for most provinces. A DRIE 1987 staff paper also stressed less reliance on grants and contributions to industry and more on local entrepreneurship, human capital, and soft infrastructure, including education.[21] Much earlier, the House of Commons Standing Committee on Regional Development, after a September 1980 visit to the Atlantic region, suggested moving to strengthen assistance to small business and industry.[22] The more specific recommendations that have been put forward over time for actions and programs that would strengthen small- and medium-sized businesses, entrepreneurship, and skills upgrading fall in one of several recognizable categories. The most popular suggestions are set out below.

Entrepreneurship Measures to improve locally based entrepreneurship, courses, seminars and training for managers; upgrading other essential skills; how to start and operate a small business; entrepreneurship as part of the educational curriculum; a greater role for post-secondary educational institutions in business education; centres for entrepreneurial development and coordinated planning for skills upgrading.

Financial Assistance The continuation of industrial incentives grants and contributions; federally funded and provincially delivered cash grants; advance payments on grants; the use of generally available assistance instruments, such as equity investment, loan guarantees, and repayable advances to reduce the possibility of countervail action by trading partners; special tax breaks, tax-free capital accumulation, tax-free debt instruments, municipal bonds, venture capital and stock savings plans; investors/business opportunities brokering and development corporations.

Services Increase the availability and decentralization of information and management services; promote regionally rooted service industries, computers and telecommunications; develop user-friendly services; ensure a supporting network of suppliers and service businesses; develop and support financial counselling, business planning, marketing, data processing, consulting engineering, food and catering services, public relations and child care; accept the need for public sector investment; extend small-business incentives programs to the service sector and provide soft and institutional infrastructure.

These are some of the ideas more frequently put forward for improving the business and entrepreneurial climate in the less economically favoured regions of the country.[23] Other related recommendations advocate local sourcing, special efforts to develop locally based manufacturing and service industries, the development of marketing expertise in the region, including support of market research and development centres, and greater access to national and international marketing information. Business spin-offs from research and development fostered in regionally located centres of excellence and building on natural attributes such as the resource industries are also promoted. On a more selective basis, hard infrastructure for incubator and industrial malls, transportation improvement, tourism enhancement, and urban development remain popular. Although resources fall outside the purview of small business and entrepreneurship as such, emphasis is still placed on having resource enhancement, exploitation, and value added take place within the region rather than elsewhere, thus acting as important catalysts for the development of supporting small businesses and services in the region.

Most of these proposals have been around for many years, which is not to diminish their value or importance. Most have been employed at one time or another, frequently being resurrected through the "reinventing the wheel" syndrome or because they were worth another try. The focus on service industries and a supporting services infrastructure is perhaps stronger now than in the past, when there was so much else to do. All of the existing federal departments and agencies that carry a regional development mandate, along with provincial governments, program in most of the foregoing areas. In its day, DREE was a prominent exponent of most of these approaches. It led the way in the introduction of some and moved through the hierarchy of levels of sophistication from hard infrastructure to high technology, skills upgrading, new forms of financial assistance, and service industries support. The ad hoc application of so many of these schemes diminished their usefulness in bringing improved economic circumstances to the peripheral regions. Placed in a more coordinated context, they have a much greater chance of success and can be the basis of a concerted attack on regional development problems.

TECHNOLOGY

Technology is the recognized key to economic progress. Its diffusion is cited as a factor that enhances or detracts from competitiveness, and the peripheral regions are generally considered to be slower at technological adaptation than the more central parts of the country.[24] "High-tech" industry has come to imply an economic panacea for industry sectors and regions alike. Every province has wanted its own centres of micro-electronics, bio-technological exploration, electronics and aerospace research and development, and the attendant feeder industries to these glamour sectors. A more rational outlook has emerged, however, as the reality has hit home that every province, or even Canada, cannot support all sectors. Some regions have been wise enough to concentrate on technologies that are seen as native to the region. As early as 1978, the Atlantic Development Council urged governments to meet the technological challenge of the 1980s, specifically recommending that federal centres of excellence in fisheries, marine technology, metallurgy, communications research, and alternate energy research be located in the region.[25]

Technology, the availability of skills, access to domestic and international markets, and tough international competition dictate a large degree of selectivity with respect to what and where Canada pursues the natural or induced growth of economic sectors.

The adaptation of existing industries to higher levels of efficiency through the application of new technology is a realistic basis for Canada's technological aspirations, even more so for the technological aspirations of its peripheral regions. At the same time, emerging fields of endeavour based on technology should not be overlooked if Canada is to stake a claim in the global marketplace. Canada and its regions cannot afford to abandon existing economic foundations, even if they may be in decline vis-à-vis the service industries sector. All of the existing manufacturing and processing sectors, the latter of particular importance to peripheral areas, lend themselves to the use of technological improvement to increase their competitive position, something that has already been taking place with and without government assistance.[26]

The Task Force on Regional Development Assessement stated that structural improvement in the regions required a more proactive and sustained role for government, in concert with the private sector and research institutions. New areas of technological specialization needed to be pursued, implying risk, additional costs, and greater decentralization of research and procurement by both government and private industry. The task force stressed the need for a greater role for post-secondary educational institutions and suggested that provincial research organizations might have to be encouraged to evolve a role for themselves that the private sector might be seen to fill elsewhere. It was impressed by the National Research Council Industrial Research Assistance Program (IRAP) and its possible use as a model for technology diffusion to smaller firms.[27]

The newly arrived information technology and service industries sectors are dissolving traditional world trading patterns and hold the key to whether Canada and its regions progress, fall backward, or hold their own in economic development terms. The location of enterprises to develop these new and exciting fields will to a significant extent determine the future status of Canada's regions. The Task Force on Regional Development Assessment said, "In many ways, regional competition and comparative advantage in Canada will be based on economic competition and specialization among urban centres in which the most dynamic centres will be those most richly endowed with knowledge-based infrastructure and networks," and "Knowledge-based industry investment gravitates to centres that are endowed with a supporting infrastructure of research institutions."[28]

Without development—of a suitable kind—and the adoption of technological advances in the regions, strongly supported by governments, the peripheral areas of the country will fall behind. The consequence will be an even heavier and much more deleterious burden on the transfer system and a reduced participation by the people of these regions in the future of Canada. The problem centres on how to integrate the peripheral regions into the mainstream of technological revolution.

INFORMATION TECHNOLOGY AND SERVICE INDUSTRIES

Barry Lesser and Pamela Hall posed the question "What will be the impact or implications of the information economy on the spatial

236

distribution of economic activity among Canada's regions?" and provided their own answer: "It is theoretically possible for disadvantaged regions either to gain or lose relative to more advantaged regions through the introduction/application of the technology of the information age ... it is most likely that the Atlantic provinces will lose ... if market forces alone are left to decide the outcome."[29] The Federal-Provincial Task Force on Regional Development Assessement also identified the potential role that innovation and technology could play in the structural improvement of weaker economies, but warned that market factors alone could drive a new regional disparity related to technological endowment.[30]

Information, as a product in its own right and as the output of service industries, aided by telecommunications technology, is a two-way street for the peripheral regions of Canada. Information and service industries outputs can be transmitted out from a region, but they can also get in. Coffey and McRae refer to two schools of thought on the subject, one that says new information and communications technology permit the decentralization of office-based activities, the other that these technologies free office functions from the necessity of proximity to the operations they direct. They conclude that the evidence supports the premise that centralization has accompanied technological advances, particularly with reference to the producer services component of the service industries sector.[31]

These conclusions are based on a central location benefits theory, coupled with the accepted wisdom that peripheral regions trail the rest of the country in adopting new technologies. Lack of regional technological capacity, lower skills and education levels, smaller regional markets, and a lower level of support services such as computer maintenance, consultants, and training facilities all militate against the region.[32] Barry Lesser lists the low population base and levels of educational attainment in the Atlantic region, its higher-than-average and growing rural population (technology has an urban bias), a proportionally lower level of management/administrative positions than nationally (the centralizing tendency of the management function), and a lower level of a number of service industries in the region to indicate the difficulty it faces in competing with more mature centres of technology development.[33] Nationally, Lesser and Hall said there was no information technology policy, making it impossible to construct a regional policy.[34] Since that time ISTC created an information technology branch in an effort to bring some order into its approach to the sector with emphasis on the diffusion of such technology. Some attention has been paid to the regional dimension. The service industries also have a home in ISTC's Service Industries Branch. It was instrumental in launching (despite a high level of skepticism and disinterest) the $2.4-million service industries study series that is described later.

The role of telecommunications in advancing regional economies was examined in Atlantic Canada as early as 1973–74. Under a DREE-initiated three-part consultant study, a computer/communications industry development project was proposed to develop a federal-provincial vehicle to oversee the fostering of such a capability within the region.[35] A task force and workshops involved the four provincial governments, seven federal departments, and nine private sector companies. The idea was to design a system comprising a number of interrelated elements, including application software development, community data-processing centres, user and supplier training, and a data communications network with operating-system software and hardware. The primary benefit would be a regional network linked to a national network, with a high-technology, high-information capacity, and extensive software and training capability. This ambitious idea was not completed. It would be interesting to speculate whether its implementation would have changed the face of the Atlantic economy in the intervening years.

A related DREE Atlantic initiative was launched in the 1973–78 period in an attempt to interest the three larger provinces in a combined effort of computer technology development, coupled with some of its telecommunications aspects, with a view to building the region's capability for its own self-sufficiency and for export. Provincial interest was not high, again because of so many other pressing needs. Newfoundland, however, entered a cooperative arrangement with DREE by which it developed a government-sponsored computer institute, one of the more advanced computer capabilities in the region at the time.

In summing up their theoretical framework, Lesser and Hall said that modern telecommunications infrastructure is a prerequisite to any contribution that this science could make to a regional economy. It was their opinion that were the regional economy left to market forces, there would be a tendency to centralization; without government involvement, regional disparities would exacerbate. Lesser and Hall concluded that government would have to play a part if it desired to influence the spatial growth of the information economy, and that it should start with a national policy. In regional development terms, the emphasis would have to shift to the services sector, and there would have to be a greater diffusion of computer technology in the (Atlantic) region, through counselling programs for business users, new applications research, improved services for the sector, shared facilities, and skills upgrading.[36] We will see a remarkable similarity between telecommunications services and other producer services, as more broadly defined, in the following section.

Service Industries and Regional Development

On the basis that footloose industries are amenable to locating in peripheral regions, attention has been given to the possible contribution of service industries to regional development. In 1986, the federal Department of Regional Industrial Expansion (now Industry, Science and Technology) sponsored a $2.4-million research program into the service industries sectors that resulted in over eighty individual studies. A departmental industry consultation paper dated June 6, 1989, observed that there was no evidence that the growth of the service sector was contributing to a reduction of regional disparities in Canada.[37] The research backing up this departmental observation suggested that the service sector was having a worse than neutral impact on regional economies. In fact, it seemed that the fast-growing service industries sector had a negative impact on regional development, threatening to diminish opportunities in the regions.

It has been well established that service industries represent the growth sector of developed nations, far outpacing manufacturing and processing in terms of job creation and rate of growth.[38] Service industries are usually placed in three descriptive categories: consumer services, producer or business services, and public services. The research conducted revealed that the producer services grouping, comprising those functions that serve as inputs into the production of goods or other services, was the most rapidly growing sector in most developed economies. This led ISTC to conclude that Canada could not have a world-class economy without a world-class producer services sector. Not only was producer services a growth sector, it was playing an increasingly important role in improving productivity and competitiveness in Canadian industry. Its products were increasingly sold in combination with goods and as elements of customized solutions to specialized needs, and firms were expanding their contracting-out of a range of service needs not requiring firm-specific knowledge.[39]

The potential for regional economic growth from the producer services component of the service sector is based on its rapidly increasing importance in the national economy, its required presence if regional economies are to have any chance of even keeping up, let alone grow, its possible footloose nature, and its potential for effecting change. Coffey and McRae introduced some sobering thoughts on the subject. They accept the theory that a significant portion of producer services are either basic or export-oriented activities that are highly responsive to external demand. They then probe the likelihood of "whether high order producer services, those capable of contributing to the development of a region, are sufficiently footloose to locate in peripheral regions or, at least, outside of large metropolitan areas." They conclude, on the basis of their analysis of centralization, deconcentration, and decentralization of corporate behaviour, that it is unlikely.[40] The essence of Coffey and McRae's argument is one that we have seen before regarding locational incentives—the clustering or agglomeration effect, the desire to be where others are, whether of your own kind or of your suppliers', and the role of headquarters decision making in multiregional and multinational firms. Coffey and McRae suggest that headquarters decision making is the norm in developed economies and that even with peripheral plant locations, the regional producer services firms find it difficult to break into the multi-establishment firm market. They conclude, "Neither an analysis of spatial patterns across a broad set of countries, nor an exploration of the question from a more conceptual perspective indicates that there is much cause for optimism concerning the capacity for producer services to have an impact upon the level of economic development in peripheral regions."[41]

The generally identified disadvantages associated with regional economies are well known to policy makers and practitioners of regional development. They provide the definition for regional disparity—remoteness from central markets and underdeveloped transportation and communication modes, sparsely distributed population and small domestic markets, statistically lower education and skills levels, lower levels of managerial capability, loss of expertise from the region, a lagging adoption of new technologies, a lack of marketing expertise, and an insufficient supporting infrastructure to help overcome many of these deficiencies.[42] Coupled with these indigenous disadvantages are all the strengths that the competition carries in these areas—larger markets and firm size, higher skills levels, modern infrastructure, the use of latest technologies, and the very important benefits of networking. The regional situation is further aggravated by an even more difficult problem, that of being overlooked in a purely market-driven environment. Manufacturing, processing, and service industries corporate decisions are taken in a centralized decision-making mode, national companies choose to purchase their goods and services nationally rather than to pursue regional acquisition policies, the regional operations of national financial and other institutions are thwarted from taking risks on local entrepreneurs (even though local managers know them far better than do headquarters), and firms in peripheral regions are frequently required to meet more stringent financial security requirements than in other parts of the country. These attitudinal barriers may be the most difficult to overcome.

Notwithstanding the conventional wisdom on the strikes against regional economies' sharing in the new technology-dominated marketplaces of the nation and the world, things may not be as bad as they are made out to be. This book has described just how much progress has been made over the years in improving regional infrastructures of every kind, of upgrading the still-important resource base, and in diversifying the industrial sector. Transfer payments, undesirable as they may be in terms of the dependency syndrome, have enabled the consumers and the governments of the peripheral regions to participate at a very high level in the national wealth and to contribute to it.

We need not be completely pessimistic about the role for producer services or the more broadly based service industries sector in improving regional economies. Fortunately, governments and agencies such as ACOA, WD, and ISTC seem unwilling to give up on this exceptionally important opportunity without a fight. The consumer and public services components of the service sector are accepted elements of regional economies and receive sufficient attention to ensure a climate within which they can remain abreast of technological developments. The resource- and manufacturing-based activities of the peripheral regions can become significantly more efficient and competitive with a determined effort to adopt the technologies of producer services and to have those services developed within the regions. Coffey and McRae acknowledge this possibility, stressing the need to develop the demand side and the supply side of producer services together. In speculating on forms of (government) assistance to improve the chances of success for regional services development, they emphasize the necessity of providing information and marketing support, financial assistance for firms' establishment, and education assistance to ensure the availability of the skills upon which to build a technologically competent economy. ISTC also acknowledged a potential for service industries in regional development if initiatives were undertaken in the context of an appropriate framework.

In service industries, therefore, including telecommunications and the important producer services component, there is no option but to strive for their implantation in regional economies—without them, the regions can only regress. This is a legitimate area for government involvement. The most pressing need is for infrastructure—physical and on a shared basis, computers and telecommunications facilities—for learning centres in all the areas where deficiencies exist: skills, technologies, marketing, and business finance. A coordinated approach to ensuring a service industries support network is also a function for government, as is a selective incentives program to encourage new firm formation in the regions. This is an area for a truly proactive stance on the part of government agencies or some recognized institution or association that can speak for this economic grouping. There must be an effort made to encourage national firms to develop regionally, to seek out new applications for these technologies in the regions, and to vigorously promote their use by the manufacturing, processing, and service industries that already form the base of regional economies.

There is a role for federal departments such as ISTC, Communications Canada, CEIC, Fisheries and Oceans, the National Research Council, and others that have acknowledged expertise in their fields. Failing a return to a one-department dedicated approach to regional development, federal effort should be led by ACOA, WD, and ISTC, which have the program instruments for direct intervention in regional economies. Their record in the use of these instruments has been spotty, with a high percentage of their financial involvement going to firms in no apparent conformity to an overall policy framework and with a majority of assistance going to firms in manufacturing, processing, and non-producer services sectors. Yet some support has been provided for important infrastructure, and some producer services firms have been the recipients of assistance. What appears to be lacking is an overall coordination of effort as part of a recognizable game plan and a more proactive posture to nudge the sector itself, and the users of its services, to greater involvement. This has to change if the producer services sector is to take root in peripheral regions.

FREE TRADE AND REGIONAL DEVELOPMENT

The Canada-US Free Trade Agreement (FTA), the most topical and widely debated issue of 1988 and widely dissected and analysed since then, is a subject deserving book-length attention in its own right. It will be given only brief review with respect to its influence on regional economies. The FTA came into force January 1, 1989, and its impact on Canadian business and on Canadian competitiveness in the North American context received both positive and negative comment. Views on its potential impact on regional economies were mixed. The Canadian government had given assurances of its ability to continue to assist the less economically favoured regions of the country under the FTA.[43] Efforts were made during negotiations to reach consensus on rules governing subsidies employed by the two countries, with possible exemptions for regional development purposes, but these rules did not materialize. The domestic laws of both governments continued to prevail, and experience was to show that both governments had every intention of using them if circumstances so dictated.[44]

The dispute-resolution mechanism set up under the FTA has responsibility for ruling on questions of subsidy or incentives, and this could impinge on regional economies. US actions taken after the FTA was agreed upon that were detrimental to Canadian regional interests dimmed any optimism regarding Canada's ability to remain immune to US trade sanctions. In his last days in office, President Ronald Reagan authorized a two-year extension of the tariffs on West Coast shingles and shakes, a safeguard action that had been arbitrarily imposed on Canadian industry and that was found to be detrimental to both countries. In the first week after the FTA came into effect, US pork producers were lobbying for tariffs against Canadian pork products, a dispute that continued well into 1991, with an outcome favourable to Canada that was hailed as a victory for the dispute-resolution mechanism. Both Canada and the US delayed scheduled tariff cuts on plywood because of their difference of opinion on standards. Trade officials on both sides of the border suggested that this was how it should be, the issue not being whether there would be disputes but rather how such disputes were handled. A spate of plant closures and layoff announcements in Canada, occurring close to the effective date of the trade agreement, did little to help the mood of those already suspicious of the FTA. The bickering between Canada and the United States continued right through 1991, when Canada's removal of an internal 15 percent surtax on softwood lumber precipitated a retaliatory action by the US government. Both countries aired grievances before the General Agreement on Tariffs and Trade (GATT), each threatening retaliation against trade actions of the other.[45]

On May 24, 1989, Washington submitted the first formal request under the FTA, asking that a trade panel be set up to consider a dispute concerning the BC salmon and herring fisheries. The US listed a number of other trade irritants, including Canada's slowness in moving to engage the subsidies negotiations.[46] Canadian companies were also requesting dispute-resolution panels in a number of product categories. Their suspicions were further inflamed when the US International Trade Commission ruled against Canadian steel imports in August 1989, triggering stiff import penalties. Canadian producers retaliated by commissioning a report that concluded that US steel companies benefited from a range of subsidies and concessions worth $30 billion. Many of these problem areas, including the high-profile forest, fisheries, and steel sectors, carried direct regional implications, with their resolution for or against Canada of real significance to regional economies.

US retaliatory action against Canada's special regional development programs remained as an unexercised threat through the first years of the FTA. The Economic Council of Canada, referring to the new development agencies of ACOA and WD in its twenty-fourth annual review, 1987, expressed the opinion that the grants they administer were possible targets of US countervail action. The council qualified its comment by adding that those grants aimed at relocating investment in Canada would be less likely to be the subject of international sanction than those aimed at attracting investment to Canada. The Macdonald Commission, in concluding that free trade would be good for all regions of Canada, suggested that the interregional effects of trade policies are either masked or diluted because of the mobility of factors of production between regions and the ownership of interregional assets.[47] This resurrects the belief that labour mobility is not detrimental to the regions and implies that any asset-specific injury caused by free trade may not be felt in the region if the ownership resides outside the region. If regionally based assets were to be shut down as a result of free trade, the corrective action to offset such a situation could be the outward mobility of labour—hardly advantageous in terms of a contribution to peripheral regional economies.

One year after the free-trade agreement came into effect, the official position of the federal government was that it was too early to evaluate its impact on the Canadian economy. Three years later, however, Industry and Trade Minister Michael Wilson was to give it credit for softening the Canadian recession and opening access to US markets. Those in favour of the FTA cited employment growth of 250,000 as evidence that any deleterious effect of the agreement through direct job loss was more than offset by new employment, much of which could legitimately be attributed to free trade.

The Canadian Labour Congress (CLC) estimated losses as up to 105,000 jobs and more than 258 companies in the first year of the agreement. Analysis of data revealed that approximately 62 percent of the losses were in Ontario and Qubec, approximately 11 percent for the Atlantic provinces and the West and some 27 percent not identified by region. Overall, job loss in economically disadvantaged regions was calculated at about 20 percent, and this did not include losses attributable to the problems of the coastal fish-processing plants.[48] The data were highly qualified in terms of actual and predicted job loss and permanent or temporary job loss. Although most of the loss in the central provinces occurred in the urban areas, the rural and remote areas of the two provinces were significantly represented. By 1991 the CLC and the Liberal Party of Canada were claiming that the job loss of over 250,000 was attributable to the FTA, a claim widely denounced by the Canadian Manufacturers' Association. Economists suggested instead that the manufacturing sector, particularly in Ontario, was going through a fundamental restructuring caused by the recession, government policy, interest rates, the high value of the Canadian dollar, and world competitive conditions.[49] A *Financial Post* review of regional economies seemed to subscribe to the restructuring theory, citing seventy-five plant closings in a six-month period and 97,000 jobs lost in Ontario in a one-year period ending July 1990. It did not assign blame to the free trade agreement.[50]

The numbers surrounding employment gain or loss and conclusions on the degree to which such employment shifts have been influenced by the FTA are suspect and open to a range of interpretations. Similarly, the impact of the free-trade agreement on regional economies cannot be presumed to mirror the national picture. Many of the reported plant closures and layoffs occurred in the nation's industrial heartland. In the regions, some of the perceived adverse effects of the FTA occurred in the resource sectors, but by no means all. Plant closures and relocations in the regions included chemicals, pharmaceuticals, lawn-mowers, thermostatic controls, insulation, printing, and food processing.

Maude Barlow, in a devastating attack on the FTA, the Mulroney government, and big business in Canada and the US, put forward the proposition that the FTA was the work of the corporate elite in North America. She suggested that Canada was prepared to sacrifice regional development programs during the trade negotiations but the US refused so as not to tie its hands in subsequent discussions on subsidies.[51]

A Royal Bank retrospective on the FTA lent some credibility to Barlow's contention that the FTA was a creature of, and of prime benefit to, North American corporate leaders. Its *econoscope* special issue review of the first year of the trade agreement was an unabashed, completely uncritical endorsement of the agreement, extolling all its virtues, speaking almost entirely of the benefits to companies as opposed to people, and in respect of employment impact concluding that "jobs lost appear to have been more than compensated for by expanded employment opportunities in other sectors." The bank continued its unmitigated endorsement of the free-trade agreement in its second-year review, concluding that shifts in the structure of manufacturing industry in Canada were more influenced by recession, interest rates, labour costs, and the strong Canadian dollar than by the FTA.[52]

As 1990 came to a close, the Mulroney government had relegated the Canada-US Free Trade Agreement to the back burner. The extravagant claims of 1988–89 had faded, and except within the context of

Canada's apprehensive participation in the trilateral (Canada, Mexico, and the US) continental trade discussions, little was heard of the FTA until a year later, when the controversy over its impact on the Canadian economy erupted with renewed vigour. In December 1991, Gordon Ritchie, the Canadian deputy chief trade negotiator of the FTA, scolded the US for not honouring the spirit of the agreement. The charge was rejected by the Americans and Trade Minister Michael Wilson. As US punitive trade actions in softwood lumber and under the Automotive Pact signalled increased US aggressiveness in an election year, however, Prime Minister Mulroney took up Ritchie's charge, accusing American government officials of pettiness and harassment. The subsidies issue was rearing its head in a way that extended beyond agency programs in support of regional development, to cloud the entire range of Canada-US trade relations, and the regions could only look on with increasing concern. One thing was certain; any punitive US trade actions against Canada would reverberate through the regional economies.[53]

Chapter Eight

Conclusions

OPTIONS

Federal regional development policies have included centralized explicit regional development programs, provincial implementation of federally designed schemes, rural-based efforts, targeted industrial programming, the growth-pole concept, federal-provincial design and management of regional development initiatives, decentralized federal administration, explicit and ad hoc organizational forms, dedicated development agencies dating from the 1960s, and almost continuous change of policy direction. Federal departments with no dedicated regional development mandate have pursued national policies that have enhanced or contradicted regional economic progress. All policies have found their expression in program, management, and organizational terms. On the evidence, it has to be concluded that decentralized program design, management, and implementation, if effected within a national context, are likely to provide the greatest return for effort. Where do we go from here?

Despite the array of policy, program, and project suggestions that have been directed to resolving economic discrepancies between Canada's regions, there is little likelihood of anything coming along that has not already been tried. Governments are not going to be venturesome when it comes to redirecting national social and economic policies for the exclusive purpose of adjusting the fundamentals of regional economies—adverse political reaction alone would negate such actions. The level of funding allocated for explicit regional development purposes continues to garner comment, but there is only so much that can be expended in this regard without subsuming other federal and provincial government mandates in the name of regional development. It is not the amount of money available, but how it is used, that counts.

What, then, is left for politicians and bureaucrats in the ongoing pursuit of solutions to Canada's perennial regional development problems? When new ideas are scarce and governments are unable to exhibit the fortitude to stay with a particular policy thrust long enough to prove it effective, they frequently turn to two standbys—instruments (of programming) and (organizational) structures, underpinned with the philosophy of coordination. One of the most solid and enduring recommendations for improving regional economies focuses on the importance of coordination between departments and between governments—coupled with improved communication between all parties that may have an impact on regional economic circumstances.[1]

STRUCTURES

Organizational structures, which rarely receive their precise definition before they are in place, are expected to overcome a lot of policy deficiencies. They are frequently an afterthought, following policy, program, and functional requirements. One of the most perplexing problems encountered in trying to structure an organization for regional development purposes is determining whether it is to have a coordinating, overseer, policy, or operational role, or all or some of these responsibilities. The form that results will be drastically different in each case. Ian McAllister saw DREE being transformed into a small, senior, policy agency or board, reporting to a senior minister, with no programming responsibility and a prime function of persuading other government departments to execute regional development program responsibilities. It would formulate guidelines and monitor the performance of these departments, which would operate against a set of DREE-identified regional development targets. There would also be provision for federal-provincial collaboration and private sector advice.[2]

Aucoin and Bakvis saw the problem in a somewhat different light in 1985, being content to specify that the cabinet decision-making process needed to be organized so that cabinet would receive specific advice on the needs and opportunities of regions as they related to national policy. They added that the administration and implementation of national policies, decisions, and programs required coordination at the regional level and that the responsibility for regional economic development policy required separation from sectoral policy determination.[3]

In 1986 Donald Savoie spoke of a new organization that "would thus depart from tradition, in combining the capacities of a central agency with that of a program and research body." He talked about an agency with solely a regional development mandate (DREE), its own minister at the table (DREE), a department that cuts across jurisdictional lines (DREE), and one that managed the regional development fund (the DREE budget, in the DREE days). It could define strategies, negotiate them with provincial governments (DREE), and ensure a regional dimension in federal policies and programs. "It could play a DREE-type role by providing money from the regional fund to line departments as an incentive to do new and needed things."[4] (DREE in parentheses above is author's emphasis. In other words, DREE fulfilled all of the requirements of Savoie's "new" organization for regional development.) Savoie also envisaged the agency developing programs on its own in the absence of proposals from line departments, transferring them to other departments when the programs were mature and when departments demonstrated they understood the objectives of the programs. DREE was doing this at an accelerated rate by the time it was brought to an end in 1982. Pieces of Savoie's proposal are found in the make-up of the Atlantic Canada Opportunities Agency, which followed in 1987, and none of the elements are significantly different from what DREE did or had the mandate to do.

ACOA was originally conceived as a small agency, with a staff of no more than a hundred, with a prime responsibility for coordination of federal efforts, and with most programming carried out by federal and provincial departments. It would play an active role in opportunity identification and the preparation of industrial profiles and corporate industrial and economic intelligence. It would study devices to enhance regional economies, such as tax incentives, and assist soft and hard infrastructure in support of its objectives.[5] ACOA is an example of how a concept can be adulterated. The agency became much larger than first recommended, playing every conceivable role for regional development, including developing direct business incentives programs. Whether it is any better at coordinating the activities of other government departments than a single line department would be has yet to be demonstrated.[6]

Of the many structural suggestions since 1982, several of them tried, none has proved superior to DREE, not because DREE itself was flawless, but because no consideration was given to whether the DREE model could have been improved upon.

INSTRUMENTS

Over the decades during which governments have pursued various policies of regional development and practised a range of strategies for their implementation, the instruments to be used, the tools of the trade, have never been a problem—this despite the number of times politicians and bureaucrats alike have tried to hide behind the argument that there was no program in place to do one thing or another. Legitimate activities to legitimately enhance regional economies, not pet political projects, can always be accomplished. There is always a legal way to effect regional development plans, a legal way to turn a policy into action.

The distinct programs that have been put in place over the years for regional development purposes have been many, some carrying full legislative authority in their own name through acts of Parliament, others carried forward under departmental mandates and Estimates Vote wording. The list of program acronyms is formidable — ADA, ARDA, ADB, ADIA, and AEP to FRED, ILAP, IRDP, and RDIA — with any number of other interesting letter assemblies in between. The most innovative and flexible approach devised, however, found its expression in the GDAS (later ERDAS) and the subsidiary agreements written under them. With these vehicles it was possible to undertake any activity that would improve regional economic circumstances.

In commenting on comprehensive program concepts such as the GDA, the ERDA, and the PEI CDP, the Federal-Provincial Task Force on Regional Development Assessement said, "The apparent success and popularity of these comprehensive programs can be attributed in large measure to their regional sensitivity resulting from decentralized planning and implementation based on real knowledge and understanding of the regional economies." In comparing the ERDAS to their GDA predecessors, the task force said that the ERDAS were also comprehensive but "without a comparable capacity to marshal efforts around regionally based priorities."[7]

Federal-provincial cooperation in formulating and implementing regional development policies has received the endorsement of the most knowledgable commentators on the subject. The process to achieve the desired end-result, the GDA or ERDA agreement instrument itself, however, has continued to collect its share of criticism, usually at the political level. The DREE formula for federal-provincial collaboration worked exactly as such a cooperative system should work; neither partner was taken advantage of, no element was negotiated into an agreement that was not agreed to by both parties (even if there was give and take on its inclusion—that is the essence of negotiation), and no projects could be implemented without the written concurrence of both governments. The formula worked because the federal government had highly skilled and experienced officials involved with both negotiation and implementation who carried a meaningful level of delegated decision-making authority. This was possible because ministers, by and large, had confidence in their professionalism and judgment. The GDA, properly used, is unequivocally the best instrument yet devised for implementing regional economic development policy.

WHITHER THE FUTURE?

We cannot look intelligently to the future without reminding ourselves of the lessons of the past. Too many wheels have been reinvented in the name of regional development already, too many mistakes made by those who were presumptuous enough to think that the experiences of the past had nothing to offer. One need only look to 1982 to see the evidence of this folly. On the other hand, policy makers can be blinded by recalling only what they want to recall; the federal government in particular has been driven by its paranoia with visibility. For that reason it entered the 1990s still rethinking its regional development approach, still searching for a way to take all the credit.

Expectations

It is important to recognize both what disparity is and what it is not. It is not reasonable to expect the peripheral regions of the country to reach national levels of economic well-being, particularly as measured by quantifiable indicators. The structural base of regional economies, locational disadvantages, all those factors noted in other chapters that explain why the regions have maintained their remarkable consistency of share of national wealth and population, make it very unlikely that the regions could grow at rates of twice or more the national averages, which would be required if measurable gaps are to be closed. Sometimes their economies will spurt, as in the case of the western oil boom, but such uneven influences cannot be counted on to right the disparities dilemma.

The regions should be able to grow and prosper without worrying about being on a par with national averages. That is the objective of realistic regional development policy. As more than one person has pointed out, there are many less quantifiable benefits to living in some areas of Canada rather than in others, benefits that make the lifestyle practised the envy of other parts of the country.

To measure the success of explicit regional development efforts, one must relate them to the progress of the Canadian economy as a whole and place them in the context of all the federal government activities in the regions in which economic development is practised. Regional development policies will not counter a national or international economic downturn. Regional economies are, however, highly sensitive to national policies in virtually every field. If the explicit regional development policies and programs are dovetailed with those of other departments of government, and if the latter are sensitive to their impact on the fortunes of the regions, it is legitimate to expect to see significant results.

There is no way to design a benefit-cost formula to accurately assess long-term regional development policies. The individual projects and programs executed under the aegis of those policies, however, are measurable, and the sum of those evaluations will give a very good indication of whether policies are on the right track. The important proviso is time, the one thing that governments do not think they have. Without adequate time to make mistakes and make corrections, there is little hope of any regional development policy surviving long enough to prove its worth. The federal-provincial approach incarnated in the GDA (and the ERDA and other name changes) lasted longer than most, in concept if not in form. It endured through eight years with DREE and another ten years under MSERD, all departments of government, and the dedicated agencies created in 1987. The approach came under heavy attack in 1990, with actors at the political level still not understanding its value and still perplexed over how to use it. Unfortunately, its use was convoluted after its initial success by the repeated structural changes that governments experimented with after 1982. Nevertheless, the concept remains the most enduring of the many tried in the last thirty years or so.

Rather than agonize over a past failure to better evaluate the impact of dedicated regional development policies and programs, we should strive to do better in the future. Economic indicators are interesting measures of national performance, but they hold little relevance for measuring regional development effort. Evaluation of projects and programs can be improved, taking into account many more variables than most are wont to do. Evaluation must go beyond counting jobs and the cost of creating them—it must take into account earnings generated that find their way into the economy, taxes paid at all levels of government, sourcing of goods and services, sales made and markets penetrated, the attainment of educational skills, the use of technologies, and all the other influences mentioned elsewhere in this book that relate to the productivity of a region. Even the value of hard and soft infrastructure can be better assessed with the application of a little ingenuity. This is the only way to demonstrate the value of dedicated government intervention in the name of regional development. And common sense and observation are not a bad basis for judging whether something is right or wrong, is working or not working (even if this suggestion sends shudders through the veins of the purists).

Equalization and transfer payments to individuals and governments will always be with us. We might as well get used to the idea that the peripheral regions are part of this nation, and make every effort possible to ensure that they have the fullest opportunity to participate in its wealth and contribute to its future. Transfers need not carry a negative connotation, but care must be taken that they are not employed in a way that creates new, or perpetuates existing, dependency syndromes. Regional development can help offset this debiliating consequence of transfers, and that is where the effort must be concentrated. With improved economic circumstances, equalization and transfer regimes, particularly for individuals, can be modified and tailored to reflect more reliable employment opportunities and a climate more conducive to economic growth. Induced or coerced mobility is not a solution to regional economic inequalities.[8] Governments should remain neutral on the mobility issue.

What to Do?

The in-vogue concept of helping people to help themselves represents a fundamentally correct approach to regional development—it was the basic philosophy of DREE at a time when it meant building the basis of an economy and its supporting infrastructure so that entrepreneurial talent had a chance to succeed. The concept can now be taken further in the more precise areas identified in chapter 7 and elsewhere in this book. It should incorporate the principles of building on comparative advantage and, with the realization that there are not going to be wondrous new remedies, helping people do better the things they already know how to do. There need be no limitations imposed by these criteria, but they serve to delineate the ordering of priorities. The involvement of government must be in support of positive adjustment. Some four million Canadians change jobs every year, mostly without government intervention. Positive adjustment can facilitate economic rehabilitation with a minimum of disruption, if the government support systems are properly employed and if they avoid backing declining sectors and companies.

The availability of hard and soft infrastructure and information is the basis of successful regional economic development. The hard infrastructure provides the wherewithal upon which to build the talent, the systems, the knowledge, and the businesses for domestic markets and international competition. The soft infrastructure—the technologies, computer networks, telecommunications systems, and the training

and education to use what is available in the most competitive way—
bring it all together. There is a role for governments in providing those
things that need the horizontal coordination and the funding that cannot
easily be provided, at least in the initial stages, by the private sector.
Government can be the catalyst for a move in these directions, leading
the private sector until it becomes advanced enough for legitimate
profit-motivated participation.

Small business has come in for its share of attention vis-à-vis its
ability to contribute to the national economy and its promise as the
prime determinant in creating employment and wealth in the peripheral
regions. Federal and provincial programs, including assistance for the
provision of supporting infrastructure, are heavily tilted to the small-
and medium-sized business sector. The sector itself, however, warns
that conflicting government actions and financing difficulties are detrimental to the SME grouping. The federal goods and services tax so
widely debated in 1989 and put into effect on January 1, 1991, was
considered a real threat to small business. There were concerns about
its impact on sales and the administrative burden entailed in collecting
and remitting the tax. The sector does not exempt any level of government in its criticism of the number and level of taxes imposed and
of the regulatory and paper burden that it finds so crippling. Attempts
have periodically been made to attack the paper burden question, none
of them successful. A coordinated effort between all levels of government to streamline the number and nature of regulations, not an easy
task, could produce results that would have significant impact on the
SMES. The occasional attack on specific regulations by any one level
of government has proven that many regulations are redundant and
that impressive improvements can be obtained if the effort is made.
The February 28, 1992, federal budget announced a renewed attack
on the regulatory burden, with the launching of a department-by-
department review of regulations.[9] Small- and medium-sized businesses feel discriminated against in their search for adequate financing
for their operations. Private sector capital has moved its involvement
in small businesses significantly away from start-up situations to the
more secure expansion and buy-out categories and to large companies.
Governments at both levels have provided some relief through modest
venture capital programs and interest reduction and loan payback
schemes, but little has been done on a coordinated basis.

Very little benefit will be achieved in any of the activity areas if
they are not supported by the right kind of timely information.
Although much of this information must be developed by private
enterprise, there is an essential role for government in the provision

and dissemination of information on technology, international trade, marketing, and competitive trends, backed up by the best sector advice that a department such as Industry, Science and Technology can provide. Furthermore, government, in entering into international arrangements for information exchange and technological development, a thrust pursued more and more by ISTC and other departments, should include the regions in the distribution of such information. The position of ministers and departments can be immeasurably assisted with the provision of another kind of information—on-the-ground intelligence and analytical knowledge. The DREE annual report of 1975–76 said, "Much of the research, analysis and planning of the department is done, not so much with a view towards culmination in a specific subsidiary agreement, but to provide a background of intelligence against which other departments and the government as a whole can discuss and develop programs which complement regional development as well as individual departmental objectives." Government efforts are enhanced by on-site feedback of timely information, especially at the federal level.

How to do it—A Super-Agency

Ideally, there should be a national agency responsible for all explicit regional development activity in Canada, with a strong mandate to coordinate the impact of the policies and programs of other federal departments on regional economies. Without a national master plan and a "super-agency" to oversee it, an effective national policy on regional development will not be possible. Without an influence on the major policy instruments of government, a national declaration of intent, such as that made by Prime Minister Trudeau on January 12, 1982, will fall short of the target. Instructing departments to be sensitive to the regional implications of their policies, actions, and intentions is not enough. Departments will never put a regional development objective ahead of their own mandate—after all, they are measured on the basis of their success in executing their assigned responsibilities. Constant attention needs to be paid to what these departments do in regional development terms. An effective regional development policy requires, above all, a national will that such a policy succeed and a continuity of commitment by the government, as represented by the cabinet and especially by those ministers who control the key departments. It is not sufficient, or practical, to speak of bringing regional development issues to cabinet for resolution on some kind of ad hoc operational basis. This remains too passive an

255

approach. It would place ministers in an untenable position and, in the absence of an overall policy framework, would make it virtually impossible to have issues decided in any rational way.

If ministers are sincere in wanting to improve regional economies and if the government could garner country-wide public support for such an intent, a dedicated agency would be the most appropriate instrument. It would study the impact of every federal government policy on Canada's peripheral regions and develop action plans and alternative courses of action for each major policy sector, from monetary and fiscal policy to transportation and all the sectors in between. Every proposal would be costed and the implications of proceeding or not proceeding with any one would be assessed, including an assessment of the impact on the regions, the national economy, and other related policy areas. The agency would monitor departmental progress against a master plan within a prescribed time frame. Although the master plan would be costed, it would not automatically imply additional budgetary requirements. Departments would have helped to construct the master plan, perhaps with staff seconded to the agency. Master plan intentions, or decisions, if supported by cabinet, would be integrated with departmental policies, and any contradiction with regional development objectives for that sector would be resolved before consideration by cabinet.

To work, such a formula would require ongoing support at the political level, the lack of which has encumbered more than one otherwise good approach to regional development. This implies that there must be one minister in cabinet to represent all regional development effort in Canada. Three or four ministers, as is the case with the regional agencies and ISTC, along with other ministers whose departments may be managing subsidiary agreements, make for uneven representation and unnecessary confrontation at that level. Ministers and their departments would have to be convinced that national and regional policies could be harmonized at little cost to "national efficiency" (which frequently presumes lower standards of services for peripheral regions). The possibility of a deliberate, all-encompassing, national policy for regional economic development in Canada will be greeted with skepticism, even by some who may have called for it.[10] Yet a workable strategy for a national effort to improve the economies of the peripheral regions cannot exist in isolation from a coherent approach to the Canadian economy as a whole.[11]

The proposal for a nationally constituted regional development super-agency differs from Thorburn's proposition for a federal-provincial institution on economic development in a significant way—it has a federal, as contrasted to a federal-provincial, bias.[12] A national approach to regional development, as proposed, would have difficulty in functioning if the agency were constituted on a federal-provincial basis. The uneven strength of the provinces would be reflected in the less economically favoured members of the federation feeling at the mercy of the stronger ones, as well as being continually reminded of their poor-cousin status. The stronger members would also not have the same level of interest in the subject as would the weaker. Thorburn's economic development institution, or commission, on the other hand, should work differently, since every province would have a vital interest in its mandate and each would likely have a somewhat more equal (but still not equal) voice on the components of an economic development strategy for Canada, some of which might be region-neutral. Nevertheless, Thorburn's proposal is a bold one, with clear implications for regional economies, and a national regional development agency would have to take full account of such a forum if it were to exist. Given the direction followed by the federal government as it headed into the 1990s, however, real cooperation with the provinces appeared to be on the decline and would not foreshadow the kind of entente between the two levels of government envisaged by Thorburn.

The existence of a single nationally structured and managed super-agency focusing on regional economies raises the question of the appropriateness of existing dedicated organizations such as the Atlantic Canada Opportunities Agency, the Department of Western Economic Diversification, and similar (in intent) structures in Ontario and Quebec. A separate program-delivery department for regional development could still exist, in its own right, but would require a capability to coordinate its actions nationally and to operate within the framework of a national policy. Such a department of government would continue the dedicated effort to improve economic conditions in the peripheral regions, employing region-specific structures such as ACOA if it so wished. Along with the provinces, under a clearly defined mandate framework, the department would do those things that generally are still beyond the mandate, and sometimes the competence, of other federal departments. If ACOA and WD are to remain in place, they must be placed in a national context and within the framework of one umbrella entity.[13]

The national agency concept conjures up the Ministry of State for Economic and Regional Development, but there are many differences. MSERD was hampered by its quasi-operational position in the hierarchy of government, its structure, and its lack of convincing influence with federal line departments. There was no master plan and insufficient national coordination. The regionally based FEDCs, obliged to generate provincial strategies under the guise of "regions," did that, and the resultant ERDA subsidiary agreements revealed the absence of a truly regional approach and the lack of a federal policy. MSERD did not work and there is no reason to believe that its reincarnation would be any more successful. There was nothing greatly wrong with the concept, it simply broke down in application.

The declaration of a national priority for regional development in Canada, the realization of which could be a super-agency, would face formidable obstacles in the Canadian structure of government. Such a super-agency would find it difficult to maintain its priority status and command the attention required to do its job, which is why most such entities, or good ideas, falter. The complexity of the environment in which it existed, the competition for attention, the lack of an effective mechanism to enforce its clout, and flagging political support would all militate against it. Other than being the brainchild of cabinet at its birth, it would have no natural political constituency. Nevertheless, sufficient cabinet and prime ministerial support, resolutely maintained, could overcome almost all of the problem areas cited.

The Federal-Provincial Imperative

Regional development is very much a matter of federal-provincial relations. In 1990 the federal government reverted to its policy of reduced joint activity and favoured direct program delivery, oriented in large measure to individual companies, associations, and institutions. Nonetheless, effective regional development can best proceed in cooperation with the provinces. And the concept of region need not be an obstacle. Provincial orientations are quite adequate for many kinds of initiatives in most of the priority areas mentioned earlier. There are, however, other situations where a multi-provincial thrust is more appropriate and where a federal coordinating role could be effective. In Atlantic Canada and the West, for example, it is unlikely that each individual province would be able to justify its own training centre in marketing, scientific and engineering technologies, telecommunications and computer technologies, management training, and other disciplines essential to the region. There would not be enough clients for each province to support its own facility, nor would it be easy to attract a sufficient number of qualified instructors. The location of such infrastructure within a multi-provincial region could be negotiated between the governments and the other participants involved, with attention paid to equal treatment of the provinces but the positioning of facilities, which may be clearly identified with particular places, decided on a logical basis.

258

In the Atlantic region, ocean technology in Nova Scotia and Newfoundland (meriting location in more than one province) and forest industries in New Brunswick (the most forest-industries-dependent province in the region) are two examples of logical infrastructure positioning. Halifax must be a prime candidate for footloose disciplines such as training and location-neutral technical centres because of its central location, the synergy with existing institutions, and the possible ease of attracting teaching expertise (open to dispute). Western Canada has its similar logical centres for the location of agricultural and energy-based skills-related training facilities and for the advancement of medical, microelectronics, and similar sectors that have been encouraged in that region.

Where there is federal-provincial collaboration, it is not necessary to make an issue of who delivers programs that evolve from regional development policies. In most instances it is obvious which level of government is best suited and best equipped to deliver the goods.[14] Only the visiblity issue impinges on the logic of this argument. The provinces have the jurisdiction and the know-how to carry the implementation responsibility in many of the resource sectors (my view is that the federal government should be out of this domain) and to contract for municipal services and industrial infrastructure. The provinces are also equipped to perform the contracting function for the more sophisticated institutional infrastructure that supports the training and technical centres incorporated in the newer regional development policies, especially if undertaken jointly with the federal government. The federal government should concentrate on the generic, horizontal infrastructure requirements of the regions. It can enter into direct arrangements with the private sector, institutions, associations, and other representative bodies for the establishment and operation of supporting infrastructure facilities, if it so wishes. If it chooses to do so, it is desirable that its actions be correlated with those of provincial authorities, particularly in areas of recognized provincial jurisdiction. Obviously, overlap should be avoided.

The provinces are generally good at delivering SMEs incentives programs, but the federal agencies have largely pre-empted that field, a direction that portends inherent danger. The federal government should not be involved with company-specific incentives in most cases (the exceptions being those in support of broad strategies within a sector-specific department such as ISTC). The private sector may very well be characterized accurately as the engine of growth in most economies, including the regions, but it cannot be expected to have a regional conscience. The best that can be said is that governments should strive to improve the environment for doing business in the regions so as to attract private sector companies, resident or potential, thereby improving the economy. Assistance for business and industrial services and infrastructure of benefit to all companies in a particular region removes the crowding-out and distortion potential inherent in firm-specific contributions. Such support can be tailored much more precisely to general physical infrastructure (industrial parks, access roads, training and centres of excellence institutions) and to hard and soft infrastructure in support of research and development, technology diffusion, skills upgrading, marketing, financial expertise, and anything else that makes sense. This is how centres of excellence, increased productivity and competitiveness, new product development, and market penetration are accomplished.[15]

The national government also has a role to play in implementation that cannot be performed by the provinces. The federal government can orchestrate the inter- and intraregional initiatives that are more and more essential in the kind of regional development that should now be practised by governments. It can ensure national communications and information networks, and it is probably still better than the provinces at meaningful economic and opportunity analysis. Most of all, the federal government can maintain a core of sectoral expertise in all the areas important to regional economies—technical and marketing trends, business information, telecommunications, and international trade. Streamlined information dissemination and easy access for the client body (provincial governments and the private sector) to such information is only possible through some form of dedicated national agency. This is where the federal level could shine—in guaranteeing this body of knowledge and expertise and its availability.

On another extreme, the Beaudoin-Dobbie report on the Constitution, in its recommendations on the devolution of authorities to provinces and negotiated bilateral agreements to recognize provincial leadership in resources and certain other jurisdictions, also suggested that regional development be considered for similar treatment. Liberal members of the committee dissented, saying such an approach would not respect national priorities for regional development.[16] This is not the first time it has been suggested that the federal government remove itself from direct involvement in the field, and the provinces would perhaps agree, but only if block funding were made available to finance provincial regional development efforts. The idea has little merit and is seriously deficient in addressing some level of national consistency that would still be necessary to prevent injurious interprovincial competition.

It is unfortunate that the federal government cannot let go of its obsession with receiving public credit (most often media attention) for its regional development efforts. The provinces are also not immune from this malady. If the national government insists on its visibility, or more accurately, if politicians wish to have their names continuously in the news, this can be accommodated. The provinces are not the culprit in this regard. The integrity of the public information provisions in federal-provincial agreements, which specify the arrangements to be followed by both governments, can be ensured by officials for just about any project. Officials in the field are usually in the best position to recommend the kind and degree of attention that any particular situation merits, but they need the authority to take decisions on the content and timing of news releases. There is nothing as stale as yesterday's news. Politicians would do well to heed officials' advice on the need for a government presence, and at what level of seniority, for a given event. Contrary to popular belief, Ottawa-based ministerial and information services staff will usually not be nearly as sensitive as departmental officials are about the nature of a local media happening. Finally, there should be an end to news releases that no one reads or that are so complicated the media only extracts the essential facts. It is surprising that information specialists cannot recognize that a news release that concentrates on politicians, sometimes quoting up to four MPs or ministers, works against the goal of gaining media attention.

Ironically, after years of the federal government's employing every trick in the book to gain political visibility at the constituency level, Deputy Prime Minister Don Mazankowski announced, shortly after the February 25, 1992, budget, that the practice of MPs making announcements and carrying cheques back to their ridings was to cease. Referring to tax-weary Canadians, he said, "They say, 'Don't try to fool me. It's my money you're fooling around with.'"[17]

THE DECADE OF THE NINETIES

The 1970s and 1980s saw intense regional development efforts by governments. What of the 1990s? Do the politicians any longer really care, or are current efforts simply a posturing to placate regional voters? Have circumstances so changed over the years that a dedicated regional development policy is no longer pertinent, given the many priorities that cry out for attention at the federal level and the economic realities that prevail nationally and internationally? If the effort is to continue, what is the best approach?

The organization to give effect to regional development policy and programming must operate under some form of national umbrella for country-wide cohesiveness, with significant and unencumbered decision-making authority at the operational level in the regions. Instruments can be developed to give program effect to any policy decision. Federal-provincial devices are best employed where the two governments both have an interest in the initiative being pursued. As a minimum, some level of consultation should be ensured between governments to avoid costly duplication and counterproductive actions.

The Spirit of DREE

Although DREE may not have been a total success or a panacea for all of Canada's regional development problems, it improved regional economies and influenced federal government regional development policy. If it had had anything like the longevity of many other government instruments of federal policy (departments), it would have made even more headway towards reaching its objectives. DREE, in its all-too-short existence, succeeded as a discrete expression of a regional development strategy within the framework that was circumscribed for it. The DREE model contained most of the elements required to develop, pursue, coordinate, and implement regional development policy in Canada. It had the planning capacity to identify, with the provinces or on its own, development opportunities and the constraints to development. It had the skills and expertise to negotiate the content of initiatives and the knowledge required for program implementation. It was working towards, and would have perfected, better and more reliable techniques to evaluate the degree of success of its efforts. And it had in place the departmental coordination process to head off injurious interregional actions. To be more successful, DREE required a strengthening of the one element that admittedly did not work as well as intended: government-wide coordination of effort. In terms of its own programming, however, its interdepartmental coordination function had substantially improved over its life, and it made more gains than generally acknowledged in influencing the actions of other departments.

The premature ending of DREE and the reorganization of economic departments in 1982 was a mistake. Almost everything identified in 1987 as necessary to the economic development in Canada's regions was in use or in the planning stage in DREE in 1981. The loss of DREE's momentum and coordinated strategic regional development programming constituted a serious setback to federal economic development efforts in Canada in the interval of 1982–87. DREE could have been left in place in 1982 and MSERD could still have become a strengthened MSED to monitor the economic and regional development programs of departments, but with no operational or even program coordinating role of its own. The dedicated department must maintain the coordinating role as part of its responsibility. As 1981 came to a close, DREE was poised to carry regional development through the 1980s in a direction that reflected careful assessment of existing and predicted circumstances. It could have done the same for the 1990s.

There is nothing mysterious about the DREE model. It was based on a decentralized structure and real delegated decision-making authority, executed in a national framework. It believed in federal-provincial cooperation and interdepartmental collaboration. It practised economic analysis and opportunity identification in the regions, usually sharing its information with provincial governments. Such an approach could work today, but only if it had one other essential attribute present in the DREE era—a high level of trust between ministers and officials and a minimum of political interference in day-to-day operations and decision making. In other words, it was a way of doing business that has not re-emerged in any of the experiments in regional development that followed 1982. As an entity dedicated to explicit regional development in Canada, the DREE model remains second only to a workable national regional development agency. DREE was as close as we have yet come to getting it right.

Regionalism, if not regional development, is a fact of life at the national level and will remain so throughout the 1990s. The pendulum is swinging towards a focus on national issues, an approach that must take account of regional points of view but will not be driven or defined by regional imperatives as such. Regional development is now in competition with other national and regional priorities, including the environment, deficit reduction, and global competition, coupled with a scarcity of resources to do all the things that the populace wants done. The once-sacred billion-dollar-plus budgets of ACOA and WD, which were to be added to existing levels of expenditures for regional development in the peripheral regions, have been eroded by central agencies and through re-profiling of assigned funding over a greater number of years.

The Atlantic Canada Opportunities Agency and the Department of Western Economic Diversification, operating as truly "regional" agencies that concentrate on support to small- and medium-sized businesses and act as the federal arms for generic programming, can still have an impact on the regions. But they still must fit into a national framework. This does not mean program design in Ottawa; that responsibility stays in the regions, at the community level if necessary, but with some measure of national coordination and knowledge sharing.

Separate agencies cannot hope to be greatly effective in coordinating the activities of other departments, especially if they do not have a means of ensuring interregional coordination. If the federal preoccupation with direct program activity is maintained in the 1990s, then the role of the agencies in federal-provincial relations and in consummating cooperation agreements will change; the agencies' ability to pursue what should be their most important activity, that of upgrading supporting business and community infrastructure, may be inhibited.

The peripheral regions of Canada have made impressive economic gains since the 1960s. There is still much to be accomplished. The reasons for the improvement are many, including national economic growth and dedicated regional development effort. It has not yet been possible to quantify the benefit-cost of the explicit effort made, nor is it ever likely to be so. What is important is that the commitment has been maintained, sometimes intensively, as in the DREE period, other times less so, over the intervening years.

Less satisfactory has been the reluctance of successive governments to stay a determined course of action long enough to reap full benefits from the experience gained. For the future, the single major policy decision is whether to continue a distinct regional development philosophy or to presume that the national, and even more so the international environment will make specific actions for strengthening regional economies redundant. The latter attitude could understandably be envisaged if Canada's political leadership reaches the conclusion that the nation's prospects are so positive that the regions will be carried along, or, conversely, that national and international circumstances would erase the effectiveness of explicit regional development initiatives. I do not hold that either eventuality is yet close enough to obviate the effectivenss of continued regional development effort. I hope to see a more sincere effort by the national government to aid and encourage the regions to bring themselves closer to the economic mainstream of Canada. One way of doing that has been described in this book.

Appendix 1

Comparison of GDA and ERDA

GENERAL DEVELOPMENT AGREEMENTS	ECONOMIC AND REGIONAL DEVELOPMENT AGREEMENTS

Newfoundland, February 1, 1974
Increase number and quality of, and access to, jobs and the opportunity to live in the area of choice.

Newfoundland, May 4, 1984
Eliminate disparities; people to participate in and benefit from opportunities; contribute to national economy; adopt long-term policies, diversification, efficiency and productivity.

Resource utilization and value added, resources marketing, tourism, development infrastructure, geographic location and ocean science and technology, business and labour force capability, increased output, construction, housing and manufacturing.

Resource sector adjustment, further processing and diversification, tourism, infrastructure, ocean industries, offshore oil and gas and related spin-offs, energy intensive industries, import replacement, transportation improvement, skills upgrading.

Nova Scotia, September 12, 1974
Job opportunities, earned income and quality of life, develop dynamic economy.

Nova Scotia, June 11, 1984
Job opportunities, earned income; promote economic growth to support social and cultural well-being; enhance development throughout the province; contribute to the national economy.

Optimum utilization of resource industries, rural and urban development, communications, distribution, transportation, business and personal

Increase productivity via technology, trade, quality products and services, and market development, human resource development, private sector

services, high-tech and ocean industry, offshore oil and gas spin-offs,
energy resources and distribution
systems, tourism and development
infrastructure.

New Brunswick, April 23, 1974
Reduce gap in earned income per
capita; raise income; increase productivity; reduce out-migration;
upgrade labour force; focus on economic distribution and viable diversified communities.

Improve resource utilization, productivity, management, marketing,
value added and product diversification; increase product value in the
manufacturing sector with labour
skills and technology; encourage
small business, tourism and service
industries; infrastructure support for
economic, community, and area
development.

PEI CDP, March 7, 1969
Phase I 1.4.69–31.3.75
Phase II 1.4.75–31.3.81
Phase III 1.4.81–31.3.84
Foster conditions under which people could create viable economic
enterprises; generate self-sustaining
private sector employment, add
value to the island's resources and
improve social well-being; concentrate on economic, rural, and community development, social
adjustment, and infrastructure support.

Resource management and utilization, tourism, educational opportunities, skills up-grading, manufacturing
and processing productivity, housing,
health and welfare services, highway
transportation and municipal and
industrial infrastructure.

investment, offshore oil and gas
spin-offs, resources and manufacturing industries productivity improvement, ocean-related and high-tech
industries and small business, tourism, and service industries.

New Brunswick, April 13, 1984
Reduce gap in earned income per
capita; increase growth rate of provincial output; reduce vulnerability
to international and national down-
turns; regions of province to contribute to economic growth.

Contribute to resources sectors,
value added, diversify via high
growth, high tech manufacturing and
service firms; stress competitiveness; adopt new technologies, products and processes, upgrade skills
and resource management;
strengthen transportation, communications, marketing and energy conservation and supply.

Prince Edward Island, June 13,
1984

Stabilize and diversify the economic
base of the province and its communities; encourage balanced growth,
employment and income opportunities; contribute to the national economy; utilize human resources;
concentrate on comparative advantage, output, marketing, investment,
management, skills upgrading, and
new technology.

Direct strategy to capital incentives,
research and development, marketing
and selected infrastructure; increase
productivity; reduce barriers to
development, notably high-energy
costs and inadequate transportation
infrastructure.

Initiate Manitoba Northlands Socio-
economic Development Program; develop agricultural lands south of Winnipeg; improve trade and service centre communities; build manufac-uring base, resource sectors proc-ssing and servicing capacity; xpand secondary urban centres and ural communities, regional assem-ly, distribution and servicing func-on of Winnipeg and other urban ntres; consider industrial and mmunity infrastructure, skills grading.

Address productivity and competi-tiveness of the industrial base, growth in output and earned income, disparities within Manitoba; priority for economic expansion and invest-ment; focus on agriculture, manufac-turing and services; see Winnipeg as the hub of economic development; enhance public and private invest-ment; give attention to factors of production, market development, human resource utilization, transpor-tation, the water resource, service sector, technological change.

skatchewan, February 11, 1974
celerate economic development
job creation; people to partici-
e in economic development;
rsify economic base.

Saskatchewan, January 30, 1984
Further economic and regional devel-opment; increase job and income opportunities; people to participate in economic development; remove barri-ers; foster diversification.

ss balanced rural-urban growth;
nce natural resources; increase
ortunities in the North, including
r transportation and communi-
ns; examine steel complex for
West, steel- and metal-related
stries, forest resources, agricul-
raw materials output and fur-
rocessing; develop Qu'Appelle
y.

Improve international competitive-ness of agricultural products, potash, minerals, fuels, forestry, and other resource sectors; concentrate on pro-ductivity, investment, market devel-opment, removal of structural and economic constraints.

ta, March 4, 1974
ve job opportunity and access
-advantaged areas; promote
rban balance, distribution of
pment and priorities for socio-
nic development.

Alberta, June 8, 1984
Foster environment to capitalize on strengths; develop human resources, balanced regional development, dis-tribution of economic benefits; diversify economy.

ize resource utilization; pro-
ommunity development in
jor urban service centres and
mmunities, incentives to
usiness, housing, sewage and
nfrastructure, management of
ince's natural and wildlife
es.

Recognize natural resources (natural gas, oil sands, heavy oil, coal, food processing and forest products); stress value added, skills upgrading and utilization, small business, tour-ism, export promotion and commer-cialization of research and development.

Quebec, March 15, 1974
Consolidate employment in traditional sectors; improve standard of living, industrial and urban structure of Quebec; people to participate in development; balanced development in relation to Canada; emphasize human resource utilization; reduce unemployment but do not encourage out-migration; increase productivity, entrepreneurship.

Emphasize resource sectors productivity, diversification, utilization, management, marketing, and impact on manufacturing; promote new enterprises and modernization; accelerate transformation of the industrial structure; support tourism, air freight transportation, finance, research, and municipal infrastructure.

Ontario, February 26, 1974
Promote employment and access; emphasize less-favoured regions; reinforce policies and priorities in identified areas and sectors. In the North, facilitate urban and rural development; support municipal facilities and services; group processing industries; diversify single-industry communities; improve transportation, communication; support SMEs and skills upgrading; coordinate industrial incentives programs of governments; assist projects in manufacturing and tourism.

Manitoba, June 5, 1974
Improve income and employment opportunities and chance to live in area of choice; encourage northern development.

Quebec, December
Improve employme
and incomes; peop
in development; cr
to achieve econom
enhance comparat
productive enterp
consultation and
between governm
human resources
industrial base.

Emphasize reso
tivity, diversifi
management, r
ogy; encourag
tage; help maj
problems; attr
port investme
ment, market
science and t
nications and
software, an
structure.

Ontario, N
Enhance e
developme
developme
national e
regional c
the North
potential
diversify
the Nort
industry
technolc
labour
resourc
tor, an

Manit
Enhar
devel
ment
econ
quat

British Columbia, March 28, 1974

Improve job opportunity and access in less-advantaged areas; promote balanced distribution of benefits of development; recognize erratic nature of the resource-based economy and danger of overconcentration in the lower Mainland.

Stress directed sectoral and spatial diversification, key industries, human resource development, social and economic overhead investments, underutilized, uncommitted resources in the northwest, the Kootenays and the northeast; support value added resource base, transportation services, manufacturing, recreational development.

British Columbia, November 23, 1984

Improve job opportunity, productivity, wealth creation; promote economic potential of regions and diversification; recognize raw materials endowment, energy, transportation, institutional infrastructure, skilled labour force, and geographic location.

Build on strengths; remove impediments; improve productivity; reduce costs; enhance resource management, processing technologies, value added, new products and markets; create centre of excellence in resource management, extraction, processing, transportation technology, and equipment; develop Vancouver as centre of finance, business services, travel, trade, cultural, medical and educational activities, transportation.

Appendix 2

Representative Projects

FOREST EXPLOITATION

Forest lands management, acquisition, private woodlot management agreements, woodlands and forests inventories, multiple land use development, green houses, nurseries, seedlings cultivation, experimental and production plantings, cable logging, steep slope logging, harvesting research, access roads, resource protection technology, insect infestation protection programs, incentives to harvest decaying resources first, forest fire detection and suppression systems, water bomber refits, forest industries improved productivity measures, better raw material utilization in sawmills and secondary wood products industries.

MINERALS EXPLOITATION

Minerals resource inventories, resource management, geoscientific surveying and mapping, minerals core storage and classification, laboratory services, geological/geochemical surveys, commercial minerals exploitation.

AGRICULTURE

Agricultural land-use planning, consolidation and development, water conservation, family farm programs and extension services, agriculture service centres, business and management counselling, marketing assistance, skills upgrading and on-farm training, technology transfer and innovative demonstration projects, on-farm grain storage facilities and central grain drying, grading and storage, on-farm feed processing, high-energy and protein feed grain development, livestock production improvements, veterinarian and other services, horticultural development, soil and crop analysis, refrigerated transportation systems.

FISHERIES

Fisheries marine service centres, haul-out slips, mechanized landing systems, community stages and publicly owned landing facilities, ice-making, cool/cold storage facilities, fish-handling systems, aquaculture, fish-plant water supply systems.

TOURISM

Tourism community infrastructure, national parks improvement, destination development, attractions upgrading, historical restorations, accommodation upgrading incentives, marketing assistance, packaged tours and tourism service programs, tourist reservation system, visitor information centres and programs, Kings Landing, Village Acadien, Shippigan Marine Centre, Qu'Appelle Valley.

COMMUNITY DEVELOPMENT

Community development, community infrastructure, remote areas infrastructure, spatial development, integrated regional planning, targeted resource development for community/rural support, transportation systems planning, intercommunity roads, grants to rural development associations, incentives to small enterprises and crafts, housing assistance, education and medical services, communication services.

URBAN DEVELOPMENT

Urban development, regional water supply systems, arterial transportation links, urban core development, housing, hotel and trade centres support, waterfront redevelopment and services, computerized traffic management centre, ports development, containerization handling systems, Newfoundland Institute of Marine Technology, Maritime Forestry Complex, New Brunswick North-East Institute of Technology.

TRANSPORTATION

Secondary road networks, collector systems, highways to remote areas, roads to resources.

INDUSTRY

Industrial opportunity identification, industrial development commissions, management and marketing support, market development centre, manpower development, small-business incentives programs, industrial incentives programs, venture capital funding, industrial parks and services, industrial and incubator malls, industrial infrastructure, dry docks, ship construction and repair, steel mill modernization, pulp and paper mill modernization, mill conversions, pilot plant and experimental facilities and equipment, airline simulator facility, steel and metals fabrication, Michelin, Sysco, Abitibi-Price, Kruger, CIP.

OCEAN INDUSTRIES

Oceans research and development, Ocean Industry Offices, cold water research, technological development and commercialization, incentives for marine-related industries, capital and marketing assistance, ocean industries trade associations support, ocean industry park and incubator mall.

ENERGY

Energy system planning program, energy load management project, demonstration alternate energy devices, co-generation projects, industrial energy retrofitting, energy test centre, financial assistance for energy projects.

OTHER

Development of service industries capability in surveying, mapping and land registration, resource planning, distribution services, labour education and management training.

Notes

INTRODUCTION

1 Harvey Lithwick produced a widely quoted construction of regional economies over the forty-year postwar period, in which he relates federal government
policy positions on regional development to economic performance in the country
as a whole. See Lithwick, "Regional Development Policies." See also the Royal
Commission on the Economic Union and Development Prospects for Canada
(hereafter cited as Macdonald Commission), *Disparities and Interregional Adjustment*, chap. 3 (Lithwick).

2 This was during the Diefenbaker era. Ibid., pp. 125, 127.

3 In 1972 J. P. Francis characterized this surge of activity: "The programs
introduced were rather a reflection of the kinds of problems and special needs of
particular parts of the country than of an attempt to evolve a general regional
development strategy and program. ... In retrospect, the approach to the problems
of regional economic disparity in the 1960s amounted to an attempt to deal with
them on a rather ad hoc basis, in response to the strongest needs and pressures
at the time" (DREE, "Federal Regional Development Policies," by J. P. Francis
pp. 9–10).

4 As referenced by Phidd and Doern, *The Politics and Management of Canadian Economic Policy*, pp. 322, 323. Phidd and Doern rationalized the federal
program initiatives of PFRA, ARDA, FRED, and ADB by saying that the different
programs revealed the heterogeneity rather than the homogeneity of Canada's
regions and the necessity for a decentralized planning strategy. They expressed
the view that governments were attempting to extend these earlier programs by
expanding the rural base, emphasizing the economic and social dimensions of
regional development, and expanding activity throughout the country, rather than
restricting it to specific regions (pp. 315, 316).

5 Kent, *A Public Purpose*, p. 418. Kent said this despite the fact that he and
Jean Marchand were unable to get the super-ministry that they had wanted to
ensure that such a role could be exercised.

6 Ibid., p. 419.

7 Ibid., p. 422.

8 Department of Regional Economic Expansion (DREE), "Federal Regional Development Policies," by J. P. Francis pp. 9–10.

9 Ibid.

CHAPTER 1

1 Measurable indicators remained in fashion into the 1980s. The Atlantic Development Council, in "The Atlantic Region of Canada" (pp. 217–26), called for specific targets to close disparity gaps by 1991. It proposed job creation between 350,000 and 400,000, unemployment of 5 percent, per capita income at 90 percent of the national average, and a participation rate equal to the level existing nationally in the year of the report (1978). Ian McAllister (*Policy Options*, March 1980) suggested goals for per capita income and participation rate at 85 percent of the national average and the declaration of a state of economic emergency for any province with an unemployment rate more than two to three points above the national rate. In 1982 the Atlantic Provinces Economic Council, in "An Analysis of the Reorganization for Economic Development" (p. 34) said that goals and objectives for regional economic development must be defined in terms of moving such indicators as unemployment rates, participation rates, earnings, and per capita income closer to the Canadian average. APEC was also one of several that suggested that governments were apprehensive about quantifiable targets against which their performance could be measured. APEC regularly comments on the disparity question in its newsletters (see vol. 33, nos. 5 and 6 [June–October 1989]).

2 DREE, "Federal Regional Development Policies," by J. P. Francis pp. 10–11.

3 Federal-Provincial Task Force on Regional Development Assessment, *Report*, p. 1.

4 Macdonald Commission, *Disparities and Interregional Adjustment*, chap. 3 (Lithwick), pp. 109–10.

5 Senate Standing Committee on National Finance, in its report *Government Policy and Regional Development* (pp. 24, 26), said that the federal government should focus less on the differences between the provinces and that the most effective way to attack regional disparities was to define the economic potential of the less-developed regions and to encourage development of that potential. Donald Savoie said of Atlantic Canadians, "From their point of view, the central purpose of federal regional development policy should have been and should still be to deal with the structural deficiencies of their region" (Savoie, "Establishing the Atlantic Canada Opportunities Agency," p. 15). In 1989, the agency itself described its mission as creating a strategic partnership with Atlantic Canadians to foster a renewal of entrepreneurial spirit and stimulating long-term economic development to increase earned incomes and improve employment opportunities (*Fredericton Daily Gleaner*, July 7, 1989).

6 Senate Standing Committee on National Finance, in *Government Policy and Regional Development* (pp. 19–20), said, "The Committee has found its inquiry into the subject of regional disparities both challenging and frustrating ... frustrating because testimony has made it evident that there are no solutions waiting to be discovered."

7 Philip Mathias, *Forced Growth*, pp. ix, x.

8 Senate Standing Committee on National Finance, *Government Policy and Regional Growth*, pp. 33, 34. See also Charles J. McMillan, *Standing Up to the Future*, p. 7.

9 See Macdonald Commission, *Domestic Policies and the International Economic Environment*, chap. 9 (DRIE), for a discussion of influences bearing on the Canadian scene that are pertinent to regional circumstances.

10 Lesser and Hall, *Telecommunications Services and Regional Development*.

11 Coffey and Polèse, eds., *Still Living Together*, p. 115.

12 Savoie, *Regional Economic Development*, p. 150; and Richard Higgins, in Senate Standing Committee on National Finance, *Proceedings*, November 21, 1978, p. 7.

13 Higgins, in Senate Standing Committee on National Finance, *Proceedings*, November 21, 1978, p. 7.

14 The value of the growth-pole concept to the Maritime provinces was resurrected by Charles J. McMillan in his 1989 report to the Council of Maritime Premiers, *Standing Up to the Future*, p. 29.

15 Savoie, *Regional Economic Development*, pp. 6–8; Economic Council of Canada, *Living Together*, chap. 3; and Courchene, "Avenues of Adjustment," pp. 145–84.

16 Although Donald Savoie said that it had fallen out of favour by the 1970s, it remained alive and well at the end of the 1980s (Savoie, *Regional Economic Development*, p. 135).

17 Ibid., pp. 136, 137.

18 Polèse, "Patterns of Regional Economic Development," p. 28.

19 Macdonald Commission, *Disparities and Interregional Adjustment*, chap. 3 (Lithwick), pp. 143–44.

20 McMillan, *Standing Up to the Future*, p. 19.

21 Ibid., p. 21.

22 "It is an illusion to believe that regional disparities can be meaningfully ameliorated in the context of a sluggish national economy" (Courchene, "A Market Perspective on Regional Disparities," p. 517); and "Successful regional adjustment within a faltering national economy is a non-starter" and "Overall policy must run with the regional strengths, not against them" (Courchene, "Canadian Regional Policy," p. 54).

23 Savoie, *Regional Economic Development*, p. 153. He also suggested that national sectoral policies and regional strategies be developed simultaneously (p. 156).

24 Macdonald Commission, *Report*, vol. 3, p. 217.

25 Federal-Provincial Task Force on Regional Development Assessment, "Report," p. 31.

26 Savoie, *Regional Economic Development*, p. 153.

27 The Federal-Provincial Task Force on Regional Development Assessment (*Report*, pp. x, 28) observed that joint planning and programming between the two levels of government presented an effective mechanism for reconciling national policies and regional development. It identified the need for regionally based intelligence for senior officials, the incorporation of such intelligence into

the decision-making process of departments, the incorporation of regional development objectives into the priority-setting process of ministers, and a significant degree of delegated departmental decision making in the regions to permit on-site flexibility in program implementation.

28 Donald Savoie suggested that regional development in Canada is a balancing act, requiring politicians to arbitrate decisions between regions or between regional and national policies, which, he assumes, are (always) in conflict. "The central government, in promoting regional economic development, must attempt to strike a proper balance between, on the one hand, the pursuit of national objectives through national policies and, on the other, the promotion of regional economic development through special regional policies and programs. *These two goals are conflicting*, not only because to make special provisions for one region is often to oppose the implementation of national policies, but also because to promote economic development in one region is to assist that region in competing with other regions of the federation" (Savoie, "Politicians and Approaches to Regional Development," p. 130).

29 Thorburn, *Planning and the Economy*, p. 78.

30 Ministry of State for Economic Development, "Agenda for Economic Development in the 1980s," October 20, 1980.

31 Interest-rate complaints reached a high level of stridency at a February 27, 1989, meeting between provincial premiers and Prime Minister Mulroney, with even Ontario chiming in. It was the premiers of more distant provinces, however, who were particularly exercised. Nonetheless, Bank of Canada Governor John Crow held fast, saying that "there is no useful sense in which we can have a monetary policy that is differentiated by regions" (*Globe and Mail*, March 9, 1989, p. B1). Crow said that in an economy with one exchange rate and free movement of capital, it was not possible to have different interest rates in different parts of the country (*Globe and Mail*, October 30, 1989, p. 6). With interest rates continuing to climb, Premier Peterson of Ontario returned to the attack on May 2, 1990, accusing the governor of the Bank of Canada and the federal finance minister of striving to drive the country into a recession (*Ottawa Citizen*, May 2, 1990, p. D7). By October, the recession had taken hold in Canada, with Crow and Wilson still holding to their positions. Interest rates increased to the end of the year, then started their decline. Crow reiterated his view that monetary policy was "indivisible" in face of the government's constitutional package of September 24, 1991, which proposed greater regional input into such policy making.

32 Polèse, "Patterns of Regional Economic Development."

33 Canada has not been alone in maintaining long-term patterns in the economic relationship between its regions. An analysis undertaken by the US Commerce Department's Bureau of Economic Analysis, covering the period 1929–87, revealed that, in terms of per capita income, economic differences between regions of the United States had stayed within five percentage points of the national average to 1979. From that date, however, the measure had widened in several regions, reaching 13 percent in the southeast in 1987. The study attributed the change to different economic structures, with high-technology and service

industries regions outpacing those based on agriculture and heavy manufacturing (*Globe and Mail*, August 21, 1988).

34 See Savoie, "Establishing the Atlantic Canada Opportunities Agency," pp. 6–8; Savoie, *Regional Economic Development*, pp. 107–18; and Federal-Provincial Task Force on Regional Development Assessment, "Report," Annex 3, p. 51.

35 Federal-Provincial Task Force on Regional Development Assessment, *Report*, Annex 3.

36 Courchene, "A Market Perspective on Regional Disparities," pp. 506, 509.

37 Polèse, "Patterns of Regional Economic Development," pp. 23–24.

38 Polèse, "Regional Disparity, Migration and Economic Adjustment," pp. 519, 520.

39 Ibid., p. 520.

40 Ibid., p. 523.

41 Ibid., p. 524.

42 Senate Standing Committee on National Finance, *Government Policy and Regional Development*, p. 48.

43 Economic Council of Canada (ECC), *Newfoundland*, p. 56.

44 Ibid., p. 58.

45 Ibid. The Economic Council was somewhat more ambivalent in its earlier study, *Living Together: A Study of Regional Disparities* (pp. 178, 212). At that time, it seemed to accept the theory that out-migration "would certainly be beneficial," but went on to say it was not that effective. It also drew a distinction between migration resulting from a one-time loss of employment of large proportion (a shut-down) and employment loss of a more persistent and pervasive nature.

46 Courchene, "A Market Perspective on Regional Disparities," pp. 510, 517.

47 ECC, *Newfoundland*, p. 156.

48 Yves Rabeau, "Regional Efficiency," p. 383.

49 Courchene suggests that there is an inefficient outcome from excessive migration to resource-rich regions because of the influence on wage rates; thus, he is theoretically arguing against adjustment (Courchene, "A Market Perspective on Regional Disparities," p. 514).

50 Rabeau, "Regional Efficiency," p. 384.

51 Kent, *A Public Purpose*, p. 83.

52 Ibid., p. 293.

53 Savoie, *Federal-Provincial Collaboration*, p. 2.

54 Thorburn, *Planning and the Economy*, p. 192.

55 Kernaghan and Siegel, *Public Administration in Canada*, p. 386.

56 Leslie, *Federal State, National Economy*, p. 71.

57 Savoie, *Federal-Provincial Collaboration*, p. 159. Savoie repeated his accusations five years later in *Regional Economic Development* (pp. 11, 16).

58 Leslie, *Federal State, National Economy*, p. 44.

59 Milne, *Tug of War*, p. 135.

60 Leslie, *Federal State, National Economy*, p. 45.

61 Ibid., p. 48.

62 Ibid., p. 49.

63 Milne, *Tug of War*, pp. 120–21.

64 Leslie, *Federal State, National Economy*, pp. 64–71.

65 Anthony Careless, in describing the heavy-handed style of management in the earlier DREE days, says, "The second novelty in DREE was that its scope of operations was to be as wide as Ottawa deemed the case under treatment to be. Constitutionally-assigned jurisdictions had to be treated as expendable luxuries if the provinces expected federal assistance for their problems. Experience in the past certainly suggested that the narrow departmental and constitutional constraints had robbed regional development programs of their full effectiveness. Thus, although the federal government in the late sixties was increasingly more willing to divert its funds to the reduction of regional disparities, this was to be without consideration of the formal divisions of the Canadian constitution" (Careless, *Initiative and Response*, p. 169).

66 Leslie, *Federal State, National Economy*, p. 72.

67 Ibid., pp. 86–103.

68 Ibid., p. 91.

69 Milne, *Tug of War*, p. 119.

70 Ibid. In 1989 the Conservative government of the day chose to use the federal-provincial development agreements to criticize some provincial economic development positions. See chapter 5.

71 Atlantic Development Council (ADC), "The Atlantic Region of Canada," pp. 27, 61; and Atlantic Provinces Economic Council (APEC), *An Analysis of the Reorganization for Economic Development*, pp. 34–36. APEC also suggested designating federal regional development financial commitments by province and public accountability of such commitments. Even the Macdonald Commission called for a significant increase in the federal financial commitment to regional development (*Report*, vol. 3, p. 220).

72 Macdonald Commission, *Report*, vol. 3, p. 396.

73 Savoie, *Federal-Provincial Collaboration*, p. 165.

74 Ibid.

75 Savoie and Chenier, "The State and Development," p. 407.

76 James McNiven, "The Efficiency-Equity Tradeoff," pp. 434–35.

77 That is not to say that the money would not be well spent—only that the federal government would be written out of the equation. The provinces are generally very good at identifying opportunities and the constraints that can prevent them from being realized.

78 Savoie, *Federal-Provincial Collaboration*, p. 165; Savoie, *Regional Economic Development*, p. 157; and Higgins, quoted in Senate Standing Committee on National Finance, *Proceedings*, November 21, 1978, no. 3, p. 3:11.

79 Ian McAllister, in "How to Remake DREE," proposed a federal-provincial regional development fund for each province, funded 75:25 federal-provincial, with no programming responsibilities of its own and managed by a board of directors whose prime responsibility would be to persuade departments of both governments to implement projects for regional development purposes, first from their own budgets, secondly from the fund. Seven years later, in "Establishing the Atlantic Canada Opportunities Agency" (pp. 65–67), Donald Savoie proposed, in addition to a budget for the agency, an Atlantic Canada investment fund of at least $240 million, which could be used for supplementary ERDA funding, the

topping up of existing federal programs, and other activities of benefit to the Atlantic region. The fund would screen proposals against a set of approval criteria. Savoie does not suggest who would have managed such a fund.

80 Even the Ministry of State for Economic and Regional Development, a central agency put in place with its own minister during the 1982 reorganization of economic departments, did not satisfy this requirement, as its allegiance went beyond regional development. This is the other side of the coin of the criticism expressed at the time that the 1982 reorganization left regional development without a voice in cabinet.

CHAPTER 2

1 House of Commons, *Debates* (Mr Trudeau introducing Bill C-173, a government organization bill) February 27, 1969, p. 6016.

2 House of Commons, *Debates*, March 20, 1969, pp. 6893–95.

3 Kent, *A Public Purpose*, pp. 415–20; and Savoie, *Regional Economic Development*, pp. 30–32 (based on conversations with Jean Marchand).

4 Kent, *A Public Purpose*, p. 418.

5 Tom Kent describes the decentralization and higher levels of delegated decision making that took place in the reorganization of Manpower and Immigration in 1966. Operational responsibility was placed in the field under directors exercising real authority. He says that "the Manpower structure was the first major experiment in decentralization within the federal bureaucracy" and adds that "it might almost be taken as a mark of soundness in the organization that the number of senior officials outside Ottawa should exceed the number in Ottawa" (Kent, *A Public Purpose*, pp. 398–99). Tom Kent's approach to a decentralized department is recorded differently by Anthony Careless in *Initiative and Response* (pp. 86–87). He reports that Kent, on becoming deputy minister of the new DREE, retained most of the control in Ottawa, removed signing authorities from the field, kept his regional officials in the dark, and made it clear that development of new strategy or policy commitments to the provinces would be executed in Ottawa, with decentralization covering only administrative and tactical matters.

6 Doug Love gives the composition of regional staff as 29 percent from existing provincial offices, 22 percent from Ottawa head offices, and 49 percent new recruitment, largely from within the regions (Love, "The Continuing Relevance of DREE Decentralization," p. 441).

7 Phidd and Doern, *The Politics and Management of Canadian Economic Policy*, pp. 338, 345.

8 Milne, in describing the Trudeau government's effort to apply its centralist federalism in economic policy, says, "Perhaps the most revealing of the use of economic policy for the rational pursuit of federal purposes, however, was the experience with regional economic development. After years of Conservative and Liberal ad hoc attempts at promoting economic development in the poorer provinces and regimes, the Trudeau government broadened federal development policy with the Department of Regional Economic Expansion (DREE) in 1969. Here the earlier objectives of reducing regional disparities were expanded to include not only stricter federal control over planning objectives, administrative efficiency

and programs, but a closer fit with preferred federal political goals. Higher federal visibility in the provinces, the counteracting of economic provincialism and the gradual development of a direct relationship between Ottawa and recepients of federal services in the provinces were to be encouraged." Milne acknowledged a relaxing of these measures in 1973 (Milne, *Tug of War*, p. 124).

9 House of Commons Standing Committee on Regional Development, *Proceedings*, no. 2, April 10, 1973, p. 2:11.

10 Ibid.

11 Prime Minister's Office, "Reorganization for Economic Development."

12 Careless, *Initiative and Response*, p. 165. Careless also says that the motivation behind DREE reflected three federal government priorities: efficiency in federal expenditures, greater public visibility, and federal policies directed towards definite federal goals.

13 Savoie, *Federal-Provincial Collaboration*, p. 165.

14 Ibid., p. 128.

15 Ibid., p. 3.

16 The views expressed in this review are based on the personal experience of the author, encompassing the management of regional operations and daily contacts over an eight-year period with individuals, provincial premiers and federal ministers, members of Parliament and provincial legislatures, federal and provincial officials at every level of the hierarchy, leading businesspeople, small entrepreneurs, and representatives of institutions and associations.

17 Donald Savoie perpetuates this myth in his 1986 book, *Regional Economic Development*, when he refers to the exclusive responsibility of DREE provincial office officials in identifying and pursuing development opportunities with provincial governments (p. 50) and when he says that provincials offices have "full responsibility for all stages of programs from research analysis to program formulation and implementation, and thence to evaluation and revision" (p. 51).

18 Subsidiary agreements were selectively submitted to cabinet committee as early as 1976.

19 Thorburn, *Planning and the Economy*, p. 102.

20 As suggested by Savoie, *Federal-Provincial Collaboration*, p. 108.

21 See Love, "The Continuing Relevance of DREE Decentralization," p. 442.

22 Donald Savoie, in *Federal-Provincial Collaboration* (p. 122), refers to provincial officials boasting of their new-found authority under the Canada–New Brunswick GDA. If this were the case in provincial administrations, which is questionable, it did not obtain on the federal side. There would be several reasons for this—among them, federal officials in general are accustomed to exercising delegated authority and they would be unlikely to boast about those very bureaucratic practices that were criticized for slowing the decision-making process.

23 Savoie, *Federal-Provincial Collaboration*, p. 145.

24 Ibid., p. 110.

25 Ibid., p. 119.

26 Donald Savoie seemed to believe this when he asked where the GDA fit into the continuing struggles of bureaucracies to expand their spheres of influence. He also quotes Alan C. Cairns and federal officials to the same effect (Savoie,

Federal-Provincial Collaboration, pp. 5, 7). Years later, the empire-building syndrome was still troubling Savoie. In the early pages of *The Politics of Public Spending*, he appeared convinced that it still prevailed (p. 11), but less so upon reflection later in the book (p. 206).

27 J. D. Love, DREE deputy minister during and after the policy and planning phases for the GDA and departmental decentralization, afterwards said that the process of decision making was substantially decentralized without any significant loss of control by the deputy minister or the minister or the government. See Love, "The Continuing Relevance of DREE Decentralization," p. 440.

28 There is much dispute about the part played by bureaucrats in the governmental process. Officials may—where they have superior knowledge; where they must give selective policy advice; or where ministers either have confidence in them, are weak, or are overworked—play a de facto policy decision-making role, but the principle of ministerial authority remains valid. Thus, if Tom Kent exercised the (political) power attributed to him by Anthony Careless, and there is little doubt that he did, it was an aberration rather than the standard (Careless, *Initiative and Response*, p. 86).

29 Lithwick, "Regional Policy: The Embodiment of Contradictions," p. 255.

30 Savoie, *Federal-Provincial Collaboration*, p. 132.

31 Love, "The Continuing Relevance of DREE Decentralization," p. 442.

32 Savoie, *Regional Economic Development*, p. 56. When asked for views on the role of the proposed Atlantic Canada Opportunities Agency in 1987, Savoie had second thoughts on the nature of federal-provincial agreements. On business development, he suggested that "the agency should consider signing business development agreements with all four provinces. It is not possible nor in fact advisable to spell out in detail the contents of the agreements. What works in one province may not work in another; therefore, each package should be tailored to the economic circumstances of the individual province." In this instance, Savoie was not shy of advocating the tailoring of strategies to fit prevailing circumstances, nor was he hesitant in abandoning his suggestion for region-wide initiatives fitted into national frameworks. See Savoie, "Establishing the Atlantic Canada Opportunities Agency," p. 43.

33 Unpublished communication, DREE files.

34 Savoie, "Politicians and Approaches to Regional Development," p. 130.

35 Many other meetings also involved politicians of both levels of government. Discussions of GDA initiatives in the Atlantic region involved Roméo LeBlanc, Eugene Whelan, Gerald Regan (as a federal minister), Allan MacEachen, Bennett Campbell (as a federal minister), William Rompkey, Brian Tobin, Gary McCauly, Maurice Dionne, Maurice Harquail, Herb Breau, Russell McLellan, and David Dingwall, to name but a few. Initiatives discussed included a separate subsidiary agreement to modernize the Consolidated-Bathurst mill at Bathurst, NB, a total Cape Breton economic review leading to several major projects, including the $100-million Sysco agreement, a number of infrastructure agreements, including highways in New Brunswick, and others of similar vein. Both federal and provincial politicians, including ministers, regularly discussed proposed and pending initiatives with DREE officials.

36 Savoie, *Federal-Provincial Collaboration*, p. 134.

37 Ibid., p. 145.

38 As cited in Savoie, *Federal-Provincial Collaboration*, p. 8.

39 As early as 1973–74, DREE Newfoundland rejected three proposed subsidiary agreements in their final stages of development for not meeting federal and agreed-upon criteria of quality and relevance. DREE steadfastly refused Nova Scotia's proposals for highways involvement. As program development matured in the Atlantic, DREE adopted a policy of supporting only project-specific related infrastructure.

40 One of the largest agreements signed in Newfoundland, the $68-million St John's Urban Agreement, was shared 65:35 between the two governments. Other examples include the Halifax-Dartmouth Agreement ($110 million at 72:28), NS Agriculture ($48 million at 62:38), Michelin Tires ($56 million at 75:25), and Ocean Industries ($35 million at 65:35). New Brunswick highways agreements were virtually all signed at a 75:25 ratio, with 70:30 used in the $51-million NB Arterials Agreement. The $95-million Northeast NB Agreement was signed at 70:30. Similar examples can be found in the other DREE regions. Most planning agreements were cost-shared at 50:50.

41 Milne, *Tug of War*, p. 125.

42 Savoie, *Federal-Provincial Collaboration*, pp. 91–92.

43 This procedural point was the subject of substantial discussion at a meeting of the House of Commons Standing Committee on Regional Development; see *Proceedings*, no. 22, April 2, 1981, p. 22:5.

44 *Globe and Mail*, June 8, 1979.

45 This delegated authority placed a significant responsibility on officials, and it has been suggested that in one province, at least, that authority led to surreptitious arrangements between federal and provincial officials to accomplish their goals to the exclusion of the wishes of other departments and perhaps even ministers. There is no evidence, other than hearsay, to support this contention. See Savoie, *Federal-Provincial Collaboration*, pp. 99, 122.

46 Ibid., p. 138. Savoie says, "It will also be recalled that during the course of a fiscal year, funds can be transferred between subsidiary agreements." This was not possible and was not done. Savoie subsequently acknowledges (Savoie, *The Politics of Public Spending in Canada*, p. 28).

47 The DREE Act did, nevertheless, direct that in cooperation with other departments DREE was to formulate plans for the economic expansion and social adjustment of special areas and "provide for co-ordination in the implementation of those plans by departments, branches and agencies of the government of Canada and carry out such parts of those plans as cannot suitably be undertaken by such other departments, branches and agencies."

48 The program activity was described at a meeting of the House of Commons Standing Committee on Regional Development; see *Proceedings*, no. 12, May 4, 1977, p. 12:15.

49 House of Commons Standing Committee on Fisheries and Forestry, *Proceedings*, no. 59, May 25, 1982, p. 59:48.

50 The task force, headed by Michael Kirby, studied the condition of the East Coast fishery and resulted in the report "Navigating Troubled Waters, A New

Policy for the Atlantic Fisheries" (December 1982). DREE provided the task force considerable information on fish-processing capacity in the Atlantic, plus critical comment on its work.

51 Agriculture; Canada Mortgage and Housing; Employment and Immigration Canada; Energy, Mines and Resources; Environment Canada; Health and Welfare Canada; Indian and Northern Affairs; Industry, Trade and Commerce; Tourism and Transport Canada (DREE, annual reports, 1975–76 through 1982–83).

52 House of Commons, *Debates*, December 14, 1978, p. 2136.

53 Agriculture Canada, CMHC, CEIC, Tourism, the Coast Guard, DFO, EMR, Environment Canada, Finance, ITC, Parks Canada, and Public Works Canada.

54 As recently as 1986, Donald Savoie continued to say that "other federal departments and agencies were simply not participating" (Savoie, *Regional Economic Development*, p. 57).

55 Courchene, "Canadian Regional Policy," p. 54; and Lithwick, "Regional Development Policies," p. 143.

56 Savoie, *Federal-Provincial Collaboration*, p. 21.

57 Ibid., p. 151.

58 Ibid., p. 153.

59 Ibid., pp. 66, 108.

60 Savoie, in *Regional Economic Development* (p. 153), says, "There has been virtually no effort to determine what a province or an area can do efficiently in relation to other regions. The GDA ... appear to present ten separate and autonomous policies." He suggests that such a policy orientation could give rise to costly interprovincial competition. However, he emphasizes that "what is required in one region may not be required in another" (p. 137). In "Establishing the Atlantic Canada Opportunities Agency," Savoie quotes the provinces as making the point that no two provinces face the same problems in terms of level of development (p. 28).

61 Nader, "An Economic Regionalization of Canada," p. 135.

62 In discussing this question, Michael Jenkin says, "The attempt by many peripheral provinces to increase the processing of local resources does not appreciably affect central Canadian manufacturing. This is because most resource production is destined for foreign markets in the first place and it is foreign, rather than domestic firms which are denied the added possibilities in further processing the resource ... with the exception of Prince Edward Island, no province relies on the rest of the Canadian market for more than a third of its shipments of resources and primary products. ... In addition, further processing of raw materials benefits the entire country because it creates new markets for central Canadian suppliers of capital equipment and services" (Jenkins, *The Challenge of Diversity*, p. 87).

63 Savoie, *Regional Economic Development*, p. 138.

64 Perhaps this is what Savoie has in mind when he says that "it is widely accepted that the consequences of interprovincial competition in the field of economic development are particularly damaging" (Savoie, *Federal-Provincial Collaboration*, p. 153).

65 Donald Savoie, in "Establishing the Atlantic Canada Opportunities Agency" (p. 43), agrees that "interprovincial competition for projects rarely surfaces with

aspiring or small local entrepreneurs or locally owned medium-sized businesses."

66 Donald Savoie, in discussing the handling of large projects in Atlantic Canada in 1987, stressed the importance of the federal government taking a lead position in project assessment, the assignment of sector specialists to the evaluation, and the use of the federal-provincial subsidiary agreement instrument as a vehicle. This is exactly what DREE did in its time, a number of years earlier (ibid., p. 42).

67 The widely reported controversy between ministers Herb Gray of ITC and Pierre De Bané of DREE over the location of a possible Volkswagen facility in Canada was said to have contributed to the eventual merger of the two departments. Volkswagen had proposed establishing a new parts plant in Barrie, Ontario, and presumed it would have access to the government's duty-remission program for remission of duties on automobile imports. De Bané proposed that if Volkswagen rejected his suggestions and incentives to locate in either Montreal or Halifax, it should be denied duty-remission eligibility. It was really a non-issue, as Volkswagen had no intention of locating anywhere other than where its own analysis dictated. Cabinet supported Herb Gray against the DREE minister.

68 Donald Savoie says that "the political cost of the GDA approach is extremely high in that it operates in such a fashion that traditions of accountability—at least in New Brunswick—are affected, patterns of relations between ministers and their officials are altered, and public and interest group participation is discouraged" (Savoie, *Federal-Provincial Collaboration*, p. 128). He makes frequent reference to the use by officials of authorities delegated to them and of ministerial frustration so engendered. For examples, see pages 104, 123–24, 147–49, and 157.

69 In 1988 the federal government established, by act of Parliament, the Atlantic Canada Opportunities Agency and the Department of Western Economic Diversification, with strong mandates for regional economic development. DRIE (later ISTC) continued to be responsible for the provinces of Ontario and Quebec. Expectations at the time were very high.

70 Savoie, *Federal-Provincial Collaboration*, pp. 121, 122.

71 Michael Jenkin, in examining the quality of intergovernmental relations, warns that formal institutional arrangements are not a substitute for effective action. He differentiates between process and substance in the following way: "On the process side, the elements which seem to have encouraged harmonious federal-provincial relations include, first, shared professional norms and commitments which allow policy issues to be reduced to technical questions, and second, formal or informal networks connecting officials and ministers from different jurisdictions. ... Successful intergovernmental negotiations also depend in particular on the degree to which the governments involved are flexible about achieving objectives and the degree to which they are willing to involve the other level of government at an early stage." Jenkin also refers specifically to the GDA subsidiary agreements as an example of how such a process worked in practice and how it afforded the federal government the opportunity to influence provincial policy (Jenkin, *The Challenge of Diversity*, pp. 104–5, 137–39).

72 Savoie, *Federal-Provincial Collaboration*, pp. 9, 11.

73 Ibid., p. 9.

74 Ibid., pp. 122, 144.

75 Ibid., p. 137.

76 Ibid., p. 158.

77 Ibid., p. 132, 34.

78 Ibid., p. 135.

79 This was discussed in the Atlantic region context at the House of Commons Standing Committee of Regional Development (*Proceedings*, no. 4, June 6, 1980, p. 4:24).

80 Ibid., no. 6, May 31, 1978, p. 6:25.

81 Savoie, *Federal-Provincial Collaboration*, pp. 120, 136, 137.

82 Ibid., p. 137.

83 As reported in ibid.

84 Savoie, "Politicians and Approaches to Regional Development," p. 223.

85 Even though the DREE/ITC merger had been announced early in 1982, DREE Atlantic continued to operate under its existing management and maintained its regional office presence until the beginning of October, when the assistant deputy minister was formally transferred to Ottawa.

86 *Times-Transcript* (Moncton), June 7, 1977, p. 29.

87 In a speech by the president of APEC to the Moncton Rotary Club, January 26, 1981, reported in the Saint John *Telegraph-Journal*, January 27, 1981.

88 House of Commons Standing Committee on Regional Development, *Proceedings*, no. 3, April 4, 1978, p. 3:9.

89 Ibid., no. 22, April 2, 1981, p. 22:8.

90 Ibid., p. 22:4.

91 Ibid., p. 22:13.

CHAPTER 3

1 Phidd and Doern, *The Politics and Management of Canadian Economic Policy*, p. 354.

2 Ibid., p. 354.

3 Ibid., p. 356.

4 Senate Standing Committee on National Finance, *Government Policy and Regional Development*, pp. 68, 69.

5 Federal-Provincial Task Force on Regional Development Assessment, *Report*, p. 43.

6 Internal DREE Atlantic strategic policy and resources deployment paper, January 5, 1979.

7 In the Atlantic, the figures were 18 percent and 5 percent respectively. By this time the region had been blanketed by first- and second-generation resource agreements, federal resource departments were in closer harmony with their provincial counterparts, and the DREE industrial development subsidiary agreements permitted the flexibility the department needed to pursue resource value added program directions. In 1981 the Canadian Construction Association was formally advised of the DREE policy to phase out its support of highway construction and that message was also disseminated via the media.

8 Senate Standing Committee on National Finance, *Government Policy and Regional Development*, pp. 37, 38.

9 Federal-Provincial Task Force on Regional Development Assessment, *Report*, p. 10.

10 "Even ardent conservatives agree that government spending on infrastructure is critical to a healthy economy" (Conservative economist Gary Becker, in *Business Week*, as quoted in the *Globe and Mail*, October 18, 1988, p. B8). A US banker commented on the state of disrepair of infrastructure in that country: "The infrastructure and capital structure of the United States have deteriorated to a point where it is adversely affecting commerce, industry, productivity, and competitiveness in global markets. Bridges, highways, mass transit systems, airports, water supply systems, waste disposal systems, and other public works are in dire need of repair, upgrading, or expansion ... Improving the infrastructure is clearly of critical importance ... for the long-term economic vitality of U.S. industry" *Globe and Mail*, December 21, 1989, p. B2.

11 DREE, "Atlantic Region Industrial Parks."

12 *Globe and Mail*, May 15, 1989, p. C3.

13 An event related to the ocean industry initiative was a recommendation by the deputy minister of the Canadian Employment and Immigration Commission that DREE chair an interdepartmental committee on offshore oil and gas developments and related industrial opportunities, modelled on the Cape Breton Interdepartmental Task Force chaired by the DREE ADM Atlantic.

14 On September 29, 1987, the federal minister of fisheries and oceans announced a new oceans policy and strategy and the establishment of a National Marine Council industry advisory group (activated in March 1988) to advise the minister on ocean-related policies, provide private sector views on the ocean economy, and provide a forum for the exchange of views and the assembly of ideas on government proposals. The oceans policy also revealed that no central department of government held sole responsibility for ocean-related policies and programs (fourteen departments and seventy-five relevant programs were involved, including the DREE- and DRIE-launched initiatives of the past).

15 The Federal-Provincial Task Force on Regional Development Assessment said this of urban centres: "There is substantial evidence that the growth of urban centres plays a major role in development, from the standpoint of developing a critical mass and network of businesses and labour market skills and also in terms of creating the amenities necessary to attract investors and employees" (*Report*, p. 10).

16 Much of this work was assigned to consultants who worked in close collaboration with senior regional office and DREE provincial office officials. Conclusions relating to these three areas were summarized in a DREE report, "Support for Indigenous Development, Atlantic Region," by Audlen Projects Limited, dated November 30, 1974.

17 Ibid., p. 5.

18 As late as 1990, this was still the case. In reaction to a severe downturn in the Atlantic fishery, the federal government announced a $584-million assistance package, which was intended to promote diversification out of the fishery and community self-help measures. (*Ottawa Citizen*, May 3, 1990, p. A3, and May 8, 1990, pp. A1, A4). This was followed in October 1991 by a further $39-million aid package.

19 The theory that a department cannot perform a somewhat central agency coordinating and monitoring function and at the same time operate its own programs was contradicted by the establishment of the Atlantic Canada Opportunities Agency and the Department of Western Economic Diversification in 1987. Both roles were implanted in the two agencies, with the disadvantage of no national policy cohesion.

20 House of Commons, *Debates*, December 14, 1978, p. 2134.

21 A prevailing theme of suggestions in the 1960s and 1970s was the coordination of federal policies and actions in regional development. Lessard was reacting to these ideas, as well as embracing the logic of the argument itself. Phidd and Doern posed the problem as "the diversity of interests which must be captured in formulating regional policies, impose new strains on the various governmental structures operating in the regions and they constitute a major component of the demand for more horizontal coordinating mechanisms to handle problems which cut across departmental lines." Their solution was a set of alternatives based on boards and crown corporations, a coordination role for Treasury Board, the de-concentration of federal departments, so they would be more regionally sensitive, a strengthened Atlantic Development Board (disbanded by this time), and a national development strategy (Phidd and Doern, *The Politics and Management of Canadian Economic Policy*, pp. 316, 324).

22 First Ministers' Conference, November 27–29, 1978, Ottawa, agenda item no. 4.6, regional development document no. 800-9/087.

23 Ibid., agenda item no. 4.1-(4).

24 "My government will ask you to support programs which build upon the strengths of the regions of Canada. Legislation will be placed before you to strengthen the mandate of the Department of Regional Economic Expansion" (Speech from the Throne, October 9, 1979).

25 Donald Savoie describes De Bané's restlessness with progress in reducing disparities in Canada before and during his DREE period (Savoie, *Regional Economic Development*, pp. 67–70).

26 Moncton (regional headquarters), Fredericton (provincial main office), and Bathurst (sub-office) in New Brunswick; Halifax, Nova Scotia; Charlottetown, PEI; and St John's and Happy Valley/Goose Bay (sub-office) in Newfoundland. Subsequently, sub-provincial offices were established in Sydney, Nova Scotia, and Corner Brook, Newfoundland. A modest DREE presence also existed in Summerside, PEI.

27 De Bané wrote to all the premiers, over several weeks in 1981, in the name of his cabinet colleagues. The letter sought the cooperation of the premiers in ensuring observation of the subsidiary-agreement guidelines for joint public announcements. It noted the requirement for joint coverage under tender and contract awards, jointly identified descriptive literature, and DREE presence or mention at official openings and speaking engagements. This protocol was to be observed by either party, with neither trying to pre-empt the other. In closing, he threatened to refuse agreement cost-sharing where this protocol was not observed.

28 Doern, "The Political Administration of Government Reorganization," pp. 34–56.

29 Donald Savoie, in *Regional Economic Development* (p. 127), says that many

Atlantic and Quebec MPs had asked for adjustment to DREE programs to give more federal visibility and had stated that if that were not possible, the department should be disbanded.

30 Macdonald Commission, *Regional Responsiveness*, chap. 2 (Aucoin and Bakvis), p. 104.

31 As late as 1989, federal Industry Minister Harvie Andre was complaining that the provinces were taking all the credit while the federal government "doled" out all the money (*Ottawa Citizen*, April 20, 1989, p. A4).

32 Quoted in Beer, "Life after DREE."

33 During one all-day journey to New Brunswick in 1978 by ministers Marcel Lessard and Eugene Whelan (Whelan did collaborate with DREE, despite some of his public utterances), the latter expounded on how little program or signing authority he had compared to DREE officials (and probably Agriculture Canada officials, as well, when it came to project-specific actions).

34 Savoie, *Regional Economic Development*, pp. 74–75. (See this volume, note 67, chap. 2.)

35 In 1970–71, with DREE only just launched, the fear that economic slowdown would take the emphasis away from regional development was voiced by the department's first deputy minister, Tom Kent (Kent, *A Public Purpose*, p. 423).

36 Aucoin and Bakvis, *The Centralization-Decentralization Conundrum*," p. 17.

37 Doern, "The Political Administration of Government Reorganization," p. 43.

38 There were two task forces formed shortly after the merger announcement, one on program integration (the Marshall Task Force) and one on resources integration, including organizational structures, headed by Bert Laframboise, on secondment from Treasury Board.

39 House of Commons, Standing Committee on Regional Development, *Proceedings*, no. 37, May 11, 1982, pp. 37:25, 26.

40 Ibid., p. 37:21.

41 Savoie, "Establishing the Atlantic Canada Opportunities Agency," p. 25.

42 Doern, "The Political Administration of Government Reorganization," p. 52.

CHAPTER 4

1 Prime Minister's Office, "Reorganization for Economic Development."

2 Almost every government reorganization based on merger presumes savings in personnel, no matter how onerous the new mandate. DRIE was expected to save person-years through the merging of the common services (personnel, finance, and administration) of DREE and ITC and in some program-delivery categories — this notwithstanding its regional and national mandate and its attempt to play a more meaningful role in helping Canadian business to be more competitive internationally.

3 Kent, *A Public Purpose*, p. 420.

4 This point was also underlined by Premier Hatfield of New Brunswick in a comment recorded June 6, 1984, in the Moncton *Times-Transcript*.

5 Macdonald Commission, *Report*, vol. 3, p. 216.

6 Ibid., p. 219.

7 Ibid., p. 220.

8 Ibid., p. 395.

9 Ibid., p. 470.

10 This was a point on which Donald Jamieson was very adamant when minister of DREE. It is also a prevailing view in many federal circles (senior departmental staff conference, Winnipeg, February 9–11, 1975).

11 Others have been more explicit in their criticism of the Macdonald Commission's work as related to industrial and regional development policies. Peter Leslie declares, in referring to the commission's suggestion that, in the absence of a national economic development policy, regional development be practised mainly through provincial initiatives supported by federal grants: "Surely it is politically unrealistic to suppose that Ottawa could do for stagnating regions, by bankrolling provincial programs, what it abjures for the whole country." Leslie then describes the ingredients necessary for a policy of redistribution, effectively calling for a national policy of economic development (Leslie, *Federal State, National Economy*, p. 180; see also ibid., pp. 171–80, for the context of the Macdonald Commission discussion). Michael Bradfield says of the Macdonald Commission: "Their regional policies reflect their basic assumptions of competitive markets, mobile factors and products, and distortions in labour markets because of social policies" — assumptions Bradfield had already attacked elsewhere in his analysis of the commission's work as being unsound (Bradfield, "Review Essay," pp. 125–37).

12 Government of Canada and the Governments of the Provinces and the Territories, "Intergovernmental Position Paper on the Principles and Framework for Regional Economic Development."

13 Prime Minister's Office, "Reorganization for Economic Development."

14 Love, "The Continuing Relevance of DREE Decentralization," p. 448.

15 Donald Savoie was to recommend this approach again in 1987 in his proposals for the establishment of the Atlantic Canada Opportunities Agency (Savoie, "Establishing the Atlantic Canada Opportunities Agency," p. 63).

16 Kent, *A Public Purpose*, p. 296.

17 Macdonald Commission, *Regional Responsiviness*, chap. 2 (Aucoin and Bakvis), p. 77.

18 Ibid., pp. 77–79.

19 Ibid., pp. 90–91.

20 The Council of Maritime Premiers, at its meeting of February 8 and 9, 1982, both publicly and privately registered strong concern with announced federal intentions for unilateral action in the provinces, not only in the field of economic development, but even in respect of municipalities and universities (*Chronicle-Herald* [Halifax], February 10, 1982).

21 Macdonald Commission, *Regional Responsiveness*, chap. 2 (Aucoin and Bakvis), p. 101.

22 Ibid., p. 104.

23 Aucoin and Bakvis, "Organizational Differentiation and Integration," pp. 363, 366–68.

24 Under DREE, over 90 percent of the RDIP cases were decided at either the provincial or regional level, with only the very largest submitted to an Ottawa-based interdepartmental committee that then made recommendations to the minister. On balance, ministers and the government received better publicity under DREE than thereafter.

25 Savoie, "Establishing the Atlantic Canada Opportunities Agency," p. 30.

26 Donald Savoie was to later suggest that one reason for the foundering of the devolution idea was a concern by officials with potential job loss (Savoie, *The Politics of Public Spending in Canada*, p. 207). In the case of DRIE, there were two reasons for the idea's not working: (1) the concern of not only ministers but MPs with loss of visibility in the granting of hundreds of small incentives grants and (2) the reluctance of provinces to accept the federal government's wish to retain some involvement in the process of determining the framework within which projects would be assessed.

27 Macdonald Commission, *Regional Responsiveness*, chap. 2 (Aucoin and Bakvis), p. 104.

28 By late 1989 serious consideration was being given to downplaying the joint ERDAS; subsidiary agreements were now referred to as "cooperation agreements," and the emphasis of federal activity was swinging back to direct program delivery. In 1982, in a retrospective on the GDA, the Senate Standing Committee on National Finance acknowledged that the GDA had "become everybody's favourite whipping boy, being blamed for situations that are intrinsic in a federal system." The committee said it deplored the decision to let the GDAS lapse, adding, "In the Committee's judgement, the GDA concept was balanced and well adapted to the political situation in Canada, although it needed some tightening up" (Senate Standing Committee on National Finance, *Government Policy and Regional Development*, pp. 80–81).

29 Macdonald Commission, *Regional Responsiveness*, chap. 2 (Aucoin and Bakvis), p. 103.

30 It was said that the Mulroney government had decided to de-emphasize the direct delivery aspects of the ERDAS, and there is evidence that it was not as aggressive as its predecessor in trying to use the instrument for this purpose. At the same time, direct delivery was considered one way of improving visibility, something the Conservatives desperately wanted to accomplish. What the government did was to put in place unique federal entities such as ACOA and WD (Western Diversification), based in large part on unilateral delivery, by which whatever credit or blame that was to accrue came to the federal level. By late 1989, in apparent frustration over the prominent role of provincial governments in both program content and visiblity, the government decided to move to a series of federal theme priorities under renamed "cooperation agreements," with cost-sharing dictated by the presence of federal program priorities in the agreements, some direct delivery, and renewed efforts of visibility.

31 Macdonald Commission, *Regional Responsiveness*, chap. 2 (Aucoin and Bakvis), p. 104.

32 *Winnipeg Free Press*, April 23, 1989, p. 1.

33 Ibid.

34 Macdonald Commission, *Regional Responsiveness*, chap. 2 (Aucoin and

Bakvis), p. 53. Donald Savoie drew on this premise in his report "Establishing the Atlantic Canada Opportunities Agency" (p. 4).

35 Careless, *Initiative and Response*, p. 168.

36 Aucoin and Bakvis, *The Centralization-Decentralization Conundrum*, p. 72. Aucoin and Bakvis make an important distinction between deconcentration, a physical phenomenon, and decentralization of decision-making authority. The first has been the practice of many federal government departments over the years, but unaccompanied by the second. Conversely, authority can be decentralized within one location, as is also the practice of some federal departments within the Ottawa enclave.

37 Ibid., p. 75.

38 Ibid.

39 The Federal-Provincial Task Force on Regional Development Assessment, said, "The success of regional development programming has been related to the degree of decentralization, both federal and provincial, and the experience of officials in developing and managing meaningful programs. The success of a program depends critically on practical and workable design at the local level" (*Report*, p. 12).

40 Savoie, "The Toppling of DREE," p. 333.

41 Ibid., p. 335.

42 Ibid., pp. 335–36; and idem, *Regional Economic Development*, p. 133.

43 Savoie, "The Toppling of DREE," p. 334; and idem, *Regional Economic Development*, pp. 128–29.

44 Savoie, "The Toppling of DREE," p. 335.

45 Phidd and Doern, *The Politics and Management of Canadian Economic Policy*, p. 357.

46 Senate Standing Senate Committee on National Finance, *Government Policy and Regional Development*, pp. 69, 72, 73.

47 Lithwick, "Regional Policy," pp. 264–66.

48 "As for the new approach to working with the provinces implicit in the January 1982 statement, we have serious concerns (Senate Standing Senate Committee on National Finance, *Government Policy and Regional Development*, p. 70).

49 Savoie, "Establishing the Atlantic Canada Opportunities Agency," pp. 69, 70.

50 Donald Savoie expressed some optimism for the reorganization at the beginning. Mitchell Beer says, "Savoie thinks the reorganization has a chance of achieving that goal (regional inequities becoming a central priority in Ottawa's planning) by ... replacing the old system of GDAs with ... new and simpler sets of agreements with the provinces, involving a wider range of federal departments" (Beer, "Life after DREE.")

51 Savoie, "Establishing the Atlantic Canada Opportunities Agency," p. 3.

52 Savoie, "Politicians and Approaches to Regional Development," p. 224. Savoie held a similar opinion of the 1969 DREE legislation. In a 1986 backward-looking assessment, he said that the DREE Act lacked precision on such goals as increasing income levels or improving productivity; further, the geographic dimension of special areas was not laid out, and no targets to be reached were identified (Savoie, *Regional Economic Development*, p. 35).

53 Ibid., p. 227. Savoie returned to the subject of departmental legislation some years later. In reciting the factors that made it difficult to write legislation in a precise and restrictive fashion, he said, "No longer is it possible to predict problems and situations that may crop up within six months, let alone a few years down the road. If the legislation is restrictive, the department will be unable to deal with unanticipated issues. Going back to parliament to amend its enabling legislation is not an option, given the crowded legislative agenda" (Savoie, *The Politics of Public Spending in Canada*, p. 205).

54 Timothy Plumptre has elaborated this point with reference to pre-1960s practice: "This custodial view of the public servant's role was reinforced by the detailed regulations and procedures which for years characterized many of the laws passed by Parliament ... Parliament instructed public servants not only upon goals to be achieved but also upon how work was to be done. Little discretion was permitted to deal with special cases or circumstances, little room for managerial judgement ... members of Parliament often created legislation that was ponderous, complicated and difficult to administer" (Plumptre, *Beyond the Bottom Line*, pp. 87, 135).

55 While some of Savoie's concerns were covered in the two acts to follow that created ACOA and the Department of Western Economic Diversification, most were not. The flexibility remained and the references to comparative advantage and areas for sectoral attention were imprecise, with no quantitative targets given.

CHAPTER 5

1 Federal-Provincial Task Force on Regional Development Assessment, *Report*.

2 Ibid. The report was tabled in November 1987.

3 Prime Minister's Office, news release, June 6, 1987.

4 Speech to the New Brunswick Economic Council, quoted in the *Financial Times*, June 15, 1987.

5 Ibid.

6 House of Commons, *Debates*, vol. 129, no. 236, January 18, 1988, p. 11985.

7 Atlantic Canada Opportunities Agency (ACOA), *Report of the Minister for the Fiscal Year 1988–89*.

8 *Daily Gleaner* (Fredericton), January 28, 1988, p. 5.

9 ACOA, press release, February 15, 1988. On February 27, 1990, ACOA announced modifications to the Action Program to include supplier development costs associated with bid preparations and market development costs, including design, packaging, promotional material, and professional salaries as eligible program expenses.

10 As of March 31, 1989, the staff complement was 324 (ACOA, *Report of the Minister for Fiscal Year 1988–89*).

11 Savoie, "Establishing the Atlantic Canada Opportunities Agency," p. 73.

12 House of Commons, *Debates*, vol. 129, no. 236, January 18, 1988, pp. 11993, 11994, 12009.

13 House of Commons, *Debates*, vol. 129, no. 237, January 19, 1988, p. 12044. Note also that although announced in January 1982, the government

organization bill effecting the merger that created the new Department of Regional Industrial Expansion was not passed until December 1983.

14 *Globe and Mail*, February 27, 1988; and *Telegraph Journal* (Saint John), November 12, 1987, p. A5.

15 *Daily Gleaner* (Fredericton), January 28, 1988, p. 5.

16 Ibid. By March 1988 the Atlantic premiers wanted to discuss the operations of ACOA directly with the prime minister. They were concerned about conflict between ACOA and provincial small-business programming, incrementality, and where the decision making was really taking place (*Globe and Mail*, March 1, 1988, p. 3). Donald Savoie had also recommended that ACOA should avoid a direct programming role, with the provinces substantially delivering small- and medium-sized business programs (Savoie, "Establishing the Atlantic Canada Opportunities Agency," pp. 43, 75). The suggestion was quickly dismissed by John Crosbie (*Globe and Mail*, March 2, 1988, p. A5.).

17 *Ottawa Citizen*, May 20, 1989, p. A5.

18 New Brunswick speech from the Throne, March 14, 1989, as reported in the *Globe and Mail*, March 15, 1989, p. A3.

19 Sources include ACOA, *Report of the Minister for the Fiscal Year 1988–89*, and ACOA, speaking notes for the president for an address to the Greater Moncton Chamber of Commerce, November 8, 1989.

20 In fiscal year 1988–89, 76.7 percent of approved projects had a value of less than $200 thousand and 96.7 percent were under $2 million. The 4,550 projects under $2 million were offered 46.5 percent of the funding (ACOA, *Report of the Minister for Fiscal Year 1988–89*, Figure 6, p. 56).

21 ACOA was not, and is not, averse to trying to attract companies from other provinces, something that DREE had been criticized for and a practice that Donald Savoie had disparaged in his report "Establishing the Atlantic Canada Opportunities Agency." In its earliest days ACOA placed ads in Ontario papers and distributed glossy brochures extolling the virtues of locating in Atlantic Canada. In 1990 the new head of ACOA said, "The agency is looking at ways to persuade companies in Southern Ontario's Golden Horseshoe to relocate in Atlantic Canada," and opined that if he were an Ontario businessman he would be sorely tempted to do so (*Globe and Mail*, February 13, 1990, p. B1).

22 Those familiar with the case would find noteworthy ACOA's combined $10.9-million contribution and interest buy-down assistance to Wink Industries Ltd. towards its establishing a fabricating facility in Caraquet, NB, in a plant donated by the province, along with $3.8 million of loans and loan guarantees. This sounds like a repeat of the ill-fated Cirtex textiles operation, originally located in the same building, that eventually went bankrupt at a high cost to both levels of government. Both are examples of incentives being given to operations with no natural reasons to locate in the regions in question—a practice that has not worked well in previous experience.

23 Prime Minister's Office, news release, August 4, 1987.

24 Ibid.

25 This latter principle bears a striking resemblance to one of the objectives of the Newfoundland and Manitoba General Development Agreements of 1974:

"[to] increase opportunities for people to live in the area of their choice with improved (real) standards of living."

26 *Globe and Mail*, August 6, 1987.

27 House of Commons, *Debates*, March 1, 1988, pp. 13277–82.

28 Office of the Solicitor General of Canada, news release, May 9, 1988.

29 *Journal de Montréal*, November 25, 1987.

30 Canada, "Rapport Committee Consultative au Committee Ministériel sur le Développement de la Région Montréal," November 6, 1986.

31 *Globe and Mail*, "Report on Business," February 25, 1988, p. B7.

32 Office of the Minister of Regional Industrial Expansion, Canada-Quebec news release, June 9, 1988.

33 Services des communications de l'Office de planification et de développement du Québec, "A l'Heure de l'Entreprise Régionale," (see in particular page 51).

34 *Financial Post*, May 11, 1987, p. 13.

35 Industry Science and Technology Canada (ISTC), "Meeting the Challenge." See also Bill C-3, an act to establish the Department of Industry, Science and Technology. In March 1990 the deputy minister of ISTC simplified the priorities of the department; the emphasis was put on fostering expansion in export trade and the application of technology.

36 In each of Canada's regions, commitments and expenditures under the GDAS and the next generation ERDAS reached many billions of dollars of federal funding alone by 1987, along with commitments of the same order of magnitude by provincial governments. To March 31, 1982, DREE's last independent year, federal and provincial commitments under the GDAS approximated $5.6 billion. Since that time, well in excess of $3 billion have been committed under the ERDAS. At March 31, 1989, subsidiary agreements in force in the Atlantic provinces totalled $2.23 billion in value.

37 House of Commons, *Debates*, vol. 129, no. 236, January 18, 1988, p. 11985.

38 It is difficult to strike an average figure for a financial incentives program based either on annual commitments or on actual expenditures. Some relationship between commitments and expenditures can be developed over a longer period of time. Usually, actual cash flow runs at less than the annual commitment level, as project payout always occurs one or more years after a commitment is made. It would take a complicated model to match individual project payout to project commitment, aggregated over time. The data were drawn from the annual reports of DREE and DRIE, 1978–79 through 1986–87.

39 *Daily Gleaner* (Fredericton), January 28, 1988, p. 5.

40 ACOA reported 76.7 percent of approved projects and 17.7 percent of funding directed to projects of less than $200 thousand in 1988–89. Projects under $2 million accounted for 96.7 percent of applications, and 46.5 percent of funding (ACOA, *Report of the Minister for the Fiscal Year 1988–89*).

41 Anecdotally, ACOA, "with all due politesse," said, in turning down Nova Scotia's proposal for financing the Halifax Metropolitan area and cleaning up Halifax harbour, that its $1.05 billion budget "was not for infrastructure" (*Daily Gleaner* [Fredericton], January 28, 1988, p. 5). In 1988–89, an agreement was

concluded with Nova Scotia to "put in place a $196 million waste water treatment system for Halifax Harbour" (ACOA, *Report of the Minister for the Fiscal Year 1988–89*).

42 The question of allocation of funding by province was debated at length in the House of Commons on third reading of the ACOA Bill, April 27, 1988, p. 14881–84.

43 Government of Newfoundland and Labrador, "Preliminary Discussion Paper on the Atlantic Canada Opportunities Agency."

44 *Globe and Mail*, March 21, 1989, p. B6. More than a year later, the two governments were still at odds over the size and cost-sharing aspects of a new forestry agreement, with Canada wanting over 50 percent B.C. participation on a $200-million agreement and the province remaining adamant on the equal cost-sharing formula and proposing a five-year, $400-million deal (*Financial Post*, August 21, 1990, p. 3; August 23, 1990, p. 4). Finally, the federal government signed an agreement with B.C. in March, 1991, but at a substantially reduced share; $100 million over five years, one-third less than its previous five-year involvement.

45 *Ottawa Citizen*, March 22, 1989, p. B6; March 25, p. A1, A2.

46 *Chronicle-Herald* (Halifax), April 7, 1989, p. 1.

47 *Financial Post*, May 1, 1989, p. 15; May 8, 1989, p. 19.

48 Department of Finance, budget papers, pp. 67, 68, 69.

49 *Globe and Mail*, May 17, 1989, p. A11; *Financial Post*, May 17, 1989, p. 1; and *Ottawa Citizen*, May 20, 1989, p. B4.

50 This restriction was lifted in the February 20, 1990, budget, and projects with eligible costs of up to $20 million were reinstated for consideration. In March 1990, direct contributions under $100,000 were exempted from the government's grants repayment provision.

51 *Globe and Mail*, June 21, 1989, p. B5.

52 ACOA, *Report of the Minister for the Fiscal Year 1988–89*.

53 ACOA is also responsible for special federal financial assistance schemes in the Atlantic provinces. It was assigned the management of a $90-million economic diversification program aimed at alleviating job loss caused by a downturn in the fisheries in 1990.

54 ACOA did have its supporters. After Sinclair Stevens was forced to step down as DRIE minister in 1986, the people of Cape Breton hosted a party in his honour as an expression of thanks for the attention he had given that island. The Industrial Cape Breton Board of Trade gave full marks to ACOA for bringing new opportunity to the region, and the agency's man in charge concurred, although he recognized the contribution made by earlier programs (*Financial Post*, March 20, 1989, p. 7). One highly touted Cape Breton project, and rightly so, was a federal transport contract to Micronav Limited for an airport microwave landing system, worth at least $50 million and potentially much more. The contract was awarded in the name of regional development (*Globe and Mail*, August 29, 1989, p. B3). The spadework for the Micronav initiative, including federal financial support, predated ACOA by several years, and it was the persistance of DREE officials, in face of considerable opposition from other departments, that kept the project alive.

55 Canadian Intergovernmental Conference Secretariat, "Barriers to Interprovincial Trade," document number 800-24/060, Annual Conference of First Ministers, Toronto, Ontario, November 26–27, 1987.

56 A year after the committee on trade barriers was formed, agreement on a restricted procurement protocol, covering goods tendering over $25,000 (not public works or services) was announced (*Globe and Mail*, September 20, 1988, p. B11). It was not ratified by all provinces until August 1991. Still exempt were beer and wine, crown corporations, and several other single-province practices. In December 1989 the Atlantic provinces signed a regional free-trade zone agreement (*Globe and Mail*, December 21, p. B5). In September 1990 Premier McKenna of New Brunswick spoke of Maritime economic union (*Globe and Mail*, September 14, 1990, p. A16). The Canadian Manufacturers' Association called for the elimination of barriers by 1993 (*Financial Post*, April 17, 1991, p. 6). The federal government announced its intended greater involvement with the issue in the Speech from the Throne, May 14, 1991, and followed that with a barriers-elimination proposal in its September 24, 1991, constitutional reform package.

57 House of Commons, *Debates*, vol. 129, no. 236, January 18, 1988, p. 11985.

58 ACOA reported some success in its advocacy role in its "Report of the Minister for Fiscal Year 1988–89." It indicated its participation in developing Canada's position on the definition of subsidies under the FTA, its promotion of federal procurement to stimulate the regional economy, and its full representation on major crown procurement committees dealing with purchases of over $100 million.

59 *Financial Post*, July 26, 1988, p. 48.

60 Savoie, Donald J., *ACOA: Transition to Maturity* (February 1991), pp. 43, 44, 45, 60, 66–68, 74, 76, 77, 81, 84. For a further insight into the difficulties experienced by ACOA in effecting its mandate, see Savoie, *Regional Economic Development*, 2nd ed., pp. 136–39.

61 Such actions were a repudiation of the government's 1984 declaration that it would stay out of the marketplace. They were also in apparent contradiction with the policy that Michel Côté had tried to enunciate two and a half years later, in May 1987 (*Financial Post*, May 11, 1987, p. 13).

62 *Globe and Mail*, March 17, 1989, p. A4.

63 In June 1989 the company announced a $218-million expansion of its facilities. Canada and Quebec subsequently provided $50 million of loan assistance for a further five years to 1994, with interest to be repaid only on profit and only on a portion of the loan balance, so that the interest paid will be negligible over the life of the loans.

64 *Globe and Mail*, "Report on Business," May 7, 1988, p. B6.

65 Western Diversification Office, Canada-Alberta news release, February 8, 1988; and *Financial Post*, February 16, 1988, p. 6.

66 *Globe and Mail*, September 9, 1988, p. B4. The Matane history is a tortuous one. Efforts had been made for over twenty years to put a mill in that location. The one-time member of Parliament from the region, now senator Pierre De Bané, tried valiantly to bring such a dream to reality. Governments were now to pay dearly if Donohue, partly owned by the Quebec government, was to have its way. It was

looking for a $20-million infrastructure grant, $8 million from each of the federal and provincial governments, $4 million from local government, a federal tax credit of $15 million (and possibly more to come), and $3 to $4 million for manpower training. The mill began operations in November 1990 and was closed for an indefinite period of time in September 1991 as a result of soft markets and prices.

67 *Globe and Mail*, February 21, 1989, p. B6; August 30, 1989, p. B9.

68 The space agency debate had been pursued for many months before a decision was announced, after the federal election of 1988, to place it in St-Hubert, Quebec. Critics decried the separation from other Ottawa-based related infrastructure and the likely loss of skilled scientists. The prime minister and the premier of Quebec both cast dispersion on the competence and motivation of those not willing to accept transfer to the new location.

69 A dramatic example of an elected government exercising its power outside Parliament occurred in October 1989 with the decision to drastically reduce passenger rail services in Canada. Despite public outcry and daily badgering in the House of Commons, the government proceeded on its chosen course; as the *Ottawa Citizen* put it: "The cuts at Via are not being approved by Parliament, but were quietly confirmed by cabinet decree today" (October 4, 1989, p. 1).

70 The project was criticized as non-viable and an election ploy. Experts said the Hibernia field was one of the most expensive in the world. In September 1989 the project was running a year late, and Newfoundland Premier Clyde Wells openly expressed his doubts about its future. In January 1990 he declared that he would leave the oil in the ground if at least one of five supermodules was not built in the province. Canada and Newfoundland offered a new benefits package to ensure that objective (*Globe and Mail*, July 18, 1988, p. A2; June 9, 1989, p. B1; July 18, 1989 [the anniversary date], pp. A7, B1, B3; September 13, 1989, p. B3; January 12, 1990, p. B6; and *Financial Post*, March 24, 1989, p. 1; September 18, 1989, p. 5; January 24, 1990, p. 3). By May, Wells had rejected the consortium (Mobil Oil, Petro Canada, Gulf, and Chevron Resources) decision to build only one module in the province (*Financial Post*, May 21, 1990, p. 6). Finally, ten years after the oil discovery and after several missed deadlines, a $5.2-billion Hibernia agreement was initialled in Newfoundland on September 17, 1990, ensuring one of five construction modules for the province and over $3 billion of construction for Canadian firms. Bill C-44, providing for $2.7 billion of federal participation in the project, was passed by the House on October 4, 1990, and by the Senate on October 29, 1990.

71 See ACOA data in note 40, this chapter.

72 ACOA was also accused of being politically motivated during the period just prior to the November 21, 1988, federal election. Data were quoted in the *Globe and Mail* (June 21, 1989) purporting to prove that $155.9 million, close to the agency's total annual budget, was committed in the two months prior to the election, with almost two-thirds going to twenty-five companies, including such giants as the Irving Pulp and Paper Company and a Weston's subsidiary company.

73 Provincial governments must be of two minds with regard to federally led regional development policy. On the one hand, large dollar amounts are involved and these can not easily be rejected by certain of the provinces. Conversely, the federal approach leaves the provinces with reduced bargaining power. Quebec, not

willing to acquiesce to a direct federal approach, has won its point. In Atlantic Canada, the federal government is capable of outspending the provinces on dedicated regional development activities. Although most provincial governments feel that they hold prime jurisdiction and responsibility for regional development, they cannot afford to reject the intent of the federal government to improve regional economies. The provinces are more comfortable, however, if they are seen to be part of the action, to have meaningful input into the determination of priorities, and to engage in cost-sharing of those activities carried out under subsidiary agreements.

74 The ACOA Act stipulates a quinquennial report by the Agency to provide an evaluation of activities and the impact on regional disparity — section 21.(2). Two years after ACOA came into being, it claimed that the projects it assisted accounted for almost one-third of jobs created, one-third of business investment, and one-quarter of new business formations in the goods-producing sector in the Atlantic region over the previous years (*Daily Gleaner* [Fredericton], July 7, 1989, p. 3; see also ACOA, "Report of the Minister for the Fiscal Year 1988–89").

75 David Milne, in *Tug of War*, discusses federal efforts to turn back provincial power, the destruction of DREE being one result (pp. 131, 132), and concludes: "One long-term consequence of these federal-provincial wars, especially where they involve massive uprooting of earlier bureaucratic arrangements and practices such as those operating under the old GDA agreements under DREE, is that functioning patterns of trust and cooperation between federal and provincial officials are simply destroyed. Since regional economic development necessarily requires intergovernmental collaboration, whatever the 'high' politics of federalism, these patterns will somehow have to be developed under whatever kind of bureaucratic regime. As J. Stefan Dupré has argued, it would be far better to perfect and improve those working relationships to achieve additional objectives than it would be to pull them down and start again" (p. 135).

76 The debate on the government's approach to regional development continued in Atlantic Canada. Industrial commissioners lauded ACOA-type assistance for business; the Atlantic wing of the Canadian Federation of Independent Businesses (CFIB) said the region was strewn with unsuccessful businesses created solely to take advantage of government handouts, and manufacturers complained of unfair assistance to competitors and to the services sector. A CFIB survey of members revealed about one-fifth unaware of the agency and one-half not interested in it. There was some support for government assistance for the "soft" side of its mandate, including advocacy, development of management skills, and coordination and dissemination of research efforts (*Globe and Mail*, February 13, 14, 1990, p. B1). A CFIB survey of its western members revealed that 59 percent were unaware of the Department of Western Diversification and only 5 percent of the remainder said they were interested in its assistance. Less than 1 percent of survey respondents said they had received WD financing (*Globe and Mail*, September 14, 1990, p. B3).

CHAPTER 6

1 The Federal-Provincial Task Force on Regional Development Assessment (*Report*, p. 2) suggested that regional development should be viewed as the

economic development of the regions and that there should be focus less on disparities among provinces and more on efforts to maximize growth in all the regions or provinces, based on their strengths. In its report, the Macdonald Commission said "it is time to stop viewing inequalities simply in terms of per capita income differences" (vol. 3, p. 215). Courchene commented: "The aspect of regional disparities seen as the most important, and the one which has received most policy attention, is the difference in interregional per capita incomes or factor payments. But do such differences represent a problem requiring government action? ... The direction of, and motivation for, economic policy measures, however, should not depend on the degree to which economic variables can be measured" (Courchene and Melvin, "Canadian Regional Policy," pp. 61, 62). Donald Savoie, a one-time supporter of measurable indices, subsequently said, "Current goals of alleviating regional disparities, as measured by unemployment rates and per capita income, date back to the 1960s. ... Some governments still cling to the notion that Ottawa should commit itself to alleviating regional disparities, as measured by unemployment rates and per capita income. ... New regional development initiatives should be defined according to more realistic criteria than has been the case thus far" (Savoie, "Courchene and Regional Development," p. 74; see also idem, *Regional Economic Development*, p. 149). Sometime later Savoie introduced the idea of an entrepreneurial index, to measure the entrepreneurial dynamic of a region, in other words, a forward-looking approach to assessing regional potential (*Regional Economic Development*, 2nd ed., p. 203.

2 Treasury Board Secretariat, "Draft Guidelines for Program Evaluation."

3 DREE Atlantic staff memorandum to management, August 31, 1978.

4 The province of New Brunswick, in a submission to the Senate Standing Committee on National Finance, October 21, 1980, expressed its concern in the following way: "It is the Province's concern that DREE activity to date will be evaluated on the basis of the short-term, quick return syndrome. ... It is impossible in the decision-making process of government to adequately quantify the long-term impact of economic development measures. But economic development is a long-term process and adequate time must be allowed to assess the full impact of such measures."

5 APEC, *Industrial Incentives Programs in the Atlantic Region*, p. 133.

6 This was a departmental task force whose mandate was to look at the integration of the programs of DREE and ITC and make recommendations on new program directions. It reported in March 1982.

7 The objective "identification of industries that have potential for growth in designated regions and special areas" had been deleted by the time of the 1974–75 Main Estimates.

8 DREE, "Report on Regional Development Incentives, July 1, 1969–December 31, 1982."

9 Data for the IRDP analysis were drawn from the 1988–89 IRDP annual report, and for the employment analysis, from reports 1984–85 through 1988–89. The jobs data were displayed by both program element and by tier. For all years but 1985–86 the totals corresponded. In that year the "tiers" data were higher and were used, for consistency purposes, in developing percentage relationships.

10 APEC, *Industrial Incentives Programs in the Atlantic Region*, p. 135.

11 DREE, annual reports.

12 Savoie, *Regional Economic Development*, p. 123.

13 In its twenty-fourth annual review, the council qualified its earlier opinion: "In general, we are not much enamoured by many of the regional and industrial programs now in place. With respect to regional industrial grants, while we are on record as having said, in an earlier analysis, that 'the value of the jobs created appears to outweigh the inefficiency involved in locating production inappropriately,' we generally share the view of the Macdonald Commission that, at best, 'it may be that the policies have prevented regional imbalance from getting worse'" (ECC, "Reaching Outward," p. 48). Although the Macdonald Commission comment was preceded by some discussion on industrial incentives (vol. 3, p. 213), it seemed to be more a generic comment in nature than a direct reference to company incentives.

14 Quoted from ECC, *Living Together*, Appendix B, pp. 237, 238.

15 Springate, "Regional Development Incentives Grants and the Government of Canada," p. 128.

16 Ibid., pp. 287, 288.

17 Mathias, *Forced Growth*, pp. 7, 9, and all chapters for the cases analysis.

18 Woodward, "The Capital Bias of DREE Incentives," pp. 2, 4, 7, 16. See also Woodward, "Effective Locational Subsidies."

19 Data were extracted from the DREE monthly incentives reports to Parliament, 1981 and 1982, and the DRIE Industrial and Regional Development Program annual reports, 1984–85 through 1988–89.

20 Careless, *Initiative and Response*, p. 169. Although Careless appears to be discussing DREE activities in a broader sense of financial assistance, his reference in specific to industrial activity.

21 Lithwick, "Regional Development Policies," p. 144.

22 Donald Savoie, in *Regional Economic Development* (p. 159), suggests that "evaluation criteria ... should be tied to the creation of employment and movement away from dependence on transfer payments." By itself, this is an inadequate criterion. Savoie's view that incentives "should cover manufacturing and processing industries and primary resource processing and service facilities that correspond to a region's economic circumstances" would appear to preclude the introduction of new technologies and management and marketing skills essential to a competitive economic environment, as well as economic diversification. The reference to a movement away from transfer payment dependency is puzzling. That is the underlying premise of all targeted regional economic development policies and employment policies, but tying firm-specific cash grants to macroeconomic transfer payments policy in any operational sense is hardly practical.

23 Savoie makes an erroneous assumption when he compares the cost of administering the RDIP to *all* DREE overhead costs, saying, "A regional incentives program entails considerable administrative costs. ... An expensive bureaucratic structure has to be maintained to deliver, monitor, audit ... the program." He then compares DREE's *total* expenditures on grants to business, which he estimates as $118 million annually, to total *DRIE* administrative costs of $220 million in 1984–85, several years later (Savoie, *Regional Economic Development*, p. 163;

and idem, "Cash Incentives versus Tax Incentives for Regional Development," p. 6).

24 Savoie nevertheless falls into the trap of many other commentators on DREE when he focuses on direct incentives programs to the extent of saying, "Canada's (industrial) incentives program remains the cornerstone of the federal government's involvement in regional development" (Savoie, *Regional Economic Development*, p. 157). Even in 1986, this was not true. Although the IRDP was a major program instrument of DRIE, it had considerably less impact on the peripheral regions than the subsidiary agreements by now being written by many federal departments. Only if incentives are given the widest possible interpretation could Savoie's statement be considered accurate.

25 DREE, Main Estimates, 1971–72 through 1973–74.

26 DREE and DRIE, Main Estimates, 1971–72 through 1986–87.

27 See note 23, this chapter.

28 Tupper, *Public Money in the Private Sector*," chap. 5 and p. 57.

29 Ibid., pp. 58, 60.

30 Ibid., p. 80.

31 Ibid., p. 91.

32 Department Industry, Trade and Commerce (Canada), unpublished staff paper, October 1977.

33 Bernard Bonin and Roger Verreault, "The Multinational Firm and Regional Development," p. 161. To underline the contradiction on the value of incentives, Bonin and Verreault cited a 1968 British Board of Trade Study that showed that foreign-based companies (non-British) moving plants to the US in the 1945–65 period tended to locate them in developed areas to a greater degree than did British companies.

34 Tupper, in *Public Money in the Private Sector*, quotes a Michelin executive on incentives: "They were certainly not the reason for our coming to Canada or for our settling in Nova Scotia. That said, it is not something to be neglected. But obviously, a company which enters an important market ... and intending to stay in that market on a long-term basis, could not be swayed ... by different degrees of assistance. It is well to have that assistance ... but that could not be the basis of the decision" (p. 62). Tupper suggests that another reason for the Michelin decision was a weak trade union movement in Nova Scotia. The $52-million deal negotiated with Michelin in 1979–80 for a new facility in Waterville, NS, bringing a forecasted 1,860 jobs, was considered by federal officials to allow Nova Scotia to compete with US state interests, since the union threat in the US was non-existent. Michelin clearly wanted a Canadian access to the US market and for some years was willing to pay a premium in terms of countervail against their tire exports. The company also found the Nova Scotia labour force to be one of the most productive in its worldwide system. Federal officials felt the incentives offered to Michelin played an important part in convincing the corporate management to proceed in Nova Scotia, with the eventual benefits to the economy, both regionally and nationally, far outweighing the value of the incentives.

35 Semple, "Regional Analysis of Corporate Decision Making within the Canadian Economy," Table 1, p. 204.

36 Ibid., tables 3–6.

37 Ibid., Table 6, p. 216.

38 Ibid., Table 7.

39 Ibid., Table 10, p. 227. Semple relates the population of an area, or city, to the percentage of national revenues or assets controlled by all corporations in the area. He factors in foreign control revenues and assets percentages to provide a composite index.

40 Ken Norrie, quoted in Tupper, *Public Money in the Private Sector*, is even more forthright on this question in saying, "The geographically peripheral areas of the country are just not feasible sites to naturally attract most types of secondary industry. ... Hinterland regions do not become industrial centres in a market economy, and the distribution of manufacturing industries across Canada is a simple reflection of this fact" (p. 48).

41 The *Financial Post* (January 9, 1989, pp. 11–16) discusses the locational question in the context of free trade.

42 Semple, "Regional Analysis of Corporate Decision-Making," p. 233.

43 Federal-Provincial Task Force on Regional Development Assessment, *Report*, p. 43.

44 *Globe and Mail*, April 14, 1989.

45 Ibid., February 9, 1989, p. B6.

46 Ibid., March 1, 1989, p. B13.

47 Ibid., March 3, 1989, p. B7.

48 Ibid., February 24, 1989, p. B3.

49 Ibid., January 23, 1990, p. B6; *Ottawa Citizen*, January 23, 1990, p. 38; idem, January 26, 1990, p. B8; and *Globe and Mail*, January 31, 1990, p. B5.

50 *Financial Post*, October 12, 1990, p. 8.

51 DREE, "Economic Development Prospects in the Atlantic Region," one of a series of reports (blue books) on development prospects in the regions of Canada, December 1979, p. 3.

52 Ibid., pp. 3–10.

53 House of Commons, Standing Committee on Regional Development, *Proceedings*, no. 22, April 2, 1981.

54 DREE, unpublished Atlantic Canada regional strategy paper, November 3, 1981.

55 APEC, "An Analysis of the Reorganization for Economic Development," pp. 13, 14.

56 Federal-Provincial Task Force on Regional Development Assessement, *Report*, pp. 3–4.

57 Ibid., p. 43.

58 Savoie, "Establishing the Atlantic Canada Opportunities Agency," pp. 16, 54.

59 The Macdonald Commission, *Report*, vol. 3, p. 198.

CHAPTER 7

1 Federal-Provincial Task Force on Regional Development Assessment, *Report*, p. 27.

2 Courchene and Melvin, "Canadian Regional Policy," p. 56. For some of

Courchene's earlier, and supporting, views on adjustment, see Courchene, "Avenues of Adjustment," pp. 50–58.

3 ECC, *Newfoundland*, p. 1.

4 Senate Standing Committee on National Finance, *Government Policy and Regional Development*, p. 101.

5 Federal-Provincial Task Force on Regional Development Assessment, *Report*, p. 33.

6 Courchene and Melvin, "Canadian Regional Policy," p. 60.

7 As witnessed by the Conservative government's rejection of the Forget Commission report on unemployment insurance in 1987.

8 See Ralph Matthews, "Two Alternative Explanations of the Problem of Regional Dependency in Canada," pp. 63–84.

9 Atlantic Development Council, "The Atlantic Region of Canada," p. 53; ECC, *Living Together*, p. 220, recommendation 3; and idem, *Newfoundland*, p. 161, recommendation 1.

10 Polèse, "Regional Disparity, Migration and Economic Adjustment," p. 524.

11 Savoie, *Regional Economic Development*, pp. 161–63; Savoie and Chenier, "The State and Development," p. 419; and Savoie, "Establishing the Atlantic Canada Opportunities Agency," pp. 55, 57.

12 Federal-Provincial Task Force on Regional Development Assessment, *Report*, p. 39.

13 Kent, *A Public Purpose*, pp. 419–20. Kent returned to this theme twenty years later in extolling the importance of local input to what he calls "community conservation" (Kent, *Getting Ready for 1999*, pp. 135–38). Kent does not, however, recognize the importance of having some indigenous strength on which to build, and even more significantly, the need for stong local leadership to make it work.

14 Kent, *A Public Purpose*, p. 432.

15 Federal-Provincial Task Force on Regional Development Assessment, *Report*, pp. 33, 42.

16 APEC, "An Analysis of the Reorganization for Economic Development," p. 34. The council stressed that development plans for slow-growth areas must promote the growth of an industrial base.

17 Savoie, "Establishing the Atlantic Canada Opportunities Agency," pp. 38–39.

18 ECC, *Newfoundland*, p. 126.

19 Donald Savoie proposed measures to raise educational and knowledge levels of a population and initiatives to foster entrepreneurial talent (Savoie, "Courchene and Regional Development," p. 75). He also proposed a joint analysis of the educational and training needs of the Atlantic provinces through the combined efforts of the federal and provincial governments, universities and community colleges, business, and labour (Savoie, "Establishing the Atlantic Canada Opportunities Agency," p. 53). The Federal-Provincial Task Force on Regional Development Assessment presented a provincial government perspective for a more conducive policy, program, and regulatory environment for the formation of new small business: more attention to education and training, support for marketing, trade development, and technological advance, and adaptation of contemporary

infrastructure for economic and business development (*Report*, pp. 34, 35).

20 *Daily Gleaner* (Fredericton), April 10, 1987, in reporting the Liberal leader's response to the New Brunswick Throne Speech. I have not as a practice included political views or intentions when referencing proposals to improve regional economies—unfortunately, they are usually met with suspicion by most readers. An exception has been made in this case because McKenna had just developed his own agenda for economic improvement in New Brunswick; albeit it still carried political connotations. It is beyond the purview of this book to assess his success in implementing his ideas after he assumed the premiership of New Brunswick.

21 DRIE, unpublished staff paper, 1987.

22 House of Commons Standing Committee on Regional Development, in presenting recommendations to the DREE minister with regard to the study of Main Estimates 1980–81.

23 Sources include the Atlantic Development Council, the Atlantic Provinces Economic Council, the Federal-Provincial Task Force on Regional Development Assessment, Frank McKenna as New Brunswick opposition leader, New Brunswick presentation to the Senate Standing Committee on National Finance (*Government Policy and Regional Development*), Charles J. McMillan's report to the Council of Maritime Premiers (Standing Up to the Future), Donald Savoie, in several writings, unpublished DREE and DRIE staff papers, and discussions with federal and provincial officials.

24 Macdonald Commission, *Report*, vol. 3, pp. 217–18.

25 Atlantic Development Council, "The Atlantic Region of Canada," pp. 65, 68, 182.

26 The Senate Standing Committee on National Finance, in its 1982 report *Government Policy and Regional Development* (pp. 58–59), said, "There is very little wrong with being hewers of wood and drawers of water, especially when these resources come from a sector of the economy that generally employs the most sophisticated technology and enjoys the highest productivity of all sectors." It added, "But it should not be forgotten that technology is the key to resource development and that there can be spin-offs of supporting service industries and sophisticated manufacturing."

27 Federal-Provincial Task Force on Regional Development Assessment, *Report*, pp. 38–40.

28 Ibid., pp. 33, 42.

29 Lesser and Hall, *Telecommunications Services and Regional Development*, pp. 137–38.

30 Federal Provincial Task Force Report on Regional Development Assessment, *Report*, p. 39.

31 Coffey and McRae, *Service Industries in Regional Development*, pp. 122–23. Coffey and Mario Polèse also discussed the interurban location of office activities in "The Interurban Location of Office Activities." They said that in their locational choice office activities have a tendency to climb the urban hierarchy as their size increases. They stressed that the spatial distribution of such activities may be highly influenced by where professionals and managers prefer to live. They suggested no clear-cut conclusion on the office location question but

were skeptical of the ability of the national government to influence office locations, particularly to peripheral regions. They concluded: "There seems to be general agreement among researchers that it is only the programmed or standardized activities that are able to be effectively dispersed to the periphery; in the case of higher-order non-programmed functions, urban centres at the top of the hierarchy tend to reinforce both their own growth and the centralization of these functions due to their advantageous positions for controlling economic interaction" (pp. 98–99).

32 Lesser and Hall, *Telecommunications Services and Regional Development*, p. 138; and Coffey and McRae, *Service Industries in Regional Development*, p. 123.

33 Barry Lesser, "Technological Change and Regional Development," p. 343.

34 Lesser and Hall, *Telecommunications Services and Regional Development*, p. 141.

35 DREE, "Support for Indigenous Development, Atlantic Region," by Audlen Projects Limited, pp. 30–32.

36 Lesser and Hall, *Telecommunications Services and Regional Development*, pp. 82, 166, 167. For a more complete discussion of telecommunications services as a critical component of the information economy, see also chapters 3 ("Theoretical Framework") and 5 ("Policy Implications").

37 ISTC, "The Service Sector in the Canadian Economy-Industry Consultation Paper," p. 10.

38 The views on this question are by no means unanimous. Issue has been taken on the degree of independence of service industries and the quality of jobs in the sector. Even the data vary, with one source quoting manufacturing jobs as 28.9 percent of all jobs in 1989, another claiming a reduction to only 17 percent in that same year. There is a greater level of agreement on job growth in services. The Economic Council of Canada says that jobs in the service sectors are polarized into good or bad, with no in-between. Good jobs are classified in transportation, communications, business services, finance, insurance, wholesale trade, and real estate. Bad jobs fall in retail trade, personal services, food, and accommodation. The Canadian Manufacturers' Association claims that the service sectors cannot survive without a strong goods-producing sector and that manufacturing contracting-out of service-related jobs has distorted the relative positions of the two groups, to the detriment of manufacturing jobs statistics and the enhancement of service jobs (*Financial Post*, March 5, 1990, p. 7; and *Globe and Mail*, April 16, 1990, pp. B1, B4).

39 ISTC, "The Service Sector in the Canadian Economy," pp. 6–7.

40 Coffey and McRae, *Service Industries in Regional Development*, pp. 116, 118.

41 Ibid., pp. 120, 123.

42 The Macdonald Commission (*Report*, vol. 3, p. 203) recites a number of these same factors as the reason for the productivity gap that explains the earnings differential between different regions in Canada. See also the Senate Standing Finance Committee, *Government Policy and Regional Development*, p. 48.

43 House of Commons, *Debates*, vol. 129, no. 236, January 18, 1988, p. 11987. Prime Minister Mulroney wrote to Premier Buchanan of Nova Scotia

on December 30, 1987: "When these negotiations with the U.S. began, I wanted to ensure that our ability to promote regional development policies was preserved. We have done that. I can assure you further that we will continue to maintain our capacity for regional development programs in the course of negotiations intended to develop a new North American regime on trade remedy rules. In short, the federal government remains fully committed to programs and measures which will deal effectively with regional disparities."

44 The 1987 trade negotiations never came close to reaching a meeting of minds on business subsidies because of what Canada's chief trade negotiator described as unbridgeable differences in trade philosophies between the two countries. Canada held to the position that any subsidy provisions would have to respect Canada's right to provide for regional development, research and development, and small-business needs in this country. It appeared certain that both countries would take up to the full seven years provided under the FTA to resolve the business subsidies dispute, notwithstanding early efforts to put some mechanism in place.

45 *Globe and Mail*, April 13, 1989, p. B1; May 3, 1989, p. A8.

46 Ibid., May 25, 1989, p. B5. The trade panel on BC salmon and herring reported in October 1989, and both sides chose to interpret the findings to their advantage, leading officials to further pessimism on how the dispute-resolution mechanism was going to resolve issues on which both countries held entrenched points of view (*Globe and Mail*, November 10, 1989, p. B1).

47 Macdonald Commission, *Report*, vol. 1, pp. 330–31. See also Watson, "The Regional Consequences of Free(r) Trade with the United States."

48 *Globe and Mail*, December 6, 1989, p. A5; January 2, 1990, p. A7; January 3, 1990, p. A8; *Financial Post*, December 4, 1989, pp. 1, 4; and *Ottawa Citizen*, January 20, 1990, p. B5; May 3, p. D11. See also Barlow, *Parcel of Rogues*, Appendix, pp. 206–34.

49 *Ottawa Citizen*, December 13, 1990, p. C1; and *Financial Post*, December 18, p. 6; 20 December, 1990, p. 44.

50 *Financial Post*, "Report on the Nation," p. 16.

51 Barlow was undoubtedly overstating her point in suggesting that whole communities and regions were being deserted, with deep cuts to the budgets of ACOA and WD and reduced effort in forestry, fish processing, and tourism (Barlow, *Parcel of Rogues*, pp. 31, 88, 91).

52 Royal Bank *econoscope*, 1990, pp. 2, 16; and *econoscope*, special edition, "Free Trade: Second Year Review," February 1991.

53 *Ottawa Citizen*, December 17, 1991, p. A1; December 18, 1991, p. A3; March 20, 1992, p. D11.

CHAPTER 8

1 Atlantic Development Council, in "Economic Strategy for the Eighties" (p. 54), stressed the need for the people and governments of the Atlantic region to strengthen consultative and organizational arrangements; Ian McAllister, in *Policy Options*, recommended that regional development be viewed in terms of the (federal) government's overall goals being taken into account in the budget

and that all federal agencies be given regional guidelines and targets; Savoie, in *Federal-Provincial Collaboration*, said, "A strong case can be made for suggesting to the federal government that it should look more inwardly in its attempt to alleviate regional economic disparities" (p. 165); and the Atlantic Provinces Economic Council review of the "Reorganization for Economic Development" (pp. 34–35), proposed regional guidelines for federal line departments and compensating fiscal policy for any adverse impact of national policies on regional economies.

2 McAllister, "How to Remake DREE."

3 Macdonald Commission, *Regional Responsiveness*, chap. 2 (Aucoin and Bakvis), p. 109.

4 Savoie, *Regional Economic Development*, pp. 164, 165. The suggestion was made in his discussion on the difficulty of convincing line departments to deviate from entrenched positions and the need for an organization that could cut across jurisdictional lines.

5 Savoie, "Establishing the Atlantic Canada Opportunities Agency," pp. 45–48, 76, 78.

6 In the fall of 1989, the agency concluded it had still not effected adequate federal departmental cooperation and had not wrested the lead from the provinces in determining regional development policy. This led to a new enunciation of federal theme objectives: cost-sharing based on federal priorities, a return to direct federal program delivery, and a renewed effort to promote federal visibility (source: public announcements and discussions with officials).

7 Federal-Provincial Task Force Report on Regional Development Assessment, *Report*, May 1987, p. 11.

8 Almost thirty years after rejecting mobility as a solution to regional development problems (see note 51, chapter 1), Tom Kent proposed a voluntary mobility assistance program. In so doing, however, he said, "Rightly, people in the Atlantic region reject the view common among economists and others in central Canada, that 'the' solution to the region's problems is continued out-migration." Then he added, "A program with that deliberate purpose is not only politically unthinkable; its economic and social effects would be disastrous" (Kent, *Getting Ready for 1999*, p. 134).

9 Budget papers, 1992, p. 97.

10 Many will not have forgotten the abortive attempts by the federal government since 1972, or before, to develop an industrial development strategy for Canada and the eventual abandonment of the effort. Canada has not been particularly warm to long-term planning of its economy, as the Economic Council of Canada learned in its early years (Thorburn, *Planning and the Economy*, p. 89).

11 This point was dramatically reinforced when the government proposed sweeping new constitutional powers for itself in the management of the economic union, qualified by an override requiring the concurrence of at least seven of the provinces representing 50 percent of the population. The proposal met a cool reception from the provinces and was discarded in the subsequent Beaudoin-Dobbie report on the Constitution (Government of Canada, "Shaping Canada's Future Together").

12 Thorburn, *Planning and the Economy*, pp. 213–18. Also note the similarity

between Thorburn's proposal and that found in "Shaping Canada's Future Together" for an independent agency to monitor and evaluate the macroeconomic policies of the federal and provincial governments and financed jointly by the two levels of government.

13 Donald Savoie, in writing the proposal "Establishing the Atlantic Canada Opportunities Agency" (p. 62), speaks of the agency having the ability to assess a selection of national programs for regional impact and suggests that the agency should have the capacity to assess the regional distribution of all departmental financial allocations. If this line of thought is carried to its logical conclusion, each of the four regional approaches now being practised in Canada should do the same thing—hardly an efficient use of resources and not a practice to which other departments would be very receptive. This kind of function must be coordinated on a national scale and is one particularly suited to Treasury Board. Unfortunately, for many years that organization has resisted any move to make it responsible for such a task.

14 Dom Jamieson commented on the problems for federal politicians caused by the blurring of lines of responsibility between the two levels of government that occurred in a range of cost-sharing schemes introduced from Pearson onwards "to channel federal funds into everything from regional development to urban transit and housing." He said, "Federal governments have created a stout rod with which they are constantly being beaten" (Jamieson, *No Place for Fools: The Political Memoirs of Don Jamieson*, vol. 1, pp. 197, 198).

15 There may be some justification for up-front assistance to companies engaged in high-risk, special technology fields that accord with an agreed-upon strategic plan for a regional economy. Such assistance could be conditionally repayable, although this may not be cost-effective. If such a venture succeeds, its contribution to the region in the areas intended would far outweigh the repayment of funds advanced. Similarly, start-up assistance for the very small indigenous venture so essential at the community level, which is so frequently discriminated against by lending institutions, may be justified.

16 Canada, Special Joint Committee on a Renewed Canada, *Report* (the Beaudoin-Dobbie Report), February 29, 1992, Supply and Services Canada; *Ottawa Citizen*, March 1, 1992, p. A4.

17 *Ottawa Citizen*, March 1, 1992, p. B8.

References

Atlantic Canada Opportunites Agency (ACOA). "A Comprehensive Study of Opinions about the Atlantic Canada Opportunities Agency." Opinion research carried out by PIR Management Services Consulting Group, Halifax, Nova Scotia, October 1988.

–. Press release ("Action Program"), Moncton, NB, February 1988.

–. Press release ("Modifications to ACOA's Action Program, Moncton, NB, February 1990.

–. "Report of the Minister for the Fiscal Year 1988–89," Moncton, NB, August 1989; *Annual Report 1990–91.*

–. Speaking notes for the president for an address to the APEC Conference, Moncton, NB, October 1989.

–. Speaking notes for the president for an address to the Greater Moncton Chamber of Commerce, Moncton, NB, November 1989.

–. "Transition to Maturity," by Donald J. Savoie. February 1991.

Atlantic Development Council (ADC). "The Atlantic Region of Canada: Economic Development Strategy for the Eighties." November 1978.

Atlantic Provinces Economic Council (APEC). *An Analysis of the Reorganization for Economic Development.* Halifax, 1982.

–. *Atlantic Canada Today.* 2nd ed. Halifax: APEC, 1977.

–. *The Atlantic Vision-1990: A Development Strategy for the 1980's.* Halifax: APEC, 1979.

–. "Federal Spending in Atlantic Canada: An Examination of Key Components." APEC Atlantic report, October 1989.

–. "The Federal Role in Atlantic Canada: Remarks to the APEC Annual Meeting and Conference," by J. Fred Morley. Moncton, October 4, 1989.

–. *Industrial Incentives Programs in the Atlantic Region.* Halifax: APEC, October, 1976.

–. Newsletters, various. See for example vol. 33, nos. 5 and 6 (June–October 1989).

Aucoin, Peter, and Herman Bakvis. *The Centralization-Decentralization Conundrum: Organization and Management in the Canadian Government.* Halifax: Institute for Research on Public Policy, 1988.

–. "Organizational Differentiation and Integration: The Case of Regional Economic Development Policy in Canada." *Canadian Public Administration* 27, no. 3 (1984): 348–71.

Barlow, Maude. *Parcel of Rogues: How Free Trade Is Failing Canada.* Toronto: Key Porter Books, 1990.

Beer, Mitchell. "Life after DREE." *Atlantic Insight*, April 1982.

Bonin, Bernard, and Roger Verreault. "The Multinational Firm and Regional Development." In *Still Living Together*, edited by Coffey and Polèse.

Bradfield, Michael. "Review Essay: Macdonald Royal Commission Report." *Canadian Journal of Regional Science* 9, no. 1 (1986): 125–47.

Brown, Douglas M., and Ronald L. Watts, eds. *Canada: The State of the Federation 1989.* Kingston: Institute of Intergovernmental Relations, Queen's University, 1989.

Canada. "Prosperity through Competitiveness." Consultation paper, Supply and Services Canada, cat. no. C2-177/1991E.

–. "Rapport du Comité Consultatif au Comité Ministériel sur le Développement de la Région de Montréal." Ottawa, November 6, 1986.

Careless, Anthony. *Initiative and Response: The Adaptation of Canadian Federalism to Regional Economic Development.* Canadian Public Administration series. Montreal: McGill-Queen's University Press, 1977.

Carmichael, Edward A. "New Stresses on Confederation: Diverging Regional Economies." C.D. Howe Institute, observation no. 28, June 1986.

Coffey, William J. "Structural Changes in the Canadian Space-Economy." In *Still Living Together*, edited by Coffey and Polèse.

Coffey, William J., and James J. McRae. *Service Industries in Regional Development.* Institute for Research on Public Policy, 1989.

Coffey, William J., and Polèse, Mario. "The Interurban Location of Office Activities: A Framework for Analysis." In *The Canadian Economy*, edited by Savoie, pp. 85–103.

Coffey, William J., and Mario Polèse, eds. *Still Living Together: Recent Trends and Future Directions in Canadian Regional Development.* Montreal: Institute for Research on Public Policy, 1987.

Courchene, Thomas J. "Avenues of Adjustment: The Transfer System and Regional Disparities." In *The Canadian Economy*, edited by Savoie, pp. 25–62.

–. "A Market Perspective on Regional Disparities." *Canadian Public Policy* 7, no. 4 (1981): 506–18.

Courchene, Thomas J., and James R. Melvin. "Canadian Regional Policy: Lessons from the Past and Prospects for the Future." *Canadian Journal of Regional Science* 9, no. 1 (1986): 49–67.

Department of Finance (Canada). Budget papers, May 23, 1985, February 26, 1986, June 18, 1987, February 10, 1988, April 27, 1989, February 20, 1990, February 26, 1991, February 25, 1992.

–. "The Canada–U.S. Free Trade Agreement: An Economic Assessment." January 1988.

–. *Economic Development for Canada in the 1980s.* Ottawa, November 1981.

–. "Towards a Sustained Expansion: Canada's Economic Prospects, 1986–1991." Ottawa, February 1986.

Department of Regional Economic Expansion (Canada). Annual reports, 1975–76 through 1982–83.

–. "Atlantic Region Industrial Parks—An Assessment of Economic Impact." Atlantic region occasional paper, October 1979.

–. *Economic Circumstances and Opportunities in the Provinces of Canada* (the yellow books), 1973.

–. *Economic Development Prospects in the Provinces of Canada* (the blue books), 1979.

–. "Federal Regional Development Policies," by J. P. Francis. Paper presented at the Regional Economic Development Conference, University of Ottawa, March 1972.

–. Main Estimates, 1971–72 through 73–74.

–. Monthly reports to Parliament, 1981 and 1982.

–. "Regional Development: Some Issues and Conceptual Problems," by J. P. Francis and N.G. Pillai. Ottawa, June 1979.

–. "Regional Poverty and Change," by Gunter Schramm, Canadian Council on Rural Development. Catalogue no. RE14-2/76, 1973.

–. "Report on Regional Development Incentives, July 1, 1969–December 31, 1982," and DREE Monthly Reports to Parliament 1981 and 1982.

–. "Single-Sector Communities," revised 1979.

–. "Social Science and Regional Development," by J. D. Love. Paper presented to the National Social Science Conference, Ottawa, November 1975.

–. "Support for Indigenous Development, Atlantic Region," by Audlen Projects Limited, Nova Scotia. November 1974.

–. Unpublished papers, various, 1974–82.

Department of Regional Industrial Expansion (Canada). Annual reports, 1984–85 through 1988–89.

–. Industrial and Regional Development Program annual reports, 1984–85 through 1988–89.

–. Main Estimates, 1984–85 through 86–87.

–. Unpublished papers, various, 1982–89.

Department of Industry, Trade and Commerce and Regional Industrial Expansion (Canada). "Program Review Task Force Report." March 1982.

Department of Western Economic Diversification (Canada). News releases, 1987–89; annual reports, 1989–91.

Doern, G. Bruce. "The Political Administration of Government Reorganization: The Merger of DREE and ITC." *Canadian Public Administration* 30, no. 1 (1987): 34–56.

Economic Council of Canada (ECC). "The Bottom Line: Technology, Trade, and Income Growth." 1983.

–. *Living Together: A Study of Regional Disparities.* 1977.

–. *Newfoundland: From Dependency to Self-reliance.* 1980.

–. "Reaching Outward." Twenty-fourth annual review, 1987.

–. "Western Transition," 1984.

Emanuel, A. *Organization for Economic Co-operation and Development. Issues of Regional Policies.* Paris: OECD, 1973.

External Affairs Canada. "The Canada–U.S. Free Trade Agreement." 1987.

REFERENCES

−. "The Canada–U.S. Free Trade Agreement Synopsis." 1987.

−. "Canadian Trade Negotiations." December 1985.

Federal-Provincial Task Force on Regional Development Assessment. *Report of the Federal-Provincial Task Force on Regional Development Assessment.* May 1987.

Financial Post. "Report on the Nation: Canada: an Uneasy Alliance of Regions," October 1990.

First Ministers Conferences: November 27–29, 1978; November 26–27, 1987; November 9–10, 1989.

Government of Canada. "Canadian Federalism and Economic Union: Partnership for Prosperity." Supply and Services Canada, cat. no. CP 22-27/1991E, 1991.

−. "Shaping Canada's Future Together: Proposals." Supply and Services Canada, cat. no. CP 22-24/1991E, 1991.

Government of Canada and the Governments of the Provinces and the Territories. "Intergovernmental Position Paper on the Principles and Framework for Regional Economic Development," June 1985.

Government of Newfoundland and Labrador. "Preliminary Discussion Paper on the Atlantic Canada Opportunities Agency," St John's, December 2, 1986.

Grubel, Herbert G., ed. *Conceptual Issues in Service Sector Research: A Symposium.* Vancouver: Fraser Institute, 1987.

House of Commons. *Debates.* 28th Parliament, 1st Session, vol. 6 and 7, February 19–April 26, 1969.

−. *Debates.* 29th Parliament, 1st Session, 1973–74.

−. *Debates.* 30th Parliament, four sessions: September 30, 1974, through March 26, 1979.

−. *Debates.* 33rd Parliament, 2nd Session, January–August 1988.

−. Standing Committee on Fisheries and Forestry. *Minutes of Proceedings and Evidence*, May 25, 1982.

−. Standing Committee on Regional Development. *Minutes of Proceedings and Evidence*, 29th Parliament, 1st Session, nos. 1–14. 2nd Session, nos. 1–5, 1973–74.

−. Standing Committee on Regional Development. *Minutes of Proceedings and Evidence*, 30th Parliament, 2nd Session, nos. 11–13, 1976–77.

−. Standing Committee on Regional Development. *Minutes of Proceedings and Evidence*, 30th Parliament, 3rd Session, nos. 2, 3, 5, 6, 7, 1977–78.

−. Standing Committee on Regional Development. *Minutes of Proceedings and Evidence*, 31st Parliament, 1st Session, nos. 2, 6, 1979.

−. Standing Committee on Regional Development. *Minutes of Proceedings and Evidence*, 32nd Parliament, 1st Session, nos. 3, 4, 15, 16, 17, 22, 23, 37, 38, 1980–82.

−. Standing Committee on Regional Industrial Expansion. *Minutes of Proceedings and Evidence*, 33rd Parliament, 1st Session, nos. 1–3; 2nd Session, nos. 1–10, 1984–87.

Industry, Science and Technology Canada (ISTC). "Meeting the Challenge: Industry, Science and Technology in Canada." Consultation document of the

314

Department of Regional Industrial Expansion and the Ministry of State for Science and Technology, undated, ca. 1988.

–. "Regional Disparity in Canada 1989." Occasional paper no. 3, July 1989.

–. "The Service Sector in the Canadian Economy." Industry consultation paper, June 1989.

Jamieson, Don. *No Place for Fools: The Political Memoirs of Don Jamieson.* Vol. 1. St John's, Nfld: Breakwater Books, 1989.

Jenkin, Michael. *The Challenge of Diversity: Industrial Policy in the Canadian Federation.* Ottawa: Science Council of Canada, 1983.

Kent, Tom. *Getting Ready for 1999: Ideas for Canada's Politics and Government.* Halifax: Institute for Research on Public Policy, 1989.

–. *A Public Purpose.* Montreal: McGill-Queen's University Press, 1988.

Kernaghan, Kenneth, and David Siegel. *Public Administration in Canada.* Toronto: Methuen, 1987.

Kirby, Michael. "Navigating Troubled Waters, A New Policy for the Atlantic Fisheries." Ottawa: Supply and Services Canada, December 1982.

Leslie, Peter. *Federal State, National Economy.* Toronto: University of Toronto Press, 1987.

–, ed. *Canada: The State of the Federation 1985, 1986.* Kingston: Institute of Intergovernmental Relations, Queen's University, 1985, 1986.

Leslie, Peter, and Ronald L. Watts, eds. *Canada: The State of the Federation 1987–88.* Kingston: Institute of Intergovernmental Relations, Queen's University, 1988.

Lesser, Barry. "Technological Change and Regional Development." In *Still Living Together*, edited by Coffey and Polèse.

Lesser, Barry, and Pamela Hall. *Telecommunications Services and Regional Development: The Case of Atlantic Canada.* Halifax: Institute for Research on Public Policy, 1987.

Lithwick, N. Harvey. "Regional Development Policies: Context and Consequences." In *Still Living Together*, edited by Coffey and Polèse.

–. "Regional Policy: The Embodiment of Contradictions." In *The Canadian Economy: A Regional Perspective*, edited by Savoie, pp. 252–68.

Love, J. D. "The Continuing Relevance of DREE Decentralization." *Canadian Public Administration* 30, no. 3 (1987): 432–49.

McAllister, Ian. "How to Remake DREE." *Policy Options*, March 1980.

Macdonald Commission. See Royal Commission on the Economic Union and Development Prospects for Canada.

McGee, R. Harley (interview). "DREE—Towards More Selective Economic Intervention." *Atlantic Canada Plus* ("Access to Government"), 1981.

McMillan, Charles J. *Standing Up to the Future: The Maritimes in the 1990s.* Report to the Council of Maritime Premiers, December 1989.

McNiven, James D. "The Efficiency-Equity Tradeoff: The Macdonald Report and Regional Development." In *Still Living Together*, edited by Coffey and Polèse.

–. "Regional Development Policy in the Next Decade." *Canadian Journal of Regional Science* 9 no. 1 (1986): 79–88.

Mathias, Philip. *Forced Growth: Five Studies of Government Involvement in the Development of Canada.* Toronto: James Lewis and Samuel, 1971.

315

REFERENCES

Matthews, Ralph. "Two Alternative Explanations of the Problem of Regional Dependency in Canada." In *The Canadian Economy: A Regional Perspective*, edited by Savoie, pp. 63–84.

Merrifield, D. Bruce. "Forces of Change Affecting High Technology Industries." *National Journal*, January 1983, 253–56.

Milne, David. *Tug of War: Ottawa and the Provinces under Trudeau and Mulroney*. Toronto: James Lorimer & Co., 1986.

Ministry of State for Economic Development (Canada). "Agenda for Economic Development in the 1980s." Ottawa, October 1980.

Ministerial Task Force on Program Review (Canada). "Economic Growth: Natural Resources." A study team report, September 1985.

–. "New Management Initiatives." May 1985.

Nader, George A. "An Economic Regionalization of Canada: The Validity of Provinces As Regions for the Conduct of Regional Economic Policy." *Canadian Journal of Regional Science* 3, no. 2 (1980): 117–38.

Phidd, Richard W., and G. Bruce Doern. *The Politics and Management of Canadian Economic Policy*. Toronto: Macmillan of Canada, 1978.

Plumptre, Timothy W. *Beyond the Bottom Line: Management in Government*. Halifax: Institute for Research on Public Policy, 1988.

Polèse, Mario. "Patterns of Regional Economic Development in Canada, Long Term Trends and Issues." In *Still Living Together*, edited by Coffey and Polèse.

–. "Regional Disparity, Migration and Economic Adjustment: A Reappraisal." *Canadian Public Policy* 7, no. 4 (1981): 519–25.

Pollard, Bruce G. *Managing the Interface: Intergovernmental Affairs Agencies in Canada*. Kingston: Institute of Intergovernmental Relations, Queen's University, 1986.

Prime Minister's Office. News release ("Reorganization for Economic Development"), January 12, 1982.

–. News release ("Atlantic Canada Opportunities Agency Announced"), June 6, 1987.

–. News release ("Western Diversification Initiative"), August 4, 1987.

Pross, A. Paul, and Susan McCorquodale. *Economic Resurgence and the Constitutional Agenda: The Case of the East Coast Fisheries*. Queen's Studies on the Future of the Canadian Communities. Kingston: Institute of Intergovernmental Relations, Queen's University, 1987.

Service des communications de l'Office de planification et de développement du Québec. "A l'Heure de l'Entreprise Régionale: Plan d'action en matière de développement régional." Québec, October 1988.

Rabeau, Yves. "Regional Efficiency and Problems of Financing the Canadian Federation." In *Still Living Together*, edited by Coffey and Polèse.

Ritchie, Gordon. "Government Aid to Industry: A Public Sector Perspective." *Canadian Public Administration* 26, no. 1 (1983).

Robson, Robert. "Canadian Single Industry Communities." A literature review and annotated bibliography, Department of Geography, Mount Allison University, Sackville, NB, December 1986.

Royal Commission on the Economic Union and Development Prospects for Canada. (Macdonald Commission). *Disparities and Interregional Adjustment*.

316

Research Study vol. 64: chap. 3, "Federal Government Regional Economic Development Policies: An Evaluation Survey," by Harvey N. Lithwick. Ottawa: Supply and Services Canada, 1986.

–. *Domestic Policies and the International Economic Environment*. Research study vol. 12: chap. 8, "The Political Economy of Business Bailouts in Canada," by Michael J. Trebilock; chap. 9, "Canada's Industrial Adjustment: Federal Government Policies and Programs," by DRIE. Ottawa: Supply and Services Canada, 1985.

–. *Regional Responsiveness and the National Administrative State*. Research study vol. 37: chap. 2, "Regional Responsiveness and Government Organization: The Case of Regional Economic Development Policy in Canada," by Peter Aucoin and Herman Bakvis. Ottawa: Supply and Services Canada, 1985.

–. *Report*. 3 vols. Ottawa: Supply and Services Canada, ca. 1985.

Royal Bank *econoscope*. "Free Trade Agreement, One-Year Retrospective." Special issue, undated.

–. "Free Trade Agreement, Second-Year Review." Special issue, vol. 15, no. 1 (February 1991).

Savoie, Donald J. "Cash Incentives versus Tax Incentives for Regional Development: Issues and Considerations." *Canadian Journal of Regional Science* 8, no. 1 (1985): 1–15.

–. "Co-operative Federalism with Democracy." *Policy Options* 3, no. 6 (1982): 54–58.

–. "Courchene and Regional Development: Beyond the Neoclassical Approach." *Canadian Journal of Regional Science* 9, no. 1 (1986): 69–77.

–. "Establishing the Atlantic Canada Opportunities Agency." Canadian Institute for Research on Regional Development, Moncton, May 1987.

–. *Federal-Provincial Collaboration: The Canada–New Brunswick General Development Agreement*. Canadian Public Administration series. Montreal: McGill-Queen's University Press, 1981.

–. "The General Development Agreement Approach to the Bureaucratization of Provincial Governments in the Atlantic Provinces." *Canadian Public Administration* 24, no. 1 (1981): 116–31.

–. "Politicians and Approaches to Regional Development: The Canadian Experience." *Canadian Journal of Regional Science* 10, no. 2 (1987).

–. *The Politics of Public Spending in Canada*. Toronto: University of Toronto Press, 1990.

–. *Regional Economic Development: Canada's Search for Solutions*. Toronto: University of Toronto Press, 1986; Second Edition, 1992.

–. "The Toppling of DREE and Prospects for Regional Economic Development." *Canadian Public Policy* 10, no. 3 (1984): 328–37.

–, ed. *The Canadian Economy: A Regional Perspective*. Toronto: Methuen, 1986.

Savoie, Donald J., and John Chénier. "The State and Development: The Politics of Regional Development Policy." In *Still Living Together*, edited by Coffey and Polèse.

Semple, Keith R. "Regional Analysis of Corporate Decision Making within the Canadian Economy." In *Still Living Together*, edited by Coffey and Polèse.

Senate. *Debates*, July 7–July 26, 1988.

REFERENCES

–. Standing Committee on National Finance. *Minutes of Proceedings and Evidence*, no. 10, November 21, 1978; October 21, 1980.

–. Standing Committee on National Finance. *Minutes of Proceedings and Evidence*, nos. 34, 35, 37, 38, June 1988.

–. Standing Committee on National Finance. *Report of the Standing Senate Committee on National Finance on Government Policy and Regional Development.* 32nd Parliament, 1st Session, September 1982.

Springate, David J. V. "Regional Development Incentives Grants and the Government of Canada: A Case Study of the Effect of Regional Development Incentives on the Investment Decisions of Manufacturing Firms." PhD Thesis, Harvard University, 1972.

Stevenson, Garth. *Unfulfilled Union: Canadian Federalism and National Unity.* Rev. ed. Canadian Controversies series. Toronto: Gage Publishing, 1982.

Thorburn, H. G. *Planning and the Economy: Building Federal-Provincial Consensus.* Toronto: Canadian Institute for Economic Policy, James Lorimer & Co., 1984.

Treasury Board Secretariat. "Draft Guidelines for Program Evaluation," January 31, 1978.

Tupper, Allan. *Public Money in the Private Sector: Industrial Assistance Policy and Canadian Federalism.* Kingston: Institute of Intergovernmental Relations, Queen's University, 1982.

Watson, William G. "The Regional Consequences of Free(r) Trade with the United States." In *Still Living Together*, edited by Coffey and Polèse.

Woodward, Robert S. "The Capital Bias of DREE Incentives." University of Western Ontario, July 1973.

–. "Effective Location Subsidies: An Evaluation of DREE Industrial Incentives." University of Western Ontario, November 1973.

Woolstencroft, Timothy B. *Organizing Intergovernmental Relations.* Kingston: Institute of Intergovernmental Relations, Queen's University, 1982.

NEWSPAPERS

The Chronicle-Herald (Halifax)
Daily Gleaner (Fredericton)
The Financial Post
The Gazette (Montreal)
The Globe and Mail
The Ottawa Citizen
The Times-Transcript (Moncton)

Index